Parallel Functional Languages and Compilers

ACM PRESS

Editor-in-Chief:

Peter Wegner, *Brown University*

ACM Press books represent a collaboration between the Association for Computing Machinery (ACM) and Addison-Wesley Publishing Company to develop and publish a broad range of new works. These works generally fall into one of four series.

Frontier Series. Books focused on novel and exploratory material at the leading edge of computer science and practice.

Anthology Series. Collected works of general interest to computer professionals and/or society at large.

Tutorial Series. Introductory books to help nonspecialists quickly grasp either the general concepts or the needed details of some specific topic.

History Series. Books documenting past developments in the field and linking them to the present.

In addition, ACM Press books include selected conference and workshop proceedings.

Parallel Functional Languages and Compilers

Edited by

Boleslaw K. Szymanski

Rensselaer Polytechnic Institute

ACM PRESS
New York, New York

ADDISON-WESLEY PUBLISHING COMPANY
Reading, Massachusetts • Menlo Park, California • New York
Don Mills, Ontario • Wokingham, England • Amsterdam • Bonn
Sydney • Singapore • Tokyo • Madrid • San Juan • Milan • Paris

Library of Congress Cataloging-in-Publication Data

Parallel functional languages and compilers/edited by Boleslaw K. Szymanski.
    p.   cm.—(ACM Press frontier series)
Includes index.
ISBN 0-201-52243-8
    1. Parallel programming (Computer science) 2. Functional
programming languages. 3. Compilers (Computer programs)
I. Szymanski, Boleslaw K. II. Series.
QA76.642.P37 1991   90-20902
005.2–dc20   CIP

1 2 3 4 5 6 7 8 9 10-MA-9594939291

Contributors

E. A. Ashcroft
Department of Computer Science
Arizona State University
Tempe, Arizona

Marina Chen
Department of Computer Science
Yale University
New Haven, Connecticut

Young-il Choo
Department of Computer Science
Yale University
New Haven, Connecticut

Kattamuri Ekanadham
IBM Thomas J. Watson Research Center
Yorktown Heights, New York

A. A. Faustini
Department of Computer Science
Arizona State University
Tempe, Arizona

Paul Hudak
Department of Computer Science
Yale University
New Haven, Connecticut

R. Jagannathan
Computer Science Laboratory
SRI International
Menlo Park, California

Jingke Li
Department of Computer Science
Yale University
New Haven, Connecticut

Vivek Sarkar
IBM Palo Alto Scientific Center
Palo Alto, California

Stephen K. Skedzielewski
Amdahl-Key Computer Laboratory
Fremont, California

Boleslaw Szymanski
Department of Computer Science
Rensselaer Polytechnic Institute
Troy, New York

Preface

This is a book for the parallel software user or designer who has become tired of the traditional programming languages and has wondered whether there is a better way to write parallel programs. The book is also aimed at students and researchers in parallel programming, languages, and compiler design, – topics in which parallel functional programming is an issue of growing importance. The book provides insight into the current state of parallel functional language design and into techniques developed for efficient implementations of these languages. It provides enough details about the languages presented here to enable readers to decide whether the approaches discussed in the book are suitable to their particular problems.

Parallel programming has become an important part of computer science and software engineering. In the parallel processing environment, functional languages preserve all the advantages that they have over traditional languages in sequential programming – for example, simple, clean semantics and a high level of abstraction from implementation details. Moreover, compilation and generation of an efficient parallel code are usually easier for functional programs than for programs written in traditional high-level languages, a significant reverse of their relation from sequential programming. Because of such factors, the importance of functional programming in parallel processing has been growing. There is already a mounting wealth of theory and experience in using such languages, in implementing sophisticated translators for them, and in supporting them on various parallel architectures. Many of the new languages have been widely publicized in articles in computer science archival journals and conference proceedings. However, there is no introduction and overview of parallel functional languages available to the rank-and-file users of supercomputers and parallel machines. This book attempts to fill that gap.

Functional programming languages can be designed differently, incorporating different styles of writing programs. This book attempts to capture that richness of approaches by presenting a new language in each chapter. The chapters are not intended to be a manual for the languages described. (Readers interested in the details of a particular language should refer to the appropriate monographic publications). Instead, each chapter has been written as an introduction to the language and an illustration of its associated style of programming. The main purpose of this book is to provide the reader with a general understanding and appreciation of the different approaches to designing parallel languages based on functional programming. Hence, the concluding chapter discusses the broadly understood language issues, such as application areas, semantics, exposition of parallelism, determinacy, abstraction mechanisms, models of execution, supported architectures, and implementation efficiency. In addition, many program examples are presented throughout the book, and one program – LU decomposition of the matrix – is included in each chapter and written in all presented languages to help the reader in comparing the different approaches.

Based on a review of the state-of-the-art research in the subject of parallel functional languages, the authors of the most significant projects have been invited to write a chapter describing their approach. As a result, this book reflects the work of authors representing different backgrounds and approaches. Chapter 2, which discusses intensional programming in Lucid, has been written jointly by E.A. Ashcroft (co-author of Lucid) and A. Faustini from Arizona State University, and R. Jagannthan from the Computer Science Laboratory at SRI International. Chapter 3, which presents Equational Programming Language based on recurrence relations, was written by Boleslaw Szymanski (designer of the language) from Rensselaer Polytechnic Institute. Chapter 4, on SISAL, was written by Stephen Skedzielewski from Amdahl Key Computer Laboratory and the University of California at Davis/Livermore. In Chapter 5, Paul Hudak of Yale University discusses his idea of parafunctional programming in Haskell. The data-flow approach represented by the language Id is described in Chapter 6 by Kattamuri Ekanadham of IBM Thomas J. Watson Research Center. Chapter 7, which describes Crystal, was written by a group from Yale University: Marina Chen (author of the language), Young-il Choo, and Jingke Li. The parallelizing Fortran compiler called PTRAN, which was developed at IBM, is presented by Vivek Sarkar of Palo Alto Scientific, a member of the developing team. The final chapter provides language comparisons and concluding remarks. It was written jointly by all the authors of this book

The views presented in each chapter are those of their authors and do not necessarily express the views of other authors or the institutions that employ them. All languages presented here have existing compilers for at least one commonly used parallel computer. Some of them are ready for widespread use.

As the editor of this book, I would like to thank all the contributing authors for their efforts and timely response to my requests for new versions of their chapters and for their contributions to the concluding chapter. I am also indebted to the reviewers: David Notkin, David Wise, Hamilton Richards, and Guy Steele. Their comments improved the quality of all chapters and helped to integrate the entire book. Special thanks go to Peter Gordon, my editor at Addison-Wesley Publishing Company, for his encouragement and support of this project.

Contents

1

Introduction

Boleslaw K. Szymanski

Software development in conventional programming languages is more complex for parallel computers than for sequential machines in at least two aspects: program correctness and efficiency. Parallel program correctness requires the execution results to be independent of the number and speed of processors running the program. This requirement can be satisfied only if the parallel tasks are independent of each other or properly synchronized, if a dependence exists. Synchronization design and verification are the major sources of difficulty in assessing parallel program correctness.

The focus on software efficiency in parallel program design increases the complexity of software development. Efficiency of the parallel implementation is usually measured by dividing the speed-up of the parallel program (relative to its sequential version) by the number of processors used. Thus, to achieve a reasonable efficiency, the idling of processors must be kept low. In the presence of synchronization, this task requires proper load balancing. The balancing (and also the debugging) can be done reliably only after the software has been developed, resulting in costly post-development tuning.

In Flynn's well-known classification of parallel computational models [2], the von Neumann model is characterized by a single stream of instructions controlling a single stream of data (SISD). One category of parallel architectures has been created by introducing multiple data streams (SIMD), and another one by adding also multiple instruction streams (MIMD). The latter category can be divided into two subcategories based on the data access mechanism. In the shared-memory architectures, all processors have equal access to a single, global memory of the computer. In the distributed-memory architectures, each processor has a direct access to its local memory and an indirect access to the memory of other processors through an interprocess communication mechanism.

In SIMD architectures, data parallelism is used to harness parallelism [3]. A single statement is applied to the elements of a data structure distributed between the processors. Distributing data among processors, as well as finding loosely dependent data (dependence results in communication), are the major issues in this style of parallel programming. The efficiency of the computation is influenced by the match between the number of processors and the number of independently accessed pieces of data, and by the extent of the sequential code in the program. Because the typical SIMD machine consists of thousands of small, slow processors, a sequential code in the program has, according to the Amhdal law [1], a disastrous effect on the speed-up. However, correctness of data parallel programs is somewhat easier to asses than in the general parallel programs, thanks to a single thread of control.

For MIMD shared-memory machines, the major software design problems include process and data access synchronization and load balancing. Although the cost of exchanging data through shared memory is low, the number of processors is limited by the cost of supporting uniform access time to the shared memory. In MIMD distributed-memory machines, the synchronization is implicit through communication. The major problems of software design are data placement, communication overhead, load balancing and repeatability of the results for different machine configurations. Thus it is commonly assumed that distributed-memory machines pose the biggest challenge in parallel software design.

Different categories of parallel architectures have caused proliferation of dialects of standard computer languages. For example, standard C language has been extended into C* for SIMD machines [3], enriched by shared data and synchronization primitives (such as locks, barriers, and semaphores) for shared-memory machines as well as adapted to distributed-memory architectures by inclusion of communication primitives (like send and receive of different kinds). Varying parallel programming primitives for different parallel language dialects cause parallel software nonportability.

Even further from the traditional von Neumann model of a computer are dataflow and eduction architectures (see Chapter 6 on Id and Chapter 2 on Lucid). Although they allow for direct execution of the program written in an appropriate language, the efficiency of such execution and dataflow machine performance has yet to be demonstrated in practical applications. Currently available multiprocessor architectures and massively parallel computers challenge the research community to seek novel approaches to parallel programming.

Functional programming has been one of the main directions in developing new languages that directly address the challenge of parallel programming. There is already a large amount of theory and experience in using such languages, in implementing sophisticated translators for them, and supporting them on various parallel architectures. Many of the new languages have been already described in professional journals and conference proceedings and have achieved a stage at which they can be a practical alternative to the traditional languages. In this book we present six parallel functional languages: Lucid, EPL, Sisal, Haskell, Id, and Crystal, as well as a parallelizing compiler PTRAN that employs techniques developed for such languages. All the languages presented here have existing compilers for at least one popular parallel computer. Some of them are good candidates for widespread use.

There is an unquestionable need for parallel computation. This need is most acute in scientific and engineering applications that often demand computing power and speed that cannot be provided by traditional supercomputers due to the inherent limitations of a single processor. Thanks to a relatively simple, and often regular, flow of control in programs in this area, scientific and engineering computing is also an area most advanced in parallel software development (cf. benchmark codes, generic libraries of parallel subroutines, etc.). Yet, even in this area, the complexity of managing explicit parallelism and writing an efficient code remains to be a major obstacle in the widespread use of the new generations of parallel machines.

A well-designed language can shield the programmer from designing a detailed implementation, a flow of control, or a synchronization, while automatically exploiting parallelism that exists in the program. The premise of this book is that functional programming is a convenient basis for the development of the parallel programming languages that balance the division of work between the programmer and the compiler in designing parallel programs.

In functional languages, computational abstractions are expressed through functions. A first-order function takes data objects as arguments and produces new data objects as results. What is abstracted by the function is the method used to produce the new objects from the arguments.

Higher-order functions generalize this further by taking data objects as well as other functions as arguments and producing new data objects and new functions. Much of the elegance of functional languages stems from that semantics, and from the absence of operational or machine-dependent details. It can be further advanced if the referential transparency is supported by enforcing the single assignment rule. Under this rule, each variable can be assigned a value only once. Thus all references to a variable yield the same value, no matter where the reference is placed in the program. Because arguments of a function could be evaluated in any order, functional programming languages exhibit significant amounts of implicit parallelism. Compared with traditionally written software, software developed in functional languages promises to be more portable and more easily maintained over a software life cycle, even if that cycle extends over a generation of multiprocessor architectures. These properties are of the utmost importance to the long-term success of parallel processing.[1]

A key question in functional parallel programming language design is how much parallelism can be extracted automatically, and how much parallelism must rely on the programmer. The answer to this question determines the basic properties of the language, such as level of supported abstraction, typing system, execution model (strict versus non-strict semantics, or eager versus lazy evaluation), use of annotations and pragmas.

Many large codes were written long before parallel processing was easily accessible, and their methods are based on efficient, sequential algorithms. Turning such algorithms into algorithms that can be easily and efficiently parallelized is not merely a job for an "optimizing" compiler but requires reprogramming at a fairly high level of the algorithm and data structure design. In general, the task of automatically reprogramming computation into parallel programs is extremely difficult and costly except for some very restricted classes of problems. Lower level details of parallel implementation, such as identifying independent threads of control flow, spawning parallel tasks, and deciding low-level details of data representation, can be automatized. Functional languages are a good basis for building compilers capable of such automation, thanks to their simple semantics and lack of notion of the execution state. Examples of compilers that automatize the parallel code

---

[1]The same properties are also of importance in sequential programming. However, compilers of conventional languages for sequential machines are less complex and produce more efficient code than the compilers of functional languages. This advantage of conventional languages does not carry to parallel programming.

generation to various degrees are presented in the following chapters. The question then arises as to where the boundary between the low- and high-level aspects of the parallel program design should be placed. Less detailed algorithm descriptions are more portable and allow the compiler more freedom to adjust an implementation to the hardware. On the other hand, the compiler has to be more complex since it has to be able to use this implementation freedom wisely. Certainly, an ideal compiler with the computer knowledge and intelligence of the programmer would be able to match the efficiency of the most detailed programs. Since such a compiler cannot be built (at least not at the present time), the compromise is needed between expressiveness and efficiency. Omission of implementation details results in lowered efficiency only if it is above the level that can be compensated by the smart state-of-the-art compiler. This book attempts to demonstrate that the techniques developed for compiling functional languages can compensate for the lack of details such as flow of control and reassignment of variables required in the conventional languages. In that sense, the authors extend the path started by Backus, who introduced Fortran as a means for a less detailed expression of sequential programs than assembly languages. With stabilization and standardization of parallel hardware, the boundary between the low- and high-level details of parallel programming may be expected to move even further. For now, it is interesting to compare how this boundary is set in each of the languages presented here.

The book is organized as follows. In the remainder of this chapter a brief introduction of each language and its compiler is given.[2]

Chapter 2 presents an approach to parallel programming based on intensional logic. Although the concepts are illustrated in the context of a particular intensional language called Lucid, the same principles apply to other implicitly parallel languages. Lucid permits data structures such as arrays, lists, and trees to be implemented in a manner that is easily distributable. Because of Lucid's simplicity and semantic elegance, it was possible to include in the chapter nontrivial application programs— an adaptive solution to the n-body problem and LU decomposition of matrices. The authors present an analysis of the implicit parallelism available in such programs and show ways in which this parallelism can be harnessed. The fact that Lucid is not committed to any particular model of computation enables the compiler writer complete freedom to implement language features in a manner that cannot be interfered with from the user program.

---

[2]These introductions are based on material in the chapters that follow. I would like to thank the authors of those chapters for writing these introductions.

Chapter 3 describes Equational Programming Language (EPL). It is a simple functional language designed for programming scientific parallel computation. The language is defined in terms of a few constructs: generalized, jagged-edge arrays and subscripts for data structures, recurrent equations for data value definitions, ports for process interactions, and virtual processors for execution directives. In EPL, computations are represented by a collection of processes that interact through ports. Each process is specified with equations and data declarations. Equations may be annotated by virtual processors on which they are to be executed. Coarse grain parallelism is explored in EPL in terms of processes that may, if their data dependences allow it, run concurrently. Medium grain parallelism is supported by annotations; virtual processors introduced by them can be mapped on the physical processors of the architecture. Finally, fine grain parallelism may be utilized by assigning each equation instance to a different processor.

The basic techniques used in EPL compilation are data dependence analysis and data attribute propagation. In a single program, the dependences are represented in the compact form by the conditional array graph. A similar dependence graph is also created for a configuration. It shows the data dependences among processes of the computation and is used for scheduling processes and mapping them onto the processors. The chapter describes the language first, followed by program examples. Then, the compiler design and tools used in EPL implementation are discussed. Finally, conclusions and the outline of future research are given.

Chapter 4 describes Sisal, a functional language that is designed to support large-scale scientific application programming on a wide range of serial and parallel computers. To extract parallelism, Sisal programs use data-dependence information from the source program; the language has no explicit parallel control constructs. Each Sisal compiler is responsible for extracting the appropriate parallelism from a program; for example, the Sisal compiler for the Manchester dataflow machine exploits parallelism at the instruction level, while the compiler for the Cray X-MP looks for vector operations.

Another important design goal of Sisal is to guarantee repeatable results in a multiprocessor environment. This guarantee aids debugging, since the programmer cannot write a program that contains a timing error, or logically deadlocks. The chapter discusses the language and a style of expressing parallelism in Sisal. It gives several examples to illustrate the language constructs, and discusses several programming environments for Sisal program development.

Chapter 5, on para-functional programming, starts with a description of the "modern view" of functional programming as captured in

Haskell—higher-order functions, a rich polymorphic type system, and non-strict semantics (i.e., "lazy evaluation"). To express parallel computation, the chapter introduces an extension of the functional programming paradigm called *para-functional programming*. This idea is based on preserving the qualitative difference between functional behavior (i.e., what the program computes) and operational behavior (i.e., how the answer is computed). A para-functional programming language maintains the distinction between functional and operational specifications by using a metalanguage, typically manifested via annotations, to express the operational semantics.

In the case of "para-Haskell," two kinds of annotations are provided—one to express *scheduling* constraints on expression evaluation, and the other to express *mapping* of expressions onto a particular multiprocessor topology. After introducing these constructs, the chapter gives examples of their use on a variety of simple problems. In addition, implementation issues are discussed by way of describing how conventional implementations (such as graph reduction) would be modified to accommodate para-functional features. The chapter concludes with a comparison of para-functional programming with other approaches and a discussion of future research.

Chapter 6 describes Id, a dataflow functional language designed for general purpose computing, expressiveness, parallel execution, determinacy and efficiency. The importance of implicit parallelism is emphasized by discussing problems with compiler/user directed parallelizations. Automatic unraveling of parallelism is illustrated by giving rewrite rule semantics for the selected Id constructs. It is shown that these rules permit an easy translation into graph forms and that optimizations can be performed nicely on these graphs.

A brief description of a dataflow style architecture is given to show how these graphs can be efficiently executed. Problems with translating the graphs for sequential machines are discussed and several heuristic solutions are presented. Furthermore, the language takes a unique position in supporting efficient parallel computations. For instance, it directly supports array and matrix structures and provides efficient iterative constructs for their manipulation.

The chapter gives the operational semantics for the language in terms of rewrite rules. Then, a few optimizations are presented to illustrate how optimizations can be expressed in this framework. Finally, the lower level abstraction of I-structures is discussed and it is shown how they can be used to implement the higher-level abstractions.

Chapter 7, which discusses Crystal, describes how a language based on a familiar mathematical notation and lambda calculus addresses the issues of programmability and performance of parallel computers. The

Crystal research focuses on making the task of programming massively parallel machines practical while not sacrificing the efficiency of the target code. The Crystal approach to automation is to design a compiler that (1) classifies source programs according to the communication primitives and their cost on the target machine, (2) maps the data structures to distributed memory, and (3) generates parallel code with explicit communication commands. For classes of problems for which the default mapping strategies of the compiler are inadequate, the language provides special constructs for incorporating domain specific knowledge and directing the compiler in its mapping.

The chapter begins with a language description. Then, a model of parallel computation is constructed. This is followed by the definition of an equational theory of the language. The chapter also presents a metalanguage for formalizing the program transformations. To illustrate these ideas, detailed examples of the derivation of optimized programs using formal transformations are given. The authors show how to define communication metrics and to establish performance models of target machines, and how to use those models in narrowing the space of choices in a step-by-step fashion. Recognizing that many problems are dynamic in nature and must rely on runtime optimizations, the chapter illustrates two methods for such optimizations. Finally, initial performance results and further language and compiler developments are discussed.

Chapter 8 gives an overview of the PTRAN compiler developed for automatic detection of parallelism in Fortran programs and generation of parallel code for shared-memory multiprocessors. There are several connections between this work and compilers for parallel functional programming languages. Both approaches are based on implicit parallelism. The user does not specify the formation of parallel tasks, their assignment to processors, the placement of data, etc.

Control and data dependences are fundamental issues in parallelism, and they apply equally to Fortran and functional programs. The main difference is in the usage of data. Fortran supports explicit allocation and modification of data at the expense of complicating the dependence analysis necessary to reveal parallelism. Functional languages are value-oriented, which simplifies dependence analysis at the expense of complex data allocation and modification operations (with possible copying of large data structures). Renaming can be used to make a Fortran program approach a functional representation, thus trading off complexity in dependence analysis with increased cost of data allocation and modification.

The chapter describes an approach to program partitioning originally developed for Sisal, and now adapted for use in the PTRAN system. Other issues in parallel code generation—such as synchronization, software cache management, avoiding code duplication—are also discussed. The author also examines issues associated with generating executable code from the control dependence graph.

Chapter 9 is the concluding chapter that is written jointly by all authors and contains a classification of the presented languages based on the different aspects of the parallel programming language design. We first look into application areas of the languages. Next, we classify them based on their general programming properties, like typing, declarativeness, determinacy, abstraction mechanism, and order of functions allowed. The focus then moves on parallel programming aspects. We inspect properties of the presented languages in regard to the mode of execution (lazy versus eager execution, eduction), communications, explicit (user-defined) versus implicit (automatically derived) parallelism. We also discuss special constructs, such as iterations and their declarative equivalents, streams, I-structures, and arrays. A brief discussion of special architectures proposed for some languages (dataflow for Id and eduction for Lucid) follows. At the end, issues of implementation efficiency are discussed.

References

1. G.S. Almasi and A. Gottlieb, *Highly Parallel Computing*, Menlo Park, California: Benjamin/Cummings, 1989, p. 24.

2. M.J. Flynn, *Some Computer Organizations and Their Effectiveness*, IEEE Trans. on Comp. vol. C-21, 1972, pp. 948-60.

3. W.D. Hillis and G.L. Steele, Jr. *Data Parallel Algorithms*, Comm. ACM, vol. 29, 1986, pp. 1170-83.

2

An Intensional Language for Parallel Applications Programming

E. A. Ashcroft   A. A. Faustini   R. Jagannathan

2.1   Introduction

Many scientific and engineering applications demand computing power and speed that cannot be provided by traditional supercomputers because of the inherent limitations of a single processor. Thus much attention has been given to the possibility of distributing a given computation over an ensemble of cooperating processors. The programming languages used to code algorithms for such ensembles are parallel processing languages. These languages can be divided into two broad categories:

□ explicitly parallel languages
□ implicitly parallel languages

An explicitly parallel language is one in which the programmer has to explicitly state, using particular programming language constructs (fork, join, parbegin, etc.) or program annotations, those parts of the program that can be executed in parallel. This has significant advantages for the compiler technology used in implementing the language. It tells the compiler exactly where to find the parallelism in a program, which in turn can lead to an efficient implementation. Moreover, if the programmer knows how particular language features are implemented on a particular machine, then even further performance advantages can be gained.

An implicitly parallel language is one in which the programmer has little say about the way the program will be executed. The compiler technology has to completely determine a parallel execution strategy. The parallelism available in the program is implicit in the data dependencies of the program. These languages have great advantages for applications software. The programmer approaches solutions free from the details of a particular implementation and so is able to produce applications software that can be used over several generations of multiprocessor architectures. The fact that implicitly parallel languages are not committed to any particular model of computation enables the compiler writer complete freedom to implement language features in a manner that cannot be interfered with from the user program.

We are thus faced with a dilemma. Do we want implementation-oriented software that runs well on today's multiprocessors or do we want applications-oriented software that will last over generations of machines but for which there are few, if any, good parallel implementations as yet? The choice depends on our needs. We have chosen the second because we believe that in the long run it will be critical in determining the success of parallel processing.

Programming languages that are not based on a sequential model of computation—i.e., the declarative languages—can exhibit significant amounts of implicit parallelism. The declarative languages are therefore important parallel programming languages. Within the declarative paradigm, we feel that the languages based on intensional logic[11] are unique in that they permit data structures such as arrays, lists, and trees to be implemented in a manner that is easily distributable. Also, intensional programs are concise and elegant. To illustrate the concepts, we have chosen a particular intensional language, namely Lucid[13]. Lucid's simplicity and semantic elegance make possible the inclusion of nontrivial application programs—an adaptive solution to the n-body problem and programs for LU decomposition of matrices. We present an analysis of the implicit parallelism available in these programs and show ways in which we can harness this parallelism.

One of the crucial features of Lucid, and intensional languages in general, is their suitability for an implementation technique called "eduction" (which is not a misspelling of the word "education"). As we will show, Lucid *can* be thought of as a syntactically sugared functional language, but doing so, while interesting and of pedagogical value for explaining intensionality, is of little practical value because of the complexity of the corresponding functional programs and the relative inefficiency of graph reduction (the usual implementation technique for functional programs) when applied to these functional programs, as compared to eduction applied to the original Lucid programs.

2.2   Intensional Programming

Like other modern functional languages, Lucid is based on P.J. Landin's ISWIM [9]. Lucid differs from other modern functional languages in that it enables declarative programs to use intensional terms. The word "intensional" is not a misspelling of the word "intentional" (but it is pronounced the same). It is related to the word "extensional," and is taken from the work of Montague [11] on natural language semantics. Montague was instrumental in the development of a relatively new branch of mathematical logic known as intensional logic. Intensional logic is a logic in which logical terms have a meaning relative to an implicit context. Examples of context in natural language are "time" and "place." For example the assertion "it is raining" takes on different truth values depending on the temporal and spatial usage. It is probably true more often in England than in the Sahara. On the other hand, there are times when it is false in England. Using intensional logic, Montague was able to express a large subset of natural language formally. A formal treatment of a significant portion of natural language was a task that had eluded logicians for many years. Montague was able to partially succeed where so many others had failed because he was the first to realize that a "term" in natural language was an "intension" and not an "extension." The extension of a term or expression is the value that the term or expression takes in a given context. Thus an intensional term like "the President" may take on a different value in different years. "The President" can thus be thought of as a table or function that defines for each year who was president. The table or function is the "intension" associated with the term "the President." In practice we do not explicitly haul around "Almanacs" in our daily use of natural language. The "intensions" that we use encode massive amounts of data that we refer to implicitly. (Sometimes we might use absolute references such as "Jimmy Carter, the president in 1977.")

Intensionality is a simple concept that we use all the time in natural language because it simplifies communication. Words like "previous" and "next" are intensional operators. Given a context, the intensional operators "last" or "next" take you backward or forward in time. It is possible to have many other kinds of intensional operators, such as "left," "right," "up," "down," etc. Intensional programming in general and Lucid in particular attempt to bring the benefits of intensionality to computer science. Intensionality has implications for programming language constructs and their parallel implementation (see Section 2.8 on parallel implementation).

The concept of "context" used in natural language is far more general than is generally necessary in intensional programming. Lucid uses only a small set of possible contexts. We call the Lucid contexts *indexical* contexts because they can all be defined in terms of sets or sequences of natural numbers or integers. In principle there is no reason to limit intensional programming to indexical contexts, but in practice we have found that most computations can be expressed adequately using such contexts. The simplest example of a Lucid indexical context is time. In Lucid a variable can be defined to vary over a temporal context that is itself definable as a simple natural number.

Summarizing, in Lucid a variable can range over many contexts, but all these contexts must have the property that they are definable as tuples of natural numbers or integers. For example, a variable that is defined over time and two space dimensions will take on values that depend on contexts defined as 3-tuples (one natural number and two integers).

In Lucid, the extensions are simple data objects, like integers and booleans. Complex data structures are represented by intensions, as we shall see. Even though the intensions can be thought of as representing complex data structures, it is probably better not to think too much of the data structure, but rather to think of the intension, the way in which the elements depend on the context. In fact, when translating a Lucid program to a purely functional one, there are two ways to go about it. The first method, called the monolithic method, is to write a purely functional program that deals with complex data structures, like infinite lists and arrays. The second method, called the explicit-intension method, is to explicitly express the intensions as functions from objects that are contexts to simple data objects. (In the explicit-intension method, the objects in Lucid become functions and the operators and functions in Lucid that work on Lucid data objects become functions that work on functions, i.e., second-order functions.) The explicit-intension method is more natural and simple than the monolithic method, for exactly the same reason that it is better to think in terms of intensions rather than data objects. After the following introduction to Lucid, we will give purely functional descriptions of both sorts for the Lucid programs that we have introduced.

2.3   Lucid—a Parallel Processing Language

In this section, we will introduce the basic concepts of Lucid. Our goal is to provide readers with enough understanding of the language to enable them to understand the application programs presented in the rest of the chapter.

Lucid is a simple programming language in which programs are stated in terms of equations that express pure data dependencies. The simplest form of an equation is one that defines a variable to be equal to some constant (for example, a = 3.142). Sets of equations of this form are simple to understand but not very useful as a programming language. Lucid is a simple and elegant extension to this, based on intensional logic and lambda calculus[5]. As we have seen, intensional logic is a relatively modern branch of mathematical logic concerned with assertions and other expressions whose meaning depends on an implicit context. The relationship of intensional logic and programming languages is only now beginning to be understood[2]. Later in this chapter, we demonstrate the benefits of intensionality in programming languages by using Lucid to express two applications: the n-body problem and LU matrix decomposition.

The description of an algorithm usually involves the concept of temporal order. For example, an algorithm might be defined in the following terms: "We first initialize the variables, then we compute the product of the variables, after which we find a minimum and then ...." The notion of time expressed in this description is well known to programmers. It is not "real time" but relative time. Exactly the same concept exists in Lucid. To be more precise, the Lucid programmer can define a variable that begins with an initial value, which is then followed by a second value, and so on. This is in many ways a pure form of the assignment statement found in imperative languages, the difference being that in Lucid the value that a variable has at a context can never change. The temporal context changes rather than the value of a memory location. Thus when the programmer revisits the same context, the binding that was made in that context will still be valid.

The following equation defines a variable that is first 1.2 and then at successive time points is 2.5, 3.8, 5.1, and so on. In other words, *at all points* (or "times") the next value in the temporal sequence is based on the previous value plus 1.3. Example 1 shows how this is written in Lucid.

EXAMPLE 1:

```
x = 1.2 fby x + 1.3;
```

We read this as x equals 1.2 followed by (fby) x plus 1.3.

The preceding definition is an inductive definition but it is clear that the data dependency is sequential. That is, the $i + 1^{th}$ value in time depends directly on the value at the ith time. It is therefore not possible to obtain parallelism from this definition. On the other hand, if a program consists of many such definitions, it is possible to execute in parallel those equations that do not depend on each other. It is also possible to define a variable in terms of its own "future," as shown in the following example.

EXAMPLE 2:

```
x = if  now < 1000 then next x else now fi;
now = 0 fby now+1;
```

We have two equations: one defines x in terms of its own future, and the second is a counter. In the first definition we see the first usage of the temporal operator next. The value of next x is the value of x in the next time context.

The counter is called now. The reason why it is called now is that it corresponds to the temporal context of variables that use it. That is, at time 0 now is 0 and at time 1 it is 1 and so on. This is such a useful variable that it is included in the language as a built-in. Using it, a program can get at the implicit time context, when necessary. The last program illustrates another situation in which we have sequential temporal data dependencies. That is, the value of x at time 0 is dependent upon x at time 1, x at time 1 is dependent on x at time 2, and so on. The value of x at time 1000 is the value of now at that time, namely 1000.

These two examples show us that simple temporal equations have a limited form of parallelism that comes mainly from the potential of non-interacting equations that can be executed independently. How do we get more parallelism out of Lucid programs? We can extend the language from simple recursive equations to recursive function definitions. Lucid incorporates the notion of a function as in functional programming [8]. The following is an example of a function that uses the standard sieve algorithm to compute the prime numbers

EXAMPLE 3:

```
sieve(n) = n fby sieve(n whenever n mod first n ne 0);
primes = sieve(now + 2);
```

Here the parallelism associated with each recursive call can be exploited. Each call to sieve assumes that the first number, first n, in its input stream will be a prime. It outputs that number and also uses it to filter out (using the infix operator whenever) all subsequent inputs that are multiples of the first number. The resulting filtered temporal stream is then the input to another call of sieve that performs exactly the same task. (The use here of the word "then" is not meant to imply that we wait for all the infinite filtered stream to be produced before starting the second call to sieve.) Thus, if the original input is all the natural numbers starting at 2 (i.e., now+2), successive calls of sieve output the primes in increasing order. The parallelism comes from the fact that functions are always active as long as there is sufficient input in the pipelines (the pipelines being the temporal streams). It is well known that this type of parallelism can be exploited from recursive function definitions. The difference here is that we have the added benefit of pipelining through temporal streams.

The temporal operators used in the above examples are just a few of those available to the Lucid programmer. We will introduce two others that will be used in later examples. The intensional expression A asa P makes use of the infix temporal operator asa. The meaning of the temporal expression is as follows. Starting at time 0, evaluate successive temporal values of the predicate P. As soon as (hence the operator name asa) a point in time is found, say time i, at which the predicate P is true, then the value at all points in time of the expression A asa P is the value of A at this first point in time at which P became true—that is, P at time i.

The temporal expression A @t n uses the infix temporal operator @t (read as "at time"). The meaning of this operator is as follows. Evaluate n in the current time and space context then evaluate A in the time context that is the value just computed. This enables temporal expressions to be written so that a value in a particular time context can be dependent on the value in an arbitrary time context.

Pure functional programming (the lambda calculus languages) are not the only way of exploiting parallelism in declarative languages. In this chapter we discuss a novel way of exploiting the parallelism associated with intensional *space*. Algorithms can and usually do involve spatial as well as temporal contexts. Examples of this might include the current employees of a company or the current temperature in different parts of the world. Lucid permits spatial as well as temporal contexts. The simplest form of spatial context—position in one-dimensional space—gives rise to a vector, in the same way that position in time gives rise to a temporal stream. The following example defines the vector of even numbers in increasing order in Lucid.

EXAMPLE 4:

```
evens = 0 sby evens + 2;
```

Note we use sby (read as "succeeded by") to generate successive values in space. The initial value of the vector is 0, then successive values are generated from the previous value plus 2.

We can obviously have multiple space dimensions. In Lucid this is achieved by allowing the variables to depend on an arbitrary number of implicit space contexts. Thus, if we want to generate the even numbers in the second space dimension, we use the following equation.

EXAMPLE 5:

```
evens = 0 sby1 evens+2;
```

The sby1 operator is analogous to sby but for the second space dimension. Notice that the program looks almost identical to the one using the first space dimension.

So far, each equation that we have defined varies only over the time dimension or only over one of the space dimensions. In general a variable can vary in many dimensions. The following is a multidimensional version of the functional program sieve described above.

EXAMPLE 6:

```
primes = initial sieve;
sieve = N fby sieve wherever sieve mod initial sieve ne 0;
N = 2 sby N+1;
```

In this program sieve varies in both time and space and is not a function. At time 0 sieve is the vector of successive natural numbers beginning with 2. At time 1 it is the vector of successive natural numbers beginning with 3 but with all multiples of 2 removed. At time 2 it is the vector of successive natural numbers beginning with 5 but with all multiples of 2 and 3 removed, and so on. The initial values of these vectors gives the sequence primes of primes. As is the case with each function call in the functional case given above, each point in time has a sequential computation associated with it—namely the removal of the multiples of the prime found at that point in time. (In this case the Lucid built-in filter wherever is used to filter out the multiples of the prime from the spatial vector associated with each time point.)

We now begin to see other ways in which Lucid programs can exploit implicit parallelism. Figure 2.1 shows diagrammatically the prime program just described. Each of the wherever operators can be working in parallel.

For each of the temporal context shifting operators, Lucid provides analogous spatial operators. We have seen some of these in the previous

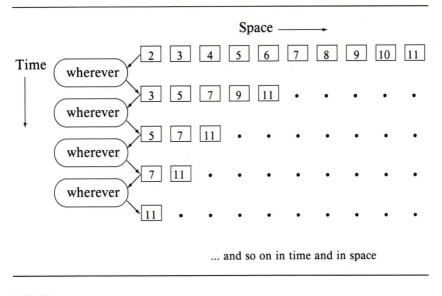

FIGURE 2.1
Diagrammatical representation of the "spatial" Primes program.

example. The following are additional spatial operators that will be used later in this chapter. We present the spatial analogs with respect to the first space dimension. The same operators exist with different names for higher space dimensions. The analog of fby is sby; the analog of next is succ. Thus x = succ succ y; means that, for all i, x at space point i is y at space point $i + 2$. The analog of the operator @t is @s (read as "at space"). Thus A @s n means evaluate n at the current time and space context and return the value of A in the context that is the current context but with the first space context being the value just computed. Note that this operator does nothing to the time context or any space context other than the first space context. Each space dimension has an @s operator that can change the space context for that dimension and no other context.

    We have two more spatial operators to introduce. The first is the prefix operator pred, read as "predecessor," which moves us backward in space. The second is the infix operator onFinding and it is the spatial analog of asa. Thus the expression A onFinding P searches the first space dimension for the first point at which the predicate P is true. The value of the expression at all points in the first space dimension will be the value of A @s i where i is the first point in space at which the predicate P is true.

Corresponding to the built-in temporal variable now we have the built-in spatial variable here. Like now, the spatial built-in here takes on the value of the space context it is used in. Thus here at space point 1 has the value 1 and at space point n has value n.

All the intensional operators introduced so far deal only with time or one space dimension. Lucid has operators that permit expressions that vary in time to be viewed as space-varying and space-varying objects to be viewed as time-varying. In this chapter we will use two operators that do this. These operators are swap and swapi. For example the expression swap here is equivalent to now and the expression swap now is equivalent to here. The operator swap*i* interchanges the time context and the dimension *i* space context.

The following equation illustrates the power of intensional programming as a notation for problem solving. It implements an iterative algorithm that is often found in numerical analysis and image processing applications. The idea is that we have a time-varying matrix. At the first point in time we are given a matrix as input. At all times after that the value of the matrix at any point in space is dependent upon (in fact, the average of) the values of its immediate neighbors at the previous point in time. In Lucid we write this as follows:

EXAMPLE 7:

```
M = given_matrix fby
      (succ M + pred M + succ1 M + pred1 M)/4;
```

This illustrates the concept of parallelism through intensionality because it clearly shows that it is possible at successive points in time to compute in parallel all points of the new matrix.

The context shifting operators just described are very structured moves that lead in general to programs that can be analyzed using formal techniques in order to prove properties about programs. Lucid also provides potentially unpredictable context shifting operators, namely @s and @t. As we have seen, these are potentially unpredictable since the expression x @s N, for example, means that we evaluate N in the current context and use its value as the space context at which to evaluate x. On the other hand, @s, for example, *can* be used in very useful and predictable ways, as in

```
pair_sum = (V + succ V) @s  (2*here);
```

The above program defines a vector pair_sum that is the result of pairwise summation of V in space. That is $(V_0 + V_1), (V_2 + V_3), (V_4 + V_5)$ and so on. Note that this is not achieved by either of the following equations:

```
shift1_sum = V + succ V;
shift2_sum = V + succ succ V;
```

The first gives us a pairwise summing of V that corresponds to $(V_0+V_1), (V_1+V_2), (V_2+V_3) \ldots$ and the second gives us a pairwise summing that corresponds to $(V_0+V_2), (V_1+V_3), (V_2+V_4) \ldots$. Note that in all of these examples addition can proceed in parallel provided that the vector V has its values ready to use. We can easily extend the pair_sum definition to produce a parallel tournament addition, as illustrated in Figure 2.2.

All of the addition operators at a given stage can be working in parallel.

The program of Figure 2.2 includes two concepts that have not yet been explained. The first is that of a Lucid where-clause (or block). There are two types of Lucid where-clauses. The first is a simple where-clause that is used to introduce auxiliary definitions of variables that can be used in the block itself or in the head of the where-clause. The following example illustrates the simple where-clause.

```
x where
   x = z+2;
   z = 1 fby z+x;
end;
```

The x before the word where is the head (or subject) of the where-clause. It directly corresponds to the value of the whole construct. The definitions within the where-clause are simply auxiliary definitions. The where-clauses can be nested and, when they are, they have almost the same scope rules as a Pascal block. The only difference is that the head of the clause that appears outside the where-end construct is also in the scope of the block.

The second type of where-clause in Lucid is one that contains declarations of variables using is current or is s_current. These blocks conform to the same scope rules as simple where-clauses do but they have an added duty. They freeze the value of the variables declared at the beginning of the where-clause. This has the effect of a subcomputation. In the program in Figure 2.2, versions, frozen in time, of the formal parameters h and n are given to H and READY. This enables the body of the function to use its own local time to process the vector H, adding together the 2^{READY} values of H. When a value is returned for the

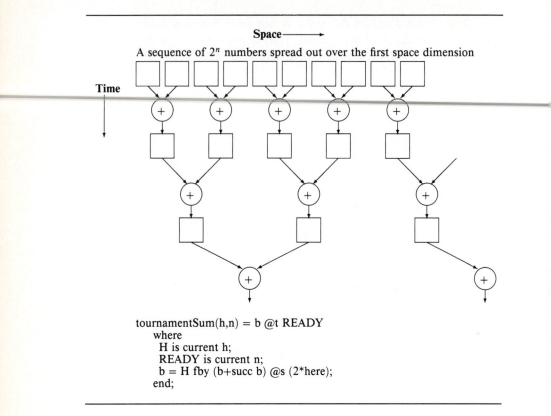

Space ⟶

A sequence of 2^n numbers spread out over the first space dimension

Time

tournamentSum(h,n) = b @t READY
    where
        H is current h;
        READY is current n;
        b = H fby (b+succ b) @s (2*here);
    end;

FIGURE 2.2
Tournament addition.

sum of vector H, it is returned as the sum of vector h for the time at which the call was made. Thus the values of the actual parameters to tournamentSum can be changing with time on the outside of the function but inside the function, for each outer time point, the values of the arguments at that time are essentially held constant while local time takes over, giving a subcomputation. This construct is probably the most difficult to explain but it is very useful in intensional programs, particularly in the design of library functions.

2.4 Functional Description of Lucid Programs

We will express the Lucid programs of the previous section in functional-program terms using the monolithic and explicit-intension methods. (We will use the language Haskell.) The reader can simply skip over this section on first reading, if desired. This section should be read in parallel with the previous section. This is because more features are added to the functional-program descriptions as more features are considered in Lucid in the previous section.

The functional programs of the two types are all obtained using two simple algorithms that work for general Lucid programs, not just for the examples given here. As a result, the functional programs given here are not the best possible and could well be improved.

PROGRAMS FOR EXAMPLE 1

Monolithic. In the monolithic method, all uses of basic operators (addition, in this case) have to be applied to all the elements of the data structures. We do this by using map.

```
x = 1.2 : (map (\a → a + 1.3) x)
```

Strictly speaking, to stay as close to the way that Lucid works as possible, the constants 1.2 and 1.3 in the Lucid program should be constant *lists* in the functional program, and we also need a version of map that works for binary functions. Thus the program should be

```
x = (car(const 1.2)): (map2 (+) x (const 1.3))
   const a = aa
     where
       aa = a : aa
map2 f c d = (f (car c)(car d)) : (map2 f (cdr c)(cdr d))
```

Explicit-Intension. In this method, x is a function rather than a list. The domain of the function is contexts, which in this case we can take as natural numbers.

```
x 0 = (const 1.2 0)
x (i+1) = (x i) + (const 1.3 i)
const k j = k
```

Notice that we have a version of const that is a second order function rather than a first order function. Despite this, we begin to see immediately that the explicit-intension method is simpler than the monolithic.

PROGRAMS FOR EXAMPLE 2

Monolithic.   We have to consider here the if-then-else operator as being a nonstrict ternary operator. As with addition, we have to apply it to all elements of structures, and, in this case, we have a version of map that works for ternary functions.

```
x = map3 f (map2 (<) now (const 1000)) (cdr x) now
   where
      f = \a b c → if a then b else c
map3 g i j k = (g (car i) (car j) (car k)) :
                             (map3 g (cdr i) (cdr j) (cdr k))
now = (car(const 0)) : (map2 (+) now (const 1))
```

The function f has been defined because it would not otherwise be clear how to map the if-then-else operator. Also, notice that the effect of next is simply obtained using cdr in the definition of x.

Explicit-Intension.   In this case it is possible to define now more simply.

```
x i = if (now i) < (const 1000 i) then (next x i)
                                  else (now i)
next y j = y (j + 1)
now k = k
```

Notice that the Lucid operator next is "implemented" as a second-order function.

PROGRAMS FOR EXAMPLE 3

In each case, we will include a definition that corresponds to the built-in Lucid operator whenever.

Monolithic.

```
primes = sieve (map2 (+) now (const 2))
sieve n = (car n) : sieve (whenever n p)
   where
      p = (map2 (ne) (map2 (mod) n (car n)) (const 0))
whenever (a:x) (true : p) = a : (whenever x p)
whenever (a:x) (false : p) = whenever x p
```

Notice that the function whenever is recursive.

Explicit-Intension.

```
primes = sieve (\i → (now i) + (const 2 i))
sieve n 0 = n 0
sieve n (j + 1) = sieve (whenever n p) j
    where
        p i = (n i) mod ((first n) i) ne (const 0 i)
whenever m q k = m (t2 k)
    where
        t2 0 = t1 0
        t2 (i + 1) = t1 ((t2 i) + 1)
        t1 h = if (q h) then h else (t1 (h + 1))
first x i = x 0
```

This program may seem harder to understand than the monolithic program because the (second-order) function whenever seems more complicated. In fact, if we had only used the recursive meaning of whenever, as is indicated in the monolithic solution, we would have got a recursive second-order function that would have been very slow. Here we have avoided second-order recursion and have got a much more efficient program. Doing a comparable thing in the monolithic method would involve avoiding recursively defined (first-order) functions. However, it does not seem possible to define whenever nonrecursively in an efficient way in the monolithic method.

PROGRAMS FOR asa

Monolithic.

```
asa (a:aa) (true : pp) = const a
asa (a:aa) (p : pp) = asa aa pp
```

Notice that the function asa is recursive.

Explicit-Intension.

```
asa A P i = X 0
    where
        X j = if (P j) then (A j) else (X (j + 1))
```

Again, we have avoided using a recursive second-order function.

PROGRAMS FOR @t

Monolithic.

```
@t A (n:nn) = (find A n) : (@t A nn)
   where
      find (a:aa) 0 = a
      find (a:aa) i+1 = find aa i
```

Here, the function @t is highly recursive.

Explicit-Intension.

```
@t A n i = A (n i)
```

The simplicity in this case is, of course, due to the fact that Lucid was designed as an intensional language.

PROGRAMS FOR EXAMPLE 4

Monolithic.   The problem here is how to distinguish, in the infinite list representation, between a sequence in time and a sequence in space. In Lucid they are different and behave differently, so that should also be the case when we use infinite lists. Perhaps the lists should have some kind of header to indicate the difference. Or perhaps, at the top level, we will have the elements at each point in time, and any one of those elements can be a list, indicating that at that time it varies in space. With this second scheme, the vector of even numbers would be

```
evens = E : evens
   where
      E = 0 : (map2 (+) E (const 2))
```

As Lucid requires, evens is the same at each point in time.

Explicit-Intension.   The problem here is to determine how we distinguish space contexts from time contexts. In fact, since things can vary in both time and space, contexts should have both time and space *components*. A context could be an object like the S-expression $((t.5)(s.13))$, which indicates the position in space (13) and the point in time (5). If either of those components is missing, it will mean that the missing component is irrelevant. For example, the vector of all even numbers would be specified as follows:

```
evens (tc : (( s.0) : []))       = const 0 (tc : (( s.0) : []))
evens (tc : (( s.(i + 1)) : [])) = X
```

```
X = (evens (tc : (( s.i) : [])))) + Y
Y = const 2 (tc : (( s.i) : []))
```

It doesn't matter what the time component (tc) is, or even whether there *is* a time component. The result depends only on the space component.

PROGRAMS FOR EXAMPLE 5

Monolithic.   Extending the "lists of lists" approach, we would use here lists of lists of lists:

```
evens = E1 : evens
   where
      E1 = E : E1
         where
            E = 0 : (map2 (+) E (const 2))
```

The lack of similarity between the monolithic programs for the programs for Examples 4 and 5 is a little disturbing, and we will see later that it causes grave difficulties.

Explicit-Intension.   Now we need to have space components for the different space dimensions, say **s0** and **s1**. (In fact, there can be an arbitrary number of components. No two can be for the same dimension, of course.)

```
evens (tc : (sc0 : (( s1.0) : C))) = S
S = const 0 (tc : (sc0 : (( s1.0) : C)))
evens (tc : (sc0 : (( s1.(i + 1)) : C))) = X
X = (evens (tc : (sc0 : (( s1.i) : C)))) + Y
Y = const 2 (tc : (sc0 : (( s1.i) : C)))
```

The problem here is that the notation for describing the (non-implicit) contexts is getting clumsy. What we really need to do is to consider contexts as sets of components and have a notation like C[**s1**, i] that denotes a context that is like C except that its **s1** component is i. The above program would then become

```
evens C[ s1, 0] = const 0 C[ s1, 0]
evens C[ s1,i + 1] = (evens C[ s1,i]) + (const 2 C[ s1,i])
```

If the explicit-intension program for the program in Example 4 were obtained by using this notation, it would look almost identical to this one.

PROGRAMS FOR EXAMPLE 6

Monolithic.

```
primes = map (car) sieve
sieve = (car N) : map2 wherever sieve p
p = map2 (ne) (map2 (mod) sieve (map (car) sieve))
(const 0) N = n : N
n = (const 2) : (map2 (+) n (const 1))
wherever (a:x) (true : p) = a : (wherever x p)
wherever (a:x) (false : p) = wherever x p
```

Notice that the function wherever is identical to the function whenever; it is just applied (in the definition of sieve) to all the elements of lists (which are themselves lists) rather than to a top-level list.

Explicit-Intension.

```
primes C[ s0, i] = sieve C[ s0, 0]
sieve C[ t, 0] = N C[ t, 0]
sieve C[ t, i + 1] = wherever sieve p C[ t, i]
p C = (sieve C) mod ((initial sieve) C) ne (const 0 C)
initial x C[ s0, i] = x C[ s0, 0]
wherever m q C[ s0, k] = m C[ s0, t2 C[ s0, k]
    where
        t2 C[ s0, 0] = t1 C[ s0, 0]
        t2 C[ s0, i + 1] = t1 C[ s0, (t2 C[ s0, i]) + 1]
        t1 C[ s0, h] = if (q C[ s0, h]) then h
                                       else (t1 C[ s0, h + 1))
```

Notice that wherever is just like the previous explicit-intension definition of whenever, only we have written contexts in the new notation.

PROGRAMS FOR OPERATOR swap

The swap operators really show the difference between the monolithic and explicit-intension methods.

Explicit-Intension.

```
swapi x C[ t, k][ si, j] = x C[ t, j][ si, k]
```

Monolithic. The program that goes here essentially has to turn a structure inside out. Writing such a program is difficult, and the program itself would be expensive to run. We will leave writing the program as an exercise for the reader.

PROGRAMS FOR EXAMPLE 7

This example, like the previous one, brings out the difference between the two methods. The explicit-intension method is relatively straightforward:

Explicit-Intension.

```
M C[ t, 0] = given_matrix C[ t, 0]
M C[ t, i + 1] = ((succ M C[ t, i]) + pred M C[ t, i])
                + (succ1 M C[ t, i]) + (pred1 M C[ t, i]))/4
succ a C[ s0, k] = a C[ s0, k + 1]
pred a C[ s0, k] = a C[ s0, k - 1]
succ1 a C[ s1, k] = a C[ s1, k + 1]
pred1 a C[ s1, k] = a C[ s1, k - 1]
```

Monolithic. The problem here is not that we have to turn a structure inside out but that we have to be able to look around in the structure in different directions, and the different dimensions are implemented differently. For example, if we were at some point in the data structure, and that structure is lists of lists of lists, as before, and we want to apply succ1, all we do is apply cdr. However, if we want to apply succ, or even next, we have to somehow get into the surrounding lists. At this point it becomes apparent that the monolithic method is much too complicated. In fact, there are features of Lucid that we have not talked about at all that are even harder to implement as monolithic functions, and we shall just give up the attempt to describe Lucid functionally, at least monolithically.

(The problems encountered by the monolithic method have been noticed in applications of other functional languages, and, as a result, it has recently been proposed that arrays be added to the new functional language Haskell. (The proposed arrays in Haskell are said to be "monolithic," but the term is used in a different sense than we have used it in this chapter.) Haskell arrays have a lot of the features of the implicit arrays in Lucid. The main difference is that array subscripts are explicit in Haskell. Haskell is not intensional.)

PROGRAM FOR DECLARATION is current

We will give an explicit-intension description of the where-clause in the definition of the function tournamentSum in Figure 2.2. It denotes a function, arbitrarily called f, defined as follows:

```
f C[ s, j][ t, i] = b C[ s, j][ t, (n C[ s, j][ t, i])]
    where
        b C[ s, j][ t, 0] = h C[ s, j][ t, i]
        b C[ s, j][ t, k + 1] = (b C[ s, 2*j][ t, k]) +
                                (b C[ s, 2*j + 1][ t, k])
```

We have taken many shortcuts here. For example, we did not use const for the number 2 or the number 1, and we did not use a definition of here. The crucial thing to notice is that b depends on the time context i for f.

This section has shown that Lucid programs can be expressed functionally. Despite this, we feel that Lucid cannot justly be accused of only being syntactic sugar for a conventional functional language. We feel that the functional versions are far less perspicacious, and Lucid programs have the benefit of having their own model of computation.

2.5   An Application in Lucid: The n-Body Problem

The main purpose of Sections 2.5 and 2.6 is to show that it is possible to program real applications in Lucid. In Section 2.7, we talk about the implicit parallelism in the applications. The applications of Lucid that we will consider are the so-called n-body problem and LU decomposition of a matrix using partial pivoting.

The Lucid program for the n-body problem is concerned with simulating the movement of a set of bodies in space, under the influence of, in this case, gravity. (The same program, with minor modifications, will work equally well for electromagnetism.) The crucial characteristic of this problem is that forces between bodies obey an inverse-square law. This means that effects between bodies are felt at large distances, and each body feels the effect of the other n−1 bodies. The traditional technique for solving this problem involves setting a time-increment "δ," and having all the bodies' positions and velocities be calculated at particular times, the successive times being separated by intervals of size δ. These successive periods at which calculations are performed are called "stages," and in the traditional technique each body's trajectory goes through the same stages. This solution is relatively easy to program in

Lucid. Here is the program:

```
[% p, v%] wherever here < n
 where
 p = p0 fby p + v*delta + (a*delta*delta)/2
         where p0 = p0x sby1 p0y sby1 p0z; end;

 v = v0 fby v + a*delta
         where v0 = v0x sby1 v0y sby1 v0z; end;

 a = initial tournamentSum(accelContrib,n)
            where
               BODY is s_current here;
               P is s_current p;
               accelContrib = if here eq BODY or here>=n
                 then 0
                 else G*mass/norm_sq(dist)*projection fi;
               dist = p - P;
                projection = dist/norm(dist);
            end;

 norm_sq(a) = sum(a*a);
 sum(a) = initial1(a + succ1(a) + succ1 succ1(a));
 norm(a) = sqrt(norm_sq(a));
 tournamentSum(h,n) = b @t powerOfTwo
       where
          H is current h;
          N is current n;
          b = H fby if width mod 2 eq 0 then b+succ b
                   else b sby b + succ b fi @s (2*here);
          width = N fby ceil(width / 2);
          powerOfTwo = now asa width eq 1;
       end;
    end
```

(The function tournamentSum in this program is different from the one shown in Figure 2.2 in that it sums an arbitrary number n of things; n need not be a power of two.)

The variables p, v, and a are defined to be the positions, velocities, and accelerations, respectively, of the various bodies. (The program outputs the positions and velocities of the bodies at successive stages in time.) The meaning of any variable, p for example, depends on the context in which it is desired. That context will say which body is being considered, which stage in the trajectory of that body is being considered, and even which dimension or direction—x, y, or z—is being considered. The crucial, and characteristic, feature of Lucid is that the context will be implicit. Contexts are not mentioned explicitly in a Lucid program; the definitions are for all contexts. For example, the one definition for p covers the positions of each body at each stage and each direction. Lucid programs are intensional.

In the following discussion it might help if we assume that we are considering some generic implicit context, C. The definitions for p and v are relatively straightforward. They are based on well-known simple equations of physics. Also, they use the Lucid operator fby ("followed by") but are easily understood. The definition of p, for example, can be understood as saying that p starts off (at the initial stage) as being p0, which has x, y, and z components, p0x, p0y, and p0z (sby means "succeeded by"). Then, at any stage, the value of p at the next stage is the value of p+v*delta+(a*delta*delta)/2 at the current stage. Equivalently, this definition of p says that if the current implicit context C says that we are at the initial stage, then the value of p in context C is the initial value p0 in the appropriate direction (that direction being specified by C). On the other hand, if C says we are at a later stage, the value of p is the value of p+v*delta+(a*delta*delta)/2 in the context corresponding to the previous stage (but to the same body and direction).

The definition for a is more complicated than that for p. To determine the (gravitational) acceleration in context C, we must use a subcomputation to sum the contributions of all the other bodies, using the masses of the other bodies and the distances (dist) to them. The function tournamentSum, in context C, adds together the values of its argument, accel_contrib, for all similar contexts, that differ from C only in the body being considered. (That is, if a context B is similar to C, it is for the same stage, and for the same direction, x, y, or z, but for a different body.) By suitably defining accel_contrib, tournamentSum(accel_contrib,n) adds together the acceleration contributions (in the C-direction) of all the n bodies that are at the same stage (as specified by C). For each of the C-similar contexts B, the value of accel_contrib depends on mass, the mass of the B-body (the body for the context B), and on dist, the distance from the B-body to the original body we were considering (the C-body). To do that, when we switch to the new context B, we need to remember the position of the C-body. That is done by the declaration P is s_current p. Its effect is to cause P to have the C-value of p in all C-similar contexts. The distance dist is then simply the difference between the position p and the position of the C-body, namely P. The rest of the definition of a should be understandable. In the denominator of the expression for accel_contrib, we use `norm_sq(dist)`, rather than just `dist*dist`, because the x component, say, of the force on a body depends on the magnitude of the distance, not just the distance in the x direction (which could be very small, even though the bodies are far apart). ("Norm" is the term used in vector algebra for the magnitude of a vector.) To get the x, y, and z components of the acceleration contribution, we have to project into the required directions the value obtained from the magnitude of the distance (hence the use of `projection`).

The program is quite short, but it is important to appreciate that it handles any number of bodies without ever referring to any of them directly, just by using generic-looking definitions. It "outputs" the positions and velocities of the various bodies at each stage. The program runs on the Lucid implementation at Arizona State University. (Figure 2.3 illustrates a plot of values produced by the program, for particular inputs.) That implementation is on a Sun/Unix system and is demand-driven. It proceeds by first asking for n, the number of bodies, and then asking for the initial positions and velocities (in each of the x, y, and z directions) of the various bodies. (The bodies will be numbered 0 through n−1.) The initial (stage 0) positions and velocities will then be printed out. It will then ask for the masses for bodies 1 through n−1, and output the position and velocity of body 0 at stage 1. It will then ask for the mass of body 0 and output all the positions and velocities of all the masses at all stages. (The output can be terminated with control-D, or the program could easily be modified to output a predetermined number of stages.) The mass of body 0 is asked for last because it is not needed until the acceleration, at stage 0, of body 1 is needed. (The acceleration, at stage 0, of body 0 is determined by the masses of bodies 1 through n−1, not of body 0.)

Figure 2.3 shows, in graphical form, the positions calculated by this program for four bodies started with different positions and velocities. For simplicity, in order to get output in two dimensions, the initial values in the z direction were all given as 0. In addition to the number of bodies, their masses, and their initial positions and velocities, the program requires the value of G, the universal gravitational constant, and `delta`, the time increment. These two values could have been built into the program, but, as written here, their values will be requested when needed in a particular context. When needed in a context different from that one, a new request will be issued. This gets tedious for G, because it really *is* a constant and should have been built into the program, but `delta` might be different for different situations and *should* be a parameter of the program. In fact, for an accurate simulation, the time interval δ has to be chosen to be small enough to ensure that the acceleration is practically constant on any body during δ, throughout its

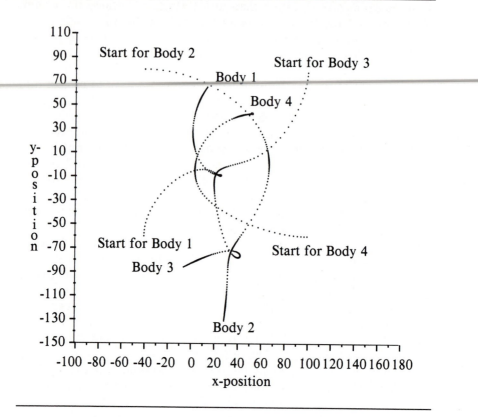

FIGURE 2.3
Trajectories calculated by the n-body program.

whole trajectory. This can be tricky. There may be situations that occur during a trajectory that call for a very small δ—for example, when
one body is rotating tightly about another—and it may not be apparent
from the initial situation that such a small δ will be necessary. The time
during a trajectory when such a small δ is needed may be quite short,
but the small δ has to be used throughout, requiring a large amount of
computation that is perhaps unnecessary.

All this suggests that it may be advantageous to have a δ that varies.
In fact, in Lucid it is more "normal" to have varying things than constant
things. It is very easy to allow δ to vary—the code already given does
not require delta to be constant! But how should it vary? The simplest
way, requiring the least change in the code, is to have delta varying

at each stage but being the same for all the bodies at each stage. The advantage of having delta the same for all bodies at each stage is that at each stage every body will be at the same real time. As a result, the Lucid program already given can be used; it need not be changed at all, except for the addition of a definition for delta! The only remaining question is the following: In what way is delta to vary?

What we can do is calculate at each stage a candidate delta for each individual body, and then take delta as the minimum of the candidates. But how do we find the candidate delta's? This question will temporarily lead us into low-level discussions of physics. As we have said, for the method of calculation to be accurate, δ should be short enough for the acceleration of any body to remain essentially constant throughout δ. The acceleration will change if the distance moved in time δ alters the force on a body appreciably, causing the body to experience a different acceleration. This can happen in two ways. The acceleration might be perpendicular to the velocity, causing the body to follow a curved trajectory, which causes a change in the direction of the acceleration. On the other hand, the acceleration may be in the same direction as (or opposite to) the velocity, causing the body to move closer to (or farther away from) the cause of the acceleration, thereby changing the force on the body, and the magnitude of the acceleration. (In most situations, the acceleration and velocity are not perpendicular to each other and both factors have to be taken into consideration, and the smaller candidate chosen.) In the first case, the ratio of the velocity and the acceleration perpendicular to it is proportional to the time taken to make a turn of a given angle. In other words, if we want to limit the angular turn to a certain amount, this ratio should be useful in limiting the time allowed. Some coefficient times the ratio is a good candidate for δ in this case.

In the second case, there does not appear to be any simple combination of acceleration and velocity of a body that can limit the time to allow for the acceleration of the body to change by a certain percentage. The acceleration is caused by some other mass at some distance away. Using just the acceleration and the velocity of the body, we cannot distinguish in the cause these two factors, mass and distance. We would *need* to distinguish them, because they have wildly different effects. If the body gets a given distance closer to the other mass in a given time, the acceleration will change more markedly if the other mass is small but very close than if it is large but far away. Therefore, to specify δ in this case we shall resort to modifying δ according to the way that the acceleration has been varying in the past. If the percentage change in acceleration from the last stage is getting too high, δ will be reduced; if it is unnecessarily low, it will be increased. We will need to "jump start" this process by specifying some initial value for δ. The second version of the n-body program will be identical to the first except that it contains, in the outer where clause, the following definition of delta:

```
delta = initial tournamentMin(candidate,n);
candidate =
  cond
    here >=n: initial candidate;
    method1<= method2: method1;
    default: method2;
  end
method1 = C*(norm(v)/aa);
method2 = jump_start sby D*delta/abs((next aa)/aa-1);
aa = norm(a);
tournamentMin(h,n) = b @t powerOfTwo
  where
    H is current h;
    N is current n;
    b = H fby if width mod 2 eq 0 then min(b, succ b)
            else b sby min(b, succ b) fi  @s (2*here);
    width = N fby ceil(width / 2);
    powerOfTwo = now asa width eq 1;
  end;
```

The definition of candidate uses two dimensionless coefficients: C, which corresponds to the first method of determining delta as explained above, and D, which corresponds to the second method. The values of C and D can be obtained by experiment. Smaller and smaller values should be tried until the trajectories of the various bodies stabilize. To get the same accuracy when comparing the two versions, the delta for Version 1 should be set to the smallest delta obtained in Version 2. When that is done, the trajectories are the same but the running times are significantly different, because, in running Version 2, the values of delta often vary by a factor of 1000! Using the smallest delta of Version 2 in Version 1 increases the running time by at least 100 times.

An interesting modification of Version 2 is obtained when we let delta vary from body to body within stages, as well as between stages. This will imply that the bodies have their own real times, and this causes a problem if we try to use the solution described before. We will not attempt to describe the modification of the program, because this chapter is supposed to describe Lucid, not the details of an application of Lucid. Suffice it to say that such modifications are easily possible and give even more savings in execution time.

2.6   Another Application: LU Decomposition

The following equations define LU decomposition without pivoting in terms of two simple recurrence relations that can be found in [5].

$$l_{i,j} = a_{i,j} - \sum_{k=1}^{j-1} l_{i,k} u_{k,j} \quad j <= i \quad i = 1, 2, 3, ..., n.$$

$$u_{i,j} = \frac{a_{i,j} - \sum_{k=1}^{i-1} l_{i,k} u_{k,j}}{l_{i,i}} \quad i < j \quad j = 2, 3, ..., n$$

The above recurrence relations can be written directly in Lucid. The lower-triangular matrix 1 and the upper triangular matrix u can be put together as one matrix (since they do not overlap):

```
if j<=i then l else u
  where

    l = A - sigma(M, j-1);
    u = (A - sigma(M, i-1))/diag(l);

    M = row(l)*col(u);

    sigma(P,n) = sum @t (n+1)
                      where
                        sum = 0 fby sum + P;
                      end;
    i = here;
    j = here1;
    row(M) = swap1 M;
    col(M) = swap M;
    diag(L) = L @s1 i;

  end;
```

Clearly, the Lucid program expresses only those data dependencies inherent in the recurrence relations. This means that any parallel implementation will not be affected by data dependencies introduced by features or constructs of the programming language. This enables a parallel implementation to exploit all the available parallelism.

The naive LU decomposition defined by the above recurrence relations and implemented by the above Lucid program will not work on singular matrices. Despite this drawback of the naive LU decomposition method, we have included it here to illustrate how it is often simple to take mathematical recurrence relations and to implement them directly as Lucid programs.

A more practical algorithm for computing LU decomposition is one based on LU decomposition with pivoting and is given to us in [7] by the following sequential, imperative program:

```
for k  ←  1 to n-1 do
        Find l such that
              | A(l,k) | = max(|A(k, k) | , ..., | A(n, k) | )
        PIV(k)  ← l    {the pivot row}
        A(PIV(k), k)  ↔  A(k, k)
        c  ← 1/A(k,k)
        for i  ← k+1 to n do
              A(i, k)  ← A(i, k) × c
        for j  ← k+1 to n do
              A(PIV(k), j)  ↔  A(k, j)
              for i  ← k+1 to n do
                    A(i, j)  ← A(i, j) -
                          A(i, k) × A(k, j)
```

This algorithm is implemented by the following Lucid program:

```
LU
  where

    LU = makeRow(firstCol(D));

    B = A fby restCols(D);

    D = if i <= k
        then swapPivRow
        else swapPivRow/pivRow sby1 restCols(swapPivRow -
            firstCol(D)*pivRow)
        fi;

    pivRow = B @s pivPt;

    swapPivRow = cond
                i eq pivPt  : B @s k;
                i eq k      : pivRow;
                default     : B;
              end;

    pivPt = tournamentMax(abs(firstCol(B)),size);

    tournamentMax(h,n) = b @t powerOfTwo
        where
          H is current h;
          N is current n;
          b = i fby if width mod 2 eq 0 then max(b, succ b)
```

```
                     else b sby max(b, succ b) fi  @s (2*i);
            width = N fby ceil(width / 2);
            powerOfTwo = now asa width eq 1;
            max(v,w) == if H @s v > H @s w then v else w fi;
          end;

      size = i onFinding iseod firstCol(A);
      firstCol(M) = initial1 M;
      restCols(M) = succ1 M;
      makeRow(C) = swap1 C;
      i = here;
      j = here1;
      k = now;
    end
```

It is interesting to compare this Lucid program and the conventional imperative program. In the Lucid program there is one "loop" that is evident, in the definition of B. The value of B is a (time) sequence of matrices, starting with the original matrix A. The next values of B are defined in terms of the current values of B, via D. Variable D is defined to be a whole new array, corresponding to the changes made to A by one pass through the outer loop of the imperative program. The first column of D will be a column of the final result, LU, and the rest of D is the next value of B. (The imperative program builds up the final result a column at a time, also.)

The outer loop of the imperative program is discernible in the indirectly recursive definition of B. None of the other loops in the imperative program correspond to recursive definitions in the Lucid program. The variable swapPivRow encapsulates all the changes made by the "interchange" operators of the imperative program. All the other changes made to A are expressed in the definition of D, without loops. All those changes can be made simultaneously. There appears to be no control structure in the program (apart from the outer loop) because no control structure is necessary. In Lucid, contexts are implicit, parallelism is implicit, and control is implicit (in data dependencies). The parallelism in the Lucid program is fine grain and implicit, whereas the task-level parallelism of the parallel implementation of the sequential program is coarse grain and would need to be explicitly specified.

2.7 Parallelism

In this section we will discuss the amount of implicit parallelism in the applications programs given above. We will assume that there is some architecture and model of computation that can exploit all the implicit parallelism, and we will discuss the execution time on such a machine. The design of such an architecture will be considered briefly in the next section.

The execution time of the n-body program, for n bodies simulated for t stages, is of order $t\ lg\ n$. At each stage, the same amount of work is needed to calculate p and v, given a, and calculating a involves summing the acceleration contributions from all the other bodies, which will depend on $lg\ n$ (using the tournament summation routine given in the program). The calculations for all the bodies at a given stage will proceed in parallel. There are t stages that have to be considered successively.

The execution time of the LU decomposition program with pivoting is of order $n\ lg\ n$ also (where the input matrix is n by n). The n columns of LU are the first columns of the matrices D. The matrices D have to be produced successively, and for each one the time taken depends only on $lg\ n$ because everything can be calculated in parallel except for finding the row that will be used for pivoting. Using the tournament maximum finding routine given in the program, the time taken for doing that will depend on $log\ n$.

Given no more than n processors for the n-body program and no more than n^2 processors for the LU decomposition program, the programs will run with constant efficiency. (It is a feature of the models of computation and architectures being considered, we believe, that they are scalable as long as they are given programs with enough parallelism.)

It is worth noting that Lucid equations can be run sequentially on a uniprocessor machine or in parallel on a multiprocessor machine without changing the program.

2.8   Efficient Execution of Lucid Programs

Efficient execution of Lucid programs requires a radically different family of computing models. The family of parallel graph reduction models used with functional programs[8, 6] is not appropriate for this purpose. In parallel graph reduction, implicit parallelism is exploited in the simultaneous reduction or rewriting of monolithic data structures. Consequently, the parallel implementation of these monolithic data structures has to follow the rewrite or reduction rules that define the data structures. This means that parallel execution is inhibited when the elements of the data structure are independent. For example, to add two vectors represented as lists in a pairwise fashion, using parallel graph reduction, would require sequential and possibly pipelined addition of elements of the two lists, even though all element pairs could really be added together independently of each other.

A Lucid program views all data intensionally. By this we mean that data is viewed as a collection of elements rather than as a monolithic data structure. A consequence of the intensional view of data is that operators on data values that are unrelated can be executed in parallel even though they may *conceptually* be part of a data structure. For example, two vectors can be added pairwise simultaneously if the elements in each list are independent of each other. This view of computation is at the heart of the family of intensional computing models that we refer to as *eduction*. The word eduction is defined in the Oxford English Dictionary as follows: "The action of drawing forth, eliciting, or developing from a state of latent, rudimentary, or potential existence; the action of educing (principles, results of calculations) from the data."

EDUCTION—A FAMILY OF INTENSIONAL COMPUTING MODELS

In eduction, each variable or term of a Lucid program denotes an unordered set of value-holders, each of which is identified by its relative conceptual position among all value-holders for that variable or term. We use the word daton to refer to a particular value-holder of a variable or term. For example v_g denotes the gth daton of the variable or term denoted by v. Note that g is the context that we refer to as the tag of the daton. Each operator of a Lucid program denotes a function that computes the values for the datons of the defining term or variable with values of datons of its argument terms and variables. A computation can be thought to be the execution of a Lucid program given a set of sequences of input daton values (over time) and a sequence (over time) of needs for values of output datons of the program.

A computing model conducts the computation in stages. A computational stage is a logical concept and does not necessarily correspond to physical time. At the initial stage, none of the values of datons except possibly for the values of input datons are defined. At each subsequent stage, some of the undefined datons are computed. Eventually, the values of needed output datons are computed. We claim that a computing model can be described using the following two characteristics.

1. Which daton values are to be computed
2. When these daton values are to be computed

Independent of the computing model, the sequence of needs for output daton values, in fact, indicates which output daton values are needed, and if an output daton value is needed, at which stage it is needed. It is important to note that all computing models implement the denotational semantics of each operator faithfully. The operational function applied to argument daton values to produce a result daton value is the same for all computing models. Furthermore, this operational function is the correct interpretation of its mathematical counterpart.

We require the computing model that we use to execute Lucid programs to be efficient. In defining efficiency, we assume that the underlying implementation has a finite amount of processing, storage, and communication resources that computations can use. An efficient computing model should exploit as much useful parallelism as possible while bounding the amount of useless parallelism exploited. We say that a daton is useful if its value determines the value of some needed output daton; otherwise, the daton is useless. Restated, an efficient model should compute as many useful daton values as possible, as soon as possible, while computing only a bounded number of useless daton values. Consider a simple intensional computing model that requires all daton values to be computed as soon as possible. We call this the eager computing model. Although the eager model exploits as much parallelism as possible, it incurs an unbounded amount of waste in the form of computed daton values that are useless. Such a model is therefore inefficient. Data-driven dataflow architectures[12, 7] are implementations of variants of the eager computing model. Inefficiencies manifest themselves in these architectures as resource bottlenecks.

Now consider the lazy intensional computing model[1]. The lazy computing model can be concretely described using the notion of demands. In particular, a daton value is demanded when it is required to be computed and the demand for the daton value is satisfied when the daton value is defined. Note that the demand for the value of a constant daton or an available input daton is satisfied immediately.

The lazy computing model can be succinctly described as follows:

□ The need for an output daton value at some stage causes the daton value to be demanded at that stage.

□ If a daton value (e_i) is demanded at some stage, then and only then are the values of all datons that are known to determine value of daton e_i demanded.

Output daton values are demanded at the stages at which they are needed. A demand for a daton value causes demands for those daton values that are known to determine it. For example, consider the following definition:

```
x = ( if p then a else b fi ) * y
```

Demand for value of x_i at stage t causes demands for values of p_i and y_i at stage $t + 1$ because values of only these datons are known to determine the value of daton x_i at stage t. Assuming that the value of p_i is defined at stage s and it is T, the daton value a_i can be demanded at stage $s + 1$ since this value is now known to determine value of x_i. We claim that the lazy computing model does not demand (and therefore compute) values of any useless daton. (A formal proof is beyond the scope of this book. Interested readers are referred to [7].) The model satisfies the condition for efficiency, which is that the amount of useless parallelism exploited should be bounded (which in the case of the lazy model is zero). However, in general, the amount of useful parallelism exploited when using the lazy model is less than optimal. This is because the model demands values of datons only when they are known to be useful in its effort to bound useless computing. For example, in the above definition of variable x, a demand for value of x_i immediately results only in a demand for value of p_i and y_i since the utility of a_i or b_i depends on the value of p_i. Furthermore, one of these values is demanded only when the value of p_i is available. If avoiding useless computing were not a concern, demand for value of x_i would immediately cause values of p_i, a_i, b_i, and y_i to be demanded, resulting in greater parallelism. It is reasonable to assume that, in an implementation of the lazy computing model, the cost of demand propagation as required by the model and the cost of executing tag-manipulation operators (such as fby, @s, succ) is lower than the cost of executing arithmetic and logic operators such as addition, multiplication, and comparison. Therefore the apparent slowdown due to demand-propagation is not significant. We illustrate how the lazy computing model effectively exploits useful parallelism inherent in the tournamentSum function shown in Figure 2.2. Assume that the time taken to process and propagate a demand and the time taken to execute tag-manipulation operators of Lucid are significantly smaller than the time taken to execute (a possibly floating-point) operation such as an arithmetic or logic operation. The tournamentSum function theoretically computes the sum of a (spatial) sequence of numbers of length n in $O[ceiling(log_2 n)]$ time, which is optimal. The processing of a demand for tournamentSum(h, n) at Lucid time t and space 0 is shown in Figure 2.4.

Initially, a demand for the sum of all numbers propagates as demands for the sum of each half of the sequence of numbers, which eventually causes demands for each of the numbers. Each pair of numbers is added together to produce a sequence of sum of pairs of numbers. This is repeated again, producing a sequence of sums of quadruples of numbers. Eventually, the sum of all numbers is computed. This is illustrated in Figure 2.5.

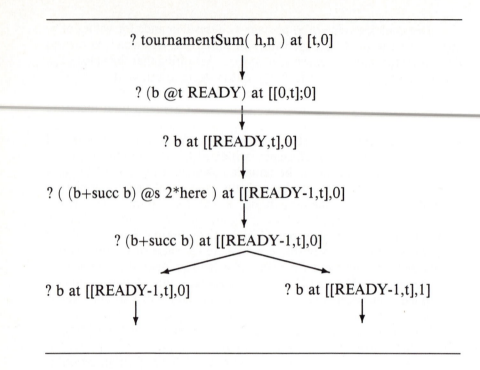

FIGURE 2.4
Propagation of demands to compute `tournamentSum( h, n)`.

Given that there are n numbers to add such that m is the smallest power of 2 no less than n, the total number of additions when using the lazy model is

$$m/2 + m/4 + \dots + 1 = m - 1.$$

These are performed by the lazy model in $log_2 m$ stages for an average parallelism of $O(m/log_2 m)$. If the eager model we referred to earlier were used, the total number of additions would have been $2m - log_2 m - 1$, which is almost twice the number of additions when using the lazy model. Since $n - 1$ is the lower bound on the number of additions to compute the sum of n numbers, the lazy model exploits useful parallelism in near-optimal time (ignoring demand propagation and tag manipulation times that we assume are nominal). The eager model does almost as many superfluous additions as useful additions while not spending any time on demand propagation.

It is possible to improve the speed of the lazy computing model by computing values of not-yet-useful datons anticipatorily. The resulting

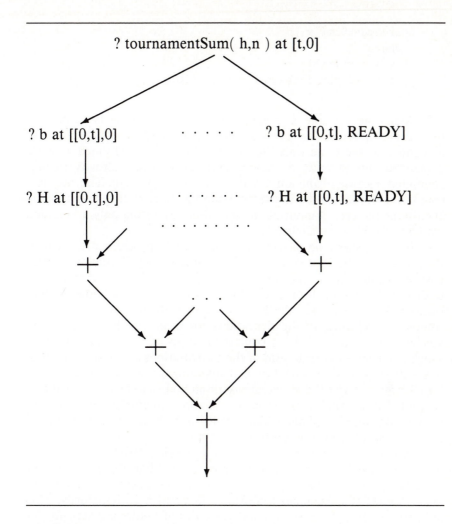

FIGURE 2.5
Computation "lattice" for `tournamentSum`.

computing model is called "eazyflow"[7]. In the eazyflow computing model, for certain variables (called "eager"), demanding a value of a daton known to be useful causes a bounded number of not-yet-useful datons (for the same variable) to also be demanded. This way when these values are demanded, they will be available sooner. Consider the following program to add the square roots of the first 2^n Fibonacci numbers, using `tournamentSum`.

```
tournamentSum( x, n )
  where
  x = sqrt(fib);
  fib = 1 sby 1 sby fib + next fib;
  end
```

Assuming variable x is eager, when a value of x_i is demanded by tournamentSum, a few extra daton values (of x_{i+1} through x_{i+b}) are demanded at the same time. So, when values of x_{i+1} through x_{i+b} are demanded subsequently by tournamentSum, they are already (being) computed because of the anticipatory demands for them. The eazyflow computing model can be shown to exploit at least as much useful parallelism as the lazy computing model, while exploiting only a bounded amount of useless parallelism[7].

Now consider the execution of the n-body program discussed in the previous section using the lazy computing model. Demanding p and v at some Lucid time, and position i for all i less than n, corresponds to demanding the position and velocity of each of the n bodies at that Lucid time. This causes the positions and velocities of bodies to be computed according to the definitions for p and v. In doing so, the acceleration of each body is computed by using the definition of a, which is the (tournament) sum of the contributions of the other bodies. In steady state, at some Lucid time, demanding the position and velocity for all bodies causes the accelerations of all bodies to be demanded and computed in parallel, and the positions and velocities of all bodies to then be computed in parallel. This results in fairly effective exploitation of useful parallelism in the n-body program.

When using the eazyflow computing model, assuming variable p and v are eager in the time dimension, demanding the position and velocity of all bodies at a given time causes the position and velocity of the bodies at subsequent times to be demanded anticipatorily. This means that when the positions and velocities of bodies are actually demanded at subsequent and possibly noncontiguous times, they would be computed much sooner than with the lazy computing model. In other words, the eazyflow computing model exploits the useful parallelism better than the lazy computing model, while incurring some bounded amount of waste.

AN ABSTRACT ARCHITECTURE

The eduction family of computing models suggests an abstract architecture that forms the basis of the "eduction evaluator," which could be a parallel hardware architecture or a distributed software interpreter.

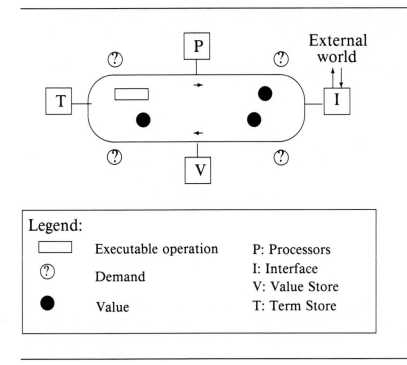

FIGURE 2.6
Abstract eduction architecture.

Such an abstract architecture is shown in Figure 2.6. The abstract architecture consists of four components: processor pool (P), interface(I), value store (V), and term store (T). The processor pool consists of a number of processing elements that are capable of executing all the basic arithmetic and logical operators of Lucid. The interface allows for the evaluator to communicate with the external world. The value store retains names of datons, their values, and status of values along with a list of demanders. The term store consists of the program being executed and a list of suspended operators waiting for values that have been demanded.

Program execution begins by a demand for value of an output daton at the switch. The demand is processed at the value store to determine if it has already been computed. If it has, the value is returned to the demander, which in this case is the external world. If not, the daton name is recorded in the value store with its status as "being computed" and the demand is sent to the term store. The appropriate operator template is created, and each value that the operator needs to execute is demanded. The demands bypass the processor pool and the interface and go directly to the value store. If the value has not been computed yet or is being computed, the demand is retained in the store so that it can be satisfied when the value is eventually computed. If the value already exists, it is returned to the term store where it is inserted into the appropriate suspended-operator template. If the arrival of a value at the term store causes a suspended operator to be executable, it is sent to the processor pool where the operator is applied. The result is sent via the switch to the value store or to the term store. A value arriving at a value store causes the value to be recorded for the appropriate daton, its status to be changed to "computed" and all pending demands for the value to be satisfied and the values to be sent to the term store.

2.9   Conclusion

We have demonstrated, using Lucid programs for the n-body problem and for LU decomposition, that it possible to write programs for parallel processing without having to say explicitly what is to be done in parallel and what is not. The declarative nature of an implicitly parallel language such as Lucid, resulting as it does in properties such as referential transparency, allows for rapid prototyping and modifiability. Moreover, if the language is intensional, as is Lucid, programs are very concise and can read much like the equations in physics that they are intended to solve (if that is the sort of application being considered). This means that the programmer can concentrate on the application (the physics, say), rather than the details of managing multiple processors.

The parallelism inherent in programs in languages such as Lucid can be extracted by using an appropriately designed architecture or by implementing the language on one of the current crop of commercially available multiprocessor systems. The latter approach has limitations because the implicit parallelism in programs that can best be discovered automatically is often of a fine-grain variety. Most of the commercially available multiprocessor architectures are really ensembles of von Neumann machines, which makes this type of parallelism more difficult to exploit in the sense that the compiler technology to do so is not very mature. If we take a prescriptive view of the situation, we can see that architectures can be designed to handle languages of the type we have been considering. In this paper we argue that there is an architecture, the eduction evaluator, that can exploit the parallelism implicit in programs such as the n-body program discussed earlier.

2.10 Acknowledgments

The authors would like to acknowledge the support of the U.S. National Science Foundation and the Mitsubishi Electric Company. They would also like to thank Liz Luntzel of SRI for patiently and diligently drawing the figures using LaTeX.

References

1. E.A. Ashcroft, *Dataflow and Eduction: Data-driven and Demand-driven Distributed Computation*, Current Trends in Concurrency, J.W. de Bakker, W-P. de Roever, and G. Rozenberg Eds., Lecture Notes in Computer Science, no. 224, pp.1-50. Springer-Verlag, 1985.

2. A.A. Faustini and W.W. Wadge, *Intensional Programming*, in *The Role of Languages in Problem Solving 2*, J.C. Boudreaux, B.W. Hamill, and R. Jernigan. Eds.), Elsevier Science Publishers B.V. (North-Holland), 1987.

3. G. Fox et al., *Solving Problems on Concurrent Processors*, vol 1, Englewood Cliffs, N.J.: Prentice-Hall, 1988.

4. C. F. Gerald, *Applied Numerical Analysis*, 2d ed. Reading, Mass.: Addison-Wesley, 1978,

5. J.R. Hindley and J.P. Seldin, *Introduction to Combinators and λ-Calculus*, London Mathematical Society, Cambridge University Press, 1986.

6. P. Hudak, *The Conception, Evolution, and Application of Functional Programming Languages*, ACM Computing Surveys, vol. 21, no. 3 (1989), pp.359-411.

7. R. Jagannathan, *A Descriptive and Prescriptive Model for Dataflow Semantics*, Technical Report Number SRI-CSL-88-5, Computer Science Laboratory, SRI International, Menlo Park, Cal., 1988.

8. S. L. Peyton Jones, *The Implementation of Functional Programming Languages*, Prentice-Hall Series in Computer Science, 1987.

9. P.J. Landin, *The Next 700 Programming Languages*, Communications of the ACM, vol. 9, no. 3 (1966), pp.157-66.

10. R.E. Lord, J.S. Kowalik, and S.P. Kumar, *Solving Linear Algebraic Equations on an MIMD Computer*, Journal of the Association for Computing Machinery, vol. 30, no.1 (January 1983), pp.103-17.

11. R. Montague, *Formal Philosophy*, Selected Papers of Richard Montague, Richmond Thomason Ed., New Haven: Yale University Press, 1974.

12. P.C. Treleaven, D.R. Brownbridge, and R.P. Hopkins, *Data-driven and Demand-driven Computer Architectures*, ACM Computing Surveys, vol. 14, no. 1 (March 1982), pp. 93–144.

13. W.W. Wadge and E.A. Ashcroft, *Lucid, the Dataflow Programming Language*, Academic Press U.K., 1985.

3

EPL—Parallel Programming with Recurrent Equations

Boleslaw K. Szymanski

3.1 Introduction

The difficulties arising in adapting and using traditional high-level languages to program parallel computations have increased interest in alternative programming paradigms, such as dataflow, assertive, reduction and logic. In many of these paradigms proposed languages belong to the larger class of functional languages.

A functional program defines a set of functions [8]. An execution of a functional program can be viewed as an application of a function to a set of values of its parameters. Since there is no notion of the program state, side effects of conventional programming languages are completely absent in the functional programs. Consequently, concurrent execution of multiple functions is permitted. The usefulness of the functional languages in parallel programming can be further advanced if the referential transparency is supported by allowing only definitions and not assignments in the program. The referential transparency simplifies compile-time program transformation, data dependence analysis, and parallelization.

In one of the novel approaches to parallel programming, called assertive paradigm [26], computations are specified as sets of assertions about properties of the solution, and not as sequences of procedural steps. Procedural solutions are automatically generated from the assertive description. Programmers are not involved in the detailed implementation, as efficiency and correctness are ensured by the underlying language translator.

Depending on the type of assertions that are used as a basis for a notation, different languages for assertive programming have been proposed. Perhaps the best known is logic programming with the Prolog language as its prime example [22]. In Prolog, assertions are expressed as Horn clauses. Automatic inference of new facts from the given rules and known facts makes it a convenient programming tool for artificial intelligence and expert systems. However, in applications in which numerical computations are involved, Prolog's usefulness is questionable because of the inconvenience of expressing numerical algorithms in that language.

Another notation for assertive programming was proposed in equational languages, where assertions are expressed as algebraic equations [4], [10], [17], [30], and [33]. Programs written in equational languages are concise, free from implementation details, and easily amenable to verification and parallel processing. Those programs, however, require a sophisticated translator to generate efficient object code. It is necessary to use global analysis and heuristic program transformations to achieve a quality translation. The role envisaged for the computer is not to execute, step by step, prescribed operations, as in procedural programming, but to find such values of unknown variables, that all stated assertions become true.

Equational languages are naturally suited to mathematical modeling. They are convenient to describe computations that involve solving systems of linear equations that may arise directly (for example, in econometric modeling [21]) or as the result of a discrete approximation of a system of differential equations. Various numerical aspects of the solution, such as the applied method, initial values, or convergence criteria, can be either generated automatically by default or may be provided by the programmer. Equational languages have also been proven to be an effective tool for describing general computational tasks [6].

3.1.1   PARALLEL SCIENTIFIC AND ENGINEERING COMPUTATIONS

Scientific and engineering computations are particularly well suited to parallel processing. It can be claimed that, so far, they have driven the area of parallel computation most aggressively. The size of the problems currently being solved in scientific and engineering computations is often limited more by the computer's ability to produce results in a reasonable time than by the user's real needs. Yet, although vast computationally, scientific and engineering computations are typically regular both in terms of control flow patterns and employed data structures. Quite often such computations comprise an iterative application of numerical algorithms to all (or the majority of) the parts of a data structure. Hence, block algorithms [28] can play an important role in decomposing large-scale computations into separate (and hopefully data independent and thus parallelizable) tasks. Typically, the data structure used in scientific and engineering computations are some variations of multidimensional arrays (sparse matrices, grids, jagged-edge arrays, and even hierarchical structures can be viewed as such). The natural language of science is based on equations and, therefore, a language for scientific and engineering computations has to, at the minimum, facilitate expressing algebraic equations.

Many of the above characteristics are satisfied by Fortran. Hence, a new language proposed in this chapter attempts to preserve those properties of Fortran that have contributed to its remarkable resiliency and widespread use in the scientific and engineering community.

Fortran was designed for uniprocessor computers. A modern scientific and engineering computation language should satisfy several additional postulates arising from the plethora of architectures on which such computations can be executed. The most important postulate is to separate the issue of execution from the meaning of the computation. In other words, the language should enable the programmer to separate "what" from "how"; the description of the meaning of the computation should be separated from the statements (if any) directing the compiler in translating the computation for execution on any particular architecture. Such a feature would also contribute to rapid prototyping and increased portability of the code.

In defining any large-scale computation, proper facilities for problem decompositions are of the utmost importance. The description of the computation in each of the decomposed subtasks should be separate from the description of the interactions between those subtasks. In conventional programming, the first description roughly corresponds to programming-in-the-small, and the second one to programming-in-the-large. The language for large-scale scientific and engineering programming should provide the means for keeping these descriptions independent.

An assignment statement—the cornerstone of any conventional programming language—is the main source of difficulty in parallel programming, since it changes the value of the variable on the left-hand side of the assignment. Thus the value of any variable at a certain point of the program execution is defined by the last executed assignment statement for this variable. Consequently, execution of any procedure that uses global variables is affected not only by the values of its parameters but also by the assignments to these global variables. Likewise, the effects of the procedure execution may include changes to the values of the global variables that have assignment statements in the procedure body. If there are parallel execution paths, each containing assignment statements for a variable, then the final value of this variable may depend on a relative speed with which those paths are executed. To avoid such side effects of the assignment statement, many parallel functional languages enforce the single assignment rule, which states that each variable can have only one value and prior to the assignment of a value, the variable is undefined.

The single assignment rule leads to declaring and operating on structures that have "excessive" dimensionality. After all, a variable that would be merely reassigned in a traditional language, in the presence of a single assignment rule, has to be viewed as a vector of values and each reassignment has to be indexed by a different subscript. However, such additional dimension of a variable is needed only in the source program. The optimizing compiler should easily be able to eliminate the additional dimension in the variable implementation [35]. If there are several candidate dimensions for elimination, the compiler can select an elimination by analyzing all data dependences in a computation. Thus it is reasonable to expect that such a selection will be at least as good as the selection made by the programmer who typically bases the decision more on intuition and the meaning of the variable than on implementation efficiency.

Finally, to enable a language compiler to explore parallelism at its lowest level, the language should also provide operators that can be applied to components of the arguments in a dataflow fashion—that is, in the order that those components become available and not in the order of their declaration.

3.1.2   EQUATIONAL PROGRAMMING LANGUAGE

This chapter presents recent work on creating and implementing a simple language for programming parallel scientific and engineering computations that is based on a few basic principles and yet satisfies the postulates discussed above. In addition, the chapter illustrates how a parallelizing compiler for this language works. The language, called

Equational Programming Language (EPL), has been developed at Rensselaer Polytechnic Institute by the author and a group of his graduate students[1].

An EPL program consists of *data declarations* and *annotated conditional equations.* Equations are defined over multidimensional jagged-edge arrays and may be annotated by *virtual processors* to which they are assigned. Data declarations are annotated by the *record* and *port* designators that are used to identify interfaces with an external environment and other programs.

In addition to programs, the EPL user can define *configurations*, which describe interconnections between ports of different processes. Configurations allow the programmer to reuse the same EPL programs in different computations. They also facilitate computation decomposition. A port creates a fair merge of its input sequences and, hence, enables the user an easy expression of nondeterminism [9] without changing a functional character of the program definition.

In addition to single-valued data structures, EPL programs contain *subscripts* that assume the range of integers as their values. Subscripts give EPL dual flavor. In the *definitional view*, they may be treated as universal quantifiers, and equations are then viewed as logical predicates. In the *operational view* they can be seen as loop control variables, and each equation is then seen as a statement nested in loops implied by its subscripts. A more detailed description of the language follows in subsequent sections.

The basic techniques used in the compilation of EPL programs are data dependence analysis and data attribute propagation. In a single program, the data dependences are represented in the compact form by the *conditional array graph.* This graph associates each dependence with its attributes, such as the distance between dependent elements, conditions under which dependence holds, and subscripts assigned to it. Both explicit data dependences (defined by the usage of one data structure in an equation defining the other), and implicit data dependences (implied, for example, by the sequentiality of the reading of incoming messages) are represented as various kinds of edges in the conditional array graph. Each node of this graph contains information about the represented entity, such as the number and the ranges of its dimensions, its type and class, and conditions guarding its definitions.

The correctness of the program is checked by verifying the consistency of the different attributes of data structures and data dependences.

[1]The author wishes to express his thanks to Jeanette Bruno, Bruce McKenney, Can Ozturan, Balaram Sinharoy, and Kevin Spier for their efforts in implementing EPL.

To accomplish this, the EPL compiler propagates data and dependence attributes along the edges of the graph.

A similar dependence graph is also created for a configuration. It shows the data dependences among the processes of the computation and is used in scheduling processes and mapping them onto the processors.

The extent of transformation required to generate the object code depends on the architecture at hand. As is the case for Lucid, which was presented in chapter 2, EPL programs can be almost directly executed on a specialized tagged dataflow architecture that consists of the following functional elements:

- **Token memory:** A memory in which each tagged value (subscripted variable) is stored after it has been read in or evaluated.

- **Matching unit:** A unit that releases an equation instance for execution when all data values needed for that equation evaluation are present in the token memory.

- **Executing unit:** One of a number of arithmetic units able to evaluate EPL operators.

The conditional array graph defines the number of copies of a value needed in the token memory for each evaluated subscripted variable. One copy is needed for each edge outgoing from the node representing the corresponding variable. Each process may have a separate dataflow machine assigned for its execution, and these machines have to be connected to exchange data through process ports. Alternatively, one dataflow machine may be allocated to the entire computation, and then ports would merely define equivalences of variables from different processes. With a sufficient number of arithmetic units, the dataflow implementation can provide the highest parallelism. However, eager scheduling of EPL computations can easily lead to an excessive demand for the token memory [1].

In Flynn's well-known classification of parallel computational models [14], the von Neumann model is characterized by a single stream of instructions controlling a single stream of data (SISD). To achieve parallelism, multiple data streams have been introduced, creating a SIMD model. A further extension is to add multiple instruction streams and this extension leads to MIMD architectures. The last category can be conveniently split on the basis of a data access mechanism into shared- and distributed-memory architectures. In the shared-memory architectures processors have an equal access to one global memory. In the distributed-memory architectures, each processor has a direct access to its local memory and indirect access to the memory of other processors.

The indirect access is typically supported through a message-passing mechanism that enables processors to communicate with each other.

For a SIMD machine, such as the Connection Machine, the major task of the EPL translation is to identify an EPL subscript that will index individual processors (i.e., a subscript that defines a domain of the computation). Equations indexed by the domain subscript will be executed in parallel on different processors. The selection of the domain subscript is influenced by the fact that a reference to an indexing expression that is different from a domain subscript implies communication of data from another processor.

Even more involving is the translation for multiple instruction multiple data (MIMD) machines. For shared-memory architectures in this class, only the allocation of equations to processors is an issue. The ports can be easily and efficiently implemented as blocks of shared memory. The efficient translation requires strong memory optimization to counterweight the effects of "excessive" dimensions that are present because of the single assignment rule enforced by the language.

For distributed-memory machines, the additional difficulty arises from data placement. In the current implementation of the EPL code generator for the Intel hypercube, it is assumed that data are distributed together with the equations that define them. This assumption makes the optimal allocation of equations to processors a more complex task.

In the following sections, the language is described first, together with a few examples. Then, the design of the EPL compiler is discussed and the tools used in the language implementation are described. Finally, a conclusion and an outline of future research are given.

3.2   The EPL Language

A computation in EPL is defined as a collection of *cooperating processes*. Each process is described by a single program in EPL. This section starts with a discussion of a process definition. Equations are described first, followed by a discussion of data structures and subscripts. Next, a description of a configuration definition is given. Finally, examples of numerical computations defined in EPL are presented. In the discussion of the language, we refer to two simple examples: computing the factorial function and listing prime numbers using a sieve.

Typically, the factorial function is defined iteratively. The factorial of the number k is expressed as the factorial of the number k−1 times k. However, this is a "sequential" algorithm in which each step depends on the previous one. Instead, we can take advantage of the fact that in the expression: $1 * 2 * 3 * \ldots n$, multiplication can be associated into binary operations in any order, including a tree-like ordering that requires $\log_2(n)$ steps in parallel:

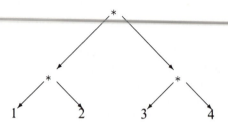

The second example involves removing (or marking) multiples of primes in the vector of natural numbers and then selecting remaining (unmarked) numbers as primes. Both examples are used in the following sections to illustrate EPL language constructs.

3.2.1   EQUATIONS

In general, an equational program consists of a set of k equations over m arrays written in the following form:

$$\mathbf{P}_1[\mathbf{I}_1] : \mathbf{A}_1[\mathbf{I}] = f_1(\ldots, \mathbf{A}_j[E_j^1], \ldots)$$

...

$$\mathbf{P}_i[\mathbf{I}_i] : \mathbf{A}_i[\mathbf{I}] = f_i(\ldots, \mathbf{A}_j[E_j^i], \ldots)$$

...

$$\mathbf{P}_k[\mathbf{I}_k] : \mathbf{A}_k[\mathbf{I}] = f_k(\ldots, \mathbf{A}_j[E_j^k], \ldots)$$

where i=1,2,...,k; j=1,2,...,m. **I** is a list of n subscripts $I_1, \ldots, I_n$, and n denotes the dimensionality of arrays. $\mathbf{I}_i$ is a sublist of list **I**. Each E_j^i is a list of n indexing expressions. Processor annotations $\mathbf{P}_1, \mathbf{P}_2 \ldots$ are discussed later in Section 3.2.5.

The set of values of the arrays $\mathbf{A}_1, \ldots, \mathbf{A}_k$ that makes all the equations hold (m-k input arrays $\mathbf{A}_{k+1}, \ldots, \mathbf{A}_m$ are assumed to be known) defines the semantics of the EPL program. As shown in [29], such a set of values is well defined if the data dependences induced by those equations do not contain cyclical dependences, the condition that can be checked during compile time for the most common cases. In particular, this condition is satisfied if the equations are recurrent—that is, each indexing expression E_j^i is in the form $I_e - c$, where c is a nonzero integer. Such semantics do not imply any particular evaluation strategy and, therefore, leave the compiler free to select the implementation.

Only arrays declared on the highest level of the EPL declarations and prefixed variables can appear in the equations. A function f_i used on the right-hand side of equation i can be a composition of conditional operators (both if-then-else and case operators are allowed), all traditional programming language operators, such as arithmetic (+,-,/,*, and taking to power **), logical (&,|,~), and relational (==,=>,<=,<,>, ~=) operators, as well as the standard built-in mathematical and string functions.

Each array element can be defined only once. If there are several equations defining an array, each equation should be defined over a disjoint subset of ranges of that variable dimensions. Potentially, the arrays can be infinite, if some ranges of their dimensions are not bounded. Verifying that each range can be associated with the condition that, when satisfied, will enable termination of computation along this range is an important part of the program consistency checking performed by the EPL compiler.

Similar equations are used in languages such as data flow languages [1], iterative languages, such as Lucid [4] (see Chapter 2), MEDEE [13] or Xloop [36], and parallel programming languages, such as Crystal [10] (see Chapter 7). On the other hand, those equations represent a special case of a mutually recursive set of function definitions when the arguments are restricted to ranges (i.e. sets of intervals of natural numbers) (cf. LISP, or FP [5]). There are several reasons for staying within the limitation of recursively defined arrays rather than allowing unrestricted recursion; the most important are as follows:

□ The area of applications that we have in mind is that of scientific computation. In this area, arrays are fundamental data structures and equations describing the relations between arrays are both natural and adequate.

□ Restricting the arguments of the defined entities to integers and imposing syntactical restrictions on the expressions that appear as subscripts on the left-hand side of the equations have enabled us to design powerful program analysis algorithms and to develop an optimizing compiler rather than an interpreter.

For associative operators, there is a reduction operator, called all, defined in EPL. This operator is applied to a vector of arguments in an eager manner. That is, it is applied to arguments in the order of their availability and not in the increasing order of the vector index. In

EPL, all can be used with +, *, &, |, ||, max, min. The all opera-
tor reduces the number of dimensions of its argument by the number of
dimensions over which reduction is made. The optional condition can
be used to select elements of the argument to which the operator should
be applied. Thus the following equations define variables psum equal to
the sum of positive elements in a[i,j], and pcnt equal to the number
of positive elements in a[i,j].

```
psum = all('+',a[i,j],i,j: a[i,j]>0);
pcnt = all('+',1,i,j: a[i,j]>0);
```

Operations on multidimensional structures are often applied piece-
wise element by element. In an equation describing such an application,
the same subscripts have to be repeated in the arguments and the result
as shown below:

```
res[sub1,...,subn] = arg1[sub1,...,subn]
                     operator arg2[sub1,...,subn];
```

The EPL language tolerates an omission of subscripts, if all multidimensional structures in the given equation have the same leftmost
subscripts omitted. Hence, the above equation can be written as:

```
res = arg1 operator arg2;
```

More importantly, the same process can be applied to different
structures by merely replacing the declarations of its input and output
files. For example, let's consider a simple equation:

```
a = b+c;
```

It can describe the sum of any two variables such as two scalars
b,c, two vectors b,c, or two arrays b,c, depending on the declarations
of a,b,c.

3.2.2   EPL DATA STRUCTURES

The basic data structure in EPL is a hierarchical multidimensional tree
structure that can be seen as a generalization of a ragged array. The root
of the declaration tree could be a *file*, a *group*, or a basic data type. The
leaves are declarations of basic (structureless) data elements. The intermediate tree nodes are groups. The basic data types are similar to those
allowed in C or any other modern language: integer types short, int,
and long; floating-point types real, double, and quad; boolean logic

and character char. Each declaration of the structure tree node consists
of the following:

□ **Level indicator:** An integer number that defines a position of the
node in the tree. A node is the root of a subtree that consists
of all nodes marked with the higher level indicators immediately
following it.

□ **Node type:** A designator such as a file, a group, or any of the basic
types.

□ **Name list:** A list that specifies data defined at the tree node. Each
name can be followed by the dimension definition that enumerates
dimension descriptors enclosed in square brackets.

The dimension descriptor may be either an integer constant that
defines the range of the corresponding dimension, or an asterisk that
indicates a variable size dimension. An asterisk can be optionally followed by a string "$<= c$", where c is a constant that defines an upper
limit of a variable size dimension. The lower limit of each dimension
is one. For example, to define a program that iteratively evaluates the
approximations of the solution of the equation x=exp(-x), we can use
the following definition:

```
group: approx[*], 1 real x, error;
x[sub1] = if sub1==1 then 0 else exp(-x[sub1-1]);
```

There is one group called approx that consists of two integer vectors: x and error. Both vectors inherit the same dimension from their
root that is a group approx. The dimension of the group is of a variable
size. It is expected that such a range is defined in the program by an
equation, such as:

```
range.approx[sub1] = if error[sub1]<0.0001 then sub1;
```

In the above definition the range is defined in terms of the values of
the variable in which it is used. Such a definition is the equivalent of the
minimalization operator and states that the range of approx is bounded
by the smallest integer for which the condition error[sub1]<0.0001 is
satisfied.

Alternatively, the range of a dimension may be inferred from other
equations that implicitly relate ranges of referenced variables. The dimension of a variable may also inherit its range from the parent structure (this is how ranges of x and error are defined) or it may be defined
by the size of the input to the process. If the range definition yields
zero, then the corresponding variable does not exist. For example, the

program listing primes can be simply stated as a vector of sieves, each
sieve removing its multiples from the input list of numbers:

```
group: list[*], 1 int nin, nout[*<=1];
int: prime;
```

```
nout[sub1,sub2]=nin[sub1,sub2];
range.nout[sub1]=if mod(nin[sub1],prime)==0 then 0 else 1;
prime=nin[1];
```

The vector list has two components, an input list of numbers nin
and output sublist nout, which may have some elements omitted (those
elements for which the corresponding range is zero). The variable prime,
which is not not a part of the group list, simply takes the first element
of the input list as the found prime.

Files.   A file declaration should be at the root of any structure that is
part of a process interface with the environment. In such a structure,
some of the levels may be annotated by a record keyword to show the
file record structure.

A file definition can be annotated with the type of the file, which
will direct its implementation. For parallel processing, the most significant type is a port file. It is used to exchange data between processes.
This exchange can take place when processes run in parallel, or for processes that interleave their execution (in the latter case, a port file is
implemented as an ordinary subroutine call). The distinction is made
during configuration processing based on types of dependences between
port variables in the global graph (see Section 3.4.5).

An input port is a collector of records (messages). It is private to
its consumer and, therefore, it can have only one consumer but several producers. Records from different producers are received by the
consumer in order of their arrival. Thus ports implement a fair merge
of their input sequences and thereby enable the programmer to express
nondeterministic computations [9]. Alternatively, the input port may be
declared as multiport and then an input record will be accepted only
if it comes from a producer specified by the (mandatory in that case)
address statement. For example, the multiport file defined below will
first read a value from the first child, and then a value from the second
child, no matter in which order they arrived at the input:

```
file: fromf(multiport),
1 record: rec[2],
  2 int: val;
```

```
address.val[sub1]=sub1;
res=val[1]/val[2];
```

The process that attempts to receive a message from an empty input port is blocked until the message arrives. Incoming messages are queued in the port without any effect on execution of the receiving process. Thus a port file allows for more parallelism than a multiport.

An output port is a producer of records for an input port or ports. The destination of the message is defined by the value of a variable created by prefixing the record name with a keyword address. For instance, the main process of the factorial example may send the lower subinterval of the total multiplication interval to its first child (i.e., the factors process) and the upper subinterval to the second one:

```
file: tof(port),
1 record: down[2],
  2 int: arg, limit;

address.down[sub1]=sub1;

limit[1]=lower_limit;
limit[2]=upper_limit;
```

An output port file always has one producer, but it can have many consumers (input ports). An address of the destination port is part of the message sent out and it is assigned to the address.record variable of the output port file in the producer process.

A port file can also be designated as input and output, and then it is used for bidirectional communication with the other process(es). Since the order of execution in EPL is not defined, without information about port interconnections, the compiler would be free to select either sending or receiving as the first operation in the process implementation. The wrong decision would lead to a deadlock, as in the following example of the server-customer computation:

```
/* server */                    /* customer */
file: request_response(port),   file: request_response(port),
      record: rec[10],                record: rec[10],
      2 int: val;                     2 int: val;

out.val=2*in.val;               out.val[sub1]=if sub1==1 then 2
                                      else in.val[sub1-1]+2;
```

Due to the data dependence of out.val on in.val in the server, the compiler will schedule message "receive" (getting in.val) before message "send". However, in the customer, the internal data dependence permits scheduling "send" and "receive" in any order, and executing "receive" first leads to a deadlock. Section 3.4.5 explains how the configurator translator identifies external dependences of this kind and how it uses them to modify the dependence graph used by the EPL compiler to prevent generation of a code that deadlocks.

In addition to being the end-user language, EPL also serves as an intermediate language in translating EPL programs into parallel code. The most general optimizations take place at the source-to-source translation stage. Direct use of the port files in an efficient way is often too cumbersome to be managed by the programmer and it can easily be replaced by the annotations that are translated by the EPL compiler into port files. A future implementation of the EPL system will include an algorithm for decomposing large EPL programs into a set of programs with ports for data exchange defined by the compiler, so there will be no need for a programmer to use port files directly.

Subscripts.   To operate on multidimensional structures, an iteration block was introduced in several functional languages [4], [13]. In the EPL language, iterations are expressed implicitly by the use of a special type of variables called *subscripts*. A subscript can assume any integer value from 1 to the range of the dimension associated with that subscript. Thus, in the EPL language, each equation with subscripts defines and refers to multidimensional structures. Subscripts are declared by simply preceding a list of subscript names with the keyword subscript:

```
subscript: i,j;
```

Each declared subscript is associated with a single range in the entire body of the program. In addition, there are ten generic subscripts denoted by the keywords sub0, sub1,...,sub9. Generic subscripts are local to each equation and, therefore, can be associated with different ranges in different equations.

The subscripts have both definitional and operational interpretations. In the former, they universally quantify the equations in which they appear. Equations are then treated as logical predicates with equality. Operationally, subscripts are loop control variables and imply nested loops around each equation in which they appear.

There is a special class of indirect indexes, called sublinear subscripts. They appear in various applications so often that a special construct devoted to them has been introduced in EPL. Formally, an indirect index s defined over the subscript i is sublinear to this subscript if it satisfies the following property:

$$0 \leq s(1) \leq 1 \text{ and } s(i) \leq s(i+1) \leq s(i)+1 \text{ for } i = 1, 2 \ldots$$

It immediately follows from this definition that the sublinear subscript s(i) starts with a value of either 0 or 1, and then, with each increase of i, it either grows by one or stays the same. Typically, there is a condition associated with each sublinear subscript; this condition dictates when the subscript increases. This is the way a sublinear subscript is defined in EPL. For example, in the sieve definition the removal of multiples of the found prime can be defined by using a sublinear subscript instead of an additional 0/1 dimension.

```
group: list[*], 1 int: nin, nout;
int: prime;

subscript: j, sublinear s(j): mod(nin[j],prime)>0;

nout[s]=nin[j];
prime=nin[1];
```

Subscripts to which the defined one is sublinear are listed in parentheses. Sublinear subscripts have an implicit range determined by the number of times the defining condition yields true.

The sublinear subscripts are convenient in expressing such typical operations, as creating the list of selected elements, operating on sparse matrices, or defining a subset of the given set. Even more important is the fact that in the implementation of the process no new iteration has to be created for computation associated with the sublinear subscript. Instead, all necessary computation can be nested in the iterations created for subscripts in terms of which the considered sublinear subscript has been defined.

Since the implementation of the sublinear subscript is so efficient, the EPL compiler attempts to recognize syntacticly structures that are used in the role of sublinear subscripts. Operations on vectors nin and nout will be implemented in a single iteration over j, even if the above program fragment were rewritten as

```
group: list[*], 1 int: nin, nout, s;
int: prime;

subscript: j;
s[j]=if j==1 then 0
     elsif mod(nin[j],prime)>0 then s[j-1]+1 else s[j-1];
```

```
nout[s[j]]=nin[j];
prime=nin[1];
```

To enforce the single assignment rule for equations that could potentially violate it, the EPL compiler generates the object code that prevents rewriting of a variable that has been already defined. In the above program, rewritting of the variable nout would be attempted for those vector nin entries that are nonprimes. To prevent such rewriting, for each element of nout, only the first assignment is executed. For example, in the first sieve prime=2, and nout[2]=3. The second assignment for j=2 that would set nout[2] to 4 is ignored. Thus, when executed, both above fragments would produce the same result.

In summary, the EPL hierarchical data structures, trees with nodes representing repeating substructures, are capable of representing data types used in other functional languages. Iterations in EPL are expressed implicitly, leaving room for the compiler to optimally arrange their scopes and nesting in the generated object code.

3.2.3 PROCESS HEADER

As previously mentioned, the computation is defined in EPL as a collection of cooperating processes. Each process is defined by an EPL program, and their cooperation is defined in the configuration language. The process definition starts with a *header*, which defines the process name and its interfaces by listing its input and output files. For a single process fact that defines a sequential evaluation of the factorial function, the following is the EPL header:

```
process: fact;
input: in;
output: out;
```

To define a process that can be invoked many times during the computation, the name of the process should be followed by the repetition indicator, as shown below:

```
process: factors[*];
        or
process: arrayproc[*,*];
```

Processes defined in that way can be created dynamically and can have multiple copies of themselves executing concurrently. Each asterisk denotes a "dimension" of a process creation. The factorial function can be calculated in parallel by a tree of concurrently executing processes called `factors` that are created by the process `main`. The following headers can be used in this definition:

```
process: main;
input: in, fromf;
output: out, tof;

process: factors[*];
input: fromf, tof;
output: tof, fromf;
```

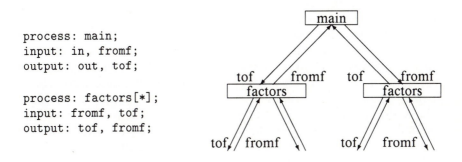

The second header implies that we have many factorial processes created by the process main, and those processes in turn can have children of their own. Process main gets the argument of the factorial function in the file `in`, and writes the result to file `out`. In addition, it uses files `tof` and `fromf` to interact with its children (the first generation factorial processes). In Section 3.2.4, we discuss how the configuration definition is used to distinguish between many different `fromf` and `tof` files created for factorial processes.

The sequential version of the factorial function can be written in EPL as follows:

```
process: fact;
input: in;
output: out;

file: in, 1 int: n;
file: out,1 int: res;
int: aux[*];

/* α1 */ range.aux = if n>1 then n else 1;
/* α2 */ aux[i] = if i==1 then 1 else aux[i-1]*i;
/* α3 */ res = last.aux;
```

Using the `all` operator, we can eliminate the variable aux and replace the above three equations by the following two:

```
range.i = if n>1 then n else 1;
res = all('*',i,i);
```

The prefix range or range(k) where k=1,2,... refers to the last (k-1 from the last, respectively) dimension of the variable that follows the prefix. Since the reference to the last element of a structure happens often, there is another prefix, namely last or last(k), that refers to the last value in the last dimension (k last dimensions, respectively) of the variable that follows this prefix. Both range and last have one (k, respectively) less dimension(s) than the variable that follows them.

The sieve computation of primes discussed earlier is inefficient, since it involves checking all natural numbers in the given range against all primes in that range. The more efficient algorithm is described below. It marks multiples of primes in the vector of odd numbers and then selects all unmarked numbers as primes. Each prime p starts marking the multiples from itself and the new markings are p elements apart in the odd number vector (so addition is used instead of more expensive mod function). Only primes smaller than the square root of the given range are used in marking. The corresponding EPL program can be written as follows:

```
process: plist;
input: in; output: list;

file: in, 1 int: limit;
file: list, 1 int: prime[*];

group: step[*], 1 int: mltp[*],zero[*],bprm;
int: lstm[*];
subscript: i,j, sublinear s(j): lstm[j]==2*j+1;

mltp[i,j] = if mltp[i,j-bprm[i]]==bprm[i] then bprm[i]
            elsif i==1 then 2*j+1 else mltp[i-1,j];
bprm[i] = if i==1 then 3 else last.zero[i-1];
zero[sub1] = mltp[sub1+(bprm-1)/2];
range.zero = if 2*sub1+1==zero[sub1] then sub1;

primes[s] = lstm[j];
lstm[j]=mltp[range.i,j];

range.mltp = limit;
range.bprm = if last.zero[i]*last.zero[i]>limit then i;
```

For each prime number bprm[i], those entries in a vector mltp[i] that are multiples of bprm[i] are set to bprm[i]. The next prime number for multiples elimination is selected by defining a subvector zero[i] of the vector mltp[i] that extends from the previous prime to the next prime entry in mltp (see the definition of range.zero).

The first four equations define an infinite computation that, if run, would produce prime numbers in the vector bprim. To make this process finite and more efficient, the next four equations define the output vector prime and the termination conditions. The resultant vector is defined by a sublinear index s that selects only prime number entries from the vector lstm. The vector lstm in turn is defined as the last column of the array mltp. Only primes whose square is less than the given limit are used in marking multiples (see the definition of range.bprm).

For simplicity of expression, equations defining range.mltp, zero, range.bprm and range.zero have some dimensions omitted.

The following two EPL programs implement the parallel version of the factorial example:

```
process: main;
input: in,fromf;
output: out,tof;

file: in, 1 int:n;
file: out, 1 int:res;
file: tof(port), 1 rec: trec[*<=2],
                 2 int: arg, limit;
file: fromf(port), 1 int: partres[*<=2];
subscript i;

range.i = if n<2 then 0 else 2;
res = if n<2 then 1 else partres[1]*partres[2];
limit[i] = (n+i-1)/2;
arg[i] = n*i/2;
```

It should be noted that the data conversions in EPL are the same as in C. In particular, a real value is rounded to the nearest integer if assigned to an integer variable. For example, if n=5, then arg[1]=2. Children of a process are created by need, when the first message is directed to them. The above process does not invoke any children when the input n is less than two, because then the range of the subscript i is zero and no structure indexed by it exists.

```
process: factors[*];
input: fromf, tof;
output: tof,fromf;
```

```
file: tof(port), 1 rec: trec[*<=2],
                 2 int: arg,limit;
file: fromf(port), 1 int: partres[*<=2];
subscript i;
```

```
range.in.trec=1;
range.out.partres=1;
range.i = if in.limit[1]>2 then 2 else 0;
limit[i] = (limit[1]+i-1)/2;
arg[i] = in.arg[1]-(i-1)*out.limit[1];
partres[1] = if limit[1]==1 then arg[1] else
             if limit[1]==2 then arg[1]*(arg[1]-1)
             else all('*',partres[i],i);
```

The range definitions in the above program state that the input
contains exactly one record, and the output has either two records or
none at all. If a variable in an input/output file is not prefixed with the
keyword in or out, then references on the left-hand side of equations
are assumed to be out and on the right-hand side to be in. The tree of
invoked processes and the exchanged values for this computation are
shown in Figure 3.1.

The description of the factorial computation that defines two processes, main and factors, is to detailed for the programmer to write,
since it requires laborious and yet mechanical splitting of equations that
define partres and res and declaring necessary port files. Section 3.2.5
discusses how equivalent computation can be described with little effort
from the programmer through the use of annotations. That section also
presents an annotated version of the prime listing program.

3.2.4   CONFIGURATION

The previously discussed process definition was incomplete, because it
did not provide information on how the locally named ports are interconnected. Such a description is provided in the configuration that
simply lists the processes participating in the computations and shows
how their ports are connected. Thus the objects of the configuration are
processes (and their aggregates) and ports. Statements of the configuration represent relations between the ports of different processes.

One attribute of the configuration nodes is of interest here. A *node
type* classifies the process as follows:

□ **Simple:** An individually defined process. This is the default node
type.

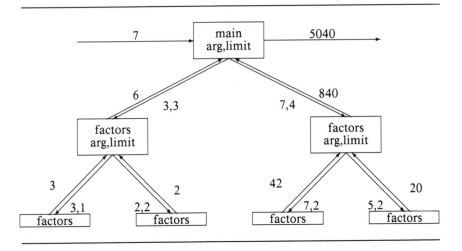

FIGURE 3.1
Processes invoked by the EPL factorial program

□ **Compound:** A group of processes for which a configuration is defined separately.

□ **Interactive:** A user communicating with the system through a terminal.

Compound nodes enable the programmer to define hierarchical configurations.

For processes created dynamically, the interconnection of ports may include parents, children, and siblings, each of them being just a copy of the same process. A parent can also be any other process in the configuration. To show interconnections of ports for dynamically created processes, the keywords parent, child, and sibling can be used in the configuration description. For example, the configuration of the parallel factorial example contains one dynamically created process factors, so it can be defined as:

```
main: tof -> tof: factors: fromf -> fromf: main;
factors: tof, fromf -> child;
factors: tof, fromf -> parent;
```

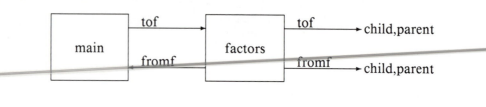

FIGURE 3.2
Graphical representation of the factorial configuration

To avoid such linearized description of the interconnections, the EPL system provides the graphical configuration language implemented under X-windows. This allows the programmer to draw the connections directly on the screen and also to check the compatibility of the exchanged port records. Figure 3.2 shows a graphical representation of the factorial configuration.

The EPL compiler optimizes the use of the main memory assigned to data structures, often replacing the entire range of an array by a window, i.e., a few elements. When such an array has to be communicated to the other processes, only that window – that is, a few records at a time, can be sent out. Therefore program optimization causes a producer to store or send as few records at a time as feasible. Similarly, a consumer has also to store and consume a minimum number of records at a time. When producer and consumer processes are concurrent, the corresponding port requires a buffer for a limited number of records. This type of data exchange implements a pipeline (also referred to as a stream). The programmer is not involved in this aspect of object code design, however the EPL compiler produces warnings for ports that cannot be implemented in that fashion.

Processes and ports are the basic building blocks of a computation in the EPL environment. A process can be viewed as a generalization of a function or a procedure. If two processes exchanging data through ports are data dependent in such a way that parallel execution is not possible, then their cooperation is implemented by a function call. However, if data dependences allow for parallel execution, both processes are invoked together and compute concurrently.

A computation can be easily modified by composing new configurations that include existing, as well as new or modified, processes and ports. Modularity based on multiple processes has been introduced in many operating systems and languages, including T.H.E. [12], Unix

[20], and CSP [16]. It has been expanded here by providing for ports that allow for one-to-many and many-to-one communications.

The easy modifiability of a configuration supports several development modes. For example, individual processes and ports may be reused as the computation is required to change. Entire independently developed computations may be easily interconnected by adding interfacing processes that convert commonly used variables from the form used in one computation to that of the other. Thus the creation of a new computation that encompasses the functions of several old computations does not require designing it from scratch.

3.2.5 ANNOTATIONS

Each equation can be annotated with a name of virtual processors assemblage (ranging from a dimensionless scalar to a multidimensional array) on which this equation is to be executed. Virtual processors can be indexed by the equation's subscripts that would identify instances of equations assigned to individual virtual processors of the assemblage. All equations annotated by the same virtual processor instance are guaranteed to be executed on the same physical processor. Depending on the ratio of physical processors to virtual processors used in annotations, one or more virtual processes can be executed on the same physical processor. Annotated equations are expended by the EPL compiler into elementary (unannotated) programs. The EPL compiler uses existing data dependences to define the port files necessary for creating an equivalent computation. For example, the parallel factorial computation can be described by a single annotated program:

```
process: main;
input: in;
output: out;

file: in, 1 int:n;
file: out, 1 int:res;
subscript: p, s;

fp[p]:f[s,p] = if s==1 then if 2*p>n then 2*p-1
                                     else (2*p-1)*2*p
              elsif 2*p>range.f[s-1] then f[s-1,2*p-1]
              else f[s-1,2*p-1]*f[s-1,2*p];
fp[p]:range(2).f = if range.f[s]==1 then s;
```

```
range.f[s] = if s==1 then (n+1)/2
                else (range.f[s-1]+1)/2;
res = last(2).f;
```

The vector of virtual processors called fp will execute the first
two equations. The computation of range(2).f in parallel is redundant,
but its recalculation is typically less costly than its broadcast from the
process main. Please note that the above program, when stripped of the
annotations, is still a correct definition of the factorial function. The
values of the array f from the unannotated program are shown below:

	values of f			
s	p=1	p=2	p=3	p=4
1	2	12	30	7
2	24	210		
3	5040			

An annotation is orthogonal to the functional description and
defines initial partitioning of the program into parallel tasks. It also
facilitates automatic partitioning since it decomposes the problem of
generating optimal size parallel tasks into two parts:

□ Finding the optimal annotation independently of the underlying
architecture, and then

□ Mapping virtual processors of the annotation into physical processors of the parallel computer at hand.

Annotations also support rapid prototyping of different parallel
solutions. The above given parallel factorial process requires excessive
communication. In each step of the computation, the process fp[p]
needs data from two siblings (numbered, respectively, 2*p-1 and 2*p).
We can decrease the volume of communication to one message per process per step, but then each process will communicate with a different
sibling in each step:

```
f[p]:f[s,p]=if s==1 then if p+range.f[s]>n then proc
                           else p*(p+range.f[s])
                elsif p+range.f[s]>range.f[s-1] then f[s-1,p]
                else f[s-1,p]*f[s-1,p+range.f[s]];
```

In each step, the processor fp[p] needs data from the processor p+range.f[s] and since the computation requires $\log_2 n$ steps, the same number of connections between processors is needed. Interestingly, the required communication pattern can be neatly embedded into the hypercube shown in Figure 3.3.

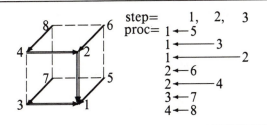

FIGURE 3.3
Factorial computation embedded into the hypercube

The prime listing program can be rewritten in such a way that multiples marking will be done in parallel. If we assume that the initial vector of primes bprm is given in input, then the corresponding process can be described as

```
process: plist;
input: in; output: list;

file: in, 1 int: limit,bprm[*];
file: list, 1 int: prime[*];

int: mltp[*,*],lstm[*];
subscript: i,j, sublinear s(j): lstm[j]==2*j+1;

        primes[s]=lstm[j];
        lstm[j]=all('min',mltp[i,j],i);
m[i]:mltp[i,j]=if mltp[i,j-bprm[i]]==bprm[i] then bprm[i]
               else 2*j+1;
m[i]:range.mltp[i]=limit;
```

Even with annotations, the program leaves the compiler some freedom to explore parallelism. For example, a vector of processors m[i] may send the calculated values of vectors mltp[i] one by one, or in groups for intervals of values of j, or the entire vector at once at the end of the computation. The above choices result in computations with different granularity and are adequate for different architectures.

3.3   LU Decomposition Example

Let's consider the following standard definition of LU decomposition without pivoting [11] for a matrix Ain, with the upper triangular matrix U transposed:

$$L_{i,j} = Ain_{i,j} - \sum_{k=1}^{j-1} L_{i,k} * U_{j,k} \; where \; j \leq i \leq n$$

$$U_{j,i} = \frac{Ain_{i,j} - \sum_{k=1}^{i-1} L_{i,k} * U_{j,k}}{l_{i,i}} \; where \; i < j \leq n$$

These two simple recurrence relations can be directly written in EPL as follows:

```
int: n;                         /* array size */
real: Ain[*,*],U[*,*],L[*,*];   /* arrays */
subscript: i,j;

range.Ain=n;                    /* omitted subscript */
range(2).Ain=n;
range.U[j]=j-1;
range.L[i]=i;

L[i,j]=if j<=i then Ain[i,j]
        -all('+',L[i,sub1]*U[j,sub1],sub1:sub1<j);
U[j,i]=if i<j then (Ain[i,j]
        -all('+',L[i,sub1]*U[j,sub1],sub1:sub1<i))/L[i,i];
```

Please note that the above range equations define L and U as triangular matrices. We had to transpose U since EPL is able to represent only lower triangular matrices, not upper ones. The definition of range.A encompasses a vector of ranges. All elements of this vector are equal to n, so the dimension in the defining equation can be safely dropped. It will be restored by the EPL compiler during program translation (but in the generated code, it will be a scalar again).

The definitions of the arrays U and L refer to both of these arrays. Using the condition analysis, the EPL compiler will be able to recognize the following:

□ In the definition of L, the reference to L[i,sub1] satisfies sub1<j (from the condition used in the all operator).

□ In the definition of L, the reference to U[j,sub1] satisfies j<=i (from the condition guarding this equation) and, as above, sub1<j.

☐ In the definition of U, the reference to L[i,sub1] satisfies sub1<i<j (from the conditions in the all and if operators); likewise reference to L[i,i] satisfies i<j.

☐ In the definition of U, the reference to U[j,sub1] satisfies sub1<i (from the condition used in the all operator).

The above inequalities ensure that the EPL compiler can generate a schedule in which all new definitions of L and U elements will refer only to already defined elements of L and U (see Section 3.4.4).

A more efficient and robust algorithm using pivoting for LU decomposition was given in [24]. The EPL implementation of this program is given below.

```
process: lu;
input: inf;
output: outf;

file: inf, 1 rec: inr1, 2 int: n,
            1 rec: inr2[*], 2 real: Ain[*];
file: outf, 1 rec: out1[*], 2 real: L[*],
            1 rec: out2[*], 2 real: U[*];
subscript: i, j, k;

range(2).Ain = n;
range.Ain = n;
range.U[i]=n-i;
range.L[i]=n-i+1;

indx[k,i] = if i<=k then k
    elsif abs(A[k,i,k])>abs(A[k,indx[k,i-1],k]) then i
    else indx[k,i-1];
PIV[k] = last.indx[k];
L[k,sub1] = A[k,sub1+k-1,k]/A[k,PIV[k],k];
U[k,sub1] = A[k,PIV[k],sub1+k];
A[k,i,j] = if k==1 then Ain[i,j]
    elsif i>k & j>k then A[k-1,i,j]-L[k-1,i]*U[k-1,j]
    elsif j==k & i==k then A[k-1,PIV[k],j]
    elsif j==k & i==PIV[k] then A[k-1,k,j]
    else A[k-1,i,j];
```

The program operates on the sequence of matrices A[i,*,*] that initially are equal to the input matrix Ain. The variable indx is used to find the largest element in the part of the vector A[k,*,k]. The position of the largest element is remembered in the variable PIV[k]. The matrices L and U are declared as triangular. An important point is that the EPL compiler will notice that the else part of the A[k,i,j] definition copies the old values onto themselves, and, therefore, the compiler will eliminate this copying [35]. As discussed in [24], the computation can be broken into the following tasks:

□ **diagonal:** Any of the k tasks (denoted as teq_k) that operate on the diagonal of the matrix A.

□ **subarray:** Tasks $t_{k,j}$ for $j > k$, that operate on the part of the matrix A.

Such partitioning of the computation can be achieved simply in EPL by breaking the definition of A into three parts and annotating the program as follows:

```
teq[k]:   indx[k,i] = if i<=k then k
                elsif abs(A[k,i,k])>abs(A[k,indx[k,i-1],k])
                then i else indx[k,i-1];
teq:      PIV = last.indx;
teq[k]:   L[k,sub1] = A[k,sub1+k-1,k]/A[k,PIV[k],k];
teq[k]:   A[k,i,k] = if i==k then A[k-1,PIV[k],k]
                elsif i==PIV[k] then A[k-1,k,k]
                else A[k-1,i,k];
t[k,sub1]:A[k,i,j] = if i>k & j>k then
                A[k-1,i,j]-L[k-1,i-k]*U[k-1,j-k];
t[k,sub1]:U[k,sub1] = A[k,PIV[k],sub1+k];
          A[k,i,j] = if i<k | j<k then A[k-1,i,j];
```

Trivial indexing expressions in the equation defining PIV have been omitted without the loss of program consistency. Since annotations do not change the meaning of the specification, the debugging and testing can be done on the sequential version, and then through experimentation with the different annotations the most suitable annotated version can be used to generate production code. It should be noted that "sequential version" means that the EPL compiler would seek parallelism in this version unguided by the programmer's annotations, so it does not necessarily have to be executed on the uniprocessor.

3.4   Implementation Issues

Equational programs require a powerful translator to generate an efficient object code. There is a need for techniques of program transformation and synthesis, data dependence analysis, and program optimization heuristics to achieve a quality translation. Optimization techniques have to provide for different features of parallel hardware, such as availability and characteristics of vector co-processors, communication interconnections and delays, shared memories, or local caches.

The overall goal in designing an implementation is to develop methods and techniques for equational program translation that are able to produce object code that equals or surpasses the efficiency of hand-written parallel programs. To make this goal attainable, we limited the forms of algebraic equations allowed in the Equational Programming Language to recurrences defined over generalized multidimensional arrays.

The overall structure of the compiler is shown in Figure 3.4. In this chapter, we will discuss only the most important parts: annotation processing, conditional array graph construction, data attribute propagation and object code scheduling in the EPL compiler and interconnection processing in the configurator.

3.4.1   ANNOTATION PROCESSING

Annotated equations are expanded by a preprocessor [27] into a collection of unannotated EPL programs. The annotation preprocessor does the following:

- □ It creates unannotated programs defined by annotated fragments of an EPL program.
- □ It determines and declares port files necessary for interconnecting computation processes into a hierarchical tree-like network.
- □ It derives data dependences between communicating processes to enable their proper synchronization.

Since each virtual processor is defined by the computation it performs, we will often refer to an annotated EPL program fragment as a virtual processor on which this fragment executes. Each virtual processor P_i produces arrays, typically used by other virtual processors, and in turn consumes arrays produced by others. Such an exchange of arrays necessitates communication and, hence, implies data dependences between processors (see Figure 3.5). To translate the annotated program into efficient, more elementary EPL programs, it is necessary to embed a spanning tree into the process dependence graph. The following three criteria are used in selecting such an embedding:

- □ **Dimension nesting:** Whenever there is a connection in the process communication graph between nodes with the different

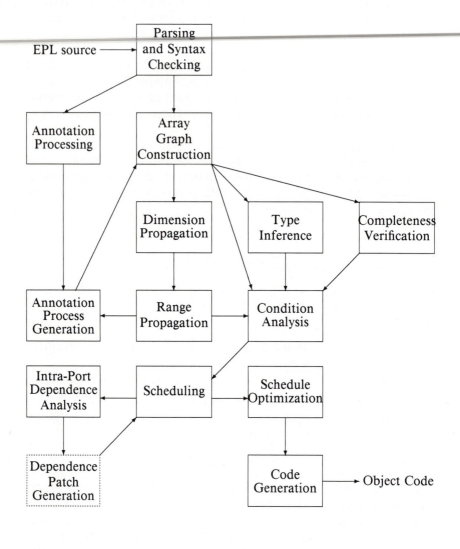

FIGURE 3.4
The structure of the EPL compiler

```
process: a1 ;
input: inf ;
output: outf ;

file: inf(disp)  , 1 rec: inr1 , 2 int : n ;
file: outf(disp) , 1 rec: out1[*], 2 real: res ;

subs: i , j , k , l , m ;
int: a[9,9] , b[9] , e , g[20] , f[20,10] , c[20,10] ,d ;

          res[i] = g[i]*d ;
P1[i]  : b[i]   = i ;
P1[i]  : d      = if i == 1 then all(+,a[i,j],i,j) endif ;
P2[i,j]: a[i,j] = b[i]*a[i,j-1] ;
P3[m]  : e      = all(+,d*g[k],k) ;
P3[m]  : g[m]   = d*k*last.c[m] ;
P4[m,k]: f[m,k] = e*m ;
P5[m,k]: c[m,k] = e*f[m,k]*f[k,m] ;
```

Sample annotated program

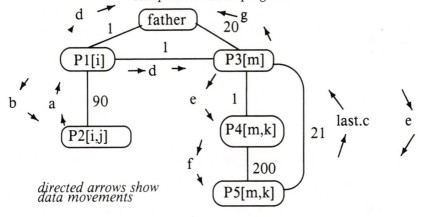

directed arrows show
data movements

Process communication graph (PCG)

FIGURE 3.5
Example of process annotations and their communication graph

dimensionality, the node with more dimensions should be located lower in the spanning tree. If, for example, processors P1[i,j] were located above the processors P2[i] in the spanning tree, the addressing and creation of child processes in P1 would involve executing an if-then statement in all $i * j$ P1 processors.

□ **Range nesting:** Processors sharing the same range should be clustered together in the spanning tree as much as possible. Variables that share ranges tend to appear in the same equations. Thus, clustering such variables together will decrease the number of cross-process references to distributed variables.

□ **data flow:** The total cost of communication of the selected spanning tree should be the minimum for all spanning trees satisfying the above two criteria.

Let G(V,E) be a process communication graph with V={v_i} as a set of nodes (processors) and E={$e_{i,j}$} as a set of edges (communications). Let c : E → R be a cost function that associates a cost $c(e_{i,j}) > 0$ with each edge $e_{i,j}$. The cost $c(e_{i,j})$ represents the volume of data being sent from the processor i to the processor j. A distance function d^T : E → N can then be associated with each spanning tree T. Let $d^T(e_{i,j})$ define the minimum number of tree edges that have to be traversed on the path from the processor i to the processor j . The cost of the spanning tree T can then be defined as:

$$C(T) = \sum_{e_{i,j} \in E} c(e_{i,j}) * d^T(e_{i,j})$$

It has been shown that this problem is equivalent to finding a proper cut-tree, which, in turn, can be done by solving | V | maximal flow problems [18]. Each maximal flow problem requires $O(|V|^3)$ applications of the Ford-Fulkerson labeling procedure. Hence, finding the solution takes $O(|V|^4)$ steps.

The three criteria discussed above led to the following algorithm for embedding a tree into the process communication graph on the basis of processor ranges:

□ For all ranges: Cluster all processors with the given range into a single node and calculate the total outflow of data from this node.

□ Select the range that has the clustered node with the minimum outflow of data and split the processors into two sets accordingly.

□ Repeat the above procedure for each split set of nodes.

An example of the efficient spanning tree selection is shown in Figure 3.6.

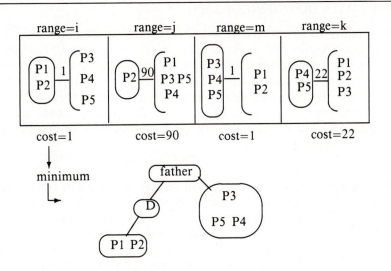

the minimum cluster chosen in the first iteration

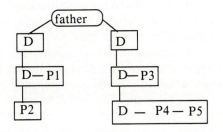

the minimum with dummy processes after all iterations

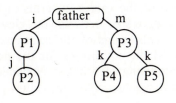

final tree selected

FIGURE 3.6
The minimum spanning tree selection

3.4.2   DATA DEPENDENCE GRAPH

The primary structure used by the EPL compiler in data flow analysis of
the source program and in object code generation is a *conditional dependence graph*. In the dependence graph, the nodes represent activities and
data structures in a computation. The edges of the graph are directed
to indicate when one data structure or activity is dependent on another.
The dependence exists if an activity (or a data value) cannot start (or
be accessed) until another activity has been executed (or another data
value has been determined).

Advantages of Condition Analysis.   An underlying decision made in the
use of data flow analysis in procedural compilers has been to ignore conditions guarding paths of flow of control. However, recognizing equivalent or exclusive guarding conditions improves the checking and optimization capabilities of the compiler. In the equational programming
environment, such recognition can be done efficiently (at least for some
common cases) because of the simple semantics of the language. The
analysis of the conditional dependences involves traversing various computational paths in the equational program and collecting a conjunctive
set of inequalities for each path. When the conjunction of the conditions
is not satisfiable, the dependences labeled by these conditions never hold
and therefore can be ignored in further analysis.

If we assume that all dependences in the dependence graph are absolute (always exist), we restrict the optimizations that the compiler may
apply and we may even cause the compiler to reject a program as un-
schedulable when it can be scheduled. A typical example of such a situation arises when the programmer is simulating phenomena that spread
outward from the defined initial region. Definitions of this type can
be found in simulations of protein folding [8], fractals, crystal growth,
shock waves, etc. A natural way to describe such behavior would be
to define the outward spread of the values in terms of conditional relations between discrete structures or between the elements of multidimensional structures. The conditions of the relations would dictate
the direction of the spread. If the conditions for the dependences are
ignored, the dependences modeling such behavior would appear to be
cyclic (due to equations that would define the values as spreading in
conflicting directions).

In the case where discrete structures are used, the values typically
grow in one direction based on a set of conditions and in the opposite
direction based on the contradictory set of conditions. By recognizing
that the conditions are contradictory, the compiler can ignore the cyclic
nature of the relations and schedule a solution.

When the behavior is patterned within a multidimensional structure, it is often defined in terms of an initial region of the structure with the rest of the values growing out from the initial region. In this situation, the structure being defined would have multiple sets of dependences: a set of dependences initializing some region and multiple recurrent dependence sets for the various growth directions. A one-directional pass through each dimension in the structure is not sufficient because of the conflicting growth directions.

With the condition analysis, the compiler can attempt to verify that the different growth directions do not overlap and that the growth is monotonic in the different directions. When this is recognized, a regional calculation of the structure can be scheduled.

We have designed and implemented algorithms for conditional dependence analysis that are polynomial in the size of the source program [8]. This is a significant improvement over methods applied in conventional languages that are exponential in the size of the input code.

The advantages of performing condition analysis are threefold:

- More efficient code is generated. Parallelism can be exposed to a greater degree if some dependences are eliminated. In addition, the equivalent conditions are tested only once and the code dependent on them is consolidated into one block.

- Storage use is optimized. The EPL compiler can use the windowing technique for representing the large dimensions through a small-sized window in memory in cases involving more complex subscript expressions.

- Program verification is improved. The single assignment rule can be enforced by checking satisfiability of the conjunction and disjunction of conditions in several equations defining the same variable. Verification of noncircularity of variable definitions is also refined in a similar manner.

EPL Conditional Array Graph.   The dependence graph that the EPL compiler uses is called the *conditional array graph*. It contains nodes representing both data elements and equations from the source program. The size of the graph is kept small by having the nodes represent aggregates. One data node in the array graph will represent all occurrences of a variable in a multidimensional structure and an equation node will represent all the evaluations of the equation. The array graph can formally be defined as

$$G = (V_G, E_G, M_G)$$

where $V_G = \{v_1, \ldots, v_n\}$ is a node set, $E_G \subseteq V_G \times V_G$ is an edge set, and $M_G : L_G = \{l_1, \ldots, l_m\} \rightarrow V_G \cup E_G$ is a labeling function. Each node v_i represents one of the following:

- **Equation:** Each equation from the program creates one node.
- **Variable:** Any variable that appears in equations is represented by a node in the graph (i.e., primitive data structures and implied data structures created by prefixing variable names with keywords range, last, or address).
- **Interface structure:** A structure declared in the program as a part of an input or output file.
- **File:** Each file creates two nodes, one representing an opening and the other a closing of the file.
- **Sublinear subscript:** A subscript explicitly defined as sublinear.

Generally, a node in the array graph represents a program activity. File nodes represent either an opening or a closing of a file, record nodes indicate a read or write operation, and equation nodes represent the evaluation of the equation. Nodes that do not trigger an activity (data nodes and sublinear subscripts) generally indicate a stage in the computation. For example, data nodes indicate that a field has been defined and is available for access.

An edge $e_{i,k}$ drawn between nodes i,k can be one of the following three types:

- **Hierarchical:** A dependence that is implied via declared structures. For example, in input structures, a record node is implied to be dependent on the file node from that structure. This dependence documents the fact that a record cannot be read until the file has been opened.
- **Data:** A dependence that is derived from equations. The node for the data element being defined is made to be dependent on the equation's node and the equation node is, in turn, made dependent on the data nodes for the data elements used in its definition (appearing on the right-hand side of the equation or in a subscripting expression on the left-hand side).
- **Parameter:** A dependence implied by the presence of range, last, and address constructs. The nodes incident to this type of edge depend on the construct involved. For example, a node for the prefix last cannot be referenced until all occurrences of the data structure that it prefixes have been calculated. The edges are drawn between such data structure nodes and the node representing the last construct.

A labeling function M defines a label for each node and edge in the graph. The node label $l_i = M(v_i)$ includes information on the type and class of the node, its dimensionality, ranges of the dimensions, and subscripts associated with these dimensions. The edge label $l_{i,k} = M(e_{i,k})$ includes conditions under which the dependence associated with the edge holds, the type of the dependence, and subscripting information.

The array graph nodes are aggregates (representing multiple occurrences of a data structure or multiple evaluations of an equation), therefore the edges are also aggregates. In order to properly schedule the activities represented by the array graph nodes, the EPL compiler needs to track the subscript expressions involved in the dependences. For example, in the array graph of the serial version of the factorial function, there are nodes for equations $\alpha 1, \alpha 2$, and $\alpha 3$, nodes for variables n, res, aux, range.aux, inr, our, two nodes for each of the files in and out (marked _open and _close, respectively), and edges between them. With $\alpha 2$ defining each i-th occurrence of aux, there is an $e_{\alpha 2, aux}$ edge labeled with i as the subscripting attribute. Also, since $\alpha 2$ refers to aux on the right-hand side of the equation, there is an $e_{aux, \alpha 2}$ edge labeled with i-1.

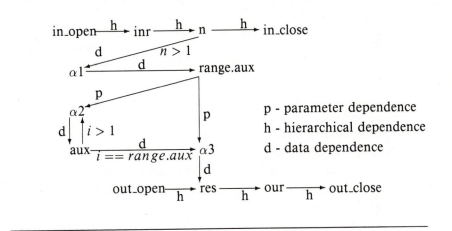

FIGURE 3.7
The conditional array graph for the factorial computation

Figure 3.7 shows the array graph for the serial version of the factorial function. There is an apparent cycle in this graph consisting of aux and $\alpha 2$; however, those nodes are aggregates. A single array graph node for aux represents all the values in the aux vector. Similarly, a single array graph node for $\alpha2$ represents all evaluations of $\alpha2$, one for each element in the aux vector. Hence, this fragment of the conditional array graph can be expanded to the following elementary dependence graph that is free of dependence cycles:

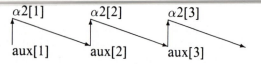

A simple analysis of subscript expressions that label the dependence edges will reveal that fact, and the EPL compiler will be able to produce an iterative solution. It would be difficult and expensive to prove such properties for compound subscript expressions. However, in many common cases the EPL compiler is able to verify that there are no dependences of data on themselves (see Section 3.4.4).

3.4.3 PROPAGATION OF ATTRIBUTES

The conditional array graph contains information about all definitions and uses of the variables in the EPL program. Checking the program and verifying that all the uses of the variable are consistent with each other involves inferring and propagating labels representing data attributes from node to node. The following general types of checks and additions take place:

- Consistency of dimensionality and subscripting, sizes of dimensions and data types of variables are checked through propagating these attributes from node to node.
- Data declaration statements are generated for variables that have been referred to in equations but have not been declared.
- A set of linear algebraic equations is identified wherever an unbreakable cycle (see Section 3.4.4) is detected in an array graph. The adequate initial values, termination conditions, and solving methods can be selected by the programmer or are supplied by default by the compiler.
- Conditions associated with each equation are propagated along the data dependences and checked for satisfiability. Once they are found unsatisfiable, the dependence associated with them is ignored. The conditions are derived from (1) conditions defined in the conditional part of the if statement, (2) conditions present in the sublinear subscript or in all operator, and (3) conditions

implied by the range definitions (i.e., for each subscript i the inequality $0 < i \leq \text{range.i}$ holds).

Experience has shown that these checks are effective in locating 80 to 90 percent of the errors (excluding syntax errors) in the development of a program [34].

An important advantage of the equational semantics of the EPL program is the fact that the condition analysis performed by the EPL compiler can use the equality implied by each equation. This equality will always appear on an equation-to-data node edge. Until the data node is scheduled, the implied equality will be kept separate from the condition. Once the data node has been scheduled, the equality is incorporated into the condition as if it were an equality relationship in the original condition. The new condition will then be propagated to the dependent equation nodes. By including the equalities implied by the equations, the compiler is able to eliminate more variables from the conditions during the final stages of the condition analysis [19].

3.4.4 SCHEDULING AND OPTIMIZATION

A schedule of equation evaluations is determined by a topological sort of an array graph. The scheduling starts with creating a component graph that consists of all the maximal strongly connected components (MSCC) in the array graph and the edges connecting the MSCC's. The component graph is therefore an acyclic directed graph. It can be topologically sorted, usually in many different ways that result in different generated object programs. It is also necessary to schedule MSCC's represented by the nodes in the component graph. Thus the component graph scheduling has to define the schedule for each node in the component graph and then to find the topological sort of the whole graph that results in the highest efficiency of the generated code.

This is done as follows. The subscripts are determined for each node in the component graph. Iterations over these subscripts must bracket the respective nodes to define all the values of the elements in the array variables. Each node must be enclosed within nested iterations if the respective equations or data arrays are of multiple dimensions. The details of the component graph node scheduling are given below in the subsection on MSCC Scheduling.

Once all the nodes have been scheduled, the architecture-dependent optimizations take place. MSCC scheduling represents a minimum ordering of the computation required to compute the correct result. The resultant component graph contains parallel paths and iterations that can be explored in parallelization.

Currently, there are three distinct optimizations done in the second stage of scheduling:

- ◻ Parallel task selection
- ◻ Horizontal partitioning for data parallelism
- ◻ Loop merging and nesting for memory optimization

Parallel Path Selection.   Since the component graph produced in the first stage of the scheduling defines a partial order, there are nodes in it that are not dependent on each other and, therefore, can be executed in parallel. Parallel tasks are created from an initial set of such nodes. Each task is then enlarged by adding nodes that are dependent only on the nodes already in this task. If the extent of parallelism obtained that way exceeds the number of available processors, tasks that require the most communication between themselves are merged together. In the opposite case, a form of horizontal partitioning is used, in which intervals of a subscript in an iteration are assigned to different processors. An extent of parallelism and, more importantly, the amount of communication needed are controlled by the size of the subscript interval. This form of parallelism is particularly suitable for shared memory architectures, since distributing an iteration does not necessitate distributing data structures. For distributed-memory machines that are based on message passing, the EPL compiler assigns data to the processor that produces it (in other words, the processor that executes an equation keeps the resulting data structure in its local memory). Thus, distributing an iteration requires distributing instances of a data structure among different processors. This is cost effective only if references to such distributed data structure are simple.[2]

Horizontal Partitioning.   In horizontal partitioning, slices are made across multidimensional data structures in such a way that data elements evaluated along each slice are independent of each other. This approach is typical of data parallelism suitable for SIMD machines; particularly for the Connection Machine [15]. In horizontal partitioning, one dimension of each data structure might be selected for projection along the processor array, with each processor then holding a single instance of that structure. Operations along that projection dimension take place in parallel [31]. In making a choice of the projection dimension for a variable, certain criteria are considered.

---

[2]Simple index references do not require any communication whereas general index expressions define complex communication patterns.

The best choice of the projection dimension for a variable will have the smallest number of expression-type references along it in the program since each reference of this type would imply a communication step. The respective forms of the expressions are also of interest. A reference that uses expressions in the form i-k or i+k, where i is a subscript and k is a constant is less costly than one that uses a more general form of expression. These special forms of references result in very regular communication patterns ("shift left" and "shift right") which, by avoiding collisions, may be performed efficiently on the Connection Machine.

The second criterion is an extent to which computations can be merged along the projection dimension, since we want the largest possible part of the program to be parallelized. Currently, the selection of the projection dimension is based on the total number of references made to it in the program. In the future implementations, a reference count will be weighted according to the complexity of each reference. We would also like to take advantage of the reduce and scan operations[3], either expressed by the EPL all operator or recognized from the syntactical pattern in the EPL program.

Memory Optimization.   In the memory optimization stage, attempts are made to enlarge the scope of created iterations. Nodes with the same range can be merged to form larger components. Merging scopes of iterations may enable sharing memory locations by elements of the same or related array variables. Let's consider a subgraph that consists of data nodes $\alpha2, \alpha3$, aux, and res in the Figure 3.7. The nodes $\alpha2$ and aux constitute one MSCC, and each of the other two nodes is a MSCC by itself. All three MSCC's have a subscript i ranging over the common range, and the equations use the subscript expressions of the form i-1 or i. If all these nodes are placed within the scope of a single iteration, the vector aux can be represented by a window of at most two elements. If it is possible to retain in memory only a window of the entire dimension of a variable, then the respective dimension is referred to as *virtual*; otherwise it is called *physical*.

Usually, there are many ways in which components can be merged (for different dimensions), each corresponding to different topological sorting of the component graph. The memory requirements of different candidate scopes of iterations serve as the criterion for selecting the optimal merging. The selection is equivalent to the NP-complete problem

---

[3]Reduce applied to a vector produces a scalar result, whereas scan results in a vector of partial results. Both operations can be executed in a time proportional to the logarithm of the vector size on the Connection Machine.

of finding a clique with the maximum weight of nodes in an undirected graph [7]. Therefore the following heuristic is used.

In each step, the algorithm merges components with the same or sublinear subscripts. The compromise is to find the lowest memory cost of mergers progressively. First, dimensions and scopes of outside iterations are determined. Then, proceeding with one iteration at a time, each already processed iteration body is scheduled, and so forth. This procedure determines both the iteration scopes and the order of nesting. The procedure may not lead to the best solution, because the outer iteration scopes are determined without analyzing the possible influence of the inner iterations on memory cost. The inner iteration scopes are optimized locally within the outer ones. However, this greatly reduces the number of alternatives that need to be considered.

The selection of the *seed component* for further mergers may also affect the selected scopes and nesting of iterations. A seed component can be picked at random and merging can then proceed with components connected to the seed by edges. Considering all orders of merging would also greatly increase the number of alternatives. However, the order of merging has little effect on large iteration scopes—which are the most important. Therefore merging along the edges that depart from the seed was selected as a good compromise.

Virtual dimensions are found by the present EPL compiler only if the subscript expressions used to reference the given variable are of the form i-k or i+k, where k is zero or a positive integer, and i is a subscript or sublinear subscript. It should be noted that elements of a window that contains more than one element have to be shifted at the end of each loop execution—that is, the first element shifted to the second position, the second to the third, etc. Alternatively, the indexes referring to elements in the window may be cyclically shifted.

Use of windows is of the utmost importance for optimization purposes [35]. Particularly important is the case of a window of size two that corresponds to indexing expressions of the form i-1. Such a dimension is called a *historical* one, because it is used in each iteration step to distinguish the current value of a structure from the previous (historical) value. For a historical dimension, part of the previous value is often transferred to a new one without any change. This is the point at which the special translation technique for *incremental* structures is applied. A structure is called incremental if the number of its elements affected by each operation is constant. Such a structure is defined by equations of the form

```
x[i,j] = if i==1 then e₀(j)
            elsif j == s₁ then e₁(x[i-1,f₁(j)])
```

```
elsif j == s₂ then e₂(x[i-1,f₂(j)])
   ⋮
elsif j == sₙ then eₙ(x[i-1,fₙ(j)])
else  x[i-1,j];
```

It is assumed that $s_1, \ldots, s_n$ do not depend on j (but they may depend on i). The expressions $e_k, k > 0$ may contain several occurrences of the form $x[i - 1, f_k(j)]$ for different $f_k(j)'$s. Furthermore, we assume that s_i for all $i \leq n$ are distinct and always within the subscript range of the second dimension of x.

With these assumptions, the following special translation has been implemented for such equations:

```
declare xw[2,*] ...
loop for i=1 ...
   if i==1 then { Initial case }
      loop for j=1 ...
            xw[1,j] = e₀(j);
   endthen { if i==1 }
   else { General case, i>1 }
      { Save needed old values in xw[2,*] }
      xw[2,f₁(s₁)] = xw[1,f₁(s₁)];
            ·
      xw[2,fₙ(sₙ)] = xw[1,fₙ(sₙ)];
      { Compute new values in xw[1,*] }
      xw[1,s₁] = e₁(xw[2,f₁(s₁)]);
            ·
      xw[1,sₙ] = eₙ(xw[2,fₙ(sₙ)]);
   endelse { i>1 }
endloop { for i }
```

It is possible to move the case of i==1 outside the loop, which then starts with i set to two. Inside the loop for the general case, there is a saving section that moves the old values needed for the current computation of x[i,*] from vector x[i-1,*] to xw[2,*]. The saving section is followed by a computation section, which evaluates values of the elements in x[i,*] and stores them in xw[1,*]. Only variables that may have changed values recently are computed, though.

A typical example of unnecessary copying is the implementation of stack or queue operations. In general, that problem arises for any structure that changes only a small part of its value in each operation. The described optimization is applicable to the mltp structure in the prime listing program. Declared as an array, the structure is implemented as a vector, with the initial assignment outside the loop. Inside the loop, only marking by the prime factor takes place and the assignment

```
mltp[i,j] = ...mltp[i-1,j]...
```

is eliminated altogether.

MSCC Scheduling.   To schedule a multinode MSCC, the EPL compiler first finds subscripts that are shared by all nodes in the MSCC. The computation represented by the MSCC has to be enclosed in the loops iterating over these subscripts. Hence, the scheduler can ignore any dependences that are labeled with the subscript expression of $i - k$ (i is a subscript or sublinear subscript, and $k \geq 0$ is a constant) for loops with an increasing loop control variable, and $i+k$ for loops with the decreasing loop control variable. Such an elimination of certain dependences may decompose an MSCC into parts that can again be enclosed into loops and decomposed further.

In the array graph of the factorial example, the only multinode MSCC contains the edges labeled with the expression $i-1$. Thus it can be easily scheduled.

In the case of MSCC's with diverging subscripts, more subtle analysis is needed. An MSCC with diverging subscripts (henceforth referred to as diverging MSCC) recursively defines some variable(s) in different evaluation directions for those subscripts. Part of the MSCC requires an ascending loop in certain dimensions, while another part requires a descending loop in the same dimensions. The EPL compiler uses the condition analysis to verify that the computation can be split into loops in different directions and that these loops can be scheduled in such a way that the recursion refers to instances of the variable(s) that have already been calculated.

Such scheduling requires that the diverging MSCC be split into separate MSCC's that share a common data. All subscript expressions for the dimension being scheduled have to be either i and $i - k$ or i and $i+k$ in each split MSCC. For each variable defined in the diverging MSCC's, the EPL compiler builds a *defined area* structure. This structure is a linked list of upper and lower bound expressions. The existence of a defined area structure indicates that the part of the dimension between the upper and lower bound expression in the structure (including the upper and lower bound) is defined.

The compiler first identifies initialization areas of the dimension that are not defined recursively and then enters them into the defined area structure. Next, it repetitively looks for diverging MSCC's with recursive equations that border on the defined areas (those are identified by their condition sets). These MSCC's are scheduled and the sections of the dimension that they define are added to the defined area structure.

Each diverging MSCC defines a subsection of an array variable that is an *entry point* node for this MSCC. The expressions for the bounds of the area being defined are derived directly from the equation conditions within the MSCC. In each diverging MSCC, there is a conditional equation defining the entry point node, called an *alternate equation*. Part of the condition in the alternate equation must specify bounds for the subscript, called the *bounding predicate*. The condition may be a disjunction of the Boolean terms, but it must have a common subscript bound expression across the disjunct terms. The bounding predicates are extracted from the equation condition and create the bounds for the diverging MSCC. The bounds for the initial defined areas are derived from the nonrecursive equation (not appearing in the MSCC but attached to an entry point node) in the same manner.

The compiler also identifies the depth of the recurrence. Part of the diverging MSCC with a negative (positive, respectively) depth is considered schedulable when its minimum (maximum, respectively) bound, offset by its depth, falls within a defined area.

Parallelism.   Parallelism is sought on three different levels in the EPL programs.

- □ **Fine grain:** Parallelism that is explored at the level of equation instances by horizontal partitioning. Each equation instance can be executed on a separate processor. Due to the limited memory assigned to each processor in the Connection Machine, the memory optimization performed by the EPL compiler through windowing and copying elimination are important parts of the SIMD EPL scheduler. To eliminate excessive communication, a *data alignment* is used to select the best displacement of data structures along the projection dimension. For example, if the only two equations in the projection dimension are

  ```
  a[i] = if i==1 then 1 else b[i-1]+2;
  b[i] = f(i);
  ```

  then the i-th processor should compute instances a[i], b[i-1]. In general, the problem is NP-complete; therefore the EPL compiler uses a heuristic for suboptimal data alignment [31].
- □ **Medium grain:** Parallelism that is sought at the level of equation clusters defined by annotations. As described above, annotations

cause the EPL compiler to generate separate programs from the annotated program fragments. Later, the configurator creates parallel computation that integrates those programs.

☐ **Coarse grain:** Parallelism that is defined by the process structure of the EPL computation. Typically, programs are defined along the functional decomposition of the computation, regardless of the decomposition execution efficiency. We have been investigating the program partitioning algorithms based on the minimum cuts through the array graph. Recursively, the program (or its parts) are bisected. The bisection is performed if the computation time of the original part is larger than the total computation time (including communication and synchronization) of the two created parts. When the bisection stops, the created parts are transformed into programs in a way similar to the transformation of annotated fragments into programs (see Section 3.4.1).

Currently, the EPL compiler produces the parallelized code for the Intel hypercube, shared-memory Balance-21000 Sequent and SIMD MasPar computers.

3.4.5 CONFIGURATION PROCESSING

The configuration is processed in three stages. The first stage involves syntactic checking and construction of a global dependence graph. The nodes of this graph are processes and ports, and the edges represent their relations. In the second stage, the semantic checking is done. Cycles in the global dependence graph are identified and the interprocess dependences are derived and processed. In the third step, the configurator schedules the entire computation and generates the command scripts for the creation of the processes and ports. Processes that consume sequential or display files are delayed until the producers of these files terminate.

Interprocess Data Dependence Analysis.   In the parallel computation, an individual process correctness is a necessary but not sufficient condition for the correctness of the entire computation. If a process has input/output ports that belong to a cycle in the configuration graph, then this process's input messages are dependent on the output messages. Such dependences (in addition to dependences imposed by the equations of a process) have to be taken into account in generating the object program for individual processes; otherwise, loss of messages, process blocking, or even a deadlock can arise.

The algorithm for finding external data dependences consists of two parts. The Internal Data Dependence Analyzer (IDDA) performs the local (process) level analysis. The External Data Dependence Analyzer (EDDA) does the global (computation) level analysis. Both parts are similar, except that the IDDA operates on the array graph, while the EDDA acts on the global dependence graph.

The following conditions are necessary for external dependences to exist in a given process:

□ The process belongs to a cycle in the global dependence graph.

□ There is a (possibly indirect) dependence of the input port records on the output port records.

Hence, in the first step EDDA lists all the processes that belong to cycles in the global graph and IDDA lists processes in which there are paths from input to output port records in the corresponding array graphs. Further analysis is restricted to the processes that appear on both lists. The IDDA and EDDA algorithms comprise the following three stages:

1. Identifying range equivalence in the variable references
2. Combining multiple edges between pairs of nodes
3. Propagating transitive dependences along the paths that connect port record nodes

Processes that belong to a cycle in the global dependence graph can execute concurrently only if they are all enclosed into the same loop of the communication sends and receives. Such processes are called *atomic*, since they cannot be broken into parts without splitting the loop. For example, if sends are done in a separate loop from receives, then all the sends have to be executed before any receive, and the successors of such nonatomic processes cannot start until its predecessors in the global dependence graph finish sending communication. Checking that the process can be enclosed into a single loop and propagating transitive dependences along the paths require identifying equivalent ranges in the variable references. The equivalence can only be derived by symbolically matching subscript references.

For example, let's examine the equation $b[i,j,k]=\ldots a[j-1,k]\ldots$. The first dimension of the variable b would not be matched to any of the dimensions of the variable a. The second dimension of b would be matched to the first dimension of a. Finally, the third dimension of b would be matched to the second dimension of a. However, the symbolic correspondence may not always be so easily determined. This is the case when references to sublinear subscripts appear or when multiple subscripts belong to the same range set. The algorithm for the matching is specific to the EPL array representation and, therefore, its detailed description is omitted here.

The second stage of the algorithm combines multiple edges between a pair of nodes into a single edge. The dependence type for each of the multiple edges is defined as a pair $<hard, soft>$ based on the form of the subscript expression that labels them as follows:

type 0: $hard$=k, $soft$= $-\infty$ (expression is a constant k);

type 1: $hard$= $-\infty$, $soft$=k (expression is of type "i-k");

type 2: $hard$= ∞, $soft$= ∞ (otherwise).

Multiple edges with types $<hard_1, soft_1>$, $<hard_2, soft_2>$, ... $<hard_n, soft_n>$, respectively, can be replaced by a single edge of the type $<\max(hard_1, hard_2, \ldots, hard_n), \max(soft_1, soft_2, \ldots, soft_n)>$. This is done for each dimension of the edge corresponding to the dimensions of the input port record. It should be noted that the above labeling of edges by dependence type is valid only after subscript references on the left-hand side of the equations have been normalized. The normalization attempts to reduce these references to a simple or sublinear subscript.

The third and final stage of the algorithm replaces a path of the dependence edges by a single direct edge with the proper dependence type. For each node v, this stage maintains a set P(v) of nodes that precede v on an already traversed path from the input port record. It also maintains a list of nodes active in each step. Initially, only the selected input port record node is active. In each step, the following is done for every active node v:

1. Let p_i, $<hard_i, soft_i>$, e_i, i=1,2...n, denote predecessors of v with already defined predecessor sets, their dependence types, and the types of their edges to v, respectively. Let $<hard_v, soft_v>$ be the previous dependence type of the node v, or $<-\infty, -\infty>$ if the node v has not been visited yet. Let $hard = \max_{i=1,2,\ldots n}\{hard_i, soft_i + e_i.hard\}$ and $soft = \max_{i=1,2\ldots n}\{soft_i + e_i.soft\}$. If $hard > hard_v$ or $soft > soft_v$ then:

   □ Set the type of the dependence of node v to
   $<\max(hard, hard_v), \max(soft, soft_v)>$
   and its predecessor set to
   $$P(v) = \bigcup_{i=1,2,\ldots n} P(p_i) \cup P(v)$$

   □ Set all the successors of v as active for the next step.

2. The previous step is repeated until there are no more active nodes, or the number of repetitions equals the number of nodes in the array graph. If the latter is the case, then the type of all the nodes active at that instance is set to $<\infty, \infty>$. This type is also propagated to all direct and indirect successors of the active nodes.

3. For each output record node that has been typed in the above steps, the resultant dependence is simply the maximum of all the *hard* and *soft* type components that the node received.

The proof of the correctness of this algorithm is straightforward and is omitted here because of the space limitation. It is clear that the longest acyclic path in the array graph is shorter than the number of nodes. Therefore any increase in the typing of nodes after that many steps of the third stage indicates the existence of cycles with a positive sum of subscript displacements. Such cycles require reading the entire input before writing any output.

The second step cannot be repeated more than V times (where V stands for the number of nodes in the array graph). Each step can process each edge at most once, so the total complexity of the third stage is $O(V * E)$, where E denotes the number of the combined (in the second stage) edges in the array graph. The third stage has to be repeated for each input record node.

The purpose of IDDA is to replace the array graph of a process by a reduced dependence graph. The nodes of this graph are port files. This is a bipartite graph with input port nodes connected to output port nodes by edges that represent the transitive closure of the dependences between the connected nodes. These edges are then used by EDDA to propagate external data dependences in the global dependence graph.

The goal of EDDA is to identify both external data dependences between process input and output port files and cycles in the global dependence graph. EDDA determines the external data dependences for a given configuration and process. This is accomplished by creating a global dependence graph and finding all dependences from output to input ports for each process (node) in this graph. Since messages sent via port files are queued at the receiver, edges in the configuration specification are always assigned a displacement of 0. Thus each configuration edge may be seen as an equation:

```
input_port_message[i] = output_port_message[i];
```

It is worthwhile to note that EDDA performs an important semantic check on the configuration specification. It determines if the message formats used by two communicating processes are compatible in terms of their dimensionalities. This is in addition to its primary goal of deriving external data dependences.

EDDA produces a *patch* file used by the intraprocess equation scheduler and code generator of the EPL compiler. This file contains a list of the additional, externally imposed data dependences (edges and their dimension types) that need to be added to the process array graph. One process may have several different patches, each associated with the different configurations in which this process participates.

A patch may have one of three possible effects on the program generated from the array graph:

- □ If there is no internal data dependence between the input and output ports connected by the patch edge, then the patch defines a new constraint on the generated program. Without the patch, port's send and receive can be scheduled in any order; whereas, with the patch, send must precede receive.

- □ If the output port is internally dependent on the input port, then an error is possible (subject to the types of existing internal and external dependences). For certain types of dependences, the configuration execution would result in a deadlock.

- □ If there is an internal data dependence of the input port on the output port, a dependence edge is already in the array graph, but the external dependence may change the type of that edge.

In each of these three cases a significant configuration dependent result has been achieved. For example, the consumer-server computation presented in Section 3.2.2 needs the patch to ensure that a deadlock-free object code will be generated by the EPL compiler.

Presently, the algorithm to propagate external data dependences regards all port dependences as unconditional. This limitation may prevent the best intra-process schedule from being generated or cause the detection of the possibility of a deadlock that, in fact, cannot arise. We plan to extend the algorithm to overcome this limitation, at least partially.

The described algorithm is an important tool in partitioning of annotated processes and in the intraprocess scheduling of parallel computations. Exploring parallelism below the process level requires process repartitioning, which in turn necessitates an analysis of externally imposed data dependences to produce correct object code for the processes involved in the computation. Such an analysis was previously performed by the programmer and the found external dependences were then explicitly added to the program. The described algorithm removes the need for programmer-performed analysis and thereby increases the reliability of the generated code.

3.5   Future Directions and Conclusions

The great challenge of concurrent programming in scientific computation is to effectively use the potential parallelism provided by a hardware. The use of an equational language for expressing computations shields the programmer from considering low-level implementation details, such as input and output operations, loop structure, and flow of control in the program. Compilation of the EPL programs, including optimization, synchronization, and parallelization algorithms and customized code generators provides the programmer with the efficient implementations for a variety of hardware.

We have implemented the prototype of the EPL compiler to investigate further applicability and efficiency of equational programming in large-scale scientific computation. Much remains to be done. One of the research topics that we have been investigating vigorously is the partitioning of large scale computations into separate parallel tasks and mapping and scheduling those tasks on various parallel architectures. An equational specification is an excellent basis for such algorithms because of its nonprocedural semantics. EPL programs can be cut and merged at will and in any order without changing the meaning of the overall computation. We are designing and investigating algorithms for finding partitionings that are optimal for the given hardware architecture in terms of the overall computation time. In addition, we analyze data dependences in each of the created processes to explore vectorization and parallelism existing below the level of individual processes. We plan to develop techniques for generating highly parallel and efficient code customized to the different computer architectures.

We have already developed the notion of a global dependence graph. This is a graph created by merging together array graphs of individual processes with a graph of configuration interconnections. A partitioning defines a cut in the global dependence graph that imposes communication between processes connected by the cut edges. The types and weights of these edges define the communication overhead imposed by the considered partitioning. Therefore the problem can be reduced to finding the optimum network cut with the prescribed number of parts (equal to the number of available processors). We will investigate and implement various heuristic solutions to this problem. We will also evaluate the efficiency (both in terms of algorithm complexity and partitioning quality) of different solutions and select the best for the implementation in the EPL compiler.

We also need to develop a simple architecture description language that will enable us to capture essential features of the computer hardware. Among the most important architectural parameters are the number and speed of processors, the configuration of the interconnection network, the speed and capacity of communication links, the distribution of the memory among processors, etc. We plan to use this language to describe various parallel computers available to us, such as the message passing Intel hypercube, the shared memory Sequent Balance 2100, and the SIMD Connection Machine and MasPar computer. We plan to generate and compare code produced by the EPL compiler for these different computers.

For regular problems, static analysis of equational programs is sufficient to achieve high-quality translation. However, for general problems many dependences cannot be resolved at compile-time. We will investigate when it is cost effective to represent such dependencies in the compact form in the object code for use during run-time to optimize execution paths that are data dependent.

Acknowledgments

This work was partially supported by the National Science Foundation under grant CCR-8613353 and grant CDA-8805910; the Office of Naval Research under contract N00014-86-K-0442; and the Army Research Office under contract DAAL03-86-K-0112 and DAAL03-90-G-0096.

References

1. W.B. Ackerman, *Data Flow Languages*, Computer, vol. 15, no. 2 (Feb. 1982) pp. 15-25.

2. G.S. Almasi and A. Gottlieb, *Highly Parallel Computing*, Menlo Park, Calif.: Benjamin/Cummings, 1989, p. 24.

3. Arvind and K.P. Gostelow, *The U Interpreter*, IEEE Comp. vol. 15, no. 2 (Feb. 1982) pp. 42-50.

4. E.A. Ashcroft and W.W. Wadge, *Lucid, A Nonprocedural Language with Iteration*, Comm. ACM. vol. 20, no. 7 (July 1977) pp. 519-26.

5. J. Backus, *Can Programming Be Liberated from the von Neumann Style? A Functional Style and Its Algebra of Programs*, Comm. ACM, vol. 21, no. 8 (Aug. 1978) pp. 613-41.

6. J. Baron, B. Szymanski, E. Lock, and N. Prywes, *An Argument for Nonprocedural Languages*, Proc. Workshop on the Role of Languages in Problem Solving-1, ed. R. Jernigan, B.W. Hamill, and D.M. Weintraub, Amsterdam: North-Holland, 1985.

7. C. Bron and J. Kerbosh, *Finding All Cliques of an Undirected Graph*, Comm. ACM, vol. 16, no. 9 (Sept. 1973) pp. 575-77.

8. J. Bruno, *Analyzing Conditional Data Dependencies in an Equational Language Compiler*, Ph.D. dissertation in computer science, Rensselaer Polytechnic Institute, Troy, N.Y. (December, 1989).

9. K.M. Chandy and J. Misra, *Parallel Program Design - A Foundation*, Reading, Mass: Addison-Wesley, 1988, p. 179.

10. M. Chen, *A Parallel Language and Its Compilation to Multiprocessor Machines or VLSI*, Proc. 13th Annual ACM Symposium on the Principles of Programming Languages, ACM, 1986, pp. 131-39.

11. G. F. Curtis, *Applied Numerical Analysis*, Reading, Mass.: Addison-Wesley, 1978.

12. E.W. Dijkstra, *The Structure of the T.H.E. Multiprogramming System*, Comm. ACM, vol. 11 (1968) pp. 341-46.

13. J.P. Fiance and J. Souquieres, *A Method and a Language for Constructing Iterative Programs*, Science of Computer Programming, vol. 5 (1985) pp. 201-18.

14. M.J. Flynn, *Some Computer Organizations and Their Effectiveness*, IEEE Trans. on Comp. vol. C-21 (1972) pp. 948-960.

15. W.D. Hillis and G.L. Steele, Jr. *Data Parallel Algorithms*, Comm. ACM, vol. 29, no. 12 (Dec. 1986) pp. 1170-83.

16. C.A.R. Hoare, *Communicating Sequential Processes*, Comm. ACM, vol. 21, no. 8 (Aug. 1978) pp. 666-77.

17. C.M. Hoffman and M.J. O'Donnell, *Programming with Equations*, ACM Trans. on Programming Languages and Systems, vol. 4, no. 1 (January 1982) pp. 83-112.

18. T.C. Hu, *Optimum Communication Spanning Trees*, SIAM Journal of Comput. (Sept 1974).

19. T. Kaufl, *Reasoning about Systems of Linear Inequalities*, Proc. Ninth International Conference on Automated Deduction, Lecture Notes in Computer Science, E. Lusk and R. Overbeek, eds, Berlin: Springer-Verlag, May 1988, pp. 563-72.

20. B.W. Kernighan and R. Pike, *The UNIX Programming Environment*, Englewood Cliffs, N.J.: Prentice-Hall, 1984.

21. L.R. Klein, *The LINK Model of World Trade with Application to 1972-1973*, in Quantitative Studies of International Economic Relations, P. Kenen, ed. Amsterdam, North Holland, 1975.

22. R.A. Kowalski, *Logic for Problem Solving*, New York: Elsevier North-Holland, 1979.

23. I. Lee, N. Prywes, and B. Szymanski, *Partitioning of Massive/Real-Time Programs for Parallel Processing*, Advances in Computers, vol. 25 (1986) pp. 215-75.

24. R.E. Lord, J.S. Kowalik, and S.P. Kumar, *Solving Linear Algebraic Equations on an MIMD Computer*, Journal ACM, vol. 30, no. 1 (January 1983) pp. 103-17.

25. J.R. McGraw, *The VAL Language: Description and Analysis*, ACM Trans. on Programming Languages and Systems, vol. 4, no. 1 (January 1982) pp. 44-82.

26. T. Moto-oka, *Overview of the Fifth Generation Computer System Project*, Proc. 10th Annual Symp. Comput. Archit. (June 1983) pp. 417-22.

27. C. Ozturan, *Expressing User-Defined Parallelism in EPL*, Master's Project, Computer Science Department, Rensselaer Polytechnic Institute, Troy, N.Y. (July, 1990).

28. B. N. Parlett and R. Schreiber, *Block Reflectors and Their Applications*, in Computing Methods in Applied Science and Engineering, vol. VII, R. Glowinski and J.L. Lions, eds., Amsterdam: Elsevier North Holland, 1986.

29. A. Pnueli, N. S. Prywes and R. Zarhi, *Scheduling Equational Specifications and Nonprocedural Programs*, in Automatic Program Construction Techniques, Bierman, Guiho and Kodratoff, eds., New York: Macmillan, 1984.

30. N. Prywes and B. Szymanski, *Programming Supercomputers in an Equational Language*, Proc. First International Conference on Supercomputing Systems, St. Petersburg, Fl. (December 1985) pp. 37-45.

31. B. Sinharoy, B. McKenney, and B. Szymanski, *Scheduling in the Equational Language Compiler*, in Languages, Compilers and Run-Time Environments for Distributed Memory Machines, J. Saltz, P. Mehrota, eds, New York: Elsevier, 1991, in press.

32. K. Spier and B. Szymanski, *Interprocess Analysis and Optimization in the Equational Language Compiler*, Proceedings of the CONPAR-90, Zurich (September 1990) Lecture Notes in Computer Science, Berlin: Springer-Verlag, 1990, pp. 287-98.

33. B. Szymanski, *Programming with Recurrent Equations*, International Journal on Supercomputing Applications, vol. 1, no. 2 (Summer 1987) pp. 44-74.

34. B. Szymanski, N. Prywes, E. Lock, and A. Pnueli, *On the Scope of Static Checking in Definitional Languages*, Proc. ACM'84 Annual Conference, San Francisco, 1984.

35. B. Szymanski and N. Prywes, *Efficient Handling of Data Structures in Definitional Languages*, Science of Computer Programming, no. 3 (1988) pp. 221-45.

36. R.C. Waters, *Expressional Loops*, Proc. 10th ACM Symposium Principles of Programming Languages, ACM, 1983, pp. 1-10.

4

Sisal

Stephen K. Skedzielewski

4.1   Introduction

Parallel processors are one approach to building faster computers. They are successful when they are able to solve larger problems than those that are solved using conventional, sequential machines, or when they provide faster solutions than conventional machines. Programming a parallel computer should be no harder than programming a uniprocessor, yet experience shows that it can be much harder.

Why?

Basically, many of our conventional programming environments are not designed for programming in a parallel world. Programming a parallel processor is really no harder than programming a uniprocessor when programming tools help us avoid common pitfalls.

Applications programmers have traditionally been shielded from problems that arise from asynchronous events. These events are commonplace in the world of operating systems, for example, and programmers in that world are aware of the difficulties that they bring. The main difficulty occurs during debugging, where it may be impossible to recreate the exact conditions that caused the failure. The problem is often

time-dependent and the act of debugging can disturb the timing enough
to cause it to disappear.

A parallel processor, then, brings these problems to the applications programmer. The existence of operating systems shows that programming in the presence of asynchronous events is possible. However,
operating systems are considerably harder to write and maintain than
applications programs. One of the goals of a parallel processor should
be to make the programmer more productive; instead, we seem to be
creating problems where none existed. A tenet of this chapter is:

> A well-designed language can shield the programmer from
> timing problems while automatically exploiting any paral-
> lelism expressed in the program.

We should not expect a compiler to find and exploit parallelism
where there is none. Many large codes were written long before parallel processing was easily accessible, and their methods are based on
efficient, sequential algorithms. Turning such algorithms into efficient,
parallel algorithms is not merely a job for an "optimizing" compiler. It
requires reprogramming at a fairly high level. This chapter promotes a
style of programming and a language. Both will help the programmer
express parallelism in the program and will help the compiler automatically exploit the parallelism in a way that is guaranteed to be repeatable
and debuggable.

The Sisal language is designed to be a notation for expressing solutions to large-scale, scientific problems. In contrast to conventional *imperative* languages, Sisal belongs to a class of languages called *applicative
languages*, which share the following characteristics:

- **Expression-based (or function-based):** Expressions and functions
  are *single-valued* mappings from a range to a domain. They are *not*
  as flexible as functions and subroutines in conventional languages
  that are procedure- or statement-based.

- **Determinate results:** It doesn't matter how many times we use a
  function; we always get the same answer for the same arguments.

- **No side-effects:** All of the inputs and results of a function or expression are local, making it easy to understand how it works. The
  only side effect of a function is to return its results to the point of
  invocation.

- **Lack of variables and global state:** Actually, the important restriction is that the name-value bindings cannot vary over time, so we
  can reason about the values without worrying about time.

Sisal is sometimes called a "single assignment" language, which is a special class of applicative languages. A name can receive a value only once in each name scope. After that assignment it becomes a read-only value, which can be shared among any number of consumers. This property eliminates one of the major causes of nondeterminacy, the *race condition*.

To illustrate a race condition, consider the following two pieces of code written in an imperative language:

```
x = 2
x = x+13
print x .
```

and

```
x = 107
x = x + 1381
print x
```

Now consider the effects of running the code fragments in parallel processes. If we assume that the two processes share x, how many different pairs of values can appear? The answer is surprisingly large!

```
15,15      120,120     1488,120    1501,1488   1383,1396
15,1383    120,1488    1488,1488   1501,1501   1396,15
15,1396    120,1501    1488,1501   1383,15     1396,1383
15,1488    1488,15     1501,120    1383,1383   1396,1396
```

The reason for the large number of results is that at any time when x's value is fetched, three different store instructions may have immediately preceded it (one in this process and two store instructions in the other process). Because we obtain the value twice in each process, we generate a large number of possible execution paths.

One possible result is (15, 1488), which occurs when all of the code in the first example completes before the second example completes its first assignment. However, if the second example completes its first assignment just before the other fetches x for printing, the result is (107, 1488).

Although the above example is contrived and "obviously" a mistake, it is very easy for a programmer who is converting several thousand lines of code to accidentally generate such a mistake. Keeping track of hundreds of variable names can be tedious and prone to error. This is one area where the use of an applicative language can help, by letting the compiler keep uses of values clear and easy to understand.

Another advantage of a single-assignment form is that it clearly shows the compiler when code can be reordered or transformed. For example,

```
2.0 * (b + f(c))
```

may seem like it will always produce the same result as

```
(b + f(c)) + (b + f(c))
```

but if the execution of *f* modifies a global variable (for example, it might modify *b* or *c*) the results will differ. Compilers for applicative languages need not concern themselves with this problem, since it is impossible for a function to modify one of its arguments. Therefore some program transformations (also called "optimizations") that are unsafe in imperative languages are always safe to perform in applicative languages.

The programmer can convert sequential code to parallel code in a conventional language by taking great care to avoid such timing errors. However, the code may *still* be derived from a sequential algorithm. New algorithms may be needed to replace the sequential code with more highly parallel code. For example, we may wish to replace a good sorting algorithm like quicksort with a parallel merge sort or Batcher sort, in which the compiler can easily recognize the parallelism. It is unlikely that we would build such knowledge directly into the compiler.

If the programmer is going to rewrite the problem, we suggest converting it to an applicative language, which has the advantage of safe and automatic parallel implementation.

4.1.1   SISAL

Sisal was created by researchers from Lawrence Livermore National Laboratory, the University of Manchester, Colorado State University, and Digital Equipment Corporation. Members of this group were interested in designing and implementing an applicative language to run on their own machines, or on existing multiprocessors. Several goals emerged from the discussions on the language:

1. The language must support large-scale scientific computing.
2. Compilers for the language must be able to produce highly efficient code.
3. The language will change as a result of using the language and its implementations.

Note that Sisal is not explicitly targeted to multiprocessors. Many uniprocessors can exploit low-level parallelism, through multiple functional units or vector instructions, and these architectures will also benefit from the parallelism that can be extracted from a Sisal program.

This chapter describes Sisal Version 1.2, which is described in the reference manual dated March, 1985[9]. This chapter does not attempt to describe *all* of the features of Sisal. Rather, it will use a subset of the language as it attempts to motivate the use of Sisal in writing programs that exploit parallel computers. The interested reader is urged to obtain a copy of the reference manual.

Most of the language features are introduced by example. When examples of the syntax are given, we will use *this font to denote nonterminals* in the language and this font to represent terminal symbols.

For example, the syntax of an if-then-else-expression is written

if *BooleanExpression* then *Exp*$_1$ else *Exp*$_2$ end if

in which if, then, else, and end are terminal symbols, while *BooleanExpression, Exp*$_1$, and *Exp*$_2$ are non-terminal symbols.

4.2   Functions and Expressions

Functions and expressions are the building blocks of Sisal programs. In most situations we can freely interchange names of values, expressions, and the results of function applications.

Functions in Sisal are more closely related to mathematical functions than are functions in an imperative language. Sisal functions can map any number of inputs to any number of outputs, and the mapping is guaranteed to be single-valued. Thus a tenet of Sisal programming is as follows:

Given a fixed set of inputs, a function will *always* return the same result (if it returns at all).

The reason that such a guarantee can be made is that a function cannot modify its environment. It simply uses its inputs to compute a result. All of its inputs are explicitly given as parameters and the function's effect is limited to returning a set of result values.

The use of the word *values* is important. Sisal programs do not manipulate storage cells; rather, they manipulate values. The task of assigning values to memory cells (or registers, or cache) is left to the Sisal compiler. The performance of a Sisal program will depend heavily on the success of the compiler at memory assignment. This dependence on the compiler is analogous to giving up control of register assignment to a compiler; in most cases the compiler will do as good a job, if not a better job, than the user.

4.2.1 EXPRESSIONS

Let's begin with an example of the solution to the equation

$$Ax^2 + Bx + C = 0.$$

We begin by simply writing two expressions wherever we need the two values,

```
(-B + sqrt( B*B - 4.0*A*C ) ) / ( 2.0*A ),
(-B - sqrt( B*B - 4.0*A*C ) ) / ( 2.0*A )
```

and separating parts of a multiply-valued expression with commas. The two above expressions can be placed anywhere that we need their two values, so we could, for example, pass them as two of the arguments to a function.

```
MyFun(  (-B + sqrt( B*B - 4.0*A*C ) ) / (2.0*A ),
        (-B - sqrt( B*B - 4.0*A*C ) ) / (2.0*A ),
        X, Y )
```

Sisal expressions use a combination of infix and prefix operators. Since Sisal was designed for use by scientific programmers, it borrows many of the operators and built-in functions that one finds in languages such as Fortran and PL/I. Many of the operators are overloaded, usually to represent operations on integers, reals and doubles. However, the language will not automatically coerce the type of an operand at all, and one must take care to explicitly change the type of an expression from integer to real (or vice-versa) when necessary. The compiler will enforce this provision of the type rules, so we won't need to worry about accidentally using the wrong bit pattern, or passing the wrong type of argument to functions.

We've implicitly assumed that all of the types are compatible; in practice we'll know the types of all values before they are used. For this example, assume that we know that A, B, and C are of type real. Literal values in Sisal look much like literal values in Fortran or Pascal, and 4.0 and 2.0 are of type real. We'll now analyze the types of the values in a bottom-up manner; all expressions in Sisal can have their type determined in such a manner.

□ *4.0* and *A* are real, therefore *4.0*A* must be real

□ *C* is real, therefore *4.0*A*C* must be real

□ Since *B* is real, so must *B*B* and *B*B - 4.0*A*C*

□ *sqrt(B*B - 4.0*A*C)* is real

□ and so on, until we infer that

□ *(-B + sqrt(B*B - 4.0*A*C)) / (2.0*A)* is real

Thus we know that the type of expression is real. This is a very simple type inference system, but it allows some type declarations to be optional. The programmer can explicitly declare the type of a name, and the Sisal compiler will check to ensure that the type inferred for the expression matches the explicit type.

Expressions may reveal opportunities to exploit fine-grain parallelism. For example, a CPU with a pipelined multiplication unit could overlap the computations of $B*B$, $4.0*A*C$, and $2.0*A$. Such parallelism is often available in scientific programs and is very easily identified by the Sisal compiler.

4.2.2 FUNCTIONS

Expressions can become functions by "abstracting out" the values that comprise the expression. The abstract quantities are called *parameters*, and Sisal will require that the programmer explicitly assign types to all of them at compile-time. This requirement will allow our simple type inference mechanism to have a type declaration for each name that it encounters in an expression.

We can write the expressions in the previous example as a function by providing a wrapper around them. The wrapper explicitly gives the types of each of the named values, as well as giving the types of the results. The expressions that we wrote previously provide those results. The type information gives the compiler the ability to infer and check the types of all of the expressions and subexpressions in the function body.

```
%%% Simplistic version of the quadratic equation solver
%%%
function QSolve( A, B, C: real returns real, real )
   (-B + sqrt( B*B - 4.0*A*C ) ) / (2.0*A ),
   (-B - sqrt( B*B - 4.0*A*C ) ) / (2.0*A )
end function %QSolve
```

The return information in the function header is compared with the types of the expressions in the body to ensure type correctness. If they disagree, the compiler signals an error.

A function becomes a value when you apply it to arguments. The syntax is similar to that of many other languages; arguments are presented as a parenthesized, comma-separated list of values. For example, we can invoke QSolve by writing QSolve(1.0, 3.0, -4.0), and QSolve will return the values 1.0 and -4.0.

Results of function calls can be passed directly to other functions, and this leads to an interesting form of referential transparency. We can then pass these two result values as part of another parameter list: QSolve(QSolve(1.0, -3.0, -4.0), 4.0) becomes QSolve(1.0, -4.0, 4.0), which returns 2.0, 2.0. If the language required functions to return a single list of values, we will be forced to write the code to change the return list into the argument list. In Sisal we simply nest one function application within the other and the compiler passes the results of one call as arguments to the other.

Functions comprise expressions, so they have the same opportunities for parallel execution as expressions. In addition, some Sisal compilers have spawned each function application as a parallel task on a multiprocessor. However, experience [18] shows that only *some* of the function calls should be run in parallel, since the cost of spawning a function is fairly large (even when the runtime system avoids operating system intervention) and often there is little other work to be done in parallel.

4.2.3 ASSIGNMENTS IN AN APPLICATIVE LANGUAGE

Assignment in an applicative language binds a name to a value. This binding is subtly different than assignment in an imperative language, where the assignment places a value in a memory location named in the assignment. An applicative name-value binding will continue to hold for the duration of the current name scope.

Name-value bindings can be introduced in a Sisal program in the let expression and the for expression. To continue with the previous example, we could write the quadratic equation solver as

```
%%% Version of the quadratic equation solver that uses names
%%%
function QSolve( A, B, C: real returns real, real )
let
   Disc := B*B - 4.0*A*C
in
   ( -B + sqrt( Disc ) ) / ( 2.0*A ),
   ( -B - sqrt( Disc ) ) / ( 2.0*A )
end let
end function %QSolve
```

The scope of the name Disc extends *from the point of definition* to the matching end let. We could continue to define more names in the let-expression, but as the next example shows, at some point the names cease adding information to the code:

```
%%% Version of the quadratic equation solver that uses more names
%%%
function QSolve( A, B, C: real returns real, real )
let
  Disc := B*B - 4.0*A*C;
  D := sqrt( Disc );
  TwoA := 2.0 * A
in
  ( -B + D ) / ( TwoA ),
  ( -B - D ) / ( TwoA )
end let
end function %QSolve
```

Programmers may be accustomed to defining names to hold common subexpressions, rather than for describing their value, but most Sisal compilers do a good job of detecting common subexpressions. Identical code will be generated for each of the versions of *QSolve* that have been given.

Two restrictions on the use of names are important. First, names may receive only one definition in a name scope (single-assignment). Second, the order of the definitions in a let-expression in Sisal is important; you may not use a name before it is defined.

"Definition before use" is a simple concept to present to new users and provides a simple way to ensure noncircularity. However, "definition before use" is not absolutely necessary from a language design standpoint. At the end of the name scope, the compiler can ensure that you have definitions for all names referenced within that scope. The execution order would still be determined by the data dependence present in the Sisal expressions.

4.2.4   ALTERNATION

Perhaps the easiest "control" expression in Sisal expresses alternation. Alternation in Sisal is written using the if-then-else expression; it can be cascaded to several tests and alternate return values:

> if *BooleanExpression* then Exp_1 else Exp_2 end if
> if $BExpression_1$ then Exp_1 elseif $BExpression_2$ then Exp_2
> else Exp_3 end if

The idea of a "conditional expression" is not new. The expression was present in Algol-60 and appears in the C language. In an applicative language, it has the following restrictions:

1. The number of results must agree in all then and else clauses.
2. The types of each result must agree in all then and else clauses.
3. Each test must be an expression of Boolean type and have exactly one result.
4. Any number of elseif clauses may be added between Exp_1 and end if.

The type of the if-then-else-expression is the same as the type of each of its alternate results.

The previous example could be modified to treat complex results in a special way:

```
%%% Version of the quadratic equation solver that catches complex
%%% results
function QSolve( A, B, C: real returns real, real )
let
    Disc := B*B - 4.0*A*C
in
    if Disc > 0.0 then
            ( -B + sqrt( Disc ) ) / ( 2.0*A ),
            ( -B - sqrt( Disc ) ) / ( 2.0*A )
    else
            0.0, 0.0
    end if end let
end function %QSolve
```

Alternation offers an interesting possibility for parallel execution. A compiler could attempt to minimize the runtime of a program by initiating both clauses of an if-then-else-expression before the result of the Boolean expression has been computed. Such *greedy* evaluation might allow the exeuction of the test and the results to overlap. However, we run the risk that the calculations will compete for resources (CPU, memory) and we cannot always be sure that greedy evaluation will lead to shorter runtimes. One benefit of the single-assignment rule is that since neither clause of the expression can modify its environment, we will not need to "undo" any of the speculative work if it is not needed.

4.2.5   ITERATIVE EXPRESSIONS

The Sisal language contains three ways to express iteration: recursive functions, iteration expressions, and forall expressions. The decision of which form to use will depend on the amount of parallelism that the programmer wishes to express, as well as on personal style. However, all three methods support the four main parts of an iteration: initialization, test, update, and return values.

We'll use a simple sum and then Gaussian iteration as examples of iteration expressions.

Iteration.   The syntax of an iteration expression in Sisal resembles the syntax of an iteration statement in an imperative language, but its semantics are quite different. The difference occurs in the use of value names. In an imperative language the name of a loop value is coincident with its memory cell; any assignment to its name changes all subsequent references to the new value. Assignment in an applicative iteration does *not* change a memory cell but creates a *new* name-value binding in a new scope.

Each "trip through the loop" creates a new scope, much like the new scope that is opened upon each application of a recursive function. Each trip also carries forward the old bindings of all loop values but accesses them as old *name*. Here is a simple example of a loop that computes a sum of cubes:

```
for initial
I := 0;
Sum3 := 0
while I < N repeat
I := old I + 1;
Sum3 := old Sum3 + I*I*I
returns value of Sum3
end for
```

The iteration expression in Sisal uses four clauses to distinguish the parts of the iteration: the initialization, test, body, and return values.

Initialization.   The initialization clause declares all iteration names and gives them a value in the initial name scope. These values can be used in later assignments in the initial clause, in the test clause, or in the first application of the body, when the name is prefixed by old. The syntax is

> for initial *assignments*

Test.   The two forms of a test clause (continue when true, continue when false) are available in Sisal. The test clause can be placed either before or after the repeat clause. The position of the test determines whether it occurs before or after the first application of the body of the iteration.

>   while *Boolean expression*
>   until *Boolean expression*

A test that uses while will terminate the iteration as soon as the test value becomes false. A test that uses until will terminate the iteration as soon as the test value becomes true.

Body. The repeat clause contains new instances of all loop names, uses of old values, and name bindings for temporary values. Like the initial clause, name bindings must follow the "definition before use" rule. Multiple assignments are separated by semicolons, just as in a let-in expression.

>   repeat *assignments*

Return Values. The returns clause identifies the value of the entire for initial expression. Many forms of return values are possible, but the most common is

>   returns value of *expression*

which returns the value to which the loop name was last bound. Another common form is

>   returns value of *reduction expression*

where *reduction* can be either sum, product, least, or greatest (see Section 4.2.5). Any number of return values can be specified.

Example. Another example of an iteration is a square root function that uses Gaussian iteration. The mathematical formula of the series of approximations is

$$a_{i+1} = (x/a_i + a_i)/2.$$

In this example we will begin with $a_0 = x/2$. Many Sisal implementations include square root and a number of other mathematical functions as predefined functions. However, for purposes of example, suppose that we compute the square root with the following loop:

```
%%%
%%% Approximate sqrt( X )
%%% The result squared should have a relative error less than epsilon
%%%
function Sqrt( X, Epsilon: double_real
returns double_real );
   for initial
        Approx := X/2.0d0
```

```
until abs(Approx*Approx - X) < Epsilon*X repeat
      Approx := ( X/old Approx + old Approx ) / 2.0d0
returns
      value of Approx
   end for
end function % Sqrt
```

Approx is initially bound to *X/2.0d0* and that value is used in the termination test. If the approximation is not "close enough," the loop body is applied and the name old *Approx* is bound to the initial value of *Approx*. We continue the cycle of computing a new value for *Approx* and testing it for convergence until the relative error is less than *Epsilon*. At that point the final value bound to *Approx* is returned as the result of the for-expression. *Approx* will have been bound to 1+(number of times the loop body was applied) values, while old *Approx* will have received one less name-value binding.

Reduction Operators.   Reduction is a powerful tool for operating upon a series of values, such as the values repeatedly bound to a loop name in a for-expression. If we are given a series of values $v_1, v_2, \ldots, v_k$ we may *reduce* the series to a single value by applying an operation to successive pairs of numbers until only a single value remains. For example, we could apply the maximum function to (v_1, v_2), repeat it, $\max(\max(v_1, v_2), v_3)$, and continue until we have $\max(\max(\ldots \max(v_1, v_2), \ldots), v_k)$. In a similar manner we can compute the sum or product of a sequence.

Reductions can eliminate the need for values such as *Sum3* in the first example. The following expression computes the same result as the for-expression given in the section on iteration, but makes use of the sum reduction operator in Sisal.

```
for initial
   I := 0
while I < N repeat
   I := old I + 1
returns value of sum I*I*I
end for
```

The scalar reduction operators are given in Table 4.1.

Since reductions are carried out pairwise we have a choice of the association of arguments within the reduction. The (max) example reduced the leftmost arguments first, and continued to work from left-to-right at each step. Similarly, we could have begun at the right by taking $\max(v_{k-1}, v_k)$ and continuing until we reached $\max(v_0, \max(\ldots \max$

Name	Operand types	Result
sum	integer, real, double	arithmetic sum
sum	Boolean	logical "or"
product	integer, real, double	arithmetic product
product	Boolean	logical "and"
greatest	integer, real, double	greatest value
least	integer, real, double	smallest value

TABLE 4.1
SCALAR REDUCTIONS

$(v_{k-1}, v_k) \ldots))$, which is associating to the right. A third option is to build a binary tree structure for the operations. The first two values are operated upon, then the next two, etc., until all of the values have been combined once. We repeat the process on the results of the first operations until we reach a single value. For example, to sum eight values using tree-association takes three steps: $(((v_0 + v_1) + (v_2 + v_3)) + ((v_4 + v_5) + (v_6 + v_7))) \rightarrow ((r_0 + r_1) + (r_2 + r_3)) \rightarrow (s_0 + s_1) \rightarrow t_0$ where r_0, r_1, r_2, r_3 are the results of the first sums s_0 and s_1 are second-level sums, and t_0 is the final sum. Binary-tree reduction has the advantage that it can be done in $\log_2$ time steps if we have enough processors.

Since the order of the operations can make a difference in the result of operations such as floating-point addition, Sisal programmers can specify the association of the reduction within the value of clause:

value of left *Reduction Expression*
value of right *Reduction Expression*
value of tree *Reduction Expression*

If no association is given, the compiler is free to choose whichever direction it prefers. However, on a given implementation it should always choose the same direction, so that the results are repeatable and programs can be debugged. (when and unless clauses are permitted in reductions; see Section 4.2.8.)

An aside: the value of clause can also be interpreted as a reduction. The operator is "choose the second argument," so that when we generate the series of name-value bindings $nv_1, nv_2, nv_3, \ldots, nv_k$, the reduction returns nv_k. For example, the left-associative value of reduction of four values would be $(((v_0, v_1), v_2), v_3) \rightarrow ((v_1, v_2), v_3) \rightarrow (v_2, v_3) \rightarrow v_3$.

4.2.6   RECURSION

Recursive functions can be used to implement iteration (tail recursion), as well as to implement algorithms that rely on multi-way recursion (for example, walking a binary tree or another recursive data structure). Here is the simple sum example rewritten using recursive functions:

```
function Sum3( Low, High: integer
returns integer );
  if Low > High then
        0
  else
        Low*Low*Low + Sum3( Low+1, High )
  end if
end function % Sum3
```

Initialization.   The initialization occurs when values for *Low* and *High* are passed to the initial application of the recursive function. The initial value of the sum is returned when *Low > High*. Note that the only way to pass the value of *High* to all instances of *Sum3* is to pass it explicitly in the argument list; Sisal has no concept of a global value.

Test.   The test that terminates the iteration is usually found as an if expression at the outermost level of the function. It generally chooses between another recursive function application and an expression that returns the values of the iteration.

Update.   The update part of an iteration occurs in the recursive function body's if expression. The update is invoked when the test for another iteration "passes." It may perform the arithmetic inline (as in the most recent example), or it may use a let expression to bind some names to values, then use the values as parameters in the recursive call, as in the following example. This example gives a name to the sum *Accum* and computes its value before invoking itself recursively.

```
function Sum3( I, N: integer
returns integer );

    function Sum3Helper( I, N, Accum: integer
    returns integer );
        if I > N then
                Accum
        else
```

```
        let
                NewAccum := Accum + I*I*I;
                NewI := I+1
        in
                Sum3Helper( NewI, N, NewAccum )
        end let
    end if
  end function % Sum3Helper

  Sum3Helper( 1, N, 0 )

end function % Sum3
```

This version of *Sum3* needs an auxiliary function (*Sum3Helper*) because it uses a third argument (*Accum*) that is not present in the original function.

We introduced new names in the function in order to distinguish the old and new values. However, another change may affect performance. Because the first recursive version of *Sum3* delayed all additions until the end, it may need to save N temporary values before summing them. The second recursive version performs the summations before initiating the next recursive call, so it need not save each term in the summation for later use.

Return Values.   The return values are simply those values given in the "other" arm of the test expression. In the first example most of the work was done in that arm (the multiplications and summation were done as each instance of Sum3 returns). In the second example the work was done before invoking each new instance of Sum3, so the function merely returned the accumulator when the iteration terminated. The latter case more closely approximates the form of the iteration expression given previously, but neither version can make use of the reduction operators; they are only available in the other two iteration forms.

As the number of loop names and reductions increases, including the reductions that produce arrays (see Section 4.3.3 on gathering an array), so does the number of parameters to the function.

Gaussian Iteration Using Recursion.   The Gaussian iteration example can be written very straightforwardly using recursion. Once again we need an auxiliary function to initiate the recursion, as well as several parameters to hold the loop values. The return value is easy to express since this example does not compute any reductions.

```
%%%
%%% Approximate sqrt( X ) using recursion
%%% The result squared should have a relative error less
%%% than epsilon
function Sqrt( X, Epsilon: double_real
returns double_real );

    function SqrtHelper( Approx, X, Epsilon: double_real
    returns double_real );
        if abs(Approx*Approx - X) < Epsilon*X then
            Approx
        else
            SqrtHelper( ( X/Approx + Approx ) / 2.0d0, X,
            Epsilon )
        end if
    end function % SqrtHelper

    SqrtHelper( X/2.0d0, X, Epsilon )
end function % Sqrt
```

4.2.7 FORALL EXPRESSIONS

Another form of iteration, the forall expression, is not properly iteration at all but initiates several instances of *independent* loop bodies. However, the form of this expression in Sisal is very similar to the form of the iteration expression. Forall parallelism operates over a range of values, which in the Sisal language must be integers (or the integer range of array indices, as discussed in Section 4.3.4). Since each instance is independent of the others, it can be executed in parallel on an architecture that supports parallelism at the loop level. This form of parallelism is also suitable for implementation on a vector architecture.

The only interaction among loop bodies occurs at the returns part. At that point we can use the same reductions that are available in the iteration returns clause.

In Sisal, a forall expression is written as a for expression that contains no initial clause but instead gives a *generator* of values that can be used within the loop body's assignments.

Here is a simple example of a loop that computes a sum:

```
%%% Simple sum
for I in 1,N
    T := I*I*I
returns value of sum T
end for
```

The forall expression in Sisal uses three clauses to express the parts of the iteration: generator, body, and return values.

Generator.   The generator supplies both the initial values and the test condition for the expression. The generator declares an iteration name and gives the range of values to which it will be bound (once in each body). The old modifier is not allowed, since each loop body is independent from each of the others. Its syntax is

for *name* in *low, high*

Body.   The section between the range and the returns part can contain name-value bindings. Like the let or initial clause, name bindings must follow the "definition before use" rule.

Return Values.   Each of the names defined in the body of the forall expression can participate in the returns part. As in the iteration expression, a forall expression can return the value of an expression (which is defined to be the value associated with the highest value in the generated range of loop indices).

value of *Expression*
value of *Reduction Expression*

However, it is more common for the forall expression to return the value of a reduction. The following example calculates the extrema of a function over a range of integral values.

```
for I in L, H
  T := f( I )
returns
  value of least T
  value of greatest T
end for
```

4.2.8   RETURNS PARTS AND REDUCTIONS REVISITED

The returns part can explicitly filter values from consideration in the reduction (or final value). To do so, Sisal programs use an optional when or unless clause.

value of *expression* when *Boolean expression*
value of *expression* unless *Boolean expression*

These clauses can be used anywhere the value of appears — that is, in both the iterative and forall expressions. For example, if we want to change the previous example to return the first index of the least and greatest values of $f(I)$ we can augment the previous example as follows:

```
let
   L, G :=
         for I in First, Last
               T := f( I )
         returns
               value of least T
               value of greatest T
         end for
 in
    for I in First, Last
         T := f( I )
    returns
         value of least I when T=L
         value of least I when T=G
    end for
end let
```

The first for-expression finds the least and greatest values, while the second for-expression determines the smallest index that produces each of those values.

The examples of forall expressions in this section are limited because arrays have not yet been discussed. Section 4.3.4 will revisit for-expressions, using them to operate in parallel on elements of arrays.

4.2.9   PARALLELISM FROM ITERATION

We've discussed two very different forms of iteration in this section — iteration and forall-parallelism — as well as reductions. All of these features expose some parallelism.

Forall parallelism is the most explicit form of parallelism in Sisal. Each of the instances of the body can be executed in parallel and the number of iterations is known at the time we enter the loop. This information can be used to exploit parallelism on many types of architectures.

Vector machines will look for operations that match their instruction set and straightforwardly implement them. Many vector units can operate with a "masking" register, which will efficiently implement the filtering clauses in the returns part.

A pipelined, superscalar architecture can use a technique called *software pipelining* [8] to overlap the execution of several instances of the loop body and obtain high performance through this form of parallelism.

A collection of scalar processors can use the knowledge of the number of loop instances to allocate "chunks" of work (a range of indices) to each processor. This size information can allow processors in a shared-memory implementation to store their results directly into memory, since the runtime code can guarantee that each result location will be written by exactly one processor.

The extraction of parallelism from the iterative expressions is more difficult to obtain than parallelism from forall expressions. We can certainly extract the fine-grain parallelism that any collection of expressions exposes, but the hard work is to determine when multiple instances can safely overlap. This analysis usually concerns the dependence between subscripted values, and it has been studied quite heavily in the Fortran context. Such analysis would certainly be profitable in Sisal, but its impact would be less profound than in Fortran, where the user lacks the explicit "forall" expression of Sisal. The question of whether it is necessary to exploit the parallelism across iterations is a performance issue that Sisal implementers must consider.

Finally, the reduction operations can be tailored to perform efficiently on diverse architectures. Vector architectures often support these reductions directly. Multiple scalar processors may distribute the work and combine the results serially, while a dataflow architecture may directly manipulate the tag fields to efficiently implement a tree-associative reduction.

4.3   Arrays

Sisal arrays can contain zero or more *elements* that are indexed by integers. They are characterized by

- □ **Direct access**: The time cost to access any element is constant.
- □ **Dense packing**: The array contains a set of elements that are indexed over a contiguous range from a lower bound to an upper bound.
- □ **Uniform element type**: All elements of the array have the same type.
- □ **Dynamic size**: The size of an array object is not necessarily known until runtime.

The intent of Sisal arrays is to provide efficient access to potentially large arrays. Given this set of characterizations (dense packing and uniform element type), we can use address arithmetic and pointers to access an element directly, instead of using a linear access method, such as a linked list. Allowing the array bounds to vary at runtime incurs a little overhead, but it provides flexibility and allows nonrectangular arrays. The compiler can take note of special cases (such as a constant lower bound of 1) to generate the most efficient code possible.

Sisal has many means to specify an array, but five of them will be discussed in this section: the array constructor, the string constructor, the predefined array_fill function, the "array replacement" operation, and catenation.

4.3.1 ARRAY CONSTRUCTORS

Array constructors create fixed-size array values. Their syntax is

```
array [ lower bound: value, value,... ]
array: typename [ lower bound: value, value,... ]
```

Some examples of array constructors are:

```
type IntOneD = array[ integer ]
```

```
array [ 1: 1, 2, 3, 4, 5, 6, 7, 8, 9 ]
array [ 1: 'S', 't','r', 'i', 'n', 'g', 's', ' ', 'a',
           'r', 'e', ' ', 'a', 'r', 'r', 'a', 'y', 's', ' ',
           'o', 'f', ' ', 'c', 'h', 'a', 'r', 'a', 'c', 't',
           'e', 'r', 's' ]
array IntOneD [ -5: 25, 16, 9, 4, 1, 0, 1, 4, 9, 16, 25 ]
array [ L: X, Y, Z ] % L must be integer, X, Y, Z must agree
```

The lower bound of an array constructor must be an integer expression, and all of the elements must have the same type. The type name is optional, but if it is given, the compiler will compare it to the type of the array that follows within the brackets and complain if they are not equivalent.

Since Sisal uses arrays of characters to represent strings, it is convenient to have a special form for them.

```
"Strings are arrays of characters"
"Number of sides\t Area\t Volume \n "
"One can simply use a backslash to include a \""
"Nasty characters, such as \033 and \031 can be safely
included in strings "
```

To include nonprinting characters such as newline and formfeed in strings, Sisal borrows the conventions used in the C language to represent

\b	backspace
\ f	form feed
\n	newline
\r	return
\t	tab
\\	backslash
\ddd	octal digits

TABLE 4.2
SISAL ENCODINGS OF NONPRINTING CHARACTERS.

such characters. A backslash followed by a single character in the set { t,f,n,r,b, \ } is specially interpreted, as shown in Table 4.2. If the backslash is followed by a digit in the range 0-7, that digit, and at most the two following digits, are interpreted as the *octal* equivalent to the character. See Table 4.2 for a complete list of encodings available in Sisal.

Array Initialization. The predefined function array_fill is a convenient way to create boundary arrays that are all zero (or another appropriate value).

    array_fill(Length, Number, Value)

Examples of array_fill constructors are

    array_fill(1, 100, 0.0)
    array_fill(0, N-1, False)
    array_fill(1, MaxStringLength, ' ')

Since the number of elements of the array can be any integer expression, array_fill is a convenient way to initialize arrays whose size is unknown until runtime.

Replacing an Array Element. At times, we might like to modify an array by changing an element. Since we cannot modify any values in Sisal, an array-replacement expression returns an array that differs from its input at only one point.

    arrayname[Index: value]

We can imagine that *logically* we have copied the array and changed one value, but in practice, Sisal compilers detect circumstances where

Name	Type	Function
array_size	integer	Number of elements in the array
array_liml	integer	Lower Bound
array_limh	integer	Upper Bound

TABLE 4.3
PREDEFINED FUNCTIONS ON ARRAYS

array copying is not necessary and emit code that simply modifies the original array. Again, we must emphasize that we're describing *two* arrays, and if we wish to use the original value we can do so. In that case the compiler will ensure that we see two different arrays; whether it does so by copying or by other means (such as keeping a list of changes and a pointer to the original array) is not relevant to the correctness and meaning of the code. It will, however, affect the performance.

Array Catenation.   Catenation is a familiar operation on strings, so it should seem natural that Sisal includes a catenation operation on arrays.

$ArrayName_1$ || $ArrayName_2$

The lower bound of the result is the same as that of *ArrayName*$_1$. The array elements contain all of the elements of both arrays, with those of *ArrayName*$_2$ following all of those of *ArrayName*$_1$. As with other array operations, the result is *logically* distinct from either of the inputs, although clever compilers can avoid making copies.

4.3.2 ARRAY ACCESS

Sisal uses square brackets [ ] to access an element of an array — for example *A[I]*. It returns a value whose type is the basetype of the array. If the value is out of range, an error value will be returned. Using array_adjust(Array, Low, High)   a subarray, rather than a single element, is returned.

Several predefined functions are available to ask about the size or bounds of an array; some of them are given in Table 4.3.

4.3.3   MULTIDIMENSIONAL ARRAYS

Multidimensional arrays are simply arrays of arrays, which allows considerable freedom concerning the "shape" of a multidimensional array. Arrays need not be "rectangular," as is often the case in other languages. Each row of a multidimensional array can determine its own length and lower bound, and if the bounds are not uniform, the array is called "ragged." For example,

```
%%% type definitions
type OneDim = array[ real ];
type TwoDim = array[ OneDim ];
type AnotherTwoDim = array[ array[ real ] ]
% equivalent to TwoDim

%%% array constructors
let
   A := array[ 1: 2.0, 4.0, 6.0 ];
   B: OneDim := array[ 0: 0.0, 3.0, 6.0 ];
in
   array[ 1: A, B, A ]
end let
```

Both *A* and *B* are of type OneDim, while the result of the let-expression is a two dimensional array (type *TwoDim*) of nine elements. The elements have the subscripts [1,1], [1,2], [1,3], [2,0], [2,1], [2,2], [3,1], [3,2], and [3,3].

Array Results of For-Expressions.   Arrays can be returned as a result of a for-expression by using the array of *expression* clause in the returns part. Any number of arrays can be returned from either form of the for-expression (either iterative or forall).

Arrays produced by forall expressions will have an element contributed by each instance of the forall body. Indices of the array elements will range over the same values as the index of each loop. For example, if the range expression in the forall header were " for I in 1,N ," the lower bound of any arrays produced by that expression will be 1, and there will be at most N elements in the arrays.

The number of elements in the array will be the same as the number of instances of the forall body, unless a when or unless clause omits some elements. In that case, for expressions can produce arrays that have fewer elements than the number of instances of the forall body (or empty ones), but the elements will be indexed from the lowest number in the generator, *L*, up to $L + K$, where *K* values were included by when or unless clauses. For example,

```
for I in L, H
  A := sin( 2.0*Pi/360.0 * real( I-L ) / real( H-L ) )
  B := cos( 2.0*Pi/360.0 * real( I-L ) / real( H-L ) )
returns
  array of A*A
  array of B*B
end for
```

Multidimensional arrays can be easily produced by nesting forall expressions. The straightforward approach nests loops that return arrays, gathering a row from each of the inner loops into an array at the outer level. For example, the following function creates an identity array of size N. It begins by creating an array of zeros of the appropriate length in each inner scope, but returns an array that has the element on the diagonal replaced by 1.0.

```
function Ident( N: integer
returns array[ array[ real ] ] )
  for I in 1, N
      T := array_fill( 1, N, 0.0 )
  returns value of T[ I: 1.0 ] % replace the diagonal element
  end for
end function % Ident
```

```
function Modulo( N, M: integer
  for I in 1, N
      Row :=
            for J in 1, N
            returns array of mod( I*J, M )
            end for
  returns array of Row
  end for
end function % Modulo
```

The situation described by the for-expression in function Modulo is important enough that Sisal has defined a way to give both of the ranges in one expression. The form

for *Name* in *Range* [cross *Range*] ...

will create pairs (or triples, or quadruples, etc) of name-value bindings. The returns clause will often contain an array gathering clause, and the array will have as many dimensions as the for-expression had ranges. The returns clause may also contain reductions, which are performed over all the ranges, using an ordering that corresponds to the order in which explicitly nested for-expressions would have ordered the operations. The value of clause can be given, but it will return the value corresponding to the highest value in each range. The previous Modulo function can be written more concisely:

```
function ModuloPrime( N, M: integer
returns array[ array[ integer ] ] )
   for I in 1, N cross J in 1, N
   returns array of mod( I*J, M )
   end for
end function% ModuloPrime
```

4.3.4   ARRAYS AS RANGE GENERATORS

The for-expression can use an array to generate the range of a forall-style expression, The array name replaces the two integer expressions (or cross-product of ranges) in the range clause. This form is commonly used to operate on arrays in a data-parallel fashion. The syntax is

> for *ElementName* in *ArrayName*
> for *ElementName* in *ArrayName* at *IndexName*

The first form creates an instance of the for-expression for each element in the specified array. It also binds the value of the array element to *ElementName*, and that value can be referenced in the body and returns part of the expression. For example, to create an array whose elements are double the value of an input array called InputArray, we can write

```
for Elt in InputArray
returns array of 2.0*Elt
end for
```

Similarly, we can perform three-point relaxation on a one-dimensional array using the expression:

```
let
L, U := array_liml ( InputArray ), array_limh ( InputArray )
in
for Elt in InputArray at I
```

```
      NewElt :=
   if I=L then
      ( Elt + InputArray[ L+1 ] ) / 2.0
   elseif I=U then
      ( Elt + InputArray[ U-1 ] ) / 2.0
   else
      ( InputArray[ L-1 ] + Elt + InputArray[ L+1 ] ) / 3.0
   end if
returns array of NewElt
end for
end let
```

In this example we needed to know the index of each element, so we added the clause at I . If we want to process more than one dimension of a multidimensional array we can specify a list of names, rather than just one name. Doing so exposes more (potential) parallelism using another concise notation (with both dimensions able to contribute elements). For example, to transpose a square, two-dimensional array we can write

```
for Elt in A at I, J
returns array of A[ J, I ]
end for
```

This example will work only when the output array has the same shape as the input array. To handle the more general (nonsquare) case, we must explictly generate the ranges in the reverse (innermost first) order. Why? The array takes the shape of the generators, so we must generate the range of the rows first, then cross it with the range of the columns. Namely,

```
function Bounds( A: array[ real ] returns integer, integer )
array_liml( A ), array_limh( A )
end function

for J in Bounds(A[ array_liml(A)]) cross I in Bounds(A)
returns array of A[ I, J ]
end for
```

More generally, though, programs will use arrays of the same shape for both input and output. Such code has the general form

```
for Elt in A at I, J
NewElt := some_function_of( A,I,J )
returns array of NewElt
end for
```

We'll create a new array that has the same shape as the old array but contains new values that were computed using the elements of the old array.

4.3.5   PARALLELISM FROM ARRAYS

The most common source of parallelism from arrays is forall expressions that take arrays as input and produce arrays or reductions as output. Some parallelism will be expressed via catenations or explicit array constructions, but that parallelism is usually dwarfed by the parallelism present when using multidimensional arrays in for-expressions.

4.4   Streams

Another form of parallelism can be expressed by using streams rather than arrays. Streams are homogeneous data structures, like arrays, but their elements are accessible only by the use of stream_first and stream_rest functions. No subscripting or random access of a stream value is possible. This restricted form of access allows the use of elements from the head of the stream to overlap the production of some of the later elements. This overlap is not possible if we create array values, because elements of the array cannot be accessed until the entire array has been produced.

This form of parallelism is sometimes called *pipeline* parallelism, because streams can be used to express the stages in a hardware pipeline. For example, we might consider the stages in floating-point arithmetic. Floating-point arithmetic might be broken into five stages:

1. Unpack exponents and fractions.
2. Align fractions.
3. Add fractions.
4. Normalize result.
5. Pack exponent and fraction.

Each stage could operate simultaneously on a different pair of inputs, so that once the pipeline is full, the time between results is the maximum of the time for each *stage* in the pipeline, not the total time of all of the stages.

In Sisal we could write the previous example using streams:

```
type Unpacked = record[ Exponent: integer;
       Fraction: integer ];
type Sreal = stream[ real ];
type Sinteger = stream[ integer ];

global UnpackReal( A: Sreal returns Sinteger, Sinteger)
global Align( ExpA, ExpB, A, B: Sinteger returns Sinteger,
       Sinteger, Sinteger)
global StreamIntAdd( A, B: Sinteger returns Sinteger)
global Normalize( Exponent, Fraction: Sinteger returns
       Sinteger, Sinteger)
global PackReal( A, B: Sinteger returns Sreal)

function PipelinedAdd( A, B: Sreal, returns Sreal )
  let
       ExpA, FractA := UnpackReal( A );
       ExpB, FractB := UnpackReal( B );
       AlignedExp, Addend1, Addend2 := Align( ExpA, ExpB,
       FractA, FractB );
       Sum := StreamIntAdd( Addend1, Addend2 );
       NewExp, NewFraction := Normalize(AlignedExp, Sum);
  in
       PackReal( NewExp, NewFraction )
  end let
end function% PipelinedAdd
```

Every value name in *PipelinedAdd* is bound to a stream value. All values but the parameters, A and B, and the result are streams of integers, *Sinteger*. This function can create a parallel process for each function application, so up to six parallel tasks could result from *PipelinedAdd*. However, it is up to the compiler to decide whether it is profitable to do so.

4.4.1 CREATING STREAM OBJECTS

```
stream [ value₁, value₂, ..., valueₖ ]
stream StreamTypeName [ value₁, value₂, ..., valueₖ ]
```

Each of these forms of the stream constructor builds a stream of fixed size. Each *value$_i$* must be of the same type, and in the second form it must match the element type of *StreamTypeName*. The first example below creates a stream of 10 integers. The second and third examples each create an object of type *StreamOfOneDimReal*; the first stream contains three arrays and the second contains two.

```
type SOneDimReal = stream[ OneDimReal ];

stream [ 1, 1, 2, 3, 5, 8, 13, 21, 34, 55 ]
stream [ array[ 1: 1.0, 2.0 ], array[ 1: 2.0, 1.0, 2.0 ],
array[ 2: 1.0, 2.0 ] ]
stream SOneDimReal [ array[ 1: 3.0, 1.0, 4.0, 1.0 ],
array[ 1: 5.0, 9.0, 2.0, 6.0 ] ]
```

Fixed-size streams are used rather rarely. They commonly appear as arguments to stream catenation, to add a few elements to either the beginning or end of another stream. Streams are more commonly created in for-expressions. A for-expression can gather a stream in much the same manner as it gathers arrays.

stream of *value*₁ *OptionalWhenOrUnlessClause*
value of catenate *value*₂ *OptionalWhenOrUnlessClause*

These clauses can appear in both the iterative and forall forms of the for-expression (although we more commonly associate streams with iteration). The decision regarding the form of the for-expression to use is based on whether any values are shared across iterations. The *PipelinedAdd* function exploits data-parallelism, so its subfunctions can use the forall flavor of the for-expression to describe its function.

As an example of using an iterative method, consider the following function, *RandInt*. It generates a potentially unbounded number of integers as values within a stream. Implementations (compilers plus runtime systems) can either choose to evaluate this expression in a lazy manner, or use flow control between producers and consumers. They must ensure that an application of *RandInt* does not consume all of the resources (CPU and memory) to the exclusion of other executable tasks.

```
function RandInt( A, B, Seed: integer returns Sinteger )
   for initial
         X := Seed
   while true repeat
         X := mod( A * old X, B )
   returns stream of X
   end for
end function % RandInt
```

4.4.2   ACCESSING STREAM ELEMENTS

for *Element* in *S*
for *Element* in *S* at *Index*

The simplest form of stream element access occurs when the values can be consumed in a forall expression. For example, here are two of the functions referenced by *PipelinedAdd*:

```
function StreamIntAdd( A, B: Sinteger returns Sinteger)
    for AElement in A dot BElement in B
    returns stream of AElement+BElement
    end for
end function % StreamIntAdd
function Align( SXa, SXb, SA, SB: Sinteger returns Sinteger,
Sinteger, Sinteger)
%%% SA and SB must contain positive integers representing
%%% normalized values
%%% SXa and SXb contain their exponents
    for A in SA dot B in SB dot Xa in SXa dot Xb in SXb
        NewX, NewA, NewB :=
            if Xa=Xb then Xa, A, B
            elseif Xa < Xb then
                    Xb,
                    for initial Shift := Xb-Xa; SmallerA := A
                    while Shift>0 repeat
                        SmallerA := old SmallerA / 2;
                        Shift := old Shift - 1
                    returns value of SmallerA
                    end for,
                    B
            else% Xa > Xb
                    Xa, A,
                    for initial Shift := Xa-Xb; SmallerB := B
                    while Shift>0 repeat
                        SmallerB := old SmallerB / 2;
                        Shift := old Shift - 1
                    returns value of SmallerB
                    end for
            end if
    returns stream of NewX, NewA, NewB
    end for
end function % Align
```

Functions need not emit an element onto the stream on every iteration; the *OptionalWhenOrUnless* clause can mask values from the stream. The following function removes all multiples of *Value* from an integer stream:

```
function Filter(Value:integer; S:Sinteger returns Sinteger)
   for Element in S
   returns stream of Element unless mod(Element, Value) = 0
   end for
end function% Filter
```

4.4.3   OTHER OPERATIONS ON STREAMS

stream_rest(*StreamObject*)
stream_first(*StreamObject*)
StreamValueA || *StreamValueB*

The use of **stream_rest** returns a stream object that contains all but the first element of its argument, which is another stream. It is *not* a destructive operation; the original stream is still available. It commonly appears in an iterative for-expression when the function needs to remove an arbitrary number of elements during one iteration.

A copy of the value of the first element of a stream is returned by **stream_first**. It is often used in conjunction with **stream_rest** to remove the first few elements of a stream and later return the remainder of the stream.

The catenate function, ||, returns a stream that contains all of the elements of the first stream, followed by all of the elements of the second stream. It can also appear as a reduction operator in for-expressions. Here is a version of the *FlattenInt* function, which removes one level of "streamness" from a stream of streams of integers:

```
function FlattenInt(S: stream[ Sinteger ] returns Sinteger)
   for Element in S
   returns value of catenate Element
   end for
end function% FlattenInt
```

Each *Element* is a stream of arbitrary size and will contribute zero or more elements to the result. All elements of the first substream are in their original order, followed by all elements of the second substream, until all of the elements in the original stream of streams appear in the result.

An important point about the data types is apparent in *FlattenInt*. This function will accept only streams of streams of integers. If we wish to flatten a stream of streams of reals, we'll need to write and name another function.

The problem of creating new names can be easily avoided by *overloading* the name with several definitions that differ only in their input and output types. The more general solution of accepting a stream of stream of *all* types, called polymorphism, is more difficult to implement than overloading. We must worry about generating code that adapts to differing sizes of elements that compose the flattened stream. Although it is relatively easy to handle building and consuming streams, efficient implementations of other polymorphic operators, such as a generalized "+" are fairly difficult. For this reason, we are pursuing overloading, but not polymorphism, in the next version of the Sisal language (see Section 4.10.2).

4.4.4 PARALLELISM FROM STREAMS

Section 4.4 discusses the possible parallelism due to the overlap of producers and consumers of streams. This language feature arose from a very different need—the need to perform interactive input/output. Streams were originally added to the language in order to allow the user to type partial input to a program and see partial results. Since the program might not need to see *all* of its stream input, it could go off and compute some results, display them by gathering an output stream, and go back to the input stream for more input. Internal streams were a natural extension of this solution.

4.5 Records

Records and unions are used in Sisal programs in the same manner as they are in imperative programs. They group related but nonhomogeneous values together and treat them as a single data object. As with arrays, they are created all at once, using the syntax

    record [*fieldname$_1$: value$_1$; fieldname$_2$: value$_2$* ...]
    record *TypeName* [*fieldname$_1$: value$_1$; fieldname$_2$: value$_2$* ...]
    Name replace [fieldname: value]

The last form uses an extant record to produce a related record value. As with arrays, the input record R is left unchanged and another record is created using R as a template, with one field given a different value. Also as with arrays, the compiler is free to determine that no other use of R occurs within the program, in order to destructively modify R.

Some examples follow:

```
type Cartesian = record[ X: real; Y: real ]
type Polar = record[ R: real; Theta: real ]

P1 := record[ X: 5.0; Y: 5.0 ] % type Cartesian
P2 := record Cartesian[ X: 2.0; Y: -2.0 ] % type Cartesian
P3 := record[ R: 8.6; Theta: Pi/4.0 ] % type Polar
P4 := P3 replace [ R: 2.8 ] % type Polar
```

The type name is optional since the type matching rules will allow the compiler to determine the type of the record object. The type matching rule for Sisal records is fairly strict. Two types are equivalent only under the following circumstances:

1. They have the same number of fields.
2. The fields have the same names *in the same order.*
3. The types of each field are equivalent.

Thus programmers must take care to ensure that the field names are correctly ordered when they create a record object. If the order of field names is changed, a new record type is created and it will not match the original type.

4.5.1   RECORD ACCESS

Records are accessed by using "dot" notation:

RecordObject.FieldName

If R_C and R_P are record objects of type *Cartesian* and *Polar*, respectively, their fields can be referenced by $R_C.X$, $R_C.Y$, $R_P.R$ and $R_P.Theta$.

4.5.2   PARALLELISM FROM RECORDS

Records alone are not very useful in expressing parallelism, since Sisal lacks an analogue of the forall expression that operates over the fields of a record. However, they are very helpful when combined with the union data structure.

4.6   Union Types

The union in Sisal is much like the variant records of Pascal or the unions of C. Sisal union objects have an important restriction. Their use is forced by the language to be statically type correct. Thus the "tricks" used to circumvent type restrictions in other languages (for example, turning a real number into an array of Booleans or an address into an integer) will not be possible in a Sisal program. However, the union type will give us the basis for building recursive data types, which can be a useful source of parallelism.

The best way to describe the syntax of a union type is through an example. Here is a declaration of a recursive data structure called a quadtree. Each quadtree represents a matrix, but instead of breaking it into rows and columns, a quadtree divides a two-dimensional matrix into four quadrants named NE, SE, SW, and NW in the example below. Each quadrant has a power of two elements on a side and is either a Scalar (a leaf node in the recursive data type) or is a NonScalar, which contains four other Quadtrees.

```
type QuadTree = record[ Order, Padding: integer;
                        Body: QTree ];

type QTree = union[
        Scalar: real;
        NonScalar: record[ NE, SE, SW, NW: QTree ];
        ]
```

The interesting part of the declaration of *Quadtree* is that it can reference *QTree* before *QTree* has been defined.

The declaration of *QTree* defines two variants. The first represents a scalar, or a scalar times the identity matrix. As we'll see in a later example that performs addition and multiplication on these data structures, we don't need to keep the size of the QTree. The second variant of *QTree* contains four other *QTrees*.

The tagcase-expression accesses the variants of a union type and has the form

```
tagcase Name := Expression of
tag TagName₁: Expression₁;
    ...
tag TagNameₙ: Expressionₙ;
end tagcase
```

Each tag guards the expression associated with its *TagName* and all of the possible tags must be associated with some expression. Within the *Expression, Name* is bound to the value of that tag. So, to operate upon *Obj*, an object of type *QTree*, a program could include an expression like

```
tagcase Variant := Obj of
```

```
tag Scalar: Variant*2.0 % Variant is of type real
```

```
tag NonScalar: SomeFunctionReturningReal( Variant.NW )
```
% *Variant is a QTree*

```
end tagcase
```

Each tag clause returns a value of type real; hence, the tagcase-expression is of type real. When *Obj* is tagged *Scalar*, the name *Variant* is bound to *Scalar*'s real value; when *Obj* has tag *NonScalar*, *Variant* will be bound to a record of four *QTrees*. Thus, in both clauses Sisal defines the type of *Variant*, and the usual type inference can be used. The important point of this simple example is to emphasize that *Obj* and *Variant* are not the same values; one is a union value, the other is either a real value or a record value.

4.6.1   MATRIX ADDITION USING QUADTREES

Quadtrees offer several interesting qualities that we will exploit in the following example. They provide a representation for certain forms of sparse matrices, especially those forms that have large areas of zeros. In both addition and multiplication, this sparse representation will allow us to short-circuit evaluations when we notice that one of the operands is zero. Quadtrees also generate fourfold concurrency as the program descends into subtrees, which we hope the Sisal compiler will exploit. Results using quadtrees for numerical applications were reported by David Wise in [23]; the example that follows was inspired by that work.

We begin by defining a normal form for quadtrees. A quadtree is in normal form under the following circumstances:

- It is a scalar multiple of an identity matrix of any size.
- If it is not, it is a NonScalar.

$$A = \begin{pmatrix} 1 & 0 \\ 0 & 1 \end{pmatrix} \equiv 1 \cdot I = 1, \ B = \begin{pmatrix} 5 & 0 \\ 0 & 5 \end{pmatrix} \equiv 5 \cdot I = 5$$

$$C = \begin{pmatrix} 3 & 4 \\ 3 & 4 \end{pmatrix}, \quad D = \begin{pmatrix} 1 & 4 \\ 3 & 2 \end{pmatrix}, \quad E = C - D = \begin{pmatrix} 2 & 0 \\ 0 & 2 \end{pmatrix} = 2$$

In these examples, the matrices A, B and E are represented by *Scalar QTrees*, while C and D are each represented by a *NonScalar QTree* that contains four *Scalar QTrees*.

The first function shows the constructor for union objects. Both the tag and the value must be given at the same time.

%%% BuildQTree sets the four quadrants

```
function BuildQTree( NE, SE, SW, NW: QTree returns QTree )
  union QTree[ NonScalar:
                  record[ NE: NE; SE: SE; SW: SW; NW: NW ]
                  ]
end function % BuildQTree
```

The next task is to write a function, *NormalizeQ*, that takes four *QTrees* and returns a normalized *QTree*. This function is invoked each time that a new *QTree* is created, so that results like $C - D$ in the above example are converted back to the *Scalar* variant. We must nest the tagcase-expressions in order to test that both diagonals are scalars, and separately test that the off-diagonal quadrants are zero.

%%% NormalizeQ checks for NE&SW=0 and SE=NW.

```
function NormalizeQ( NE, SE, SW, NW: QTree returns QTree )
  let
        DiagonalOK :=
              tagcase NW1 := NW
              tag NonScalar: false
              tag Scalar:
                    tagcase SE1 := SE
                        tag NonScalar: false
                        tag Scalar: NW1=SE1
                    end tagcase
              end tagcase;
        Merge :=
              if DiagonalOK then
                    tagcase NE1 := NE
                    tag NonScalar: false
                    tag Scalar:
                          tagcase SW1 := SW
                            tagNonScalar: false
                            tagScalar: (NE1=0.0) & (SW1=0.0)
                          end tagcase
                    end tagcase
              else false
              end if
  in
        if Merge then NW
        else BuildQTree( NE, SE, SW, NW )
```

```
        end if
      end let
    end function  % NormalizeQ
```

The next function, *QAdd*, actually performs the addition. It is the first function to express parallelism through recursion, and it does so in three of the four combinations of *Scalar*s and *NonScalar*s. In one case *NonScalar* cross *NonScalar* we match up corresponding quadrants, but in two other cases we have a *Scalar* and a *NonScalar*. In those cases we pass the scalar value along the diagonal, which yields two recursive applications of *QAdd*, and we simply return the nonzero quadrants that are off the diagonal (since their counterparts are zero). In those cases we generate some parallelism along the diagonal, and see the benefit of short-circuiting the evaluation by doing no work off the diagonal.

```
    %%% QAdd does the real work of addition
    %%% It checks for zeros and returns the other argument
    %%%  or recursively calls itself on each quadtree
    function QAdd( A, B: QTree returns QTree )
      tagcase L := A
      tag NonScalar:
         tagcase R := B
         tag NonScalar: % NonScalar x NonScalar
           NormalizeQ( QAdd( L.NE, R.NE ), QAdd( L.SE, R.SE ),
                       QAdd( L.SW, R.SW ), QAdd( L.NW, R.NW ))
           tag Scalar: % NonScalar x Scalar
              if R=0.0 then A
              else
                    NormalizeQ( L.NE, QAdd( L.SE, B ), L.SW,
                    QAdd( L.NW, B ) )
              end if
         end tagcase
      tag Scalar:
         if L=0.0 then B
         else
              tagcase R := B
              tag Scalar: % Scalar x Scalar
                 union QTree[ Scalar: L+R ]
              tag NonScalar: % Scalar x NonScalar
                 NormalizeQ( R.NE, QAdd( A, R.SE ), R.SW,
                 QAdd( A, R.NW ) )
              end tagcase
         end if
      end tagcase
    end function% QAdd
```

The next function uses the record replace expression to create the sum. The result's *Order* and *Padding* remain the same as the input, but the *Body* is replaced by the *QTree* returned by *QAdd*.

```
%%% QuadAdd simply calls QAdd to replace
%%% the body of the Quadtree
function QuadAdd( A, B: Quadtree returns Quadtree )
  A replace [ Body: QAdd( A.Body, B.Body ) ]
end function% QuadAdd
```

4.6.2 PARALLELISM FROM UNIONS

Unions themselves offer little opportunity for parallel execution. However, they are indispensable for defining recursive data structures, which can be processed using multiway recursion. The hard problem is to effectively use that parallelism. In the quadtree addition example, relatively little work was done in each function application.

Several factors should affect how to exploit such parallelism. The available resources must not be overloaded. When the system is saturated with work, it is better to serially evaluate several function applications than to spawn new ones. We might also wish to have two versions of a recursive function, one with recursive calls that spawn new processes and another in which the recursive calls have been expanded inline, or replaced by simple call/return semantics.

4.7 An Example

The following example factors a square matrix into the product of a lower-triangular and an upper-triangular array. The example begins with type definitions for the matrix and a (one-dimensional) vector. Remember that the bounds of the array are not part of the type; rather they are a property of the object.

```
type OneDimReal = array[ real ];
type TwoDimReal = array[ OneDimReal ]
```

We'll begin by giving a helper function, *Eliminate*, which performs one step of Gaussian elimination on the matrix. It is repeatedly called by the function *Factor*.

%%% Eliminate performs one step of gaussian reduction
%%% on a matrix B.
%%% It returns a row of U and a column of L upon each call.
%%% Arguments:
%%%   M, a square matrix
%%% Results:
%%%   Row, the top row of M (the row of U)
%%%   Multipliers, the multipliers (the column of L)
%%%   array of NewRow, the remaining submatrix

```
function Eliminate( M: TwoDimReal
returns OneDimReal, OneDimReal, TwoDimReal )

    let
        Low := array_liml( M );
        N := array_limh( M );
        Multipliers :=
            for J in Low+1, N
            returns array of M[ J, Low ] / M[ Low, Low ]
            end for;
        Row := M[ Low ]
    in

        Row, Multipliers,
        for J in Low+1, N
            NewRow :=
                for K in Low+1, N
                returns array of M[ J, K ] -
                Multipliers[ J ]*Row[ K ]
                end for
        returns array of NewRow
        end for
    end let
end function% Eliminate
```

Eliminate is written to exploit forall-style parallelism during the
calculation of the *Multipliers* and the matrix of *NewRows*. Note the
shape of the array *Multipliers*; it has a lower bound of $Low+1$ and an
upper bound of N.

The computation of *NewRow* is a two-dimensional calculation in
which all of the computations are independent. Sisal's nested forall expressions expose the parallelism present here.

One form of parallelism is present in the solution but is not expressed in the previous version. As soon as each element of *Multipliers*
has been computed, the corresponding instance of the *for J* expression

could begin. This parallelism is expressed by the version of *Eliminate* below. As soon as each element of Multipliers has been placed in the stream, the outer forall expression that uses the stream can initiate another instance of its body. Since each instance of its body is a forall expression, this solution generates lots of parallelism.

%%% Version of Eliminate that exploits pipeline parallelism

```
function Eliminate( M: TwoDimReal
returns OneDimReal, OneDimReal, TwoDimReal )

    let
        Low := array_liml( M );
        N := array_limh( M );
        Multipliers, SMultipliers :=
            for J in Low+1, N
            returns array of M[ J, Low ] / M[ Low, Low ]
            returns stream of M[ J, Low ] / M[ Low, Low ]
            end for;
        Row := M[ Low ]
    in
        Row, Multipliers,
        for Mult in SMultipliers at J
            NewRow :=
                for K in Low+1, N
                returns array of M[ J+Low, K ] - Mult*Row[ K ]
                end for
        returns array of NewRow
        end for
    end let
end function% Eliminate
```

All the L and U matrices are built by repeatedly calling *Eliminate* on the reduced matrix and gathering the vectors in the triangular L and U matrices. *LUFactor* continues until it reachs a 1×1 matrix.

%%% Factor an n-by-n matrix into the product of a lower-diagonal
%%% matrix and an upper diagonal matrix (without pivoting)
%%% Arguments
%%%   M, a square matrix
%%% Results
%%%   L, the lower triangular factor
%%%   U, the upper triangular factor

```
function LUFactor( M: TwoDimReal
returns TwoDimReal, TwoDimReal )
```

```
for initial
      Row, Col, SmallerM := Eliminate( M );
      I := array_liml( M )
while I<array_limh( M ) repeat
      Row, Col, SmallerM := Eliminate( old SmallerM );
      I := old I + 1;
returns
      array of Col
      array of Row
end for
end function% LUFactor
```

LUFactor is written as an iteration, since it has a data dependence between the result of one iteration (*SmallerM*) and the following iteration (old *SmallerM*). The *array_liml* and *array_limh* functions provide the bounds of the array. We assume that all rows of the matrix have the same upper and lower bounds although we haven't explicitly guaranteed it.

The result of the iteration comprises two arrays of type TwoDim-Real. We can infer this type since we see that eliminate returns objects of type OneDimReal for Row and Column and this expression returns arrays of Rows and Columns. These are the L and U that we wish to return.

As we observed in *Eliminate*, each instance of Row and Column is one "shorter" than each row of the matrix. *LUFactor* uses Sisal's "ragged" arrays to allocate only a triangular amount of memory for each triangular array.

In order to use this factorization to solve $Ax = b$, we present two helper functions that exploit the triangular shape of L and U: *ForwardSubstitute* and *BackSubstitute*. *BackSubstitute* solves the equation $Ly = b$ and *ForwardSubstitute* solves $Ux = y$. Their composition gives us the solution to $L(Ux) = b$ or $(LU)x = b$ or $Ax = b$.

%%% *ForwardSubstitute: a forward solution of L*X = B*
%%%   *where L is a lower triangular matrix*
%%% *Arguments:*
%%%   *L, the lower factor of the matrix, stored by column*
%%%   *B, the right-hand side*
%%% *Results:*
%%%   *X, the solution of the matrix equation L*X=B*

```
function ForwardSubstitute( L: TwoDimReal; B: OneDimReal;
returns OneDimReal)
```

```
for initial
    I := 1;
    Y := array[ 1: B[ 1 ]]
while I <= array_limh( B ) repeat
    I := old I + 1;
    Y := array_addh( old Y, B[ I ] -
        for J in 1, old I
        returns value of sum L[ J, I ]*old Y[ J ]
        end for
returns value of Y
end for
end function% ForwardSubstitute
```

Each function explicitly builds the vector Y using the array_addh function rather than using an array of reduction. It must do so to access the values computed in previous iterations (old Y) within the current iteration.

%%% *BackSubstitute: a backward solution of* $U*X = Y$
%%% *where U is an upper triangular matrix*
%%% *Arguments:*
%%% *U, the upper triangular factor of the matrix,*
%%% *Y, the right-hand side*
%%% *Results:*
%%% *X, the solution of the matrix equation* $U*X = Y$

```
function BackSubstitute( U: TwoDimReal; Y: OneDimReal;
returns OneDimReal)

    for initial
        N := array_limh( Y );
        I := N;
        X := array[ N: Y[ N ] / U[ N, N ] ]
    while I > 1 repeat
        I := old I - 1;
        X := array_addl( old X, ( Y[ I ] -
            for J in I+1, N
            returns value of sum U[ I, J ]*old X[ J ]
            end for ) / U[ I, I ] )
    returns value of X
    end for
end function% BackSubstitute
```

The only parallelism exposed in *ForwardSubstitute* and *BackSubstitute* appears in the forall expressions for X and Y.

The actual solution is done by invoking the factorization and each of the substitutions in function *Solve*.

%%% Solve: perform LU decomposition and find X in A*X = B.
%%% Arguments:
%%%   A: real, square, matrix
%%%   B: real vector of the same length as a side of A
%%% Results:
%%%   X: real vector solution to A*X = B

```
function Solve( A: TwoDimReal; B: OneDimReal
returns OneDimReal )

  let
      L, U := LUFactor( A );
      Y := ForwardSubstitute( L, B );
  in
      BackSubstitute( U, Y );
  end let
end function% Solve
```

4.8   Implementation

Sisal programs can be compiled and executed in "native mode" on a wide variety of multiprocessors that range from dataflow machines to supercomputers. Compilers (producing code that runs in native mode and in parallel) have been implemented for the following machines:

- **Dataflow machines**: Manchester Prototype Dataflow Computer, CSIRO/RMIT Dataflow Computer

- **Multi-minicomputers**: Multi-VAX, Sequent Balance, Sequent Symmetry

- **Vector-multiprocessors**: Alliant, Cray-X/MP

These are "highly optimizing" compilers that produce code that executes sequentially on several of the target machines at nearly the same efficiency as programs written in conventional languages. Research into compiler algorithms to enhance Sisal program performance has been an important part of the entire project on applicative programming.

A software interpreter[21] was developed at the beginning of the project to run small programs and to study the effects of code transformations. It executes compiled Sisal programs much more slowly than the native-mode compilers, but it allows programmers to test small programs on their workstation or local sequential computer before running them on parallel machines.

4.8.1   SOURCES OF PARALLELISM

One of the strengths of the Sisal language lies in the many ways in which the programmer can express parallelism. Sisal compilers can extract parallelism from the following sources:

▫ **Loops**: Forall expressions, and iterative-style loops can generate parallelism on fine-grained parallel machines.

▫ **Function applications**: Because functions might represent large amounts of work, they are attractive candidates for parallel execution.

▫ **Multi-expressions**: Arguments to an expression, for example, can be independently evaluated. Low-level parallelism, such as that found within a single expression, can be exploited by dataflow computers and by conventional machines that overlap the execution of multiple functional units.

▫ **Streams**: Producers and consumers of streams can execute concurrently, controlled by synchronization added by the compiler.

It becomes the compiler's responsibility to decide which of these sources to exploit in a program. Differences in machine architecture may make some forms of parallelism more attractive than others. Thus a Sisal program run on different architectures may exhibit different degrees of parallelism. For example, a program that uses recursion to express parallelism may run in a highly parallel fashion on a dataflow machine but run most efficiently as a sequential program on a machine where the cost of context-switching is very high, such as the Cray-1. Alternatively, a program that expresses data-parallelism may run with a high degree of vectorization (a particular form of parallelization) on a uniprocessor vector machine, yet run as many processes on a scalar architecture.

4.8.2   SHARED-MEMORY MODEL

The initial implementations of Sisal assume a shared-memory or a uniform-address space architecture. The advantage of this assumption is that the compiler can share large data values by simply passing a pointer to the object. Each processor working on the program shares a common address space, and sets up this sharing once, as the program is initiated.

If the machines use caches to minimize memory access times, the caches are assumed to be coherent (as in the Sequent and Alliant), or they are disabled (in the multi-VAX shared memory). Therefore the compiler does not worry about keeping shared object values consistent across multiple processors.

The use of the shared-memory model is not a requirement to execute Sisal programs, but it is a simplification exploited in the first generation of Sisal compilers. It is interesting to note that the prototype dataflow computer built at the University of Manchester [7] shared several aspects of the shared-memory model. While the individual execution units received packets containing input values and result addresses, they shared the matching store, the program store, and a structure store for arrays.

4.8.3   PROCESS SCHEDULING

The initial Sisal implementations on conventional (nondataflow) computers used a single-server task queue that manipulated lightweight threads without any operating system intervention. The reason for bypassing the operating system is simply for performance. Switching operating system tasks typically takes hundreds or thousands of cycles. If Sisal programs used such a mechanism, it would be very difficult to find many tasks large enough to overcome the startup cost. If the task takes less time than the overhead to start it, it is faster to perform it sequentially.

Sisal runtime systems start up one operating system level task per processor and then maintain their own process queue. Doing so requires that the runtime system know enough about each processor to set up its runtime environment (and suspend it, if necessary). However, the cost of switching tasks is drastically reduced, to tens of instructions [3]. With such lightweight tasks, the compiler can create more parallel tasks, with the hopes of gaining lots of parallel execution.

At this point it should be obvious that the compiler must know something about the characteristics of the machine for which it is generating tasks.

4.9   Compilation Techniques

The current Sisal compilers share a common front end that translates Sisal programs into an intermediate language called IF1[22]. IF1 is an ASCII representation of a dataflow graph that uses a hierarchy to describe complex expressions, such as iterations or selections, in terms of smaller subgraphs. These graphs describe the data dependence among the pieces of a Sisal program and give the compiler very precise information about the uses of each data object.

After the IF1 has been "improved," several different techniques handle the translation to machine code. The compiler for the Manchester Dataflow Computer performed many machine-specific code transformations at the IF1 level before translating to assembly-language, where the compiler applied many low-level transformations to efficiently use the machine's instruction set. Similar techniques are used on the CSIRO/RMIT parallel systems architecture project[1].

The compiler developed at Colorado State University emits C code that is then translated by the C compiler on the host computer. The code contains calls to a Sisal runtime library, which handles the communication and synchronization among the parallel processors. The CSU compiler has an important phase in which it minimizes the amount of array copying (see Section 4.9.2), as well as other useful code transformations (see [4, 2]).

4.9.1 CLASSICAL CODE IMPROVERS

IF1 is the language in which many of the machine-independent program transformations are performed. Many of the same transformations used in imperative languages are standardly applied by the Sisal compiler. Constant folding, common subexpression elimination, loop-invariant removal (including moving loop-invariant tests out of loops) are standardly performed, since they consume very little compilation time. Results on these transformations were reported in [20] and [2].

4.9.2 UPDATE IN PLACE

The worry that Sisal programs would end up spending most of their time copying arrays was expressed shortly after such a programming style was first advocated[10]. To be sure, a naive implementation that copied an array upon every array replacement operation could incur an incredible cost [see [13] for an example of this; the time to run insertion sort became $O(n^3)$ rather than $O(n^2)$. However, research into array copy elimination has shown that very clever compilers can avoid such a penalty.

The latest Sisal compiler developed at Colorado State University analyzes programs using techniques developed by Ranelletti[14], Skedzielewski[19] and Cann and Oldehoeft[4] to minimize storage usage. These results show that array copying can be eliminated in nearly all of the cases in the benchmarks studied (benchmarks ranging from the Livermore Loops [6, 11] to complete hydrodynamics codes[5]).

4.9.3 AUTOMATIC PROGRAM PARTITIONING

The early Sisal compiler that ran on conventional multiprocessors used a simple approach to generating parallelism:

1. All functions were spawned as a task.
2. Every stream producer or consumer was spawned as a task.
3. Each forall expression was divided into a fixed number of tasks.

This method demonstrated that a large number of tasks could be generated from Sisal programs and that for many of the benchmarks, good speedups could be obtained.

As part of his doctoral dissertation, Sarkar developed a method that was selective about which forms of parallelism to exploit [15, 16, 17, 18]. He modified the Sisal interpreter to give a trace of program execution, which yielded information about the frequency of branches and the number of iterations in each for-expression. This information, along with machine characteristics such as the cost of spawning a function, was used by another phase of the compiler that decided where to exploit parallelism. It chose a subset of the function calls to run as parallel tasks and executed the others sequentially. It determined the number of sequential iterations that should be run sequentially as a task, which could vary for each for-expression. The result was a Sisal program that exploited less parallelism than the original implementation but ran considerably faster.

These transformations are crucial to the performance of a Sisal program. However, they have been shown to be effective in reducing the runtime of Sisal programs to the point where they compete with programs written in conventional languages.

Work continues on new Sisal implementations, including one for a nonshared memory system.

4.10 Future Work

The language evaluation has identified several areas in Sisal that are under consideration for change. Some of them are related to the syntax and semantics of the language; others are considered important in order to achieve even higher performance than the current language can easily yield.

4.10.1   FIRST-CLASS FUNCTION VALUES

Version 1.2 of the Sisal language treats functions as second-class objects. They can be defined only at compile time and cannot be passed as function arguments nor returned as function results. The only operation on them is to apply them to arguments. The next version of the language will promote functions to first-class status. Allowing functions to be arguments will prove useful when writing mathematical libraries as well as "plain" applications. Functions can be produced at runtime by partial applications (explained below) or by abstraction of expressions. Abstraction of expressions simply is a short form of function definition in which any names not found in the body are assumed to be defined in the current context (usually a let clause within a function). The value for these free (unbound) values will be obtained at runtime, as the function is created.

4.10.2   OVERLOADING FUNCTION NAMES

The Sisal language already allows function names, type names and values names to be overloaded. That is, a name can simultaneously denote a function, a type and a value without confusing the compiler; the context in which the name appears will distinguish the object. As mentioned in Section 4.4.3, allowing one function name to be used for several types of arguments would simplify a problem when two functions perform the same function on different types, such as pushing a value on a stack of integers, reals, records, and other types.

However, a simple relaxation of the rule for distinguishing function names will still allow us to perform type inference in expressions as is done in Version 1.2 of the language. A function name can be overloaded as long as no other function with the same name *and same argument types* has been defined. Now, each function application yields a name and a type list, whose result type has already been declared.

4.10.3   PARTIAL APPLICATION OF FUNCTIONS

Partial application of a function binds some, but not all, of the arguments to values. The result is a function with fewer arguments, but the same number of results. Two potential benefits can be gained from partial applications:

1. The compiler may be able to perform transformations to produce better code. For example, consider the following function that computes the cosine of the sum of two angles:

```
function CosineAplusB( A, B: real returns real )
 cos( A )*cos( B ) - sin( A )*sin( B )
end function
```

A simple partial application might bind the second argument to a value that can be computed at compile-time:

```
CosXplus90( X: real ) := CosineAplusB( X, pi/4.0 )
```

This partial application can be evaluated at compile time to yield

```
function CosXplus90( X: real returns real )
 cos( X )*cos( pi/4.0 ) - sin( X )*sin( pi/4.0 )
end function
```

and a clever compiler could simplify it further:

```
function CosXplus90( X: real returns real )
 -sin( X )
end function
```

Of course, it is not always possible to simplify the function at compile time. In those cases the compiler will supply the "bound" arguments automatically when the function is applied to the remaining arguments and simply use the code of the original function body.

2. General library functions become possible to write. Since Sisal functions must explicitly name all arguments, it is very difficult to write a function that needs, for example, to evaluate a derivative at a point. The problem occurs when the derivative function needs values that are present in the caller's environment. It is easy to evaluate the derivative as an expression in the caller's environment, but a function must receive these values explicitly. Since the derivative function is passed to the library routine (for example, an integration function), the library routine needs to accept a function that has more than just one variable as input. However, it cannot anticipate the number (and type) of extra arguments from all possible users.

Partial application allows us to create and pass a new function of just one argument by partial application of the original, multiple-argument function to those extra values. Thus we need to add both the ability to pass a function as an argument *and* the ability to create functions at runtime in order to create truly useful library routines.

4.10.4   RECTANGULAR ARRAYS

Although arrays of arrays are sufficient to represent multidimensional arrays, it becomes difficult to perform code transformations that could take advantage of column-wise, rather than row-wise access. In a language such as Fortran with conventional arrays, the compiler can use address arithmetic to efficiently access both down the columns and across the rows. Sisal compilers must deal with the general case of subarrays of varying size and nonuniform lower bounds, which can slow the performance.

The next version of Sisal will probably introduce a separate data type to represent rectangular arrays. These arrays will have better performance than "arrays of arrays" during element access since compilers can exploit address arithmetic and strength-reduction transformations. New operations will allow the user to specify different functions to be used, for example, on boundaries and interior points, and guarantee that they can be done in parallel.

4.10.5   GENERALIZED REDUCTIONS

Generalizing reductions to allow users to define their own reductions would add expressive power to the Sisal language. It would also add another source of parallelism when the reductions are used in forall expressions (currently, such reductions would need to be performed in a serial loop).

Some interesting issues include what to return when you try to reduce an empty array and how to express reductions that can handle different associativities. The empty reduction could return the unit value for the function (such as a "0" for addition and a "1" for multiplication), or a default value (such as error for greatest). Associativity is a problem only when you try to produce reductions where the inputs and output types of the function are not the same, such as in the array of reduction, or where the reduction function is not arbitrarily associative.

4.10.6   ERROR HANDLING

The Sisal language has an extensive set of error semantics that specify error values when either a domain or a range error occurs for *any* operation (a subject not mentioned in order to focus on the discussion of parallelism). Current architectures provide some hardware support for error detection and propagation, but they fall short of what the Sisal language specifies. For example, the IEEE floating point standard [12] will produce NaN, "not a number" upon overflow and will propagate it upon later use. However, support for an error value in the integer, character, and Boolean data types is usually not provided. Also, arithmetic faults occurring during vector operations are often quite difficult to locate precisely.

Better methods for handling the current set of Sisal error values or a different error system might result from research in this area.

References

1. D. Abramson and G. K. Egan. An overview of the RMIT/CSIRO parallel systems architecture project. *The Australian Computer Journal*, 20(3), August 1988.

2. D. C. Cann. *Compilation Techniques for High Performance Applicative Computation.* PhD thesis, Colorado State University, Computer Science Department, Fort Collins, Colo., 1989.

3. D. C. Cann, C.-C. Lee, R. R. Oldehoeft, and S. K. Skedzielewski. Sisal multiprocessing support. Technical Report UCID-21115, Lawrence Livermore National Laboratory, Livermore, Calif., 1987.

4. D. C. Cann and R. R. Oldehoeft. Reference count and copy elimination for parallel applicative computing. Technical Report CS-88-129, Computer Science Department, Colorado State University, Fort Collins, CO, November 1988.

5. W. P. Crowley, C. P. Hendrickson, and T. E. Rudy. The simple code. Technical Report UCID 17715, Lawrence Livermore National Laboratory, Livermore, Calif., Februrary 1978.

6. J. T. Feo. The Livermore Loops in Sisal. Technical Report UCID-21159, Lawrence Livermore National Laboratory, Livermore, Calif., August 1987.

7. J. R. Gurd, C. C. Kirkham, and I. Watson. The Manchester prototype dataflow computer. *Communications of the ACM*, 28(1):34–52, January 1985.

8. M. Lam. *A Systolic Array Optimizing Compiler.* PhD thesis, Carnegie Mellon University, Pittsburgh, 1987.

9. J. McGraw, S. Skedzielewski, S. Allan, R. Oldehoeft, J. Glauert, C. Kirkham, B. Noyce, and R. Thomas. Sisal: Streams and iteration in a single assignment language: Reference manual version 1.2. Manual M-146, Rev. 1, Lawrence Livermore National Laboratory, Livermore, Calif., March 1985.

10. J. R. McGraw, D. J. Kuck, and M. Wolfe. A debate: Retire Fortran? *Physics Today*, 37(5):66–75, May 1984.

11. F. H. McMahon. The Livermore Fortran kernels: A computer test of the numerical performance range. Technical Report UCRL-53745, Lawrence Livermore National Laboratory, Livermore, Calif., December 1986.

12. Standards Committee of the IEEE Computer Society. *IEEE Standard for Binary Floating-Point Arithmetic*. The Institute of Electrical and Electronics Engineers, New York, 1985.

13. R. R. Oldehoeft and D. C. Cann. Applicative parallelism on a shared memory multiprocessor. *IEEE Software*, 5(1):62–70, January 1988.

14. J. E. Ranelletti. *Graph Transformation Algorithms for Array Memory Optimization in Applicative Languages*. PhD thesis, University of California at Davis, Computer Science Department, 1987.

15. V. Sarkar and J. Hennessey. Compile-time partitioning and scheduling of parallel programs. In *Proceedings of the SIGPLAN 1986 Symposium on Compiler Construction*, pp. 17–26, June 1986.

16. V. Sarkar and J. Hennessey. Partitioning parallel programs for macro-dataflow. In *Proceedings of the ACM Conference on Lisp and Functional Programming*, pp. 202–211, August 1986.

17. V. Sarkar. *Partitioning and Scheduling Parallel Programs for Execution on Multiprocessors*. PhD thesis, Stanford University, Stanford, Calif., April 1987.

18. V. Sarkar, S. Skedzielewski, and P. Miller. An automatically partitioning compiler for Sisal. In *Proceedings of CONPAR '88*, Manchester, England, September 1988 (in press).

19. S. K. Skedzielewski and R. J. Simpson. A simple method to remove reference counting in applicative programs. UCRL 100156, University of California Lawrence Livermore National Laboratory, November 1988.

20. S. K. Skedzielewski and M. L. Welcome. Data flow graph optimization in IF1. In Jean-Pierre Jouannaud, editor, *Functional Programming Languages and Computer Architecture*, pp. 17–34. New York, Springer-Verlag, September 1985.

21. S. K. Skedzielewski, R. K. Yates, and R. R. Oldehoeft. DI: An interactive debugging interpreter for applicative languages. In *Proceedings of the ACM SIGPLAN 87 Symposium on Interpreters and Interpretive Techniques*, pp. 102–109, June 1987.

22. S. Skedzielewski and J. Glauert. IF1—an intermediate form for applicative languages. Manual M-170, Lawrence Livermore National Laboratory, Livermore, Calif., July 1985.

23. D. S. Wise. Parallel decomposition of matrix inversion using quadtrees. In *Proceedings of the 1986 International Conference on Parallel Processing*, pp. 92–99, August 1986.

5

Para-Functional Programming in Haskell

Paul Hudak

5.1   Introduction

It is probably safe to say that the main theme of this textbook is that one of the best things about functional programming languages is that they are highly suited to parallel computation.

Now, I suppose this claim is true, but it is perhaps not as true as one might think. Haskell, for example, is a modern functional language designed by a committee representative of the functional programming community, but in reality it is *not* a parallel programming language. Indeed, in many ways neither are many of the other functional languages discussed in this book. This is perhaps an odd, if not heretical, claim to make in a book on *parallel* functional programming, but there are good reasons for it, as I explain below.

Much of the elegance of functional languages stems from their abstract semantics, devoid of operational or machine-dependent detail. This property is often manifested in phrases such as "mathematical elegance," "referential transparency," and "equational reasoning." It is this abstract nature that makes functional languages so attractive to software developers, who generally wish to stay far removed from machine-specific details.

However, it is this same abstract property, this freedom from machine specific detail, that I believe makes a functional language no more a parallel language than a sequential language. Indeed, the terms "parallel" and "sequential" are themselves quite operational and thus perhaps not appropriate in describing a programming language at this highest level of abstraction.[1] Thus one argument I like to give in favor of parallel functional programming is the following: Because functional languages are not oriented toward *any* particular machine model, they are easier to compile for execution on parallel machines than conventional imperative languages, which are biased toward a sequential machine model. Of course, for the same reason, conventional imperative languages are generally easier to compile for sequential machines.

Indeed, experience bears this out. For example, in Chapter 7, which discusses Crystal, the authors describe elegant compilation and transformation techniques for functional languages executing on multiprocessors. These results would be immensely more difficult to duplicate using a sequential language such as Fortran. In contrast, efficient implementations of functional languages on sequential machines have only recently begun to appear, and only after years of hard work on sophisticated optimization techniques.

Of course, it is true that there are abstract operational semantics for functional languages that are inherently highly parallel—for example, both graph reduction and dataflow—but few implementations of functional languages accurately mimic these models. It is also true that certain functional languages, such as Id, were originally designed for a particular kind of parallel machine; in the case of Id, it was a tagged-token dataflow machine. But the most recent version of Id has adopted much of the flavor of modern functional languages, including higher-order functions (which, incidentally, are *not* easily implemented on a dataflow machine). As does the chapter on Crystal, Chapter 6 on Id shows how functional programs can be effectively interpreted as parallel programs—that is, compiled for execution on a dataflow machine—yielding high degrees of parallelism and promising to be a viable method for functional program execution. But even for a dataflow machine, the degrees of freedom in these compilation strategies are enormous; in fact

---

[1]It turns out that the terms "parallel" and "sequential" *do* have abstract semantic content, but not in the informal sense we are using here. For example, the infamous "parallel or" can be given a simple denotational semantics but is not directly implementable using a sequential machine model. Indeed, research continues on domain constructions that capture only the so-called "sequential functions," in order to give a fully abstract semantics for sequential languages. But that is another story altogether...

a sequential implementation may still faithfully capture the intended meaning of the program.

5.1.1 THE PROBLEM

So just what *is* a parallel programming language, anyway?

This is of course a difficult question to answer, but for my purposes the answer is rather simple: It is a language that allows us to express, in a reasonably natural way, a *specific parallel algorithm*. The reason I claim that most most functional languages are not parallel programming languages is that there are certain components of parallel algorithms for which these languages have no way to express. For example:

1. Specifying a specific partial ordering on program execution, whether that be with more or less parallelism than the default ordering (in other words, specifying how to *schedule* a computation).

2. Specifying on which processor in a multiprocessor architecture a particular part of a computation is to be executed (in other words, specifying how to *map* a program onto a machine).

3. Specifying particular communication or routing patterns between processors (in other words, expressing the *distribution of data* through the network).

Although certain functional languages provide ways to express these behaviors *implicitly*, very few provide *explicit* mechanisms (among those in this textbook, EPL [actually an equational language] allows for annotations to express processor mapping, and Crystal provides perhaps a "happy medium" through its index domains and distributed data structures).

Of course, one might argue that we shouldn't be concerned about these "low-level details" at all, any more than we are concerned with, for example, which registers get used on a sequential machine. But I would argue that the above kinds of behavior are far more important to performance than register usage and indeed are active components of parallel algorithm design, whereas register usage certainly is not (not even for sequential algorithms!). Furthermore, determining optimal mapping and scheduling strategies is undecideable, so smart compilation techniques might not yield the payoff that we desire. Even if they could, the complexity of the optimizations might make it very difficult for us to *reason* about parallel execution; we must trust the implementation completely.

So how do we solve this dilemma, without giving up the functional programming paradigm that we like for so many other reasons?

5.1.2   A SOLUTION

In this chapter I will introduce an extension to the functional programming paradigm, called *para-functional programming*, that allows us to express the aforementioned kinds of behavior without losing any of the well-known benefits of functional languages. The idea is based on preserving the qualitative difference between *functional* behavior (that is, *what* the program computes) and *operational* behavior (that is, *how* the answer is computed). The ideas can be adopted in any functional language, but I will express them in *Haskell*, a recently designed functional language that captures most of the major innovations in functional language research.

The basic strategy for separating the "what" from the "how" is quite simple. Existing functional languages express very well the "what" —the thing missing is the "how." Thus to add the latter in a separable way, we need linguistic extensions that are not intrinsically part of the base language, forming instead a *meta-language*. The most convenient form of meta-language for our purposes is *annotations*. Although often considered *ad hoc*, annotations can actually be quite elegant, and in our case can be given a straightforward formal semantics that is consistent with the standard semantics (see [14, 17] for details).

In the next section I will give a brief overview of the salient features of Haskell, or at least enough to get us through the para-functional programming examples discussed later. It is beyond the scope of this book to explain Haskell in all of its detail; the reader is urged to consult the Haskell Report [20] for the technical details or one of an anticipated set of tutorial documents for programming examples. It is also beyond the scope to give a detailed explanation of general functional programming techniques, but there now exist various excellent textbooks on the subject, most recently ones by Bird and Wadler [3], and Field and Harrison [9]; most of the examples in those texts can easily be translated into Haskell. A useful survey and history of functional languages, including Haskell, may be found in [16].

In Section 5.3 I will explain para-functional programming basics, starting with a description of where the parallelism in a functional program comes from to begin with, and ending with the two main kinds of para-functional behavior that we will be concerned with: *scheduling* and *mapping* programs on parallel machines. In Section 5.4 we will continue our tour of para-functional programming with a few non-trivial examples. More on para-functional programming may be found in references [19, 15].

Sections 5.6 and 5.7 finish up our discussion with comparisons to other approaches and avenues for future research.

5.2   An Overview of Haskell

Haskell is a new functional programming language, named after the logician Haskell B. Curry. It was designed by a 15-member international committee[2] representative of the "modern school" of functional programming. By "modern" I mean primarily the inclusion of the attributes (1) *non-strict semantics* (i.e., lazy evaluation) and (2) a *rich type system* including user-defined concrete and abstract datatypes and strong static type inference. Non-strict semantics was popularized by languages such as SASL [33, 34], and the type discipline was popularized by languages such as ML [23, 35]. Haskell combines these ideas into one language, together with several other novel features; in addition, it is a very *complete* language—the intent being that it is a language eminently *useable* in a broad range of applications as well as for research.

Haskell is *purely functional*, which means that it has no constructs inducing side effects to an implicit store (such as found in "almost-functional" languages such as ML). The language contains many of the recent innovations in programming language research, including higher-order functions, non-strict functions and data structures, static polymorphic type inference, user-definable concrete and abstract datatypes, pattern-matching, list comprehensions, a module system, and a rich set of primitive datatypes, including arbitrary and fixed precision integers, and complex, rational, and floating-point numbers. In addition it has several novel features that give it additional expressiveness, including an elegant form of overloading using a notion of *type classes*, a flexible I/O system that unifies the two most popular functional I/O models, and an array datatype that allows purely functional, monolithic arrays to be constructed using "array comprehensions."

Syntactically, Haskell has an "equational feel." A function is defined by a set of equations, each stating a different set of constraints on the arguments for the equation to be valid. These constraints primarily concern the structure of the arguments, and thus the process is called *pattern matching*. For example, lists are written [a,b,c] with [] being the empty list, and a list whose first element is x and whose rest is xs is

---

[2]The committee members are Arvind (MIT), Brian Boutel (Victoria University of Wellington), Jon Fairbairn (Cambridge University), Joseph Fasel (Los Alamos National Laboratory), Kevin Hammond (University of Glasgow), Paul Hudak (Yale University), John Hughes (University of Glasgow), Thomas Johnsson (Chalmers Institute of Technology), Dick Kieburtz (Oregon Graduate Center), Rishuyar Nikhil (MIT), Simon Peyton Jones (University College London), Mike Reeve (Imperial College), Philip Wadler (University of Glasgow), David Wise (Indiana University), and Jonathan Young (Yale and MIT).

denoted x:xs. Thus to define a function that tests for membership in a list, we can write

```
member x []      = False
member x (y:ys) = if x==y then True
                          else member x ys
```

Given this definition, the expression member 2 [1,2,3] returns True, whereas the expression member 0 [1,2,3] returns False. Any data structure may be pattern-matched against, including user-defined ones. Also note that function application is "curried" and associates to the left; in a conventional language one might write member(2,[1,2,3]).

A function f x = x+1 may also be defined "anonymously" with a *lambda abstraction* having form \x -> x+1; thus (\x -> x+1) 2 returns 3. In addition, any infix operator may be turned into a value by surrounding it in parentheses; thus, for example, the following equivalence holds:

```
(+) x y   ==   x + y
```

List comprehensions are a concise way to define lists and are best explained by example:

```
[ (x,y) | x<-xs, y<-ys, x>y ]
```

This expression designates the list of all pairs whose first element is from xs and second is from ys, but such that the first element is always greater than the second. Pairs are examples of *tuples*, which in Haskell are constructed in arbitrary but finite length ≥ 2 by writing "(a,b, ..., c)" (the parentheses are mandatory). Tuples may be pattern-matched like lists.

"Infinite lists" may also be defined, and thanks to lazy evaluation, only that portion of the list that is needed by some other part of the program is actually computed. For example, the infinite list of ones can be defined by

```
ones = 1 : ones
```

Thus member 1 ones returns True, whereas member 2 ones does not terminate.

The notation [a..b] denotes the list of integers from a to b, inclusive, and [a..] is the infinite ascending list of integers beginning with a. Two lists may be appended together using the infix operator ++, as in l1++l2. There are also many other standard utility functions defined on lists. Aside from the ones already discussed, the ones we need in this chapter are the following:

```
head (x:xs) = x                  -- head and tail of list
tail (x:xs) = xs


fst  (x,y)  = x                  -- first and second of pair
snd  (x,y)  = y


map f  []    = []                -- maps function f down list
map f (x:xs) = f x : map f xs


[]      ++ ys = ys               -- infix append
(x:xs) ++ ys = x : (xs++ys)


take 0  xs   = []                -- takes 1st n elements of list
take n  []   = []
take n (x:xs) = x : take (n-1) xs


foldl f a  []    = a             -- folds list from left
foldl f a (x:xs) = foldl f (f a x) xs


foldr f a  []    = a             -- folds list from right
foldr f a (x:xs) = f x (foldr f a xs)


zip (a:as) (b:bs) = (a,b) : zip as bs -- makes list of pairs
zip  as     bs    = []                -- from two lists
```

Note that comments in Haskell are preceeded with "--" and continue to the end of the line. Function application always has higher precedence than any infix operator; thus "f x : map f xs" is parsed as "(f x) : (map f xs)." Note that for foldl and foldr the following relationships hold:

```
foldl f a [x1, x2, ..., xn]  ==>
           (f ... (f (f a x1) x2) ... xn)
foldr f a [x1, x2, ..., xn]  ==>
           (f x1 (f x2 ... (f xn a) ... ))
```

Besides lists and tuples, Haskell also has arrays of a special kind, called *array comprehensions*. A two-dimensional array a is indexed at position (i,j) via the expression a!(i,j). New arrays are constructed using the primitive function array, which takes a set of bounds and a list comprehension as arguments; the list comprehension specifies the set of index/value pairs for the new array. For example,

```
array ((1,1),(n,n))
       [ ((i,j) , k*a!(i,j)) | i<-[1..n], j<-[1..n] ]
```

returns a $n \times n$ matrix, indexed from (1,1) to (n,n), and whose elements are those of the matrix a multiplied by the scalar k.

Haskell's fundamental block structuring mechanism (aside from those introduced by modules, which are beyond the scope of our discussion) is the where clause. For example,

```
x where x = y
        y = 1
```

The declarations in a where clause are lexically scoped and mutually recursive; thus their order does not matter, and the above example evaluates to 1. Also note the use of a "layout" strategy for parsing declarations. There is no need for a semicolon, or some other syntactic device, to terminate a declaration. The simple rule is that the first characters in the declarations must line up vertically with each other. For example,

```
x+y where x = a+b
          where a = 1
                b = 2
      y = 3
```

parses in the "natural way," and evaluates to 6.

This description of Haskell is necessarily brief but should be enough to make the programs given later self-explanatory. For more information on Haskell, see [20].

5.3   Para-Functional Programming Basics

Before introducing extensions to support para-functional programming, it is important to have a good understanding of the operational semantics of functional languages. After that, we will introduce two para-functional constructs—one for scheduling, the other for mapping.

5.3.1   PARALLELISM IN FUNCTIONAL PROGRAMS

In the simplest terms, because there are no side effects, any subexpression in a functional program may be evaluated in parallel with any other, without fear of non-deterministic results; in other words, the only things *limiting* parallelism are data dependencies.[3] Thus detecting the parallelism in a functional program is considered to be a trivial task (which is not to say that for a given problem there might not be a better algorithm that would expose even more parallelism; finding such better algorithms is certainly not trivial). For example, if I were to write

```
f x + g y
```

then the applications "f x" and "g y" may be evaluated in parallel. Indeed, it is not only *safe* to evaluate the two, it is in fact *mandatory* to evaluate them both *eventually*, since + is a *strict binary operator*—a technical term that captures the fact that + must know the value of both of its arguments before it can compute a result. In contrast, we can say that the conditional

```
if e1 then e2 else e3
```

is strict in e1 but not necessarily e2 or e3, since their evalutation depends on the value of e1. Still, there is nothing wrong with evaluating all three expressions in parallel, and if done is what is usually called *speculative*, or *eager*, evaluation, since there is no guarantee that all of the results will be needed. Indeed, considerable resources may be wasted with such a strategy; on the other hand, if plentiful resources are available, there may be considerable benefit to performing the speculative computation, in that the total elapsed execution time may be reduced.

A little thought should convince the reader that despite the great amount of inherent parallelism that is available in a functional program, choosing an optimal evaluation strategy can be tricky business. Compilers can help, but in general the problem is undecideable—consider, for example, the fact that choosing the optimal strategy in the case of the aforementioned conditional might rely critically on how long e1 takes to execute, yet deciding that in general is no easier than deciding if a program terminates (that is, solving the well-known halting problem).

Thus one of the para-functional mechanisms that we will introduce is a general way to control the evaluation order of subexpressions. We will discuss that in the next subsection, and follow that with the second para-functional mechanism of interest to us: How to map program to machine.

---

[3]It is the Church-Rosser Theorem [6] that states this formally for the lambda calculus, and the lambda calculus forms the basis of most functional language semantics.

5.3.2   SCHEDULED EXPRESSIONS: CONTROLLING EVALUATION ORDER

Our approach to controlling the evaluation order in a program will be first to define a *default partial order* on expression evaluation, and then to provide a mechanism for the programmer to *augment* that order in particular ways. Technically speaking, a partial order is a binary relation $\preceq$ that is reflexive, transitive, and anti-symmetric.[4] Pragmatically speaking, a partial order is an excellent notation for describing concurrency. If two events are related by $\preceq$, then there is a temporal dependency between them (meaning they must be executed sequentially); otherwise there is not (meaning they may be executed in parallel). It is a simple and intuitive idea that we can put to good use.[5]

The default evaluation strategy that we will use is the well-known "lazy" or "call-by-need" evaluation strategy, which is completely sequential, thus a *total* order, and controlled only by data dependencies and a left-to-right ordering on reducible expressions. We could have assumed a default semantics that has more parallelism than this, but for exposition it is preferable to have *all* parallelism made explicit.

The mechanism for augmenting this default evaluation strategy is a *scheduled expression*, which has the general form

```
exp   sched   sexp
```

where `sched` is a keyword, `sexp` is called the *schedule*, and `exp` is the *body* of the scheduled expression (and is just another expression).

In order to be useful, the schedule must be able to reference subexpressions in the body. We thus provide a way to *label* an expression to facilitate such references. A labelled expression has the form "`lab@exp`" where `lab` is a standard Haskell identifier (beginning with a small letter) and `exp` is any Haskell expression. The scope of a label extends lexically

---

[4]More precisely:

   □ $x \preceq x$ for all x (reflexivity).

   □ if $x \preceq y$ and $y \preceq z$ then $x \preceq z$ (transitivity).

   □ if $x \preceq y$ and $y \preceq x$ then $x = y$ (anti-symmetry).

[5]The operational semantics that we will describe can be formally stated in terms of *pomsets*, or "partially ordered multisets," as described in [17] and based on work in [30]. However, understanding such a formalization is not a prerequisite to understanding how to write para-functional programs, any more than denotational semantics is a prerequisite to understanding how to write functional programs.

outward to the innermost surrounding function definition or lambda abstraction. For convenience, if exp is itself an identifier, it may be used as the label.

Schedules define partial orders on *events*, of which for every labelled expression lab@exp there are three kinds: (1) the *demand* for exp's evaluation, denoted Dlab, (2) the *start* of exp's evaluation, denoted ^lab, and (3) the *end* of exp's evaluation, denoted lab^.

An important qualitative difference between the demand for an expression's value and either the start or end of its evaluation is that there may be *many* demands for a particular value but only *one* evaluation of it (thus conforming to lazy evaluation). Therefore we define occurrences in a schedule of the form Dlab to represent *new* demands, subject to the constraints specified in the schedule. Being new events, this is how additional parallelism is induced (and since our default evaluation strategy is sequential, it is the *only* way parallelism is achieved). In contrast, occurrences of the form ^lab or lab^ refer to the *unique event* capturing the start or end of lab's evaluation, and their presence in the schedule simply adds additional constraints to the temporal ordering between those events.

With this in mind, the structure and semantics of scheduled expressions can be defined inductively as follows:

1. Dlab, ^lab, and lab^ are schedules, for any label lab. The events that they refer to are as described in the previous paragraph, and the partial order induced is the trivial, singleton one.

2. If s1 and s2 are schedules, then so are the following:

   a. s1.s2, the *concatenation* of s1 and s2. This induces a partial order which is the union of those for s1 and s2, but with the additional constraint that every event in s1 precedes every event in s2. This is like running s1 and s2 sequentially.

   b. s1|s2, the *concurrence* of s1 and s2. This induces a partial order that is the union of those for s1 and s2 and has *no* additional constraints. This is like running s1 and s2 in parallel.

Syntactically, we define . to have higher precedence than |; in addition, we define lab (i.e., the label itself) as an abbreviation for Dlab.lab^.

The partial order of evaluation of the scheduled expression exp sched sexp is then simply defined as the union of the partial orders of exp and sexp, with the additional constraint that the start of evaluation of exp precedes all events in sexp.

Simple Examples of Scheduled Expressions.   Some simple examples should help clarify this semantics.

Consider the function application (e0 e1 e2). Using standard lazy evaluation, the expression e0 will begin evaluation first, after which the function call will be performed *without* evaluating e1 or e2. They will only be evaluated on demand from within the body of the function e0. Through the use of scheduled expressions, however, we can change this standard operational semantics in many ways. For example, we can specify the speculative evaluation of both e1 and e2 as follows:

```
(e0 m@e1 n@e2)   sched   Dm|Dn
```

This declares that demands for the evaluations of the expressions labelled m and n will begin in parallel at the point when the entire expression begins evaluation, which means that e1 and e2 will execute in parallel with each other and with the evaluation of e0.

Alternatively, we may wish to induce parallelism only at the point when e0 has completed evaluation, as in

```
(1@e0 m@e1 n@e2)   sched   1^.(Dm|Dn)
```

Here 1^ is concatenated with the concurrence of Dm and Dn, and thus specifies that e0 must complete evaluation before e1 or e2 are demanded.

As another example, note that the speculative evaluations of e1 and e2 in the last example are not required to finish before the entire expression returns its value. To require this, we would write:

```
(1@e0 m@e1 n@e2)   sched   1^.(m|n)
```

Since m and n are abbreviations for Dm.m^ and Dn.n^, respectively, e1 and e2 are required to complete before the overall expression does. Indeed, to achieve left-to-right call-by-value semantics, we would write:

```
o@(1@e0 m@e1 n@e2)   sched   1.m.n.o
```

Note that this schedule does not prohibit parallelism *within* e0, e1, or e2, of which there may be plenty.

It is important to note that in the last two examples e0 has in effect been made *strict* in both of its arguments, thus possibly changing the functional semantics of the program. As a general rule, if one only uses the demand form of labels, the program's functional semantics is guaranteed not to change, whereas using the other forms may cause divergence since some non-strict functions become strict. Indeed, certain pathological cases can be created, such as

```
1@(e1 + m@e2)   sched   1^.m^
```

Since 1^ refers to the unique event characterizing the completion of the sum, it cannot possibly happen before the summand e2 completes evaluation! On the other hand, something like:

```
1@(e1 + m@e2)   sched   1^.Dm
```

is perfectly acceptable, although completely useless. It simply specifies that once the sum has been computed, e2 is demanded *again*, which does neither harm nor good.

As can be seen, there is a surprising number of subtle ways to schedule the evaluation of an expression. Although scheduled expressions have the ability to express these various strategies, we have found that in most cases a few judicious placements of speculative demands are sufficient to get the key parallelism out of most programs. Nevertheless, the additional expressiveness is sometimes needed in critical ways. In a later section we will give more examples of the use of scheduled expressions.

5.3.3   MAPPED EXPRESSIONS: MAPPING PROGRAM TO MACHINE

Scheduled expressions allow one to control the temporal order of evaluation of expressions, but say nothing about what processing resources are used to perform the evaluations. For that reason, we arrive at our second para-functional extension: *mapped expressions*. A mapped expression has the general form:

```
exp   on   pid
```

which intuitively declares that exp is to be evaluated on the processor identified by pid (on is a keyword). The expression exp is called the *body* of the mapped expression and represents the value to which the overall expression will evaluate (and thus can be any valid Haskell expression, including another mapped expression). The expression pid must evaluate to a *processor id*. Without loss of generality, we will assume that processor ids are *integers*, and that there is some pre-defined mapping from those integers to the physical processors they denote. For example, a tree of processors might be numbered as shown in part (a) of Figure 5.1, or a mesh as shown in part (b). The advantage of using integers is

```
                                                              1
(a) "Infinite" binary tree:                              /       \
left    p = 2*p                                      2               3
right   p = 2*p+1                                   /   \           /   \
parent  p = p/2                                    4     5         6     7
                                                  / \   / \       / \   / \
                                                  .. .. .. ..     .. .. .. ..

(b) Finite mesh of size mXn          1  --  2  --  ...  --  n-1  --  n
up     p = if p>n       then p-n     |      |               |       |
down   p = if p<=mn-n then p+n      n+1 -- n+2 --  ...  -- 2n-1  --  2n
left   p = if rem (p-1) n /= 0       |      |               |       |
                    then p-1        ...    ...      ...     ...     ...
right  p = if rem  p    n /= 0       |      |               |       |
                    then p+1     mn-n+1 --  ...  --  ...  -- mn-1 --  mn

-- Note:  rem x y  is the remainder of x/y
```

FIGURE 5.1
Two possible network topologies.

that the user may manipulate them using conventional arithmetic primitives; for example, Figure 5.1 also defines functions that map processor ids to neighboring ids.[6]

Simple Examples of Mapped Expressions. As a simple example of the use of mapped expressions, consider the program fragment f x + g y. As mentioned earlier, the strict semantics of the + operator allows the two subexpressions to be evaluated in parallel, which we can specify via a scheduled expression. If in addition we wish to express precisely *where* the subexpressions are to be evaluated, we may do so using a mapped expression, as in (ignoring the scheduling for the moment):

    (f x on 0) + (g y on 1)

where 0 and 1 are processor ids.

Unfortunately, this static mapping is not very interesting. It would be better, for example, if we were able to refer to a processor *relative to the currently executing one*. Thus we provide a reserved identifier self, which when evaluated returns the id of the currently executing

[6]An alternative discipline in a type-rich language such as Haskell might be to define a primitive datatype reflecting the underlying topology.

processor. Using `self`, we can now be more creative. For example, suppose we have a mesh or tree of processors as in Figure 5.1; we may then write

```
(f x  on  left self) + (g y  on  right self)
```

to denote the computation of the two subexpressions in parallel on neighboring processors, with the sum being computed on `self`.

We can describe the behavior of `self` more precisely as follows: `self` is bound *implicitly* by mapped expressions; thus in `exp on pid`, `self` has the value `pid` in `exp`, unless it is further modified by a nested mapped expression. Although `self` is a reserved identifier that cannot be redefined, this implicit binding can be best explained using the following analogy:

```
exp  on  pid    -- is like:   exp  where  self = pid
```

However, the most important aspect of `self` is that it is *dynamically bound* in function calls. Thus in

```
( (f a  on  pid1) + (f b  on  pid2)
    where  f x = x*x                    )  on   pid3
```

a*a is computed on processor pid1, b*b on processor pid2, and the sum on processor pid3. As before, an analogy is useful in describing this behavior:

```
... f a b c ...
where  f x y z = exp
```

is like

```
... f a b c self ...
where  f x y z self = exp
```

In other words, all functions implicitly take an extra formal parameter, `self`, and all function calls use the current value of `self` as the value for the new actual parameter.

Although very useful, `self` is not always needed. In particular, mappings can be made from composite objects such as vectors and arrays to specific multiprocessor configurations. For example,

```
array  (1,n)  [ (i, f i on i) | i <- [1,n] ]
```

will produce a vector whose ith component was computed on processor i.

A given implementation of para-functional extensions to Haskell will often support a variety of "virtual" topologies. For example, it is

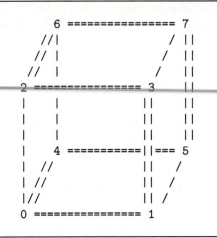

FIGURE 5.2
Embedding of ring of size 8 into 3-cube (the double line represents the ring).

possible to embed many topologies, such as trees, butterflies, meshes, tori, shuffle-exchange networks, and others, with near-optimal efficiency into a *hypercube*. Thus if one topology is most natural for a particular problem, or if an algorithm for a given topology is most familiar, it can be run on such an implementation with little or no degradation in performance.

To see how such an embedding might work, and to see in fact how it can be done by the programmer, suppose we are interested in a *ring* topology, but have at our disposal "only" a hypercube. Perhaps the simplest embedding of a ring into a hypercube is the so-called *reflected Gray-code*, captured by the following Haskell functions

```
ringtocube i = v!i
v = array (1,n) [ (i, graycode i) | i <- [1..n] ]
graycode i = if i<2 then i
                    else v!(2*mid-i-1) + mid
                 where mid = 2**(log2 i)
```

where log2 i returns the base-2 logarithm of i, rounded down to the nearest integer (the vector v is used to "cache" values of graycode i). For example, Figure 5.2 shows the embedding of a ring of size 8 into a 3-cube.

If we then change every mapped expression in our program of form "...on pid" to "...on ringtocube pid," we arrive at the desired embedding. Note that the functional code for the algorithm itself did not change at all, just the annotations. Of course, a more efficient algorithm for the hypercube might exist, or the initial data distribution might be different, and might require recoding of the main functions. Nevertheless, it is useful to be able to make topological changes such as this quickly and effortlessly.

5.4 Extended Examples

In this section I will give several examples of para-functional programming, with the goal of demonstrating the methodology on a variety of problem types, rather than coming up with the best parallel algorithm for a particular problem.

5.4.1 PARALLELIZING LISTS

Lists are a very common data structure in functional languages and, as mentioned in the overview, they are *non-strict* in Haskell, which means that their elements are computed "lazily," or "by demand." Since our default evaluation strategy for lists is sequential, and since one of the key sources of parallelism in many problems is so-called "data-level" parallelism, it is helpful to define a few auxiliary functions that eagerly evaluate the elements of lists in parallel.

The simplest such function is one that essentially *copies* the list *speculatively*, as in

```
spec_copy  []     = []
spec_copy (a:as) = a : 1@(spec_copy as)   sched  Da|Dl
```

(Recall that lone identifiers do not require labelling for use in a schedule.)

A useful variation of spec_copy is a function that only speculatively evaluates the *tails* of the list and is easily attained from the above definition by using just Dl for the schedule, intead of Da|Dl. We will call the resulting function tail_copy. Note that it results in a completely sequential evaluation—there is no parallelism within it—although it can, of course, be speculatively evaluated in a context that includes other sources of parallelism.

One disadvantage of both spec_copy and tail_copy is that they waste space by making an entirely new copy of the list. A better approach would be to try mimicking the *identity* function, rather than a copy function, but with the "side effect" of speculatively evaluating the elements. spec_eval, defined below, does just that:

```
spec_eval xs = seval xs
               where seval  []    = xs
                     seval (a:as) = seval as   sched  Da
```

Note that spec_eval, regardless of the annotation, will evaluate every tail of the list. (Such a function is said to be "tail strict"—but note that spec_copy and tail_copy are *not* tail strict.) Thus using the schedule Da|Dl in the above definition, where l is the label of the recursive call to seval (as we did in spec_copy), would not result in any more parallelism. Moving in the other direction, by eliminating the schedule altogether we arrive at a version that evaluates only the tails (and is still tail strict), and, of course, does so sequentially; we will call this function tail_eval, by analogy to tail_copy.

A final version of this function that may be useful to us is one that eagerly evaluates the heads *and* tails, as in spec_eval, but evaluates everything *sequentially*, as in tail_eval. This can be achieved by the following definition of seq_eval:

```
seq_eval xs = seval xs
              where seval  []    = xs
                    seval (a:as) = l@(seval as) sched a.l
```

Thus each head is evaluated speculatively, but its evaluation is required to complete before the tail call is begun.

As a simple example of the use of these functions, consider the simple "data-level parallelism" exhibited by mapping a function f across a list of values xs. Normally the function map would return a lazily evaluated list, but we can overcome that easily enough by writing

```
spec_eval (map f xs)
```

An important point to note is that the functions we have defined exploit parallelism exactly one level deep. For example, suppose our list is in fact a list of lists (perhaps representing a matrix), and that we wish to map the function f across each of the elements in the subsidiary lists. To induce parallelism we might naively write

```
spec_eval (map (map f) xxs)
```

as before, but this fails to evaluate the inner map speculatively. Instead, we must write

```
spec_eval (map (\ xs. spec_eval (map f xs)) xxs)
```

or, more succinctly

```
spec_eval (map (spec_eval . map f) xxs)
```

where . is the function composition operator.

But now the range of possibilities becomes clearer. For example, suppose we wish for the inner maps to be evaluated speculatively but *only when demanded from the outer map*. That's easy enough; we simply omit the outer call to spec_eval, as in

```
map (spec_eval . map f) xxs
```

It is perhaps surprising that there exist so many ways to evaluate a list in parallel! But that simply demonstrates a prevailing theme in this chapter: *parallelism is not an "all-or-nothing" proposition*.

As a final point, we note that all of these functions may be written in such a way as to map their subexpressions in a particular way on a given multiprocessor.

5.4.2   EIGHT QUEENS

The "eight queens" problem is a well-known puzzle in which one must find a chess board layout involving exactly eight queens, none of which can be captured by any other (there happen to be 92 solutions for an 8×8 board). I suspect that at least one program to solve this puzzle has been written in every language in existence! Here's one in Haskell:

```
queens n = do_row 1 empty_board []
  where do_row row board solns =
    foldl try_col solns [1..n]
    where try_col solns col =
        if legal_move board row col
        then if row==n
            then newboard:solns  -- add new solution
            else -- place queen, try next row
                do_row (row+1) newboard solns
            where newboard = update_board board row col
        else solns                -- no new solutions
```

This program has been written as if the board structure is an abstract data type with operations empty_board, update_board, and legal_move.

The search for solutions is captured in the expression do_row row board solutions, where board is a correct placement of queens in the first row-1 rows, and solutions is a list of solutions generated so far in the search. Each legal move in the current row leads to a recursive search of the next row. The only tricky part is the call to foldl in line 3, which ensures that the list of solutions of legal moves in columns 1 through k is passed on to the search in column k+1.

Although not important to us here, a simple choice for the board implementation would be to use lists as the representation type, which would result in the following code:

```
empty_board = []

update_board board row col = (row,col) : board

legal_move  []                r2 c2 = True
legal_move  ((r1,c1):board) r2 c2 =
              r1 /= r2  &&
              c1 /= c2  &&
              abs (r1-r2) /= abs (c1-c2)  &&
              legal_move board r2 c2
```

How do we parallelize this program? At first glance, since the result is just a list of solutions, it may seem that we could speculatively evaluate this list and get maximum parallelism. But this is not so, for an important reason: *each solution depends on the previous one*, in that the search for a solution eliminates certain fruitless search paths, so the algorithm waits until it finds one solution before deciding where to search next. This is a common characteristic of game tree algorithms, and means that we must initiate the parallel searches at a "deeper level" in the program; i.e., a call to spec_eval at the outermost level simply won't do.

Upon closer inspection we can see that the "broadest fork-point" in the algorithm is the call to foldl (not surprisingly) in line 3, which from Section 5.2 we know is equivalent to

```
foldl try_col solns [1, ..., n]  ==>
    (try_col ... (try_col (try_col solns 1) 2) ... n)
```

So what we really need is a speculative version of foldl, which is easily defined as

```
spec_foldl f a  []    =a
spec_foldl f a (x:xs)=spec_foldl f 1@(f a x) xs sched D1
```

Alternatively, we could just annotate the queens program directly by ensuring that the first argument to try_col is evaluated speculatively, which has the effect of ensuring that the same happens to every call to try_col:

```
queens n = do_row 1 empty_board []
  where do_row row board solns =
     foldl try_col solns [1..n]
     where try_col solns col =
        (if legal_move board row col
         then if row==n
                then newboard:solns   -- add new solution
                else -- place queen, try next row
                     do_row (row+1) newboard solns
                where newboard = update_board board row col
         else solns) sched Dsolns   -- no new solutions
```

Either approach results in a highly-parallel solution.

Of course, some additional fine-grained parallelism could be gotten from update_board and legal_move, depending on their implementations. For example, using the list representation given earlier, legal_move could be annotated as follows:

```
legal_move ((r1,c1):board) r2 c2 =
  (    r1 /= r2  &&
    l1@(c1 /= c2) &&
    l2@(abs (r1-r2) /= abs (c1-c2)) &&
    l3@(safe board r2 c2) )
  sched Dl1 | Dl2 | Dl3
```

This, in fact, is a true example of speculative parallelism, since normally not all of these tests would be needed, because the first False value in a conjunction renders the entire expression as False. Whether or not this is a worthwhile source of parallelism will depend on the processing resources available; it certainly will cause a lot of unnecessary computation but can result in a speedup if the resources are plentiful and the overhead of such small tasks is low.

5.4.3   DIVIDE AND CONQUER

Many problems can be solved as a form of "divide-and-conquer," in which a problem is recursively subdivided into two (or more) sub-problems of approximately equal size. If these sub-problems are evaluated in parallel, substantial speedups can be achieved; this strategy is the basis for many of the best-known parallel algorithms. In fact, it is possible to design a functional language based entirely on the notion of divide-and-conquer (see [27, 26]), but in this section we will limit ourselves to some simple ideas expressible directly in Haskell.

Rather than give many examples of divide-and-conquer parallelism, we will take advantage of higher-order programming and define a generic divide-and-conquer framework that can be used to solve a variety of problems. Mapping and scheduling this higher-order function results in the same mapping and scheduling for all of its instantiations.

```
divconq split combine endtest endval =
    f where
    f x = if    endtest x
          then endval x
          else combine left right   sched  Dleft|Dright
               where (l,r) = split x
                     left  = f l  on   left  self
                     right = f r  on   right self
```

Note how the recursive calls are evaluated speculatively, and mapped to the left and right children on a (virtual) tree topology. With this definition we may define, for example, "parallel factorial" by

```
pfac = divconq split combine endtest endval
       where split (lo,hi) = ((lo,mid),(mid+1,hi))
                             where mid = (low+hi)\2
             combine (l,r) = l*r
             endtest (l,r) = (l==r) || (l==r-1)
             endval  (l,r) = if l==r then l else l*r
```

5.4.4   MESSAGE PASSING ALGORITHMS

Another popular concept found in parallel algorithm design is the use of *message passing* between some notion of *processes*. This is the kind of framework typified by such parallel computing models as CSP [12, 13], CCS [24], and Actors [2].

A convenient programming idiom for expressing message passing algorithms in a functional language is the use of a *shared list* to represent the stream of messages between two processes, and *functions* to represent the processes themselves. For example, if p1 and p2 are two processes, each consuming a list of messages and producing another, then their mutual communication can be expressed via the following mutual recursion:

```
s1 = p1 s2
s2 = p2 s1
```

The calls p1 s2 and p2 s1 can be mapped onto whatever processors are appropriate. Of course, such a network of processes operating in isolation is not very useful, since there is nothing to observe! So let's assume that process p1 computes, in addition to a response list, some kind of result, thus yielding

```
result
where (s1,result) = p1 s2
      s2          = p2 s1
```

Continuing with this example, the easiest way to induce parallelism is to eagerly evaluate the two message streams in some way, and possibly to assign the two calls p1 s2 and p2 s1 to individual processors in some appropriate way. For example,

```
result
where (s1,result) = spec_eval (p1 s2)  on  pid1
      s2          = spec_eval (p2 s1)  on  pid2
```

With such a strategy, the processes would run *asynchronously*, since the lists behave as potentially unbounded buffers of messages. The only thing guaranteed is that the "arrival order" will be the same as the "sending order." Overall this strategy corresponds nicely to the Actor model.

In contrast, we may wish to synchronize the processes by insisting that a new message is not sent until the old one is received, corresponding more to a CSP or CCS model. We can accomplish this through the use of scheduled expressions, but to do so we must look a little closer at the internal stucture of the processes, where we can expect to see some kind of loop (expressed as a recursion) that, given the current "state," generates a new message and a new state upon every iteration. For example, for p2, let's assume we have something like:

```
p2 msgs = loop init_state
    where init_state = ...    -- presumably captures msgs
          loop state = (next_msg state) :
                            loop (next_state state)
```

Note that the default semantics constructs the response list lazily, and thus the elements are not computed until demanded. To ensure that new messages are not generated until the previous ones are consumed, we only have to redefine loop as follows

```
loop state =
            l@(next_msg state) : m@(loop (next_state state))
            sched  l^.^m
```

which declares very elegantly our desired result.

Of course, a better way to do this would be to somehow abstract these changes of behavior out from the processes themselves, as we did with spec_eval and friends. This can in fact be done, by the following simple definition of synch_eval:

```
synch_eval  []    =  []
synch_eval (x:xs) = (x:xs)   sched  x^.^xs
```

Note that synch_eval is just the identity function on lists but has the "side effect" of insisting that the evaluation of the tail is not begun until that of the head is finished. With this definition, we can accomplish the same results as above by making these more abstract changes to the process interconnection:

```
result
where (s1,result) = synch_eval (p1 s2)
          s2        = synch_eval (p2 s1)
```

5.4.5   MATRIX-VECTOR PRODUCT

Given the above functional programming idiom for writing message passing programs, let's construct a more sophisticated para-functional program—one that computes a matrix-vector product in parallel on a ring architecture. Although the topology of a ring is rather simple, its limited interprocessor communications make it rather difficult to use effectively, and thus algorithms for it can be rather complex, making them a good test-bed for para-functional programming.

We will assume that (1) the ring contains n processors numbered 1 through n, (2) the input matrix is represented as a list vs of n vectors (each of size n), with the ith vector residing on processor i, (3) the input vector is represented as a list xs, also distributed uniformly around the ring, and (4) we wish the result vector to be a list distributed in the same way. Although other data configurations are possible, this represents a "typical" situation in scientific computing.

Given this initial configuration, the basic idea behind the algorithm is to compute each inner product one scalar multiplication at a time,

while trying to minimize interprocessor communication. Since the ith
inner product needs to end up on processor i, it makes sense to compute
it there. To do this the ith processor needs the ith row of the matrix,
and the entire vector. Although it has all of the former, initially it has
only the ith element of the latter. Thus initially the ith processor is able
to perform only one multiplication. The vector xs can then be "shifted"
one position around the ring (requiring exactly n interprocessor "messages"), and the process is repeated, adding the products to a running
sum until an entire inner product is computed on each processor.

Using the message-passing abstraction to encode this algorithm,
we proceed as follows. First, let's consider the nature of the processes
themselves. The "initialization" data consists of an index i, a vector
v (corresponding to the ith row of the input matrix vs), and value x
(corresponding to the ith element of the input vector xs). The process
then receives as argument a stream of values ys from its "left" neighbor,
and returns as result two things: the inner product and a stream of
values for use by its "right" neighbor. In other words (i.e. in the words
of Haskell),

```
proc i v x ys = (p i msgs 0, msgs)
                where msgs = take n (x:ys)
                      p i []    acc = acc
                      p i (x:xs) acc = p (mod i n + 1)
                                         xs
                                         (acc + x*v!i)
```

Now the only thing left is to instantiate and then "connect" the processes together. To do this, it is helpful first to write out the solution
"longhand." Letting ri, ysi, vi, and xi represent the ith inner product,
message stream, row of the matrix, and element of the vector, respectively, we arrive at

```
(r1,ys1) = proc 1 v1 x1 ys2
(r2,ys2) = proc 2 v2 x2 ys3
...
(rm,ysm) = proc m vm xm ysn
(rn,ysn) = proc n vn xn ys1
```

where m==n-1. Good higher-order programming techniques then lead us
to the following solution, which uses map to obtain a closed form of the
above "network" of processes:

```
rs
where rys = map4 proc [1..n] vs xs (tail ys ++ [head ys])
      ys  = map  snd rys
      rs  = map  fst rys
```

where map4 is like map except that it takes four lists as arguments instead of one. Note the mutually recursive definition of rys and ys; this works because of lazy evaluation.

Now the only thing remaining is a set of mapping and scheduling annotations to achieve the parallel behavior that we desire. The easiest way to do that, unfortunately, is through the definitions of map, map4, and (++), which must be changed in order to achieve the proper mapping. Our final solution is:

```
(spec_eval rs
  where rys = map4 proc [1..n] vs xs
              (tail ys ++ ([head ys] on n))
       ys  = map  snd rys
       rs  = map  fst rys)
on 1
```

Note the speculative evaluation of rs—this is enough to induce evaluation of all of the processes in parallel. Also note the mapping of the entire program on the first processor; the rest of the mapping is achieved recursively through the definitions of map4, map, and (++):

```
map4 f [] bs cs ds = []
map4 f (a:as) (b:bs) (c:cs) (d:ds) =
     f a b c d : (map4 f as bs cs ds  on  self+1)

map f []     = []
map f (a:as) = f a : (map f as  on  self+1)

[]      ++ ys = ys
(x:xs) ++ ys = x : (xs++ys  on  self+1)
```

5.4.6   LU DECOMPOSITION

The last problem involved matrices but was perhaps somewhat dissatisfying in that we used lists to represent the matrices rather than arrays. In this section a more difficult problem will be solved—that of computing the "LU decomposition" of a matrix—and Haskell's *array comprehensions* (recall the discussion in Section 5.2) will be used to represent the matrices. The solution that I will present emphasizes the mathematics behind the problem, and demonstrates how the mathematical flavor of

Haskell can be used to our advantage. I will first derive a mathematical solution from the problem specification, which is then trivially translated into Haskell array comprehensions as the final "code generation" step.[7]

The problem of LU decomposition is based on solving a particular kind of linear system, described in matrix form as

$$A = L * U$$

where L and U are $n \times n$ lower- and upper-triangular matrices, respectively. Given the matrix A, our job is to compute the matrices L and U. Such matrices do not always exist, but for our purposes we will assume they do, and without loss of generality we will assume further that U is unit-diagonal, and that L is not (necessarily).

Expanding out the definition of matrix multiplication, we arrive at

$$A_{i,j} \quad = \quad \sum_{k=1}^{n} L_{i,k} * U_{k,j} \quad \text{for } i, j \in 1 \ldots n$$

But since L and U are triangular, we know that

$$L_{i,k} \quad = \quad 0 \quad \text{if } i < k$$
$$U_{k,j} \quad = \quad 0 \quad \text{if } k > j$$

thus leading to

$$A_{i,j} \quad = \quad \sum_{k=1}^{j} L_{i,k} * U_{k,j} \quad \text{for } i \in 1 \ldots n, \ j \in 1 \ldots i \qquad (1)$$
$$A_{i,j} \quad = \quad \sum_{k=1}^{i} L_{i,k} * U_{k,j} \quad \text{for } i \in 1 \ldots n, \ j \in i+1 \ldots n \qquad (2)$$

Now the goal is to solve for L and U. Expanding (1) and recalling that U is unit-diagonal, we derive

$$A_{i,j} \quad = \quad L_{i,j} * U_{j,j} + \sum_{k=1}^{j-1} L_{i,k} * U_{k,j}$$
$$= \quad L_{i,j} + \sum_{k=1}^{j-1} L_{i,k} * U_{k,j}$$

and solving for L yields

$$L_{i,j} \quad = \quad A_{i,j} - \sum_{k=1}^{j-1} L_{i,k} * U_{k,j} \quad \text{for } i \in 1 \ldots n, \ j \in 1 \ldots i$$
$$L_{i,j} \quad = \quad 0 \quad \text{for } i \in 1 \ldots n, \ j \in i+1 \ldots n$$

Similarly, expanding (2) gives

$$A_{i,j} \quad = \quad L_{i,i} * U_{i,j} + \sum_{k=1}^{i-1} L_{i,k} * U_{k,j}$$

---

[7]The solution presented here is a simplified version of one given in [18], and follows the standard derivation as found, for example, in [7].

and solving now for U we obtain

$$
\begin{array}{llll}
U_{i,j} & = & (A_{i,j} - \sum_{k=1}^{i-1} L_{i,k} * U_{k,j}) \, / \, L_{i,i} & \text{for } i \in 1 \ldots n, \ j \in i+1 \ldots n \\
U_{i,j} & = & 0 & \text{for } i \in 1 \ldots n, \ j \in 1 \ldots i-1 \\
U_{i,i} & = & 1 & \text{for } i \in 1 \ldots n
\end{array}
$$

Note the highly recursive nature of these derived specifications for the matrices L and U. In most languages one would not be able to simply forge ahead at this point and convert this recursive specification into an array, since the elements would need to be computed in a particular order; in other words, the recursive dependencies would need to be unravelled by the programmer before proceeding. In Haskell, however, arrays are *non-strict*, meaning that recursive array dependencies are perfectly acceptable as long as no circular dependencies *between elements* exist (which in this case they do not).

In addition, we can take advantage of the fact that, except for the diagonal, L is 0 whenever U is not (and vice versa), so that we can represent both arrays as one, with L's diagonal stored on the diagonal of the result and U's unit diagonal being "implicit." Calling this array lu, the resulting program is

```
lu = array ((1,n),(1,n))
       ( [ (i,j) := do_l i j  |  i<-[1..n], j<-[1..i]   ] ++
         [ (i,j) := do_u i j  |  i<-[1..n], j<-[i+1..n] ] )
do_l i j =    a!(i,j) - sum (1,j-1)
                              (\k -> lu!(i,k) * lu!(k,j))
do_u i j = ( a!(i,j) - sum (1,i-1)
                              (\k -> lu!(i,k) * lu!(k,j)) / lu!(i,i)
sum (a,b) f | a>b  = 0
            | True = f a + sum (a+1,b) f
```

Note the great similarity of this solution to the mathematical specification given earlier; except for syntax, they are identical.

The remaining task, as usual, is to induce parallelism into the code. Probably the easiest way to do this is to simply evaluate all of the elements in the array eagerly; the data dependencies between elements will be the only impediments to maximal parallelism. Since the second argument to the array primitive is a list of index/value pairs, all we need to do is evaluate this list eagerly, using one of the methods described previously. On the other hand, most compilers will try to avoid actually generating this list, so an alternative approach is to write a function that walks over the array and forces the evaluation of each element speculatively—in other words, an array version of the spec_eval function defined previously for lists. We leave such a definition to the reader.

5.5   Implementation Techniques

The single best reference to implementation techniques for functional languages is the text by Peyton Jones [29], whose emphasis is sequential implementations but nevertheless discusses the basics of parallel implementations as well and gives ample references. In addition, several of the chapters in this book should be consulted—most notably those on Id, Sisal, and Crystal.

Compiling a para-functional language for parallel execution shares many of the low-level details of compiling other functional languages, differing primarily in that the mapping and scheduling strategies are explicit in the source program, thus relieving the compiler of the burden of determining the strategies automatically. It is beyond the scope of this book to discuss these implementation techniques in detail, but a few further comments are in order.

Section 5.3.1 described where parallelism comes from in a functional program, and we argued that it was easy for a compiler to uncover the parallelism, in a large part due to the lack of side effects. To summarize, parallelism exists in a functional program whenever there exists, at some point in the evaluation process, more than one reducible expression (*redex*).

Given this parallelism, many different abstract and concrete parallel machine models have been proposed for functional languages, most based on either *graph reduction* in the lambda calculus, or *dataflow* (and these two can be argued to be duals of one another). The details vary considerably, but the essential task of every model is twofold: (1) determine how to effectively *schedule* the active redexes, and (2) determine an effective *assignment* of the scheduled redexes to the available resources.

Most parallel implementations of functional languages use dynamic methods to accomplish these tasks. For example, in a dataflow machine redexes are manifested as nodes that have received all of their tokens in a "matching store" and when activated are assigned to the next available processor through a "distribution network." In contrast, an implementation on a conventional distributed memory multiprocessor will typically have a queue of tasks for each processor, and newly created tasks will be assigned to neighboring processors using some kind of load-balancing heuristic. Special-purpose graph reduction machines use a similar strategy.

Now given any one of these models, it should not be hard to imagine how to refine it for the purpose of handling para-functional specifications. More precisely, a *scheduled expression* will dictate the scheduling strategy, and a *mapped expression* will dictate the assignment strategy. In other words, the automatic scheduling and assignment strategies, normally an essential part of these models, are essentially replaced by ones supplied by the user. This simple implementation strategy is suitable for use on almost all of the popular abstract machine models.

As an example, the implementation of para-functional Haskell being developed at Yale uses a "future-based" model of computation, where a *future* is a language construct popularized in the MultiLisp parallel dialect of Scheme [10]. The implementation at Yale uses a highly optimized version of MultiLisp called *Mul-T* [22] targeted for shared-memory MIMD machines such as the Encore Multimax. Haskell programs are compiled entirely into Mul-T code, with laziness implemented using "delays" (sequential versions of futures) and scheduled expressions implemented with futures. Mul-T has a sufficiently rich set of operations on futures to permit a direct implementation of any scheduled expression in terms of them.

On the other hand, since this implementation is for MIMD machines, mapped expressions are not relevant. However, recursive invocations of scheduled expressions can induce excessive amounts of parallelism, thus swamping the limited processing resources. For this reason a novel dynamic scheduling mechanism called "lazy futures" is used to minimize the overhead of fine-grained parallelism [25].

5.6   Related Work

5.6.1   A COMPARISON TO CSP-LIKE APPROACHES

Consider the following typical situation: A shared value v is to be computed for use in two independent subexpressions e1 and e2; the values of these subexpressions are then to be combined into a single result. In a conventional language we might express this as something like

```
begin v  := code-for-v;
      e1 := code-for-e1;        -- uses v
      e2 := code-for-e2;        -- uses v
      result := combine(e1,e2)
end;
```

and in Haskell we might write

```
combine e1 e2
where v  = code-for-v
      e1 = code-for-e1          -- uses v
      e2 = code-for-e2          -- uses v
```

Both of these programs are very clear and concise. But now suppose that this same computation is to begin and end on processor p, and the subexpressions e1 and e2 are to be executed in parallel on processors q and r, respectively. In a conventional language augmented with explicit process creation and message-passing constructs, we might write the following program:

```
process P0
    v   := code-for-v;
    send(v,P1);
    send(v,P2);
    e1 := receive(P1);
    e2 := receive(P2);
    result := combine(e1,e2)
end-process;

process P1
    v   := receive(P0);
    e1 := code-for-e1;          -- uses v
    send(e1,P0)
end-process;

process P2
    v   := receive(P0);
    e2 := code-for-e2;          -- uses v
    send(e2,P0)
end-process;
```

which is then actually *run* by executing something like

```
invoke P0 on processor p;
invoke P1 on processor q;
invoke P2 on processor r;
```

Note how the structure of the original program has been completely destroyed. Explicit processes and communications between them have been introduced to coordinate the parallel computation. The semantics of the process creation and communications constructs need to be carefully defined before the runtime behavior can be understood. This program is no longer as clear or as concise as the original one.

In contrast, a para-functional Haskell program for this same task is simply

```
((combine e1 e2) on p) sched De1|De2
where v = code-for-v
```

```
e1 = code-for-e1  on  q    -- uses v
e2 = code-for-e2  on  r    -- uses v
```

Note that if the annotations are removed, the program is identical to the one given earlier! No communications primitives or special synchronization constructs are needed to "send" the value of v to processors q and r. Instead, standard lexical scoping mechanisms accomplish it naturally and concisely. Similarly, the values of e1 and e2 are "sent back" to processor p in the same way.

The point of this comparison is that the CSP model forces one into using message-passing for *all* forms of parallelism, even in situations that do not warrant it, thus potentially destroying program modularity. It is better to have the flexibility of choosing the message-passing idiom judiciously.

5.6.2   A COMPARISON TO OTHER META-LOGICAL APPROACHES

There are a few other efforts that share our "meta-logical" approach to parallel programming—some in the context of functional languages, others in the context of logic programming languages.

Ideas similar to mapped expressions may be found in the context of logic programming, in particular Shapiro's "systolic programming" in Concurrent Prolog [31], which is in turn derived from earlier work on "turtle programs" in Logo [28]. However, there are important differences. First, both of these earlier efforts have a notion of "directionality"—that is, a notion of a process (or turtle) "navigating" through a network (or turtle world) by "facing" in a certain direction. Our approach is somewhat more general, in that such navigation is simply a special case of a particular mapping. We can "skip" from one processor to any other just as easily as to its neighbor. Another important difference, of course, is the programming paradigm on which the extensions are based. Logo is a conventional imperative language, and thus non-determinism becomes an issue in the context of parallelism. Concurrent Prolog, although often referred to as declarative and having much of the purity of a functional language, is of course based on logical relations rather than functions. The relational component in the language gives rise to "controlled" non-determinism, which is useful in contexts that require it, and in a functional language is usually obtained via explicit non-deterministic constructs.

It is interesting to note that in logic programming the success of these ideas seems to rely on the notion of "read-only variables" (as well as a "commit" operator), which are an unnecessary distinction in functional languages since in a sense *all* variables are read-only (of course, this can also be viewed as a disadvantage, since the general utility of unification is unavailable). Also, the conventional block scoping rules of functional languages seem to give an added level of control over the use of identifiers and thus over the movement of data through a network. In particular, free variables in a mapped expression may reference objects computed on any arbitrary processor. This added power slightly complicates the semantics, as does the use of higher-order functions, but we believe it is worthwhile.

Other related efforts include that of Keller and Lindstrom [21], who independently (in the context of functional databases) suggest the use of annotations very similar to our mapped expressions. Their purpose is to permit users to assign database objects to particular "sites" in a distributed network, a very useful capability.

Our scheduled expressions can be viewed as a generalization of Burton's annotations to the lambda calculus to control reduction order—in particular, to provide control over what he calls "lazy," "eager," and "parallel" execution [4]. Burton also describes annotations to *prioritize* tasks [5], which we do not do. Another related effort is that of Sridharan [32], who suggests a "semi-applicative" programming style to control evaluation order. Most recently, Darlington and While [8] suggest the use of temporal logic to control the evaluation order of a functional program. Finally, as mentioned earlier, Crystal (described in Chapter 7) uses meta-logical features to express certain kinds of parallelism.

All in all, these efforts contribute to what we think is a powerful programming paradigm in which operational and functional behavior can coexist with little adverse interaction.

5.7 Conclusions

In the preface to their seminal textbook, *Structure and Interpretation of Computer Programs* [1], Abelson and Sussman write:

> Mathematics provides a framework for dealing precisely with notions of "what is." Computation provides a framework for dealing with notions of "how to."

Indeed, as computer programmers we spend much of our time transforming abstract (although often poorly formulated) *specifications* (the "what") into concrete *implementations* (the "how").

Unfortunately, most conventional programming languages do not adequately maintain the distinction between the *what* and the *how*. Rather, the two notions are inextricably fused within the primitive constructs of the language. As a result, it is often difficult for a programmer to make a design decision concerning one without affecting the other. Abstraction techniques help a great deal in minimizing these effects, but despite our best efforts to write modular programs, it is often the case that a single design decision, or change in a previous decision, will permeate a large part of a program. As Alan Perlis once professed to would-be computer programmers, "Invent and fit; have fits and reinvent!" [1].

Functional (and other high-level) languages go a long way toward separating the what from the how, but they do so primarily by *eliminating* the how—for example, memory allocation—and such operational details are left to the compiler or runtime system. However, in the world of parallel programming the problem becomes more severe, since the "how" component becomes much larger and more complex. Not only does the coordination of many parallel processes become a rather onerous programming chore, but also many more design choices become available to the programmer—for example, the choices in mapping, scheduling, and communication described earlier. Furthermore, it is no longer the case that we can simply trust the system to manage these chores for us, their precise specification perhaps being crucial to good performance.

The basic philosophy motivating the work described in this chapter can be summarized as follows: I believe that a programmer should be able to write parallel (or for that matter, sequential) programs in a very high-level language, as close to a true specification as possible, with no concern about operational issues such as evaluation order or task granularity. Given such an "executable specification," an optimizing compiler will be able to generate reasonably efficient code for a sequential machine, and in certain cases efficient code for a parallel machine, thus supporting the notion of "rapid prototyping" [11]. However, if this is not good enough—that is, if the program does not meet the performance requirements demanded of it—then the programmer should have ways to refine the operational behavior without restructuring the whole program or completely rewriting it in some other language. The same language syntax and semantics should be maintained throughout the entire software development process. In addition, we should be able to specify the refinements to operational behavior in a way that has minimal impact on the functional behavior.

My vehicle for accomplishing these goals is, of course, a functional language. Finer control over operational issues such as evaluation order and process-to-processor mapping is accomplished quite elegantly via annotations, resulting in what I call a *para-functional programming language*. Although the use of annotations may sound somewhat *ad hoc*, in fact annotations can be given a very precise formal semantics. I prefer to think of the annotations as actually extending the semantic base of a language; they are annotations only in the sense that their removal results in a still perfectly valid functional program.

Of course, all is not rosy. Although it is usually the case that few annotations are needed, extremely fine control over parallel behavior may result in cumbersome programs. In addition, it is sometimes more convenient, even necessary, to restructure the core program for better parallel performance. I doubt that these situations can be avoided entirely, but nevertheless it is helpful to minimize them in the ways described in this chapter.

Much remains to make para-functional programming a pragmatic alternative to more conventional methods of parallel programming. At the time of this writing, an implementation of a Haskell-based para-functional language for an MIMD machine is under construction at Yale University. A similar implementation for a hypercube multiprocessor is being studied at New York University.[8]

Current research directions include the use of sophisticated programming environment techniques to support para-functional program development, such as program transformation strategies (preserving parallel behavior under functional transformations, and vice versa), version control mechanisms (using different sets of annotations for different target parallel machines), and debugging techniques (monitoring the effect of annotations on parallel performance). A good programming environment is essential for successful parallel programming.

Work is also continuing on defining the formal semantics of a para-functional language. What makes this difficult is the fact that an *operational* semantics is needed, and it is not clear what the best such framework is [14, 17].

Finally, work continues on defining the best set of meta-language features to capture the para-functional behavior of interest. In the previous section we mentioned the use of annotations to *prioritize* tasks—which can be thought of as a generalization of a scheduled expression—but there are many other variants that one could imagine. Examples include discrete-time scheduling (to specify, for example, synchronous systolic algorithms), and "hard real-time" scheduling (such as would be needed in real-time control applications).

---

[8]Enquiries regarding the availability of these implementations may be sent to The Haskell Project, Box 2158 Yale Station, New Haven, CT 06520.

5.8   Acknowledgments

I would like to thank the Department of Energy, the Defense Advanced Research Projects Agency, and the National Science Foundation for their generous support of this research under grants FG02-86ER25012, N00014-88-K-0573, and CCR-8809919, respectively. I also wish to thank the members of the Lisp and Functional Programming Research Group at Yale, who inspire much of my work and serve as my chief sounding board. In particular, thanks to Rick Mohr and Duke Briscoe for invaluable comments on an earlier draft of this manuscript.

References

1. H. Abelson, G.J. Sussman, and J. Sussman. *Structure and Interpretation of Computer Programs.* Cambridge, Mass.: MIT Press, and New York: McGraw-Hill, 1985.

2. G. Agha. *Actors: A Model of Concurrent Computation in Distributed Systems.* Cambridge, Mass.: MIT Press, 1986.

3. R. Bird and P. Wadler. *Introduction to Functional Programming.* Englewood Cliffs, N.J.: Prentice Hall, 1988.

4. F.W. Burton. Annotations to control parallelism and reduction order in the distributed evaluation of functional programs. *ACM Transactions on Programming Languages and Systems,* 6(2):159–174, April 1984.

5. F.W. Burton. Controlling speculative computation in a parallel functional language. In *International Conference on Distributed Computing Systems,* pp. 453–458, May 1985.

6. A. Church. *The Calculi of Lambda Conversion.* Princeton, N.J.: Princeton University Press, 1941.

7. G.F. Curtis. *Applied Numerical Analysis.* Reading, Mass.: Addison-Wesley, 1978.

8. J. Darlington and L. While. Controlling the behavior of functional language systems. In *Proceedings of 1987 Functional Programming Languages and Computer Architecture Conference,* pp. 278–300. Springer-Verlag LNCS 274, September 1987.

9. A.J. Field and P.G. Harrison. *Functional Programming.* Wokingham, England: Addison-Wesley, 1988.

10. R.H. Halstead Jr. Multilisp: A language for concurrent symbolic computation. *ACM Transactions on Programming Languages and Systems,* 7(4):501–538, October 1985.

11. P. Henderson. Functional programming, formal specification, and rapid prototyping. *IEEE Transactions on SW Engineering,* SE-12(2):241–250, 1986.

12. C.A.R. Hoare. Communicating sequential processes. *Comm. ACM,* 21(8):666–677, 1978.

13. C.A.R. Hoare. *Communicating Sequential Processes.* Englewood Cliffs, N.J.: Prentice-Hall, 1985.

14. P. Hudak. Denotational semantics of a para-functional programming language. *International Journal of Parallel Programming,* 15(2):103–125, April 1986.

15. P. Hudak. Para-functional programming. *Computer,* 19(8):60–71, August 1986.

16. P. Hudak. Conception, evolution, and application of functional programming languages. *ACM Computing Surveys,* 21(3):359–411, 1989.

17. P. Hudak and S. Anderson. Pomset interpretations of parallel functional programs. In *Proceedings of 1987 Functional Programming Languages and Computer Architecture Conference,* pp. 234–256. Springer Verlag LNCS 274, September 1987.

18. P. Hudak and S. Anderson. Haskell solutions to the language session problems at the 1988 Salishan High-Speed Computing Conference. Technical Report YALEU/DCS/RR-627, Yale University, Department of Computer Science, January 1988.

19. P. Hudak and L. Smith. Para-functional programming: a paradigm for programming multiprocessor systems. In *12th ACM Symposium on Principles of Programming Languages,* pp. 243–254, January 1986.

20. P. Hudak and P. Wadler, eds. Report on the programming language Haskell, a non-strict purely functional language (Version 1.0). Technical Report YALEU/DCS/RR777, Yale University, Department of Computer Science, April 1990 (to appear in SIGPLAN Notices).

21. R.M. Keller and G. Lindstrom. Approaching distributed database implementations through functional programming concepts. In *Int'l Conference on Distributed Systems,* May 1985.

22. D.A. Kranz, R.H. Halstead, and E. Mohr. Mul-T: A high-performance parallel Lisp. In *Proceedings of 1989 SIGPLAN Conference on Programming Language Design and Implementation,* pp. 81–90. ACM/SIGPLAN, June 1989.

23. R. Milner. A proposal for Standard ML. In *Proceedings 1984 ACM Conference on LISP and Functional Programming,* pp. 184–197. ACM, August 1984.

24. R. Milner. *A Calculus of Communicating Systems,* vol. 81 of *LNCS.* Berlin: Springer Verlag, 1981.

25. E. Mohr, D. Kranz, and R. Halstead. Lazy task creation: A technique for increasing the granularity of parallel programs. In *Proceedings of Symposium on Lisp and Functional Programming,* pp. 185–197, Nice, France, ACM, June 1990.

26. Z.G. Mou. *A Formal Model for Divide-and-Conquer and Its Parallel Realization.* PhD thesis, Yale University, Department of Computer Science, May 1990.

27. Z.G. Mou and P. Hudak. An algebraic model for divide-and-conquer and its parallelism. *Journal of Supercomputing,* 2(3), 1988.

28. S. Pappert. *Mindstorms: Children, Computers and Powerful Ideas.* Basic Books, 1980.

29. S.L. Peyton Jones. *The Implementation of Functional Programming Languages.* Englewood Cliffs, N.J.: Prentice-Hall, 1987.

30. V. Pratt. Modeling concurrency with partial orders. *International Journal of Parallel Programming,* 15(1):33–72, February 1986.

31. E. Shapiro. Systolic programming: A paradigm of parallel processing. Department of Applied Mathematics CS84-21, The Weizmann Institute of Science, August 1984.

32. N.S. Sridharan. Semi-applicative programming: An example. Technical report, BBN Laboratories, November 1985.

33. D.A. Turner. The semantic elegance of applicative languages. In *Proceedings of the 1981 Conference on Functional Programming Languages and Computer Architecture,* pp. 85–92. ACM, 1981.

34. D.A. Turner. Recursion equations as a programming language. In *Functional Programming and Its Applications: An Advanced Course,* pp. 1–28. Cambridge, England: Cambridge University Press, 1982.

35. A. Wikstrom. *Standard ML.* Englewood Cliffs, N.J.: Prentice-Hall, 1988.

6

A Perspective on Id

Kattamuri Ekanadham

6.1   Introduction

The functional language literature is full of exhortations about the tremendous importance of higher-level abstractions [8, 11, 23]. Typically, a language provides a primitive set of data abstractions and some means to define higher levels of data abstractions. Control (or computational) abstractions are also important for software productivity. In functional languages, the principal means of expressing computational abstractions is through functions. Typically, a function takes some data objects and produces new data objects from them. The thing that is abstracted by the function is the method used to produce the new objects from the arguments. Higher-order functions generalize this further by taking data objects as well as other functions as arguments and producing new data objects and new functions as results. The *Id*[1] language

---

[1]Id is a language that evolved over the past few years. It has fostered good principles of functional languages and has taken up a unique challenge to show that these principles can indeed be put into practice for efficient parallel execution of scientific applications. Id was designed by Professors Arvind and Nikhil at the MIT Laboratory for Computer Science and has undergone several revisions of implementations through contributions of many graduate students in

strongly supports this philosophy. Furthermore, the language takes a unique position in supporting efficient parallel computations [2]. For instance, it directly supports array and matrix structures and provides efficient iterative constructs for their manipulation.

This chapter is a comprehensive exposition of many aspects of the Id language. A reader may select excerpts depending upon the interest. It is organized as follows. Section 6.2 introduces the principal features of the language to the reader unfamiliar with it. The treatment is not exhaustive. Those features of the language that are not relevant to the focus here are not discussed—for example, type system and annotations for lazy evaluation. The chapter presents simple examples and concentrates on giving the basic tools for building higher level abstractions. Unfortunately, the power of abstractions is not completely appreciated when presented through simplified examples. Section 6.3 thus discusses three examples in detail. These are from numerical applications and are all self-contained. Going through these fairly involved examples will force you to compare how you could build similar abstractions in other languages and make a judgement on it. While going through these examples, you must bear in mind the following key questions: (a)Given the problem description, do the abstractions naturally translate into the programming abstractions or do you have to bend the concepts to conform to a rigid and less expressive programming system? (b)How much attention is being paid to expose the parallelism at the programming level and (having read the subsequent discussion on execution model) how much parallelism will indeed be exposed? (c)How can you compose these solutions in other languages to derive similar benefits? I urge you not to look at the examples as the best solutions to the problems presented but rather to look at the methodology and judge the expressive power of the language in real applications. For instance, how easy would it be to make changes to the programs if alternative algorithms or representations are chosen?

Section 6.4 gives the operational semantics for the language in terms of rewrite rules. This has a threefold purpose. First, I would like to explain the meaning of these programs clearly and in a reasonably formal framework. While I do not prove any properties of the programs

that group. The principal source of the Id language specification is [15]. The Id compiler, originally developed by Ken Traub, generates code for the TTDA dataflow machine, also designed at MIT. A simulator for the machine enables testing and running Id programs and there is a substantial body of applications written and tested. I have used Id extensively and the perspective presented here is a summary of my current understanding. Any errors and misconceptions are my own.

using the framework, they are precise enough to do so. Second, the exercise of going through these reductions will give you an intuitive picture as to how a parallel machine might execute these programs. You can get a very clear picture of the parallelism exposed at the level of basic principles, rather than look at curves for particular problems for particular sizes and so forth. Indeed, the rewrite rules mimic the execution of the programs on a fine grain parallel machine. Finally, the form of the programs for which the semantics is specified serves as a good intermediate representation for many transformations. It is devoid of many bells and whistles that are usually built into the high level language and contains the bare bones constructs, each of which have direct bearing on the implementation. The structure abstractions (lists, arrays, accumulators) could have been omitted in this representation, by including a lower level abstraction of a synchronized memory (which is actually used to implement them). However, I have chosen to retain the structure abstractions in this form, as they preserve the functionality and hence substitutions and optimizations can be expressed at this level. Section 6.5 illustrates a few optimizations to show how they can be expressed in this framework.

Section 6.6 discusses the lower level abstraction of I-structures, which is used to implement the higher level abstractions. They are non-functional. The discussion is brief, as the intention is merely to convince the reader that efficient implementation is plausible along these lines. The real question of efficiency is much deeper and is beyond the scope of this chapter.

6.2   Principal Language Features

6.2.1   FUNCTION ABSTRACTIONS

A function is defined by a simple function equation of the form

```
def newton n x = (x + n/x)/2;
```

Here newton is the name of the function. It takes two arguments—an integer n and an approximation x for its square root. It returns a better approximation using Newton's formula. Function application is denoted by a function name followed by the argument expressions that are separated by spaces. The following function returns a Boolean value that tells whether the two argument values a and b are within a specified tolerance limit epsilon. The absolute value function, abs, is applied to the difference (a-b) and the result is compared with epsilon.

```
def close? epsilon a b = abs (a-b) <= epsilon;
```

Complex expressions can be formed using blocks. A block is a set of local variable bindings followed by a result expression (prefixed by the keyword **in**). For example, the following function uses a block with bindings for two local variables y and z.

```
def approximate epsilon n x =
      {y = newton n x;
       z = if close? epsilon x y
           then y
           else approximate epsilon n y;
      in z };
def sqroot epsilon n = approximate epsilon n (n/2);
```

The value of the block expression is the value computed for z. The binding for z illustrates the familiar **if-then-else** form for a conditional. The approximate function recursively calls itself and computes better and better approximations until the tolerance limit is reached. The sqroot function computes the square root of n, starting with an initial approximation of n/2. The scope of the bindings in a block is limited to the block and the bindings can be recursive (but not circular). When blocks are nested, the usual lexical scope rules apply. Within a block, the left-hand sides of all bindings must be distinct. The order of bindings within a block is irrelevant and hence the computation of all the bindings in a block proceeds concurrently, subject to only the dependences due to the flow of data.

Iterative Constructs for Efficiency. Function calls invariably entail some overhead. Tail recursive programs can be transformed into loops, which render slightly more efficient implementations, such as moving invariant expressions out of loops and allocating resources for all the iterations at one time. Although, sometimes it may be possible to transform some tail recursive forms into loops, Id supports explicit loop constructs at the language level. The construct {**while** condition **do** body} executes the body as long as the condition holds true. For instance, the function approximate in the above example can be equivalently defined as

```
def approximate epsilon n x =
     {y = newton n x;
      in {while not (close? epsilon x y) do
                 next x = y;
                 next y = newton n y;
                 finally y}};
```

Each iteration of a loop should be viewed as a separate instantiation of a function. In this example the loop body is like a function with two inputs x and y and two outputs **next** x and **next** y. An iteration computes its outputs, **next** x and **next** y, and invokes the next iteration passing them as the corresponding inputs x and y. When the loop terminates, the final value of the loop is given by the expression following the keyword **finally**, which uses the last set of values computed. In this example, the last y is returned, discarding x. The standard alternative iterative form is also provided: {**for** i ← 1 **to** n **do** body} executes the body n times, with i bound to the value j in the jth iteration. The bounds and step size could be general expressions.

Higher Order Functions.   A crucial aspect of higher level programming is to employ abstractions at all levels. In particular, it should be possible to build new abstractions from existing abstractions—whether they are function abstractions or data abstractions. Id supports higher order functions and currying. Thus, for instance, new functions can be defined by partial applications.

```
sqroot-five-places = sqroot 0.00001;
```

Here, sqroot-five-places is a unary function, which specializes the binary function sqroot to compute the square root up to five decimal places. Thus the application (sqroot-five-places 97) is equivalent to the application (sqroot 0.00001 97).

Functions can take other functions as arguments or return them as results. This can be illustrated by the familiar example of reducing a list using some binary reduction function f. The function takes a binary reduction function and a nonempty list as arguments. Starting with the first element of the list, it applies the reduction function with every other element in the list. The standard primitive functions **hd** and **tl** select the head and tail of a list and **nil?** tests if a list is empty.

```
def reduce-list f list =
    {a = hd list;
     rest = tl list;
     in {while not (nil? rest) do
                next a = f a (hd rest);
                next rest = tl rest;
                finally a}};
sum-list = reduce-list (+)
```

The last binding in which (+) denotes the prefix form of the add operator defines sum-list as a function that takes a list of numbers as an argument and returns the sum of the elements. Function application associates to the left. Thus the expression (sqroot-five-places sum-list list) does not give the square root of the sum of the list but instead tries to apply the square root function to the sum-list function and results in error.

6.2.2   DATA ABSTRACTIONS

Four principal functional data types are supported in Id: tuples, lists, arrays, and accumulators.

Tuples.   Tuples are heterogeneous sequences of values. They are constructed by listing the values separated by commas. Tuple components are selected by pattern matching. Consider the following example:

```
def transform polar = {r, theta = polar;
                       x = r * (cos theta);
                       y = r * (sin theta);
                    in x,y};
```

The function transform takes one argument that is expected to be a two-tuple. The first equation in the block selects and binds the two components of the tuple to the two names r and theta respectively. It computes the equivalent Cartesian coordinates x and y and returns them as a single two-tuple x,y. The selection of tuple components can also be done by specifying patterns in the arguments of a function. For instance, the following is an equivalent definition:

```
def transform (r, theta) = r * (cos theta),
                           r * (sin theta);
```

Although it may be a bad programming style, mutually recursive bindings are permitted. For instance, the following bindings will not deadlock if b is a function of x alone. The values could be computed in the order b,c,a,d.

```
a, b = f x c;
c, d = g y b;
```

Lists.   Lists can be constructed using the infix operator (:) or by concatenating two lists using the infix operator (++). Components are selected by head and tail functions **hd** and **tl**. The following is a simple example that creates a list of n natural integers in the reverse order:

```
def unnatural n = {list = nil;
                in {for i ← 1 to n do
                         next list = i : list;
                         finally list}};
```

The application (unnatural 5) gives the list (5 4 3 2 1). Functional list constructions are easy when lists grow at the head. But growing a list at the tail is very expensive as it involves copying of all the elements of the list. Hence in order to produce the list (1 2 3 4 5), you must either think inversely by having the loop go from 5 down to 1 or else copy the list. Id provides a neat solution using list comprehensions (a la KRC, Miranda; see [23], appendix in [17]). For example, the following is a simple list comprehension:

def natural n = {: i ‖ i ← 1 **to** n };

The application (natural 5) gives the list (1 2 3 4 5). Clearly, the notation is very elegant. The Id implementation uses iteration from 1 to n as specified and the list is grown efficiently by adding items to the tail. This is accomplished using the implementation techniques discussed in Section 6.6. List comprehensions can have arbitrary generators and filters to select a subset of items generated. For instance, the following function gives the list of index pairs corresponding to the elements of an $n \times n$ matrix:

def index-list n = {: i,j ‖ i ← 1 **to** n & j ← 1 **to** n };

This is read as the set of all pairs (i,j) where i and j vary from 1 to n. i ← 1 **to** n and j ← 1 **to** n are called the generators and are combined by the conjunction operator &, thus forming a nested loop structure. That is, for each value of i the iterator j goes through its full range of values. Any number of generators can be specified in this manner. Each generator can also be associated with a filter as illustrated below:

def related-pairs n = {: i,j ‖ i ← 1 **to** n **when** f i
                                & j ← i **to** n **unless** g j };

This gives the list of all unordered index pairs such that the first item satisfies the property defined by f and the second does not satisfy the property defined by g.

Recurrence lists are very common in many applications and are described by the following informal identity:

recurrence-list p f x ≡ x (f x) (f (f x)) .. (f^k x)
                where p (f^i x) = true ∀ 0<=i<=k
                and p (f^{k+1} x) = false.

A recurrence list is a list of items where each item is derived from the preceding item, until a certain predicate holds true. Id does not provide this as a comprehension with special syntax. Instead, it is provided as a library function with very efficient implementation, as described in Section 6.6. The function takes three arguments: a predicate function, p, a generator function, f, and an initial element, x. Starting from the initial element, it applies the generating element and generates successive items for the list. The items are included as long as the predicate function on the item returns true. As an example, the function foo below gives the list of pairs of a number and its square, until the square exceeds a given threshold:

```
def foo n =
    {def within (i,x) = x <= n;
     def get-next (i,x) = (i+1, (i+1)*(i+1));
     in recurrence-list within get-next (1,1)}};
```

The application (foo 10) gives the list (1,1) (2,4) (3,9). Incidentally, notice the nested definition of functions. This is convenient because the inner functions can use the environment variables without having to explicitly include them as arguments. This is done automatically by λ-lifting. We will also use a slight variation of the above recurrence-list abstraction:

$$\texttt{recurrence-n-list n f x} \equiv \texttt{x (f x) (f (f x)) .. } (f^{n-1} \texttt{ x})$$

This function takes an integer n in place of the predicate function and generates a list of that many elements in the same manner.

Arrays.   An array abstraction is simply a collection of values having a one-to-one correspondence with indices within a range. Usually there is one method parameterized by the index to compute all the elements. Sometimes there may be a small collection of methods for different regions in the range. The value of an element is obtained directly by specifying its index. Efficient implementation of arrays is essential for scientific computations.

A simple example is an array comprehension shown on the right-hand side of the following definition. The result is an array whose dimensions are given after the key word **array** and whose i^{th} element is bound to the value obtained by applying the function f to i.

```
def make-array (lb,ub) f = {array (lb,ub)
                        | [i] = f i || i ← lb to ub };
```

Accessing the bounds and elements of an array is illustrated by the following function. Given an array A and a value x, the function searches the array from lower to upper bound and returns the index to the first element greater than or equal to x. If no such element is found, it returns 1 + the upper bound.

```
def search-up A x =
```

```
{i, end = array-bounds A;
 more = true;
 in {while more do
         next i, next more = if A[i] < x
                             then i+1, (i == end)
                             else i, false;
     finally i }};
```

Suppose we have a similar function, search-down, which searches the array from upper to lower bound looking for the first element smaller or equal to a given value. Now if A is a sorted array, then we can construct the function find-range that returns an index range into the array, so that the elements in that range are contained within a given interval:

```
def find-range A x y =
    (search-up A x), (search-down A y);
```

Similarly, matrices can be constructed using comprehensions. The following is a matrix in which the left and top boundary elements are set to 1, the right and bottom boundary elements are set to 0, and the interior elements are set to some number between 0 and 1.

```
T = {matrix ((1,n),(1,n))
     | [i,j] = if i==1 or j==1 then 1
               else if i==n or j==n then 0
               else (i+j)/(i*j)
               || i ← 1 to n & j ← 1 to n };
```

The symbol == denotes the relational operator for equality. The selection A[1,1] yields 1, the selection A[n,n] yields 0, and the selection A[4,4] yields 0.5, and so on. The above definition involves runtime evaluation of the conditional as each element of the matrix is created. This is inefficient and Id provides a more appealing construct as shown below:

```
A = {matrix ((1,n),(1,n))
     | [1,j] = 1 || j ← 1 to n
     | [i,1] = 1 || i ← 2 to n
     | [n,j] = 0 || j ← 2 to n
     | [i,n] = 0 || i ← 2 to n-1
     | [i,j] = (i+j)/(i*j)
               || i ← 2 to n-1 & j ← 2 to n-1 };
```

This is a provision to specify different functions to evaluate the elements in different disjoint regions of the range. The specification of the values in each region follows the special symbol | and the compiler generates one or more loops for each region as needed. All the element bindings can be done in parallel, subject only to data dependences. Notice how the index ranges are carefully specified to avoid multiple bindings of the same element. The burden of verifying that the specified regions are all disjoint is placed on the programmer, and a runtime check flags any errors. This is an unpleasant necessity for a functional framework. An imperative program can perhaps use fewer loops by taking advantage of a harmless overwrite facility.

The above scheme is much more powerful than it appears. For instance, it facilitates the construction of recursive data structures. The following definition creates an array of n Fibonacci numbers:

```
F = {array (1,n)
    | [i] = 1              || i ← 1 to 2
    | [i] = F[i-2]+F[i-1]  || i ← 3 to n };
```

The fact that F appears on both sides of the equation does not cause any problems, as explained later in the operational semantics and implementation of arrays.

As another example, consider the problem of building inverse permutations—that is, given an array B of some permutation of integers 1 to n, the problem is to construct another array A such that A[B[i]]=i for all i. It is not very convenient to build this using conventional functional structures [6]. Array comprehensions render the following easy solution for this:

```
def inverse-permute B n = {array (1,n)
                          | [B[i]] = i || i ← 1 to n };
```

Finally, another problem with functional data structures [6] is the sharing of subcomputations while generating components of two or more structures. For instance, consider the following definitions:

```
A = {array (1,n)
    | [i] = f (heavy i) || i ← 1 to n };
B = {array (1,n)
    | [i] = g (heavy i) || i ← 1 to n };
```

where f, g, heavy are some arbitrary functions. The subcomputation (heavy i) is common to both A[i] and B[i] but is computed twice unnecessarily. The problem is to program them in such a manner that the subcomputation is performed only once and the result is shared. One way to accomplish this is as follows:

```
list = {:heavy i || i ← 1 to n};
A = {array (1,n)
    | [i] = f x || x ← list };
```

```
B = {array (1,n)
     | [i] = g x ‖ x ← list };
```

However, this involves the construction of an intermediate list and traversing it twice. Id provides a family of array comprehensions that can take advantage of such sharing. For instance, we can write an equivalent program as follows:

```
def fg-pair i = {x = heavy i;
                 in (f x), (g x)};
A,B = {2-arrays (1,n)
       | [i] = fg-pair i ‖ i ← 1 to n};
```

Each generating expression produces a pair of values that are bound to the corresponding elements of A and B. Id provides a family of such abstractions like **3-arrays, 2-matrices**, etc.

Accumulators.   An accumulator is a new functional abstraction to perform unordered reduction of concurrently computed values. This cannot be efficiently implemented using any of the abstractions discussed so far. To illustrate the concept, consider the summation $\sum_{i=1}^{n}(f\ i)$, where f is some arbitrary function. This can be accomplished by the following block expression:

```
{s = 0
 in {for i ← 1 to n do
         next s = s + (f i);
         finally s }};
```

There are two issues here. First, the partial sums (that is, the values of s in successive iterations) are generated concurrently but are summed up sequentially. If we knew that the order of addition is irrelevant, they could have been summed up when they are generated. Second, and more importantly, because of single assignment restriction we are forced to allocate separate storage to hold each partial sum. Since each partial sum is used only to produce the next partial sum, it is discarded after that. If this knowledge is available to the implementation, the storage allocation for the partial sums could be avoided by updating the final sum in place. One may not readily appreciate this saving, if the storage involved is a scalar location as in the above example. But if the accumulating location is an element of a structure, the entire structure needs to be copied to update one element and this can be prohibitively expensive. The accumulator abstraction is designed to capture such information, so that efficient code can be generated. It abstracts three things: the initialization of the storage, the function used to combine a new value with an old value, and the generation of the list of values to be so combined.

In Id, such updatable storage is treated as a structure, and hence we will assume s to be an array ranging from 1 to 1. So, we can specify

```
{array (1,1)
 | [1] = 0
 accumulate (+)
 | 1 gets (f i) || i ← 1 to n }
```

The first clause creates an array of one element and initializes it to zero, as per the regular array syntax. The key word **accumulate** specifies that the following accumulations must be performed using the (+) as the combining function. The phrase y **gets** z means that the yth element of the array is accumulated using z—that is, $A[y] \leftarrow A[y] + z$. This is an imperative update of the element location. In the above example, for each i between 1 and n, the value (f i) is computed and added to the current value of the first element in the structure. The result of the expression is the final structure that contains the final value of the sum. Implicit in this specification is the requirement that intermediate values of the structure should be invisible.

A more complicated example for accumulators is histogramming—for example, to generate a lot of sample values, say integers between 1 and n and find their frequency distribution into, say k, class intervals. To do this, ideally, one would initialize an array of k elements to all zeroes. As each sample is generated, its class, j, is determined, and the jth element of the array is incremented. The reason to have an array of k elements, as opposed to having k variables, is that k can be very large and this may become unwieldy when handling an arbitrary number of them. But if a functional array is used, each increment operation must create a new copy of the array differing in just one element. The accumulator abstraction fits in very well:

```
A = {array (1,k)
     | [i] = 0 || i ← 1 to k
     accumulate (+)
     | (classify (sample i)) gets 1 || i ← 1 to n}
```

The final result of the above accumulator expression is an array of k elements, so that the ith element gives the number of samples that fall into the ith class. A total of n samples are generated and classified. In general, any binary function can be specified in place of (+). However, since the accumulations may be done out of order, the programmer must ensure that the function is commutative and associative. The notion of accumulators bears a close resemblance to logic variables [18].

6.3   Three Detailed Examples

In this section we discuss a few examples in detail to illustrate how complex problems can be expressed to easily reflect higher level abstractions. This also illustrates how little attention is needed to expose parallelism and how much parallelism is automatically exposed. I have chosen examples that are not too simple to parallelize in conventional systems. It should be noted that the emphasis in these examples is not the cleverness of the algorithms chosen but rather the manner in which abstractions in the problem domain have been captured by the function definitions and the flexibility with which they can be altered and manipulated. The parallelism is automatically exposed by the abstractions.

6.3.1   COMPUTATION OF CONVEX HULL

In the first example we compute the convex hull of a given set of points in a plane, using the Jarvis' March algorithm [19]. Intuitively, convex hull is the subset of points that, when connected in a sequence, form a rubber band around the set and will contain the entire set of points so that no line joining any two points in the set will intersect the rubber band. The points are given by their rectangular coordinates with respect to some origin and axes in the plane. A point is represented by a two-tuple of x- and y-coordinates. The following functions illustrate some simple properties of these points:

```
def lexical-small?   (x,y) (u,v) = (x < u) or
                                   (x == u) and (y < v));
def lexical-unequal? (x,y) (u,v) = (x <> u) or (y <> v);
def dir-vector       (x,y) (u,v) = (u − x), (v − y);
def determinant      (x,y) (u,v) = x * v − u * y;
def lexical-min p q = if lexical-small? p q then p else q;
def lexical-max p q = if lexical-small? p q then q else p;
```

The first function defines a notion of lexicographically small. It orders a pair of points by their x-coordinates and if they are equal, by their y-coordinates. Similarly the next function returns a boolean value indicating whether a pair of points are equal or not. The direction vector returns the coordinates of the second point relative to the first and the next function computes the value of the 2×2 determinant formed by the coordinate vectors of the two points.

The basic observation in Jarvis' March is illustrated in Figure 6.1. If P is a hull vertex, then the next hull vertex is found by scanning all the points in the set and choosing the point Q, which has minimum

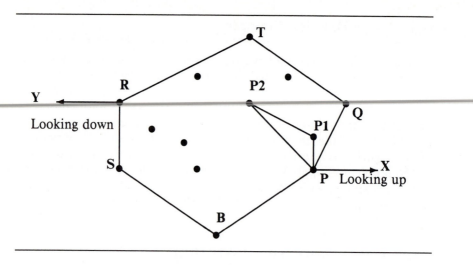

FIGURE 6.1
Jarvis' March Algorithm for Convex Hull Computation.

polar angle measured counterclockwise with respect to P as origin and
the positive x-direction at P as the reference axis. Thus, for example if
P1 and P2 are two points in the set, P1 is selected over P2, as the angle
$X\widehat{P}P1$ is smaller than the angle $X\widehat{P}P2$. This can be determined by
examining the sign of the area of the triangle formed by the two vectors
$P \rightarrow P1$ and $P \rightarrow P2$. The following function captures this notion.

```
def arg2-has-lower-angle? op oq =
    {signed-area = determinant op oq;
     in if signed-area == 0
        then resolve-collinear-case op oq
        else (signed-area < 0)};
```

The function takes two direction vectors, op and oq, of two points p and
q relative to some origin o. If the area of the enclosed triangle is positive
then p is lower than q. If the area is negative then q is lower than p. If
the area is zero, then the points are collinear with the origin and the
direction is inferred by examining four degenerate cases (omitted here
for brevity). This defines a notion of *minimality* over the set of points
and we must select the smallest point according to this criterion. There
is one caviat—if the current hull vertex is on the left side of the picture
(for example, R in Figure 6.1), then the direction of polar axis must
be reversed as shown by RY. Otherwise we will get the wrong effect.
This is captured by parameterizing the minimization function with a

sense of direction. If looking up, we take the direction vectors op and oq; otherwise we take the direction vectors po and qo as defined below:

```
def point-with-lower-angle looking-up? o p q =
    {op, oq = if looking-up?
                then (dir-vector o p), (dir-vector o q)
                else (dir-vector p o), (dir-vector q o);
     in if (arg2-has-lower-angle? op oq) then q else p};
```

Now, given a hull vertex as origin, the next hull vertex is found by reducing the list of all points to one that has minimal polar angle, as defined by the following function:

```
def next-hull-vertex looking-up? plist origin =
reduce-list (point-with-lower-angle looking-up? origin)
    plist;
```

Recall that `reduce-list` is the standard list reduction function defined in Section 6.2. The minimizing function is `point-with-lower-angle`, with the first two arguments supplied. The result is a function which takes two points p and q and returns the minimum. To build the list of hull vertices, we must march up starting at the bottom point B to the top point T and then march down from T to B. Each march builds a list of hull vertices as a recurrence—that is, a vertex being determined from the preceding vertex, which ideally fits the abstraction of `recurrence-list` defined in Section 6.2.

```
def march looking-up? plist bottom top =
    recurrence-list (lexical-unequal? top)
    (next-hull-vertex looking-up? plist)
    bottom;
```

The iteration starts with the bottom vertex and successively applies the `next-hull-vertex` function to add to the list, and the list is terminated and returned when the next vertex is the top. The following function computes the bottom and top and completes the Jarvis' March. The concatenation of the upward and downward hull vertex lists gives the complete hull.

```
def jarvis-march plist =
    {bottom = reduce-list lexical-min plist;
     top = reduce-list lexical-max plist;
     in (march true plist bottom top) ++
        (march false plist top bottom)};
```

Since the computations for all bindings in a block can proceed concurrently, the upward and downward marches automatically proceed in parallel. Of course, the parallelization can be further improved by adopting divide-and-conquer methods such as quickhull [19], which is analogous to quicksort. This involves the modification of the Jarvis-March function, to divide the point set into more than two subsets and combine the results appropriately. The determination of each successive vertex is sequential, as it is a recurrence relation expressed by the **recurrence-list** abstraction. The scanning of all the points is expressed as a sequential reduction of the list. Even then, observe that the partial computations for each point—such as computing the direction vector based on the parameter looking-up?—are automatically overlapped. Recursive doubling techniques may be used to improve this further. If the list can be subdivided easily (*e.g.*, if the lists are represented by arrays), then minima for different sublists can be computed in parallel. It should be mentioned in passing that the reduction is really an accumulation operation, except that the accumulation function is somewhat complex.

6.3.2   LU DECOMPOSITION OF A MATRIX

A classic example for parallelization is the LU decomposition of a matrix [13, 14], which is the first step in solving a system of equations, Ax=b. The matrix A is decomposed into lower and upper triangular matrices, L and U, such that Ly=b and Ux=y. The component matrices L and U are produced in the same storage replacing A by a series of linear transformations on the rows and columns.

Let $A_{k,n}$ denote a square matrix with dimensions (k,n),(k,n). Then it can be partitioned into n-k+1 disjoint sets of elements whose indices are given by band (k,n) $\cup$ band (k+1,n) $\cup \cdots$ band (n,n), where

def band (k,n) = {:k,j | j $\leftarrow$ k **to** n}++ {:i,k | i $\leftarrow$ k+1 **to** n};

Given a matrix $A_{1,n}$, its decomposition matrix, $LU_{1,n}$, is computed in n steps, where the kth step computes the kth band of $LU_{1,n}$ and a temporary matrix $A_{k+1,n}$ to be used in the next step. If B_k denotes the kth band of $LU_{1,n}$, then we have the following recurrence list:

$$(A_{2,n}, B_1), (A_{3,n}, B_2), \cdots (A_{n,n}, B_{n-1})$$

where each pair in the list is computed from the preceding pair. The last band element B_n will be $A_{n,n}$ itself. Imperative programs employ a sequential loop in which the kth iteration computes the kth pair in the above sequence and both $A_{k+1,n}$ and B_k are stored in the original matrix itself. Thus at the end of the computation, LU is produced in the same storage as A.

In a declarative program, the storage cannot be reused in this manner because of single-assignment restriction. A new matrix $A_{k,n}$ must be created corresponding to each item in the recurrence list. However, since all bands B_k are disjoint, we can store them directly in the final result matrix. This is expressed by the following set of mutually recursive bindings:

```
def decompose A =
   {(k,n),ignore = matrix-bounds A
    LU = {matrix ((k,n),(k,n))
            | [i,j] = compute-band-element T (i,j)
                  || T ← ALIST  &
                  limits,ignore = matrix-bounds T  &
                  (i,j) ← band limits};
        ALIST = recurrence-n-list n (gen-nxt-mtrx LU) A;
    in LU };
```

The computation of $A_{k+1,n}$ and B_k in each step requires the determination of a pivot element. In this example, we choose the pivot of a matrix $A_{k,n}$ to be the absolute maximum amongst all the elements in column k. Thus the pivot row number is given by the function

```
def pivot-row A =
   {(k,n),ignore = matrix-bounds A;
    def max-row i j = if (abs A[i,k]) >= (abs A[j,k])
                      then i else j;
    in reduce-list max-row {:i || i ← k to n }};
```

Given the matrix, $A_{k,n}$, the elements of the band B_k are defined as follows: In the row part of the band, the elements will be simply the corresponding elements from the pivot row of $A_{k,n}$. In the column part of the band, each element is the result of dividing the corresponding element in $A_{k,n}$ by the pivot element. Thus the $(i,j)^{th}$ element of the band is given by

```
def compute-band-element A (i,j) =
   {(k,n),ignore = matrix-bounds A;
    p = pivot-row A;
    q = if i == p then k else i;
    in if i == k then T[p,j] else T[q,j]/T[p,k] };
```

The matrix $A_{k+1,n}$ is produced from $A_{k,n}$ as follows. The $(i,j)^{th}$ element of the output matrix is the difference between the corresponding element in $A_{k,n}$ and the product of the corresponding elements in the band B_k. The band elements can be read from LU directly. This is specified by the following function:

```
def gen-nxt-mtrx LU A =
    {(k,n),ignore = matrix-bounds A;
     p = pivot-row A;
     q = if i == p then k else i;
     in {matrix ((k+1,n),(k+1,n))
          | [i,j] = A[q,j] - LU[i,k] * LU[k,j]
          || i ← k+1 to n  & j ← k+1 to n }};
```

Observe that the pivot-row of A is a constant information about A and is unnecessarily recomputed in the above two functions. This can be avoided by replacing the parameter A with a tuple consisting of the matrix and its pivot-row.

The computations of the bands and the successive elements of the ALIST proceed concurrently and stagger themselves at run time due to the dependencies. For a detailed understanding of this effect of lenient execution, the reader is invited to examine the rewrite rules of section 6.4, which show how all concurrency is exposed. It should be noted that this program incurs the cost of additional memory for the intermediate A-matrices, but does not copy any computed elements. In return, it gains the advantage of exposing all parallelism and avoids the burden of having to specify what to do in parallel or when to synchronize. In contrast, an imperative program specifies the barrier synchronizations and the parallel loops within them. As a consequence, it loses some of the pipe-line parallelism and gains by reusing the same storage because of the forced synchronizations.

6.3.3   SPARSE MATRIX MANIPULATIONS

Sparse matrices are important in many numerical computations and conventional programs using them are often hard to parallelize. Here we discuss an example to illustrate how abstractions of sparse matrices can be built just as well and how they are parallelized to the best extent. First we discuss how sparse matrices can be manipulated and later we illustrate how they can be created.

Sparse Matrix Manipulation.   Consider a square sparse matrix, S. Figure 6.2 shows a matrix with four non-zero diagonals, the dark dots indicating non-zero entries. The diagonals of S are numbered as follows: The main diagonal is numbered as zero. Starting from the main diagonal, upper diagonals are numbered 1,2, etc. and all lower diagonals are numbered as -1, -2, etc. Thus, the diagonal containing the $(i,j)^{th}$ element, is numbered $j-i$. In Figure 6.2, the 4 non-zero diagonals have the numbers -3, -1, 0, and 1. The sparse matrix S can be represented by

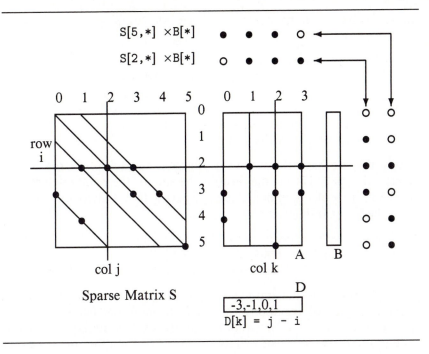

FIGURE 6.2
Representation of a Sparse Matrix S as a Pair (A,D).

the pair (A,D), where A is a matrix and D is a vector. Both S and A have the same number of rows. The number of columns in A is the number of non-zero diagonals and D has the same number of elements. D[k] gives the number of the kth non-zero diagonal. The non-zero element S[i,j] is stored at A[i,k], where D[k] = j - i.

Given the representation, (A,D), of a sparse matrix S, we examine how one of its rows is multiplied with a given vector B. For instance, in Figure 6.2, if row 2 is multiplied with B, elements in columns 1, 2, and 3 of A are multiplied respectively with elements 1, 2, and 3 of B, as indicated at the top of the figure. Similarly when row 5 is multiplied with B, elements in columns 0, 1, and 2 of A are multiplied respectively with elements 2, 4, and 5 of B. That is, we must first determine the columns from A which must participate in a multiplication with row i. The range of participating diagonal numbers is from 0-i through 5-i. We would like to get the corresponding range of column indices in A. The following function gives this index range for intersecting diagonals when only the upper or lower triangular parts of S have to be multiplied. Recall that the function find-range from section 6.2 gives the index range into an

array so that all elements in that range are contained within a given
interval.

```
def diag-range (A,D) row upper? =
    {(amin,amax),(dmin,dmax) = matrix-bounds A;
     low, high = if upper? then 1,(amax - row)
                           else (amin - row),0;
     kmin,kmax = find-range D low high;
     in kmin to kmax };
```

Using this we have the following function to multiply a row with a
vector: If upper? is true, the result is the sum of the pointwise products
of the ith row of the upper triangular part with B. Otherwise it is done
with the lower traingular part.

```
def row-times-vector (A,D) B i upper? =
    sumup-list {: A[i,k] * B[i + D[k]]
               ‖ k ← (diag-range (A,D) i upper?)};
```

We will now illustrate the Gauss-Seidel method of iteration to
solve a system of equations SX=B. Given an initial guess X^0 for the
unknown vector X, the system of equations is solved iteratively by computing successive approximations, $X^1, X^2, \cdots$ using the following relationship:

$$(Z+L) \ X^{n+1} = - \ U \ X^n + B$$

where the matrix S is decomposed into S=Z+L+U, the diagonal Z and lower
and upper triangular matrices, L and U. We assume that we are given
a sparse matrix representation (A,D), in which all three components
Z,L,U are stored in the respective portions of the matrix. For a given X,
we can compute the right-hand side vector, R, of the above equation by
multiplying each row of the upper triangular portion of (A,D) with the
vector X and subtracting the result from the corresponding element of
B. This is expressed by the following function:

```
def right-hand-side (A,D) B X =
    {(amin,amax),(dmin,dmax) = matrix-bounds A;
     in {array (amin,amax)
         | [i] = B[i] - (row-times-vector (A,D) B i true)
                        ‖ i ← amin to (amax - 1)
         | [amax] = 0.0 }};
```

The left-hand side of the equation is computed by back substitution.
That is, given the matrix (A,D) and a right-hand side vector, R, elements
of the unknown vector X are computed as a recurrence. To compute the
i^{th} element of X, we assume that we have the elements 1 through i-1 in
X. We multiply the ith row of the lower triangular portion of (A,D) with

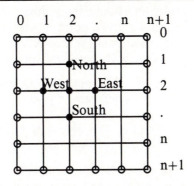

FIGURE 6.3
Interior and Boundary Points in a Grid.

X and subtract it from the ith element of R and finally divide it by the diagonal element. Two things may be noted: we reuse the earlier abstraction of mutiplying a row by a vector and we take advantage of recursive specification of an array in defining X. The function *first-higher-or-equal* from section 6.2 is used to determine the main diagonal index in the vector D. The *gauss-seidel* function computes one step of the iteration:

```
def back-substitution (A,D) R =
    {(amin,amax),(dmin,dmax) = matrix-bounds A;
     diagonal = first-higher-or-equal D 0;
     X = {array (amin,amax)
            | [i] = (R[i] - sum) / A[i,diagonal]
            ‖ i ← amin to amax   &
            sum = (row-times-vector (A,D) X i false)};
    in X };
def gauss-seidel (A,D) X B =
    back-substitution (A,D) (right-hand-side (A,D) X B);
```

Sparse Matrix Creation.   Often the creation of sparse matrices involves complications. We illustrate how some of our abstractions are useful in building the described representation of a sparse matrix from the data in a problem domain. The problem we discuss below occurs in iterative solutions to elliptic partial differential equations with Dirichlet boundary conditions in a two-dimensional rectangular region [10].

Consider an n×n grid of points, surrounded by a boundary layer which is composed of rows 0 and n+1 and columns 0 and n+1. The hollow

circles in Figure 6.3 are the boundary points. The function, inside?
below, determines whether a given point is within the grid or not. The
grid establishes the four neighbors for a node, defined by the functions,
north, south, east and west in a natural way.

```
def inside? (i,j) = (i>0) and (i<=n) and
                    (j>0) and (j<=n);
```

```
def north (i,j) = (i-1,j); def east (i,j) = (i,j+1);
def south (i,j) = (i+1,j); def west (i,j) = (i,j-1);
```

Each point (i,j) is associated with a variable $U_{i,j}$. For points (i,j) on
the boundary, the values of $U_{i,j}$ are known constants. $U_{i,j}$ for the n^2 interior points are the unknowns and must be solved using the following
n^2 equations. There is one equation for each interior grid point, specifying a stabilizing relationship with its neighboring points in the grid.
For example, a constraint, known as the *five-point stencil*, states that
the weighted sum of $U_{i,j}$ for each point and its four neighbors must be
zero. Thus, the stencil defines a list of coefficients and neighborhood
functions as follows:

```
five-point-stencil = (Cn ,north):((Cs,south) :((Ce,east):
                     ((Cw,west) :((Ci,identity): nil))));
def stencil-at (i,j) =
    {:C, f (i,j) || (C,f) ← five-point-stencil };
```

The function stencil-at gives the list of coefficients and the indices
to the corresponding neighboring points, for a given point (i,j). The
constraint at each point (i,j) reduces to the following equation:

```
sum-list {:C * U(f(i,j)) || (C,f) ← stencil-at (i,j) }= 0
```

One can see that this gives rise to a set of equations of the form SU=B,
where U is a vector of size n^2, B is a constant vector and S is a square
matrix of coefficients. This assumes that the variables $U_{i,j}$ are linearly
ordered in some manner. For instance, a natural ordering is given by
the function:

```
def linearize n (i,j) = (i-1) * n + j;
```

The stencil and the linearization determine the sparsity of the matrix
S and the functions we develop can be used with different stencil and
linearize functions. Given the boundary constants for the grid and the
functions stencil and linearize, our problem is to generate the representation (A,D) for the sparse matrix S, without actually allocating any
storage for S during this process. There are 3 steps and we discuss each
of them: (1)determine the number of non-zero diagonals and compute

D, (2)compute the elements of A and (3)compute the right-hand side vector B.

We determine the number of non-zero diagonals by enumerating all the stencil points generated by all the grid points. Each stencil point that is inside the grid contributes to a non-zero entry. We illustrate this using the accumulator abstraction. The array NZ has one entry for each diagonal and is initialized to false. Each time an entry is contributed to the diagonal we mark the entry as true. At the end the indices to the marked entries give the numbers of non-zero diagonals. We use the function list-to-array (not defined here) which returns an array of the elements in the argument list.

```
def interior-points n =
    {: (i,j) ‖ i ← 1 to n  & j ← 1 to n };
def diagonals n =
    {dmin, dmax = 1 - n*n, n*n - 1;
    NZ = {array (dmin,dmax)
            | [i] = false ‖ i ← dmin to dmax
          accumulate (or)
            | d gets true ‖ (i,j) ← interior-points n  &
                            k = linearize (i,j)  &
                            C,(ii,jj) ← stencil-at (i,j)
                            when inside? (ii,jj)  &
                            d = (linearize (ii,jj)) - k };
      in list-to-array {: i ‖ i ← dmin to dmax
                                when NZ[i] }};
```

The matrix A is constructed using similar accumulator abstraction. All entries are initialized to zero. All the stencil points are enumerated as before, and the corresponding coefficients are accumulated.

```
def sparse-matrix n D =
    {dmin,dmax = array-bounds D;
    A = {matrix (0,n*n-1),(dmin,dmax)
            | [i,k] = 0.0 ‖ i ← 0 to n*n-1  &
                            k ← dmin to dmax
          accumulate (+)
            | (i,k) gets c ‖
                    p ← interior-points n  &
                    i = linearize p  &
                    c,q ← stencil-at p when inside? q
                    j = linearize q
                    k = first-greater-or-equal D (j - i) };
      in A };
```

Finally we have to compute the right-hand side vector, B. In each equation, if a stencil point falls outside the grid, it is a constant value and gets shifted to the right-hand side. We initialize vector B to zero and subtract all such coefficients. We assume the constant values of $U_{i,j}$ on the boundary are known.

```
def boundary-points n =
    {: (0,j) || j ← 0 to n+1 }++
    {: (n+1,j) || j ← 0 to n+1 }++
    {: (i,0) || i ← 1 to n }++
    {: (i,n+1) || i ← 1 to n };
def boundary-vector n =
    {array (0,n*n-1)
    | [i] = 0.0 || i ← 0 to n*n-1
    accumulate (+)
    | i gets - c * U_{j,k}
                || p ← boundary-points n  &
                i = linearize p
                c,(j,k) ← stencil-at p
                    when not (inside? (j,k)) };
```

6.4   Operational Semantics

The semantics of Id programs is given by using an abstract reduction system [7, 22]. The distinctive feature of this specification is that the parallel nature of execution is easily understood from it. The specification also renders proofs for properties such as determinacy and efficiency (for example, avoiding multiple evaluation of the same expression, when it is substituted in many places).

Abstract Reduction System.   A program is given as a fixed set of function equations. The state of a program, at any time, is the set of variable bindings made so far and a result expression. Initially, the state consists of only the query expression. As each reduction is made, the state may be changed in three ways: adding new bindings, modifying existing bindings and modifying the result expression. The reduction system is characterized by a fixed set of rules to perform reduction. Each rule specifies a pattern to be found in the state, and a pattern to replace it under a given set of conditions. A pattern satisfying the conditions is called a *redex*. The process of replacing a redex with the new pattern is called *reduction*. When no further reductions are possible, the reduction process *terminates*. When the result expression cannot be reduced any further, it is said to have reached normal form or final *answer*. In the context of parallel processing, one can generally think that many processors could be simultaneously making reductions (on disjoint portions of the state). Hence the reduction systems are interesting only when they have the confluence property. In other words, the order in which reductions are performed does not affect the answer when it is produced.

Strict, Lenient, and Lazy Semantics. At any step in the reduction process, there can be many redexes that can be reduced. Reduction systems impose additional criteria to select a subset of the redexes that can be reduced in each step. Based on these criteria, reduction semantics can be *strict, lazy,* or *lenient* [22].

Strict semantics imposes the following three requirements during evaluation: (1) complete evaluation of all arguments before a function call, (2) complete evaluation of all components before a structure is built, and (3) concurrent evaluation of all right-hand sides in a block. Thus, in general, strict semantics may involve useless computation of some arguments or structure components that are not needed for the final answer. If some of these useless computations are nonterminating, the program fails to produce an answer, although the answer could have been produced if only necessary computation is performed. *Nonstrict* semantics does not impose any of the above restrictions. Both lazy and lenient semantics are nonstrict, but they are different, since each replaces the above three requirements with a different requirement and consequently, have some differences between them.

Lazy semantics imposes only the following single requirement: a reduction cannot be done unless it contributes to the final answer. This ensures that function arguments, structure components, and arms of a conditional are not evaluated unless they are needed. Furthermore, permitting (recursive) dependences between a set of bindings facilitates the construction of objects with unbounded sizes, and only the finite portions needed from them will be evaluated on demand. This feature is extremely useful in high-level programming (for example, see [11, 24]). Implementation of lazy semantics involves working out a scheme to determine at each stage which expressions are needed for the final answer and a *demand-propagation* scheme to initiate the evaluations when the decision is made. Consequently, lazy semantics guarantees minimal computation for a program to produce the answer (not counting the effort of the interpreter to determine which redex must be reduced next). Furthermore, termination of the computation and obtaining the final answer co-occur, as there will be no further reductions when a normal form is reached.

Lenient semantics imposes only the following single requirement: complete evaluation of the predicate before any arm of a conditional is considered. Thus unnecessary computations are avoided only when they are guarded by appropriate conditions. When encountered within the selected arm of a conditional, functions may be invoked before arguments are evaluated and structures may be built before components are evaluated. Consequently, a program may produce a final answer but may never terminate while performing unnecessary computation. That is, a lenient scheme may not produce an answer for some programs for which a lazy scheme will.

Two provisions can be made to alleviate the situation. *Weak normal forms* [21] can be defined to terminate the reduction process when a final answer is reached. Some sort of a *fair scheduling* can be enforced so that unbounded computations do not consume the resources all the time. Under these provisions, the lenient scheme produces the same answers as a lazy scheme with only a bounded amount of excess computation. Of course, error situations in the excess computations complicate matters, causing lenient and lazy schemes to have different semantics.

Despite the above observations, lenient semantics has some advantages to offer. It eliminates substantial effort in the interpreter to select the redexes in each step. It also initiates many computations eagerly (but not speculatively, as in some schemes which evaluate both arms of a conditional and discard one later), thereby increasing the opportunities for parallel execution, much more than either strict or lazy semantics can offer. Architectures [4, 5] can take advantage of eager dispatching of memory operations to mask the latency, a factor that becomes increasingly important as the parallel system grows in size. As an orthogonal issue, parallel systems also make an effort to increase the grain size of parallel tasks to take advantage of the local state in the processor. Thus a program is partitioned into a collection of sequential threads. Instead of reducing expressions, here one reduces threads. When the thread is initiated—that is, selected for reduction—all the operations in that thread will be executed in that order. Forming these threads from a program is complicated because one must worry about data dependencies. A lenient scheme needs to worry about whether the ordering will cause a deadlock, whereas a lazy scheme must also worry about whether all the operations going into the thread are needed for the final answer if the thread is initiated. Consequently, lenient schemes offer a better potential for forming longer sequential threads than lazy schemes [21]. Id has lenient semantics and is targeted for a dataflow architecture that exploits the exposed parallelism. Neither weak normal forms nor fair scheduling strategy is assumed in the current implementations.

```
program   ::= function; .. function;
function  ::= name name .. name = block
block     ::= {binding; .. binding; name, .., name}
binding   ::= name, .., name = expr, .., expr

expr      ::= constant
expr      ::= name
expr      ::= name op name
expr      ::= name name
expr      ::= if name then block else block
```

```
expr      ::= {loop name, .., name; block}
```

```
expr      ::= {tuple name, .., name}
expr      ::= {select integer name}
```

```
expr      ::= {: expr || name ← name to name}
```

```
expr      ::= {array (name,name)
                | [expr] = expr || name ← name to name}
expr      ::= name[name]
```

```
expr      ::= {array (name,name)
                | [expr] = expr || name ← name to name
              accumulate name
                | expr gets  expr || name ← name to name}
```

Note that the symbol | appearing above is a terminal symbol. It should not be confused with the disjunction operator used in the specification of grammars.

FIGURE 6.4
Grammar for Representing a Program at an Intermediate Level.

6.4.1   ID SEMANTICS

Figure 6.4 summarizes the syntax of the program forms that we use here in specifying the operational semantics as well as compiler optimizations. The syntax is very minimal as evidenced by the first few definitions, which specify programs using basic expressions and function applications. The remaining portion of Figure 6.4 consists of some control and structure abstractions that we chose to include in this level of specification to illustrate the semantics for these functional abstractions and also to discuss some optimization transformations that can be performed on them. These abstractions are kept at a minimal level just to keep the level of detail under control in this exposition and to understand the rudiments of each construct. For instance, the generator expressions can be extended to contain filter clauses and array expressions can be extended to contain many iterative clauses. One can easily augment these definitions to cover the full generality offered by the Id language.

In Figure 6.4, the terms *constant*, *name*, and *op* have the obvious forms. The basic idea is that each operation is reflected by a separate variable binding. As noted before, the program state consists of the result expression and the set of variable bindings made so far. Each time a function or a block is instantiated, a uniquely renamed version of the body is added to the state, so that we never have multiple bindings with the same name.

Substitution and Ground Values.   Basically, a reduction rule substitutes *equals for equals*, so that the resultant form is closer (in some sense) to a final irreducible form. Thus, for example, if $A = 10$; $X = A + 5$; are two bindings in the state, then we can substitute 10 for A and rewrite the second binding as $X = 10 + 5$. Similarly, we have primitive reduction rules to replace $10 + 5$ by 15 and so on. Although substitution can take place purely based on pattern matching, we often want to impose additional restrictions for efficiency. For example, if we have the bindings

$$A = B * 2; \quad X = A + 5; \quad Y = A + 6;$$

we can substitute for A and obtain

$$X = B * 2 + 5; \quad Y = B * 2 + 6;$$

However, this is inefficient, since the multiplication is unnecessarily performed twice. Reduction rules deal with this situation by introducing an additional requirement that the substituted value be a *ground value*—that is, a constant and hence will never change. So the reduction rule says

> If $A = V$ is a binding in the state and V is a ground value, then
> $$X = A + Y \quad \Rightarrow \quad X = V + Y$$

That is, the binding $X = A + Y$ can be rewritten as $X = V + Y$ only when the specified preconditions are satisfied. Implicitly, this enforces a certain ordering on the reductions—as in the above example, B and A must be reduced to constants before any attempt is made to reduce X and Y.

Testing for a ground value is a key aspect of this reduction system and as we discuss in Section 6.6, special hardware support for this at a very basic level is extremely useful. This plays a key role in controlling the order of evaluation, as can be seen by the reduction rules we give in this section. Intuitively, each name corresponds to a memory location in any implementation. Binding a ground value to a name corresponds to storing the value in that location. Since there will never be multiple bindings to the same name, this implies *single assignment*—that is, a value is stored in a location at most only one time. Substitution of a value for a name in an expression corresponds to reading the contents of that location. The reduction rules implicitly assume the ability to query the location corresponding to a name and determine if a value is present in it or not. For instance, in the above example we must be able to test whether the location for A contains a constant value or not. Furthermore, reductions imply *data-driven* execution. For example, the addition operation in $X = A + B$ can be triggered as soon as A and B are bound to ground values. This implies some sort of a synchronization in the locations for A and B to signal when the addition can be performed. Thus, an implementation may choose to store some information in the location for A and manipulate this information before the constant value is finally stored there. Thus in general, a location may contain a series of *non-ground* values and finally contain a permanent constant value. Finally, the reduction rules can enable any number of reductions to be performed in one step. Thus the semantics directly reflects the maximum potential for *parallel execution* in a program.

In the sequel, a ground value is any constant, function, or structure. A partial application of a function is also a ground value, since it is just another function. With these ground values, the semantics truly reflects data-driven execution. We will later exploit this facility (of controlling the order of evaluation using tests for ground values) further. For instance, we will introduce special non-ground values to be stored in locations and manipulated. Pre-conditions for some reduction rules may involve testing these values. The accumulator abstraction is an example of this kind. We define the successive partial sums stored in an accumulator location as non-ground values, so that they cannot be substituted. When all the accumulations are completed, we store a ground value.

Notation. We adopt the following conventions for symbols:

- □ We use X,Y,Z,... for single variable names.
- □ We use U,V,W,... for ground values.
- □ We use $a', b', ..$ for new unique names.
- □ We use α, β, .. for arbitrary patterns.
- □ The notation $\alpha^{[aa', bb', ..., cc']}$ stands for the expression α in which every occurence of the name a is replaced by a', every occurence of the name b is replaced by b', etc.

□ A reduction rule is of the form *pre-condition, pattern₁ ⇒ pattern₂*. This means that when the pre-condition is satisfied, *pattern₁* may be replaced by *pattern₂*.

□ All the reductions we specify are at the outer level of bindings contained in the state. We never have to manipulate inner blocks in this reduction process, until they are brought into a top level binding.

Substitution of Values for Names.

---

if $Y = V$ is a binding in the state and V is a ground value, then

$\alpha = Y$	$\Rightarrow$	$\alpha = V$
$\alpha = Y \; op \; \beta$	$\Rightarrow$	$\alpha = V \; op \; \beta$
$\alpha = \beta \; op \; Y$	$\Rightarrow$	$\alpha = \beta \; op \; V$
$\alpha = \textbf{if } Y \textbf{ then } \beta \textbf{ else } \gamma$	$\Rightarrow$	$\alpha = \textbf{if } V \textbf{ then } \beta \textbf{ else } \gamma$
$\alpha = Y \; \beta$	$\Rightarrow$	$\alpha = V \; \beta$
$\alpha = \{\textbf{select } \beta \; Y\}$	$\Rightarrow$	$\alpha = \{\textbf{select } \beta \; V\}$
$\alpha = \beta \; \| \; i \leftarrow Y \textbf{ to } \gamma$	$\Rightarrow$	$\alpha = \beta \; \| \; i \leftarrow V \textbf{ to } \gamma$
$\alpha = \beta \; \| \; i \leftarrow \gamma \textbf{ to } Y \; \delta$	$\Rightarrow$	$\alpha = \beta \; \| \; i \leftarrow \gamma \textbf{ to } V \; \delta$
$\alpha = \{\textbf{array } (Y, \beta) \mid \gamma\}$	$\Rightarrow$	$\alpha = \{\textbf{array } (V, \beta) \mid \gamma\}$
$\alpha = \{\textbf{array } (\beta, Y) \mid \gamma\}$	$\Rightarrow$	$\alpha = \{\textbf{array } (\beta, V) \mid \gamma\}$
$\alpha = Y[\beta]$	$\Rightarrow$	$\alpha = V[\beta]$
$\alpha = \beta[Y]$	$\Rightarrow$	$\alpha = \beta[V]$

Reduction Rule 1

Primitive Reductions.

$X = \textbf{if true then } \alpha \textbf{ else } \beta$	$\Rightarrow$	$X = \alpha$
$X = \textbf{if false then } \alpha \textbf{ else } \beta$	$\Rightarrow$	$X = \beta$

$$X_1, .., X_k = \alpha_1, .., \alpha_k \quad \Rightarrow \quad \begin{array}{l} X_1 = \alpha_1; \\ X_2 = \alpha_2; \\ .... \\ X_k = \alpha_k; \end{array}$$

if U, V, W are ground values such that $U \; op \; V \equiv W$, then

$X = U \; op \; V$	$\Rightarrow$	$X = W$

Reduction Rule 2

Notice the way conditionals are treated. Redexes within an arm of a conditional will never match the patterns we specify and hence cannot be reduced until the arm is selected.

Expanding Blocks.   When a name is bound to a block, new names are chosen and the equations in the block are consistently renamed before adding them to the state.

$$\beta = \{a_1 = \alpha_1; \,.. \, a_n = \alpha_n; \, a_{i_1}, .., a_{i_k}\} \;\; \Rightarrow \;\; \beta = a'_{i_1}, .., a'_{i_k};$$

$$a'_1 = \alpha_1^{[a_1 a'_1, .. a_n a'_n]};$$

$$....$$

$$a'_n = \alpha_n^{[a_1 a'_1, .. a_n a'_n]};$$

Reduction Rule 3

Partial Applications.   New functions can be created by *currying*—that is, by supplying fewer number of arguments than a function needs. A *closure* is a partial application of a function. We show it here as a tuple of the form $(f, a1, a2, .. ak)_{n-k}$, which remembers the function name and the arguments supplied. The subscript $n - k$ gives the remaining number of arguments to be supplied before the function can be invoked. The number of arguments k must be less than the arity, n, of the function f for this closure to be formed. In particular, $(f)_n$ is a closure with zero arguments. Id does not support nullary functions. Hence, a function name, f, is always converted to the partial application $(f)_n$. Closure creations are described by the following rules:

---

if f is the name of a function with arity n, then
$$\beta = f \; \alpha \qquad\qquad\qquad \Rightarrow \qquad \beta = (f)_n \; \alpha$$

if m > 0, then
$$\beta = (f, \alpha_1, .. \, \alpha_k)_m \; \alpha_{k+1} \qquad \Rightarrow \qquad \beta = (f, \alpha_1, .. \, \alpha_k, \alpha_{k+1})_{m-1}$$

Reduction Rule 4

Function Applications.   When the arity is satisfied, a function is instantiated as specified.

---

if $f\ a_1\ ..\ a_n = \gamma$ is a function definition, then

$$\beta = (f, \alpha_1, .. \alpha_n)_0 \qquad\qquad \Rightarrow \qquad a_1' = \alpha_1;\ ..\ ;\ a_n' = \alpha_n;$$

$$\beta = \gamma^{[a_1 a_1', a_2 a_2', ..., a_n a_n']}.$$

Reduction Rule 5

The primes indicate that new unique names are chosen for all the arguments a_i, and β is bound to the block γ after systematically renaming each occurence of a_i with its new name, a_i'. Thus function application is like obtaining a new template of the body of the function with all the formal parameters renamed and binding the new formal parameter names with the actual parameters. Notice that the rules do not require the actual parameters to be ground values. Thus function application is nonstrict, and execution of a function body commences as soon as all arguments are *specified* but not necessarily evaluated. It should also be noted that each argument expression is evaluated only once, although it may be used in many places. To illustrate this, consider the bindings.

$$X = (f, A)_1;\ Y = X\ 5;\ Z = X\ 6;$$

Even though A is still not evaluated, the closure, $(f, A)_1$, can be substituted for X, giving rise to the equations

$$Y = (f, A)_1\ 5;\ Z = (f, A)_1\ 6;$$

If f is the simple function: **def** $f\ a\ b = a+b$, then the two instantiations can take place giving the equations

$$a' = A;\ Y = a' + 5;\ a'' = A;\ Z = a'' + 6;$$

These equations remain unchanged until A is bound to a ground value, at which time that value gets substituted for both a' and a''.

Tuple Structures.   A tuple structure is a sequence of values and is created by specifying all the components. Individual components can be selected by specifying (compile-time) constant indices. The notation for tuples given in Figure 6.4 is different from what the Id language provides. We choose this notation for convenience in our exposition, and the equivalence of the two notations can be seen below:

```
X = e1,e2,e3      ≡      X = {tuple e1,e2,e3};
```

```
                          b1 = {select 1 X};
b1,b2,b3 = X;     ≡      b2 = {select 2 X};
                          b3 = {select 3 X};
```

Tuple creation and component selection are specified as follows:

---

if k is an integer constant, then
$$X = \{\textbf{tuple } \alpha_1, \ .. \ , \alpha_k\} \ \Rightarrow X = \S a'_1, ..a'_k \S \ ;$$
$$a'_1 = \alpha_1;$$
$$...$$
$$a'_k = \alpha_k;$$

if i,k are integers such that $1 <= i <= k$, *then*
$$Y = \{\textbf{select } i \ \S a_1, ..a_k \S \ \} \ \Rightarrow \ Y = a_i;$$

Reduction Rule 6

The primed symbols, $a'_1, ..a'_k$, are new unique names chosen to stand for the individual components of the tuple structure. The conglomerate, $\S a'_1, ..a'_k \S$, represents the value of the tuple structure. This is a *ground value* and can be substituted for X. The structure value can be propagated even before the individual component bindings take place. Thus, tuples are *non-strict*. A component is selected by specifying a constant index. This results in replacing the selector expression by the corresponding name of the component, as shown by the second rule. Thus a two-tuple is a *non-strict cons* and conventional list structures can be constructed using it.

Iterative Constructs.   Although iterative constructs can be viewed as semantically equivalent to tail recursive expressions, we illustrate a form of loop expression and give the rules for reducing it. Later we will use this form to specify some loop optimizations. Loop expression is defined in Figure 6.4 and has the following general form: $\{\textbf{loop } b_0, b_1, \ .. \ , b_k; \ \beta\}$, where the block β is of the form $\{binding; ..; binding; \ a_0, a_1, \ .. \ , a_k\}$. The $k + 1$ values, $b_0, b_1, \ .. \ b_k$, are the loop inputs and the loop produces an equal number of output values, $a_0, a_1, \ .. \ a_k$. The first name b_0 is taken as the input predicate value and the output predicate value is bound to a_0. Note that we use the term *input* to the loop to refer only to the circulating values and not to constant inputs to a loop. The following example illustrates the loop construct:

$$
\begin{array}{ll}
y = \{\textbf{while } b \ \textbf{do} & y = \{\textbf{loop } b, x; \\
\quad \textbf{next } b = f \ b \ x; & \quad \{b' = f \ b \ x; \\
\quad \textbf{next } x = gx; \qquad \equiv & \quad x' = g \ x; \\
\quad \textbf{finally } x\} & \quad b', x'\}\}
\end{array}
$$

The loop is supplied with initial values of b and x. If b is true, then one iteration of the loop takes place computing new values b' and x' and the loop construct is reinvoked with the new inputs. The loop terminates when the input value b is false and the output of the loop is the final value x. This is specified by the following rules:

---

*If $b_0 = $ **true** is a binding in the state, then*

$$\alpha = \{\textbf{loop}\ b_0, b_1, .., b_k;\ \beta\} \quad \Rightarrow \quad \begin{aligned} & a'_0, a'_1, .., a'_k = \beta; \\ & \alpha = \{\textbf{loop}\ a'_0, a'_1, .., a'_k; \\ & \quad\quad \beta^{[b_0 a'_0, b_1 a'_1, ..., b_k a'_k]}\} \end{aligned}$$

*If $b_0 = $ **false** is a binding in the state, then*
$$\alpha = \{\textbf{loop}\ b_0, b_1, .., b_k;\ \beta\} \quad \Rightarrow \quad \alpha = b_1, .., b_k$$

Reduction Rule 7

List Structures.   We represent a list as a sequence of two-tuples. The first component of each tuple is an element of the list and the second component of a tuple is a pointer to the next tuple in the sequence. The last tuple will have *nil* as its second component, to indicate the end. The following rules specify how a list expression is reduced. The list expression is rewritten by the first rule to a form that remembers that the tail end of the list should be marked as *nil* (indicated by the superscript $^{++\ nil}$. This form is convenient to do a concatenation of lists, as described later.

Once the iteration limits are known, two possibilities exist. If the range is null, then the name X is simply bound to the tail end, which is *nil* in this case. Otherwise, one two-tuple is constructed for each element in the range and the head of the tuple is bound to the given expression. All the tuples are linked by their tails. Standard list manipulation functions to select the elements of the list can be imagined. We can see that although the iteration clause determines the final ordering of the elements in the constructed list, the reduction steps clearly exhibit concurrency in the actual linking process. The nonstrictness of tuples facilitates the computation of all the elements in parallel and the iterative specification is a convenient way to specify the elements of the list from head to tail.

A concatenation of lists can be done using the infix operator $++$. This will, in general, imply that the first list will have to be copied. When a sub-list is used only for concatenation with another list, we can avoid the copying of the list. To facilitate this optimization, we define

$X = \{: \alpha \parallel i \leftarrow m \text{ to } n\}$ $\qquad \Rightarrow X = \{: \alpha \parallel i \leftarrow m \text{ to } n\}^{++ \; nil}$

if m,n are integers such that m > n, then
$X = \{: \alpha \parallel i \leftarrow m \text{ to } n\}^{++ \; \gamma}$ $\quad \Rightarrow X = \gamma$

if m,n are integers such that m <= n, then
$X = \{: \alpha \parallel i \leftarrow m \text{ to } n\}^{++ \; \gamma}$ $\quad \Rightarrow X = c'_m;$

$\qquad c'_m = \S a'_m, b'_m \S \; ;$
$\qquad a'_m = \alpha^{[im]};$
$\qquad b'_m = c'_{m+1};$

$\qquad c'_{m+1} = \S a'_{m+1}, b'_{m+1} \S \; ;$
$\qquad a'_{m+1} = \alpha^{[i(m+1)]};$
$\qquad b'_{m+1} = c'_{m+2};$
$\qquad \ldots$
$\qquad c'_n = \S a'_n, \gamma \S \; ;$
$\qquad a'_n = \alpha^{[in]};$

Reduction Rule 8

the following construct, which is not part of Id but is equivalent to the Id expression shown on the right.

$$
\begin{array}{ccc}
\{: \alpha_1 \parallel i \leftarrow m_1 \text{ to } n_1 & & \{: \alpha_1 \parallel i \leftarrow m_1 \text{ to } n_1\} \; ++ \\
\mid \alpha_2 \parallel i \leftarrow m_2 \text{ to } n_2 & & \{: \alpha_2 \parallel i \leftarrow m_2 \text{ to } n_2\} \; ++ \\
\mid \; \ldots & \equiv & \ldots \qquad\qquad ++ \\
\mid \alpha_k \parallel i \leftarrow m_k \text{ to } n_k\} & & \{: \alpha_k \parallel i \leftarrow m_k \text{ to } n_k\}
\end{array}
$$

Such a construct can be efficiently executed as shown below, without copying the sublists:

$$
\begin{array}{lll}
& & X = x'_1; \\
X = \{: \alpha_1 \parallel i \leftarrow m_1 \text{ to } n_1 & \Rightarrow & x'_1 = \{: \alpha_1 \parallel i \leftarrow m_1 \text{ to } n_1\}^{++ \; x'_2} \\
\mid \alpha_2 \parallel i \leftarrow m_2 \text{ to } n_2\} & & x'_2 = \{: \alpha_2 \parallel i \leftarrow m_2 \text{ to } n_2\}^{++ \; x'_3} \\
\mid \ldots & & \ldots \\
\mid \alpha_k \parallel i \leftarrow m_k \text{ to } n_k\} & & x'_k = \{: \alpha_k \parallel i \leftarrow m_k \text{ to } n_k\}^{++ \; nil}
\end{array}
$$

Reduction Rule 9

Array Structures.   The array structure is very similar to the tuple structure, except that both the number of components and index selectors are computable constants and may not be known at compile time. We illustrate the structure semantics for one simple case of array comprehension in Id, where we permit only one clause as shown in Figure 6.4. An array is created as shown below:

$$
\begin{aligned}
&\textit{if } m,n \textit{ are integers such that } m <= n, \textit{ then}\\
&\quad X = \{\mathbf{array}\ (m, n) && \Rightarrow && X = \langle a'_m, ..a'_n \rangle\ ;\\
&\quad \quad |\ [\alpha] = \beta\ \|\ i \leftarrow p \textbf{ to } q\} && && X[\alpha^{[ii']}] = \beta^{[ii']}\ \|\ i' \leftarrow p \textbf{ to } q;\\[4pt]
&\textit{if } p,q \textit{ are integers such that } p <= q, \textit{ then}\\
& && && b'_p = \alpha^{[ip]};\ \ \gamma[b'_p] = \beta^{[ip]};\\
&\quad \gamma[\alpha] = \beta\ \|\ i \leftarrow p \textbf{ to } q && \Rightarrow && ....\\
& && && b'_q = \alpha^{[iq]};\ \ \gamma[b'_q] = \beta^{[iq]};
\end{aligned}
$$

Reduction Rule 10

As before, the primed symbols are new unique names. The double subscript notation indicates renaming of free variables. To distinguish arrays from tuples, we use the notation, $\langle a_1, ..a_k \rangle$ to denote an array structure value, which is again a *ground value* and hence can be used for substitution. The first rule creates one new name, a'_i, for each element of the array. The array structure is also *nonstrict* and can be propagated by substituting for X, even before component values are bound. The rule also creates a schema for the component bindings. The iterator name, i, is renamed to i' to avoid any naming conflicts. The second rule expands this schema into individual bindings, one for each element. For instance, for the case $i = p$, a new name b'_p is bound to the corresponding index expression obtained by replacing i by p in α. The corresponding array element is bound to the expression obtained by replacing i by p in β. By substituting for X, index expressions of the form $X[k]$ can be reduced to $\langle a_m, ..a_n \rangle\ [k]$, which can then be reduced to the individual component names as specified by the following rules:

$$
\begin{aligned}
&\textit{if } k,m,n \textit{ are integers such that } m <= k <= n, \textit{ then}\\
&\quad \langle a_m, ..a_n \rangle\ [k] = \alpha && \Rightarrow && a_k = \alpha\\
&\quad \alpha = \langle a_m, ..a_n \rangle\ [k] && \Rightarrow && \alpha = a_k
\end{aligned}
$$

Reduction Rule 11

We can observe from the reduction rules for the arrays, that the production and consumption of values to the individual components of an array can proceed concurrently. A component value can be consumed (that is, substituted) as and when it is produced. This suggests the need for element-level synchronization in implementation. In the same vein, nonstrict arrays make it possible to construct programs in which a consumer hangs up as the corresponding component is never produced. For instance, consider the following program:

$$\{A = \{\textbf{array}\ (1,3)\ |\ [i] = i\ \|\ i \leftarrow 1\ \textbf{to}\ 2\}$$
$$\textbf{in}\quad A[3]\}$$

The array $\langle a_1, a_2, a_3 \rangle$ is created, and the components a_1 and a_2 are respectively bound to values 1 and 2. No further reductions are possible after this and the result expression a_3 does not still become a ground value. The meaning of this situation is deemed to be *undefined* or *bottom*.

Array comprehensions are truly *functional* as they have a unique value and possess the seminal property of referential transparency. For example, the program

$$X = \{\textbf{array}\ (m,n)\ |\ [\alpha] = \beta\ \|\ i \leftarrow p\ \textbf{to}\ q\}$$
$$Y = \{\textbf{array}\ (m,n)\ |\ [\alpha] = \beta\ \|\ i \leftarrow p\ \textbf{to}\ q\}$$
$$Z = f\ X\ Y;$$

is semantically equivalent to the following program:

$$X = \{\textbf{array}\ (m,n)\ |\ [\alpha] = \beta\ \|\ i \leftarrow p\ \textbf{to}\ q\}$$
$$Z = f\ X\ X;$$

The former program allocates two array structures and computes their component values twice—once for each structure. The latter program is an optimization resulting from the observation that two expressions bound to X and Y are identical and hence X and Y can be substituted as *equals for equals*. But their results are the same.

Notice that the reduction rules force the evaluation of all the component values of an array, whether they are required for the final answer or not. As pointed out earlier, this leniency may result in a nonterminating computation, although the final answer may have been computed (thus, semantically differing from a lazy scheme).

The reader can verify that the semantics can be easily extended for the more general array construct of Section 6.2.2, with different generating clauses for different regions of an array. In particular, the recursive construction of the array of Fibonacci numbers gives rise to the following excerpts of reduction sequence:

$$F = \{\textbf{array}\ (1,4)$$
$$\quad |\ [i] = 1\ \|\ i \leftarrow 1\ \textbf{to}\ 2$$
$$\quad |\ [i] = F[i-2] + F[i-1]\ \|\ i \leftarrow 3\ \textbf{to}\ 4\};$$

$\Rightarrow \quad F = \langle a_1, a_2, a_3, a_4 \rangle\ ;$
$$F[i'] = 1\ \|\ i' \leftarrow 1\ \textbf{to}\ 2$$
$$F[i''] = F[i''-2] + F[i''-1]\ \|\ i'' \leftarrow 3\ \textbf{to}\ 4;$$

$\Rightarrow \quad F = \langle a_1, a_2, a_3, a_4 \rangle\ ;$
$$i'_1 = 1;\ F[i'_1] = 1;\ i'_2 = 2;\ F[i'_2] = 1;$$
$$i''_3 = 3;\ F[i''_3] = F[i''_3 - 2] + F[i''_3 - 1];$$
$$i''_4 = 4;\ F[i''_4] = F[i''_4 - 2] + F[i''_4 - 1];$$

$\Rightarrow \quad F = \langle a_1, a_2, a_3, a_4 \rangle\ ;$
$$F[1] = 1;\ F[2] = 1;$$
$$F[3] = F[1] + F[2];\ F[4] = F[2] + F[3];$$

$\Rightarrow \quad \langle a_1, a_2, a_3, a_4 \rangle\ [1] = 1;\ \langle a_1, a_2, a_3, a_4 \rangle\ [2] = 1;$
$$\langle a_1, a_2, a_3, a_4 \rangle\ [3] = \langle a_1, a_2, a_3, a_4 \rangle\ [1] + \langle a_1, a_2, a_3, a_4 \rangle\ [2];$$
$$\langle a_1, a_2, a_3, a_4 \rangle\ [4] = \langle a_1, a_2, a_3, a_4 \rangle\ [2] + \langle a_1, a_2, a_3, a_4 \rangle\ [3];$$

$\Rightarrow \quad a_1 = 1;\ a_2 = 1;$
$$a_3 = a_1 + a_2;\ a_4 = a_2 + a_3;$$

6.4.2 STRICT ARRAYS

Now we describe a variant of array comprehension called *strict array*. This is an artifact purely for expository convenience and is not part of the Id language. We use this to simplify our forthcoming presentation of the accumulator semantics. Strict array is the same as the array comprehension presented above, except that *the array is available only after all the element bindings have been completed.* That is, the binding $X = \langle a_m, ..a_n \rangle$ cannot take effect until all components a_i are bound to ground values. One way to look at this is that we must impose additional conditions to substitute the array value for X. We accomplish this by defining a new non-ground value to be bound to X, and some rules to define when it should be converted to a ground value. We keep a count of the element bindings made, and when the required number of bindings are made, X is bound to the array value.

Syntactically, the strict array construct is identical to the array construct, except that the keyword **array** is replaced by the keyword **strict-array**. The reduction rule for the strict-array comprehension is given below:

$$
\begin{array}{l}
\textit{if m,n are integers such that } m <= n, \textit{ then} \\
\begin{array}{ll}
X = \{\textbf{strict-array}\,(m, n) \\
\quad\quad | \, [\alpha] = \beta \parallel i \leftarrow p \textbf{ to } q\}
\end{array}
\Rightarrow
\begin{array}{l}
X = \langle\!\langle n - m + 1, a'_m, ..a'_n \rangle\!\rangle \; ; \\
X' = \langle a'_m, ..a'_n \rangle \; ; \\
X[\alpha^{[ii',xx']}] = \\
\quad \beta^{[ii',xx']} \parallel i' \leftarrow p \textbf{ to } q;
\end{array}
\end{array}
$$

Reduction Rule 12

New names, a'_i, are chosen for the array elements as before. However, the name X is not bound to the array value $\langle a'_m, ..a'_n \rangle$. Instead, it is bound to a *non-ground value* $\langle\!\langle n - m + 1, a'_m, ..a'_n \rangle\!\rangle$, in which the first component, $n - m + 1$, records how many more element bindings have to be done for this to become a ground value. A new name, X', is bound to the structure value, $\langle a'_m, ..a'_n \rangle$, which is used internally for any recursive computation of array elements, as illustrated by the Fibonacci number array. Because X is a non-ground value, element bindings of the form $X[k] = V$ cannot be reduced as before. Instead we use the following rule to perform the element bindings, so that we can count them.

$$
\begin{array}{l}
\textit{if k,m,n,c are integers such that } m <= k <= n, \, c > 0 \\
\textit{and V is a ground value, then} \\
\begin{array}{ll}
X = \langle\!\langle c, a_m, ..a_n \rangle\!\rangle \; ; \\
X[k] = V;
\end{array}
\Rightarrow
\begin{array}{l}
X = \langle\!\langle c - 1, a_m, ..a_n \rangle\!\rangle \; ; \\
a_k = V;
\end{array}
\end{array}
$$

Reduction Rule 13

Finally, when the count reaches zero, then X can be bound to the array value, as shown by the following rule:

$$
X = \langle\!\langle 0, a_m, ..a_n \rangle\!\rangle \quad\quad \Rightarrow X = \langle a_m, ..a_n \rangle \; ;
$$

Reduction Rule 14

As a result, the name X is not bound to a ground value until all the n element bindings are done, each time decrementing the count by 1.

We note that this is the first time we specify a reduction rule that modifies more than one equation in one reduction step. This implies that the implementation must have some means to enforce the atomicity of updating two equations. It should be clear that the final value of X is the same deterministic array irrespective of whether **array** or **strict-array** is used. Thus strict-array is truly an array with additional restriction about when the result value should be available.

Strict Arrays Revisited.   One consequence of a strict array is that when the value of the result array is available, we can be sure that no other access to the array can be in progress. The array is created, filled, and handed to us just now and until we pass it further, no one else has access to it. (That is, the reference count to the array is 1 when its final value is available.) This is a very useful information and under certain circumstances, we can utilize this information to modify the array in place without losing determinacy. To this end, we define yet another artifact that takes a strict array as input and returns the same strict array after performing concurrently all specified modifications to it.

Obviously, we cannot permit any arbitrary modifications, or else we will lose determinacy. For instance, we cannot have recurrences in the modifications—that is, the new value of an element cannot depend on the value (new or old) of another element because this would imply that the modifications must be performed in a certain order and the program must specify this. However, we can permit self recursion—that is, the new value of an element is a function of its old value. Now, if all the self-recursive modifications are on disjoint elements, then determinacy can be guaranteed. Alternatively, multiple self-recursive modifications on an element can be permitted if the modifying function is associative and commutative, so that the order of modifications does not matter. We will assume this and specify the following rule for reducing a strict-array construct intended for modification:

$$X = \{\textbf{strict-array}\ \langle a_m, ..a_n \rangle \qquad \Rightarrow \qquad X = \langle\!\langle q - p + 1, a_m, ..a_n \rangle\!\rangle\ ;$$
$$|\ [\alpha] = \textbf{gets}\ \ \beta\ \|\ i \leftarrow p\ \textbf{to}\ q\} \qquad \qquad X[\alpha^{[ii']}] =$$
$$\textbf{gets}\ \ \beta^{[ii']}\ \|\ i' \leftarrow p\ \textbf{to}\ q;$$

Reduction Rule 15

Here the strict-array construct takes a strict array, $\langle a_m, ..a_n \rangle$, in place of dimensions. So we do not create a new array and instead take the given array in which all elements have been assumed to be initialized. The element binding clause has the new phrase $[\alpha]$ **gets** β, where β will be of the form $op\ V$ and the effect is to replace the element $X[\alpha]$ by the value $op\ V\ X[\alpha]$. As before, the name X is bound to a hidden non-ground value, $\langle\!\langle c, f, a_m, ..a_n \rangle\!\rangle$. The count, c, is set to the number of bindings specified in the construct (because the number of modifications to be made may be different from the size). (Comparing this with Rule 12, there is no X' here, because we disallow recursion.) The element modifications must decrement the count as specified below:

> *if k,m,n,c are integers such that* $m <= k <= n, c > 0$
> *and U,V,W are ground values, such that* $U\ op\ V \equiv W$, *then*
> $$X = \langle\!\langle c, a_m, ..a_n \rangle\!\rangle\ ;\qquad\qquad X = \langle\!\langle c - 1, a_m, ..a_n \rangle\!\rangle\ ;$$
> $$a_k = V;\qquad\qquad\qquad\Rightarrow\qquad a_k = W;$$
> $$X[k] = \textbf{gets}\ op\ U;$$
>
> **Reduction Rule 16**

Note that the precondition must check three equations: the equation for X containing the count, the equation specifying the new binding for the component a_k, and the existing binding for the component a_k. The reduction decrements the count in the equation for X, replaces the old equation for a_k with the new value, and *deletes the new binding equation from the state*. The last step is important since we do not want to execute the same action again. X will be bound with the final value of the array as before, when the count reaches zero.

The determinacy of the structure value in this construct requires the following two conditions to be satisfied:

1. The construct must have exclusive access to its input structure. That is, when this construct is activated, no other program component can have access to it, and such access is granted only after this construct completes execution.
2. The operation *op* in the **gets** clause must be commutative and associative, and it must be a simple operation to be performed atomically as part of the memory update.

6.4.3 ACCUMULATORS

Using strict arrays, we can specify the semantics for an accumulator construct. We define a simple version of the accumulator, as shown in Figure 6.4, which has only one clause (extension to multiple clauses is straightforward). We will have appropriate rules for substitution of values to names in these constructs. The rule for reducing the accumulator expression is shown below.

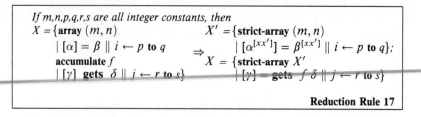

If m,n,p,q,r,s are all integer constants, then

$X = \{\textbf{array }(m, n)$

$\quad | [\alpha] = \beta \| i \leftarrow p \text{ to } q$

$\quad \textbf{accumulate } f$

$\quad | [\gamma] \textbf{ gets } \delta \| j \leftarrow r \text{ to } s\}$

$\Rightarrow$

$X' = \{\textbf{strict-array }(m, n)$

$\quad | [\alpha^{[xx']}] = \beta^{[xx']} \| i \leftarrow p \text{ to } q\};$

$X = \{\textbf{strict-array } X'$

$\quad | [\gamma] \textbf{ gets } f\, \delta \| j \leftarrow r \text{ to } s\}$

Reduction Rule 17

The array X' is a strict-array which will be returned after all the initializations are done. Since X' is a new name used nowhere else except in the equation for X, it is guaranteed that when X' is bound to the value, no other program component has access to it. The name X is also a strict-array, thereby guaranteeing that its value is not available until all the modifications are completed. Thus the accumulator value will be deterministic if the function f is commutative and associative. Also note that if all the elements that are to be modified are not initialized to begin with, the reduction process will not yield a result value. Similarly, if a number of initializations is specified that is larger than the size of the array, it results in multiple bindings to the same name, which is considered as an error value for the whole program.

6.5   Optimizing Transformations

As discussed in [20, 21], one of the advantages of the intermediate forms is that many optimizations can be performed on this form itself. Subsequently it was observed in [1] that compiler optimizations can also be expressed as rewrite rules for the intermediate form. In this section, we illustrate these optimization transformations.

Unique Names Within Each Function.   Optimization specifications are greatly simplified if we assume that all names within a function definition are all distinct. We can always rename any program to satisfy this constraint. Such renaming involves the following.

- □ For conditional expressions, choose a new unique name for each name bound in an arm and rename all its occurences within that arm.
- □ For a loop expression, choose a new unique name for each name bound in the body of the loop and rename all its occurences within the loop.
- □ For list, array, and accumulator expressions, an iterator name must be replaced by a new unique name.

The above steps ensure that any name within a function definition will have one and only one binding. We assume this form of programs in all the optimizations specified below.

For any block, β, we define the following relation on the set of names bound in the block:

$$a \rightarrow_\beta b \quad \Leftrightarrow \quad \textit{there is a binding in } \beta, \textit{ such that}$$
$$\textit{a appears on its left-hand side and}$$
$$\textit{b appears on its right-hand side.}$$

This implies that there is a data dependence from b to a. That is, a can be reduced only after b has been reduced. We define the usual extension,

$$a \stackrel{*}{\rightarrow}_\beta b \quad \Leftrightarrow \quad a \rightarrow_\beta c_1 \rightarrow_\beta c_2 \rightarrow_\beta \; .. \; \rightarrow_\beta c_k \rightarrow_\beta b$$

This relation is easily computable and we use it in the following optimizations.

Constant Propagation.

$$\begin{array}{lcl}
\gamma = \textbf{if true then } \alpha \textbf{ else } \beta & \Rightarrow & \gamma = \alpha \\
\gamma = \textbf{if false then } \alpha \textbf{ else } \beta & \Rightarrow & \gamma = \beta
\end{array}$$

If $b_0 = \textbf{false}$ is a binding, then
$$\begin{array}{lcl}
\alpha = \{\textbf{loop } b_0, b_1, .., b_k; \; \beta\} & \Rightarrow & \alpha = b_1, .., b_k
\end{array}$$

If $f\; a_1 \; .. \; a_n = \beta; \;$ is a function definition, then
$$\begin{array}{lcl}
\alpha = f\; \beta; & \Rightarrow & \alpha = (f)_n \; \beta;
\end{array}$$

If $m > 0$, then
$$\begin{array}{lcl}
\alpha = (\beta)_m \; X; & \Rightarrow & \alpha = (\beta, X)_{m-1};
\end{array}$$

If V is a constant, and $Y = V$ is a binding, then
$$\begin{array}{lcl}
\alpha = \beta; & \Rightarrow & \alpha = \beta^{[Y\,V]};
\end{array}$$

Optimization Rule 1

The last rule relies on the fact that all inner blocks and iterator names have been renamed so that a name has only one binding in the entire program.

Inline Substitution.

> *Given the function definition:* $f\ a_1\ ..\ a_n = \beta$, *then*
>
> $$\gamma = (f, \alpha_1, .., \alpha_n)_0 \qquad \Rightarrow \qquad \gamma = \beta^{[a_1 a_1',\, a_2 a_2',\, ...\, a_n a_n']};$$
> $$a_1' = \alpha_1; \ ..; \ a_n' = \alpha_n;$$
>
> **Optimization Rule 2**

In the above rule, the primes indicate new unique names and the superscript in square brackets indicates α-renaming. Thus a full application of a function can be replaced by an instantiation of its body.

Common Subexpression Elimination.

> *If γ is any expression other than a name or constant and
> if $\alpha = \gamma$ is a binding in the state, then*
>
> $$\beta = \gamma; \qquad\qquad \Rightarrow \qquad \beta = \alpha;$$
>
> **Optimization Rule 3**

This is true because the expressions defined in the preceding sections are all truly functional and equals can be replaced by equals.

Fetch Elimination.

> *If $X = \{$**tuple** $\alpha_1, \ .. \ , \alpha_k\}$ is a binding in the state
> and i is an integer such that, $1 <= i <= k$, then*
> $$Y = \{\textbf{select } i\ x\}; \qquad \Rightarrow \quad Y = \alpha_i;$$
>
> **Optimization Rule 4**

This eliminates the selection operation. By repeated application of this rule, if all the selectors of X are replaced by the corresponding expressions, then the tuple construction itself becomes useless and is eliminated as dead code.

Hoisting Code Out of a Loop.   Recall that in the loop construct, $\{$**loop** $b_0, .., b_k; binding; ..binding; a_0, .., a_k\}$, the b's are inputs and a's are outputs of the loop. Any expression in the body that does not depend on any of the inputs or outputs must be a loop invariant and hence can be moved outside the loop. This optimization can change the termination characteristics, if the loop predicate is false to begin with.

If α is neither a constant nor a name and,

$$Y \not\xrightarrow{*}_\beta b_j, \; Y \not\xrightarrow{*}_\beta a_j, \text{ for all } 0 <= j <= k, \text{ then}$$
using a new unique name, Y', rewrite:

$$
\begin{array}{lll}
X = \{\text{loop } b_0, .., b_k; & \Rightarrow & X = \{\text{loop } b_0, .., b_k; \\
\quad Y = \alpha;..; & & \quad Y = Y';..; \\
\quad a_0, .., a_k\} & & \quad a_0, .., a_k\} \\
& Y' = \alpha; &
\end{array}
$$

Optimization Rule 5

Similarly, if an output is identical to an input (either using identical names or through equations), then it is a loop invariant and hence can be removed from the input-output list of the loop. This is expressed by the following rule. (Note that any expressions involving only this name will be moved outside the loop by the preceding rule.)

For any $0 < i <= n$, if either the names a_i and b_i are identical, or the loop body contains the following bindings for some $k >= 0$
$$a_i = x_{j_1}; \; x_{j_1} = x_{j_2}; \; ... \; x_{j_k} = b_i; \text{ then}$$

$$
\begin{array}{lll}
X = \{\text{loop } b_0, .., b_n; & \Rightarrow & X = \{\text{loop } b_0, .., b_{i-1}, b_{i+1}, .., b_n; \\
\quad .... & & \quad .... \\
\quad a_0, .., a_n\} & & \quad a_0, .., a_{i-1}, a_{i+1}, .., a_n\}
\end{array}
$$

Optimization Rule 6

Hoisting Code Out of an Array Expression. This is very similar to hoisting code out of a loop. The array expression has an implicit loop specifying the component bindings, and constant expressions from it can be moved out, as specified by the following:

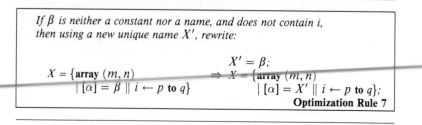

If β is neither a constant nor a name, and does not contain i,
then using a new unique name X', rewrite:

$$X' = \beta;$$

$$X = \{\textbf{array }(m, n) \qquad \Rightarrow X = \{\textbf{array }(m, n)$$
$$\mid [\alpha] = \beta \parallel i \leftarrow p \textbf{ to } q\} \qquad \mid [\alpha] = X' \parallel i \leftarrow p \textbf{ to } q\};$$

Optimization Rule 7

Hoisting Code Out of a Conditional.   When an expression appears on both
sides of a conditional, it can be computed ahead of time by moving it
outside the conditional. In addition, this eliminates the need to switch
its input values into the arms of the conditional. This is expressed by
the following rule:

If all names in β are free in **both** the two enclosing blocks,
then using a new unique name, X', rewrite:

$$X' = \beta;$$

$$\gamma = \textbf{if } \alpha \qquad\qquad \gamma = \textbf{if } \alpha$$
$$\qquad \textbf{then } \{ .. \ Y = \beta; \ .. \} \qquad \Rightarrow \qquad \textbf{then } \{ .. \ Y = X'; \ .. \}$$
$$\qquad \textbf{else } \{ .. \ Z = \beta; \ .. \}; \qquad\qquad \textbf{else } \{ .. \ Z = X'; \ .. \};$$

Optimization Rule 8

Eliminating Dead Code from a Block.   A computation within a block is
dead if it does not contribute to any of its outputs. Such code can be
eliminated without changing the meaning. This can change the termination characteristics, if the eliminated code does not terminate or causes
error.

If $c_1, .., c_m = \alpha$ is a binding in a block β,
whose outputs are $a_1, .., a_n$ and

$a_i \not\xrightarrow{*}_\beta c_j$, for all $1 <= i <= n$, $1 <= j <= m$, then
delete the binding $c_1, .., c_m = \alpha$ from β.

Optimization Rule 9

Hoisting Code Out of a Partial Application.   The intuitive idea behind this
optimization can be explained through the following example. Consider
the array expression: $\{\textbf{array }(1, m) \mid [\alpha] = (f, a_1, .., a_{n-1})_1 \ i \parallel i \leftarrow 1$
$\textbf{to } m\}$, where all the a_j are constants not depending on i. Further-
more, suppose that in the body of the function, f, there is a substantial

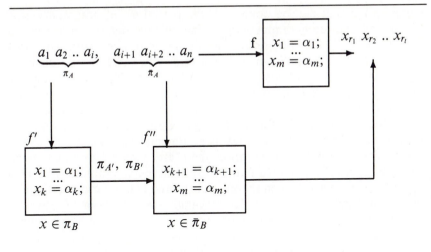

$$f \ a_1 \ a_2 \ .. \ a_n = \{x_1 = \alpha_1; \quad ... \quad x_m = \alpha_m; \quad x_{r_1}, \ .., \ x_{r_t}\}$$
$$f \ a_1 \ a_2 \ .. \ a_n \equiv f'' \ (f' \ a_1 \ .. \ a_i) \ a_{i+1} \ .. \ a_n;$$

FIGURE 6.5
Splitting a Function to Separate Partial Computation.

computation performed using only the arguments, $a_1 \ a_2 \ .. \ a_{n-1}$. All this computation will be repeated for each value of i. Splitting f will enable us to move this invariant computation outside the loop. That is, let $c_1, ..., c_k = f' \ a_1 \ a_2 \ .. \ a_{n-1}$ and replace $(f \ a_1 \ a_2 \ .. \ a_n)$ by $(f'' \ c_1 \ c_2 \ .. \ c_k \ a_n)$. Here f' and f'' are two new functions that do the appropriate things.

Figure 6.5 generalizes this further. Given the function definition, $f \ a_1 \ a_2 \ .. \ a_n = \beta$, and some integer constant $1 <= i <= n$, define the following partitions on the names appearing in the definition:

$\pi_A = \{a_1, \ .., \ a_i\}, \quad \bar{\pi}_A = \{a_{i+1}, \ .., \ a_n\}.$

$\pi_B = \{x \mid x = \alpha \ \textit{is a binding in } \beta \ \textit{and } \forall a \in \bar{\pi}_A, \ x \not\to_\beta^* a\}.$

$\bar{\pi}_B = \{x \mid x = \alpha \ \textit{is a binding in } \beta \ \textit{and } x \notin \pi_B\}.$

$\pi_{A'} = \{a \mid a \in \pi_A \ \wedge \ \exists x \in \bar{\pi}_B, \ \textit{such that } x \to_\beta a\}.$

$\pi_{B'} = \{y \mid y \in \pi_B \ \wedge \ \exists x \in \bar{\pi}_B, \ \textit{such that } x \to_\beta y$
$\qquad\qquad\qquad\qquad\qquad\qquad \textit{or } y \textit{ is an output of } \beta\}.$

The inputs $a_1 \ .. \ a_n$ to the function f are partitioned into two subsets π_A and $\bar{\pi}_A$. The assumption is that there is enough computation that can be done with the partial set of arguments π_A and the motivation is to precompute that part (so that it can be hoisted out of a loop). This is accomplished by decomposing f into two functions, f' and f'', as shown in Figure 6.5. The function f' operates on arguments π_A. Its body is simply the set of all bindings, π_B, in the block β, which depends only on the arguments π_A. Its results are a subset of the arguments $\pi_{A'}$ and a subset of the block variables, $\pi_{B'}$, which may be needed for the remaining computation. The function f'' takes these values and the remaining arguments $\bar{\pi}_A$ to compute the final results. In any implementation there are distinct costs associated with function calls and with number of arguments/results passed. This optimization is useful when there is substantial computation performed in f' and only a small number of values are sent from f' to f''. This is particularly the case in array expressions of the form: $\{\textbf{array}\ (1, m) \mid [\alpha] = (f, a_1, .., a_{n-1})_1\ i \parallel i \leftarrow 1\ \textbf{to}\ m\}$, where all the a_j are loop constants. By moving the partial computation outside the loop, there is a potential to save some recomputation. Again, this can change the termination characteristics of the program. Formally, we specify the rewrite rule as follows:

Let $f\ a_1\ a_2\ ..\ a_n = \{x_1 = \alpha_1;\ \ldots\ x_m = \alpha_m;\ x_{r_1}, .., x_{r_t}\}$
be a function definition and i is an integer $< n$.

Compute the sets:

$\pi_A = \{a_1, .., a_i\}$
$\bar{\pi}_A = \{a_{i+1}, .., a_n\}$
$\pi_B = \{x_1, .., x_k\}$
$\bar{\pi}_B = \{x_{k+1}, .., x_m\}$
$\pi_{A'} = \{a_1, .., a_p\}$
$\pi_{B'} = \{x_1, .., x_q\}$

Define the two functions:

$f'\ a_1\ ..\ a_i = \{x_1 = \alpha_1; ..; x_k = \alpha_k;\ a_1, .., a_p, x_1, .., x_q\}$
$f''\ a_1\ ..\ a_p\ x_1\ ..\ x_q\ a_{i+1}\ ..\ a_n = \{x_{k+1} = \alpha_{k+1}; ..; x_m = \alpha_m;$
$\qquad\qquad\qquad\qquad\qquad\qquad x_{r_1}, .., x_{r_t}\}$

If i, j are integers, such that $i < j <= n$, then

$$(f, \alpha_1, .., \alpha_j)_{n-j} \quad \Rightarrow \quad (f'', a'_1, .., a'_p, x'_1, .., x'_q, \alpha_{i+1}, .., \alpha_j)_{n-j}$$
$$a'_1, .., a'_p, x'_1, .., x'_q = (f', \alpha_1, .., \alpha_i)_0$$

Optimization Rule 10

It should be noted that performing the above transformation when $j < n$ alters the termination characteristics of the program. The transformation forces the evaluation of $a'_1, .., a'_p, x'_1, .., x'_q$ whether the partial application of f is later applied fully or not. Nonterminating parts of this sub-computation may be started unnecessarily. If this is a concern, the above rule must be applied only when $n = j$.

Transforming Tail Recursion Into a Loop.   Implementation of a loop construct is often more efficient than recursive function calls. Below we show a transformation to replace a tail recursive function into a loop construct. We assume that the function f computes a Boolean value for x_1 (refer to the definitions in Optimization Rule 11) and based on the value it may invoke itself or return a result. This is specified by having the output, δ, of the function f as a conditional form, in which the then-clause invokes f again. Thus the loop must circulate the Boolean value x_1 and all the arguments $a_1, .., a_n$ to the function. But, the final result expression, γ, may use some of the names, $x_2, .., x_m$, computed in the last iteration. Here we assume all of them are used (and this can be simplified using the relation $\rightarrow$ as in Optimization Rule 10). Hence, the loop will circulate all the names $x_1, .., x_m, a_1, .., a_n$. Initially we compute the values of $x_1, .., x_m$ and invoke the loop. The loop body computes the new variables y_j and new argument values $c_1, .., c_n$ as defined in the block β. The final values of x_i and a_j are used in the block γ to compute the final results. Formally, this is expressed by the following rule:

Let $f\ a_1\ a_2\ ..\ a_n = \{x_1 = \alpha_1;\ \ ...\ \ x_m = \alpha_m; \delta = \alpha;\ \delta\}$
be a function definition where,
$\quad \alpha = \textbf{if}\ x_1\ \textbf{then}\ \beta\ \textbf{else}\ \gamma$
$\quad \beta = \{y_1 = \beta_1;\ ..;\ y_k = \beta_k;\ \beta_0 = (f, c_1, .., c_n)_0;\ \beta_0\}$
$\quad \gamma = \{z_1 = \gamma_1;\ ..;\ z_l = \gamma_l;\ \gamma_0\}$

Then, rewrite the definition of function f as follows:
$\quad f\ a_1\ ..\ a_n = \{x_1 = \alpha_1;\ \ ...\ \ x_m = \alpha_m;$
$\qquad\qquad\qquad x_2', .., x_m', a_1', .., a_n' =$
$\qquad\qquad\qquad\qquad \{\textbf{loop}\ x_1, .., x_m, a_1, .., a_n;$
$\qquad\qquad\qquad\qquad y_1 = \beta_1;\ ..;\ y_k = \beta_k;$
$\qquad\qquad\qquad\qquad x_1' = \alpha_1^{[x_1 x_1', ..., x_m x_m']};$

$\qquad\qquad\qquad\qquad x_m' = \alpha_m^{[x_1 x_1', ..., x_m x_m']};$
$\qquad\qquad\qquad\qquad c_1' = c_1^{[x_1 x_1', ..., x_m x_m']};$

$\qquad\qquad\qquad\qquad c_n' = c_n^{[x_1 x_1', ..., x_m x_m']};$
$\qquad\qquad\qquad\qquad x_1', .., x_m', c_1', .., c_n'\};$
$\qquad\qquad x_1' = \textbf{false};$
$\qquad\qquad z_1 = \gamma_1^{[x_1 x_1', ..., x_m x_m', a_1 a_1', ..., a_n a_n']};$

$\qquad\qquad z_l = \gamma_l^{[x_1 x_1', ..., x_m x_m', a_1 a_1', ..., a_n a_n']};$
$\qquad\qquad \gamma_0\}$

Optimization Rule 11

6.6   Implementation Considerations

6.6.1   PARALLEL MACHINES

The rewrite rules of Section 6.4 suggest a natural implementation on a parallel machine in which the granularity of a task is as small as a single instruction. Dataflow architectures [5] take this approach. While actual implementations may vary in detail (*e.g.,* tasks may carry information along with them or they may store them in a preallocated place), the general spirit of it can be described by the following conceptualized view.

Memory Model.   Each new name created during the reduction process corresponds to a new location allocated in the memory. Thus the memory must have the ability to allocate locations dynamically. Also, substitution for a name in an expression must take place when the name has been bound to a ground value. This implies that the memory must be able to tag each location to reflect whether a ground value is present or not. Furthermore, attempts to read a ground value for substitution must be made to wait until such a value is present. The following operations capture these notions:

- □ **allocate** n : Allocates n contiguous locations and returns the address of the first location.
- □ **fetch** a i : Suspends until location $a + i$ contains a ground value and then returns its contents.
- □ **store** a i v : Stores the ground value v into location $a + i$ and activates any suspended fetches from this location.

Each new binding added to the state corresponds to a parallel task. The mission of a task is to reduce the right-hand side to a ground value and then to store it in the location corresponding to the left-hand side. For example, when the binding $X = Y + Z$; is added to the state, the machine initiates a new task whose program consists of the sequence of steps:

$$r1 = \textbf{fetch } Y \ 0; \ \ r2 = \textbf{fetch } Z \ 0; \ \ r3 = r1 + r2; \ \ \textbf{store } X \ 0 \ r3;$$

The names $r1, r2, r3$ refer to some local state of the task. Thus the task may wait during the first two steps, then perform the addition using the operand values $r1$ and $r2$, and finally store the result in the target location and terminate. There are architectures that can optimize this whole sequence into a single instruction [12, 16]. Expansion of a block means that new locations are allocated for all the names bound in the block and a new parallel task is initiated for each binding. A conditional expression translates into a task that fetches the condition value and based on it, initiates the block from the appropriate arm of the conditional. A function application is translated into a task that checks the arity of the function. If the arity is satisfied, the new block is initiated. Otherwise, it constructs the new partial function and stores it into the left-hand side location. There must be some strategy to represent the partial functions. Usually, they are stored as lists remembering the function name and the operands collected so far.

Loops. The loop expression can, of course, be simply rewritten into an equivalent recursive function definition. However, the objective is to take advantage of the fact that it will be repeated many times. Several schemes are possible for loop implementation. Here we outline one simple method that uses the following additional features in the machine:

- □ Some scheme to detect the termination of all tasks within an iteration.
- □ An operation to **reset** the tag of a location for reuse.

Using these features, we can outline a simple scheme that preallocates the locations for a fixed number of iterations ahead of time. Recall that the loop expression takes $k + 1$ input values, $b_0^i, ..b_k^i$, and produces $k + 1$ output values, $a_0^i, ..a_k^i$. In addition, we add a synchronization location, s^i, for each iteration (its use is explained below). So, a total of $2k + 3$ locations are used by an iteration to communicate with its neighboring iterations. The idea is to somehow make this communication implicit (as opposed to using the general function calling mechanism to pass arguments and return results). One simple strategy is to imagine some q agents executing concurrently and they take up one iteration at a time in a cyclic manner. (The choice of q is made from resource constraints and is outside the scope of the current discussion.) That is, the agent i executes loop iterations i, $q + i$, $2q + i$, etc. When a loop is initiated, a contiguous block of $q * (2k + 3)$ locations are preallocated, so that each agent knows exactly where its results should go. The scheme works as follows:

- □ The location s^i is used to ensure that agent i does not commence iteration $q + i$ before the iteration i terminates and so on. The actual value contained in s^i is irrelevant—presence of data in s^i indicates that agent i is ready to take up the next iteration. Initially all s^i are set to true.
- □ Agent i commences its execution by reading the location b_0^i. It may wait until the fetch is successful.

- If b_0^i is false, then the loop is terminated by providing the values of $b_1^i, ..b_k^i$ as the result of the loop.
- If b_0^i is true, the loop body is expanded. Locations $b_0^i, ..b_k^i$ are used for inputs and output values are produced in locations $a_0^i, ..a_k^i$.
- It reads location s^{i+1}, waiting if necessary for this purpose. This read operation ensures that agent $i+1$ has completed its previous execution. Then the location s^{i+1} is reset.
- The values from $a_0^i, ..a_k^i$ are stored into $b_0^{i+1}, ..b_k^{i+1}$.
- It then waits until all other tasks in this iteration are completed.
- Locations $b_0^i, ..b_k^i$ are all reset.
- True is stored into location s^i.
- The agent repeats the algorithm.

Several variations are possible. For instance, sending input values to iteration $i+1$ can be done at any stage in the body, provided that s^{i+1} is checked before doing so (for example, see [5]). When the loop terminates, a similar mechanism can be used to trigger the deallocation of the entire block of locations allocated for this loop.

Structures.   Structure allocations, fetches, and stores take the following obvious forms: The task for the binding $X = \langle a_1, ..a_m \rangle$ performs $r1 =$ **allocate** m; **store** X 0 $r1$. The task for the binding $Y = X[k]$ performs $r1 =$ **fetch** X k; **store** Y 0 $r1$. Similarly, the task for $X[k] = Y$ performs $r1 =$ **fetch** Y 0; **store** X k $r1$. While array comprehension is functional in the sense that its result is a constant structure with well-defined values (that will never change), its implementation is via the parallel tasks described above. Here one task creates a structure and passes the address to other tasks which use it for accessing the structure components. The functionality is obviously lost at the implementation level. However, determinacy is still preserved at the implementation level because of the single-binding restriction for any location. These are *I-structures* as elaborated in [6]. They are crucial for efficiently implementing some of the abstractions we described earlier. In order to reinforce their place in the implementation, we elaborate a few examples.

Consider for example, the construction of the list $\{: i \mid i \leftarrow 1 \textbf{ to } n\}$. It is not easy to construct this with a conventional functional *cons* operator, as it will only build the list in the reverse order. We might implement this using the concept of open lists [3], as illustrated by the following algorithm:

$$L = \{: i \mid i \leftarrow 1 \text{ to } n\} \quad \equiv$$

$$\{a = \textbf{allocate } 2;$$
$$\textbf{store } a \; 0 \; 1;$$
$$b = \{\textbf{for } i \leftarrow 2 \text{ to } n \textbf{ do}$$
$$\quad c = \textbf{allocate } 2;$$
$$\quad \textbf{store } c \; 0 \; i;$$
$$\quad \textbf{store } a \; 1 \; c;$$
$$\quad \textbf{next } a = c;$$
$$\quad \textbf{finally } a\};$$
$$\textbf{store } b \; 1 \; \textbf{nil};$$
$$\textbf{in } a\};$$

The memory cell cannot be a basic functional abstraction, because no meaning could be given to the allocate operation without the associated fetch and store operations.   Besides, **store** is purely a side effect and not an expression. Hence, in order to provide the above list abstraction, we must make the entire code atomic—or as a primitive operation whose internal stages are invisible to the rest of the program. For instance, the entire code can be made sequential and the result is made available only after the whole thing is constructed. This will preclude the concurrent operation of the readers and writers of this list. Use of I-structures provides such concurrency, as can be seen from the above implementation.

There is yet another advantage to the above implementation scheme. It facilitates building recursive structures. Consider the following implementation of the array comprehension:

$$A = \{ \quad \textbf{array } (0, n)$$
$$\quad \mid [0] = 1$$
$$\quad \mid [i] = A[i-1] + 1 \parallel i \leftarrow 1 \text{ to } n\};$$

$$A = \textbf{allocate } (n+1);$$
$$\textbf{store } A \; 0 \; 1;$$
$$\{\textbf{for } i \leftarrow 1 \text{ to } n \textbf{ do}$$
$$\quad x = \textbf{fetch } A \; i;$$
$$\quad y = x + 1;$$
$$\quad \textbf{store } A \; i \; y\};$$

As the entire loop consists of only side effects, the whole loop is a side effect. The name A is bound to the address and is passed around freely and the store operations can fetch the contents of elements filled in earlier. Building this abstraction by sequentializing the code calls for a precise ordering of the store operations. This is difficult if the dependences are not regular. The I-structure solution works for any type of interdependences, as long as the definition is not circular. The same arguments hold true for the recurrence-list abstraction for lists and so on.

Separation of the **allocate** and **store** operations for the I-structures has another advantage. Whenever two corresponding elements of a pair of structures have some computation in common, their **store** operations can be performed together in the task that computes the shared value. This is illustrated by the **2-arrays** abstraction in Section 6.2.2. The reader can see that in its implementation, the two allocate operations take place outside the loop. Each iteration computes the shared value and then stores it in the corresponding elements of the two structures. Id provides a variety of such abstractions, **k-nd-arrays**, for various dimensions, n, and for various composites, k. However, there are bound to be other abstractions that are similar in nature—namely, those that make good functional abstractions—but cannot be built out of functional building blocks.

One such example appears in the LU decomposition example in Section 6.3. The last step in this example computes the matrix lu. The pivot vector piv must also be computed (not included in the program). Both of them share the *list* of three-tuples, giving the band-generator function, the pivot row, and the sub-matrix. The band-generator function is needed for building the matrix lu and the pivot row numbers are needed to build the vector piv. There is no abstraction that can be built at the language level to make use of this sharing. Hence, in the example, we built the *list* and passed it to the matrix and array abstractions. One can see that if it is programmed at the I-structure level, this can be avoided by placing the **store** *pivot row* operations in the outer loop of the matrix computation. The Id language actually makes the I-structure primitives available to the programmer for efficient building of arbitrary abstractions. Of course, functionality cannot be guaranteed for this use.

Making the I-structure cell a basic block is useful for building many efficient abstractions involving lists and arrays. However, the accumulator abstraction cannot be built with them. The principal difference is that the accumulator abstraction requires repeated imperative updates for a cell and some control over when its value can be read by tasks. The key feature required in memory is an atomic update of at least two locations—one for the count and one for the array element. Efficient implementation of accumulators is a subject of further study.

6.6.2 SEQUENTIAL MACHINES

Although the preceding model of parallel computation exposes all possible parallelism during execution, it forces synchronization at the instruction level. For instance, if we were to charge one unit of cost for each interrogation made during a **fetch** operation, the synchronization cost is tremendous. The undesirable feature is that in many cases we can determine that synchronization is unnecessary, but the model does not provide the means to take advantage of it. As a trivial example, if we have the bindings $X = Y + Z$; $W = X + 5$, it is pointless to dispatch the task for the second binding before the task for the first binding completes. If indeed the second task is dispatched after the first terminates, it is unnecessary to make the check to see if X has a ground value in it or not. Consequently, this raises the question as to how many such unnecessary synchronizations can be eliminated, by forming threads of sub-programs, where each thread executes sequentially as in a von Neumann machine [21]. Conventional pipelined machines with efficient access to local state can take advantage of longer threads [9, 12]. Several strategies are possible for partitioning the programs into threads.

In general, partitioning involves some form of dependence analysis of the flow of information between operations. Depending upon the sophistication of the analysis, the dependence information between any two operations, a and b, can be of three types: b depends upon the outcome of a, in which case they can be sequenced in that order; b does not depend on a, in which case they can be put in any threads; b may depend on a sometimes (perhaps data-dependent), in which case they cannot be put in the same thread. Analysis of these methods and their efficient implementations are subjects of current study.

Acknowledgments.   I thank Ken Traub and Paul Suhler for patiently reading the draft and providing useful comments. I thank Ramesh Natarajan for helpful discussions on the sparse matrix problem.

References

1. Ariola, Z.M. and Arvind "P-TAC: A Parallel Intermediate Language," *Proceedings of the Functional Programming Languages and Computer Architectures, London* (September 1989).

2. Arvind and K. Ekanadham "Future Scientific Programming on Parallel Machines," *Journal of Parallel and Distributed Computing*, 5 Academic Press (December 1988).

3. Arvind, S. Heller, and R.S. Nikhil "Programming Generality and Parallel Computers," *Proceedings of Fourth International Symposium on Biological and Artificial Intelligence Systems*, Trento, Italy (September 1988).

4. Arvind and R.A. Iannucci "Two Fundamental Issues in Multi-processing," *Proceedings of DFVLR Conference on Parallel Processing in Science and Engineering, Bonn-bad*, West Germany (June 1987).

5. Arvind and R.S. Nikhil "Executing a Program on the MIT Tagged-Token Dataflow Architecture," *Proceedings of the PARLE Conference*, Eindhoven, The Netherlands. Springer-Verlag LNCS 259 (June 1987).

6. Arvind, R.S. Nikhil, and K.K. Pingali "I-structures: Data Structures for Parallel Computing," *Proceedings of Workshop on Graph Reduction*, Santa Fe, New Mexico. Springer-Verlag LNCS 279 (September 1986).

7. Arvind, R.S. Nikhil, and K.K. Pingali "Id Nouveau Reference Manual, Part II: Semantics," *Technical Report, MIT Laboratory for Computer Science*, Cambridge (April 1987).

8. Backus, J. "Can Programming Be Liberated from von Neumann Style? A Functional Style and Algebra of Programs," *Communications of ACM*, vol. 21, no 8 (August 1978).

9. Buehrer, R.E. and K. Ekanadham "Incorporating Dataflow Ideas into von Neumann Processors for Parallel Execution," *IEEE Transactions on Computers*, C-36, 12 (December 1987).

10. Hageman, L.A. and D.M. Young *Applied Iterative Methods*, New York: Academic Press, 1981.

11. Hughes, J. "Why Functional Programming Matters," *The Computer Journal*, vol. 32, no. 2 (February 1989).

12. Iannucci, R.A. "A Dataflow/von Neumann Hybrid Architecture," Ph.D. Diss. LCS TR-418, MIT Laboratory for Computer Science, Cambridge, Mass. (May 1988).

13. Karp, A. H. "Programming for Parallelism," *Computer*, vol. 20, no. 5 (May 1987).

14. Lord, R.E., J.S. Kowalik, and S.P. Kumar "Solving Linear Algebraic Equations on an MIMD Computer," *Journal of the Association for Computing Machinery*, vol. 30, no. 1 (January 1983).

15. Nikhil, R.S. *ID (Version 88.1) Reference Manual*, Computation Structures Group Memo 284, MIT Laboratory for Computer Science, Cambridge, Mass. (August 1988).

16. Papadopoulos, G.M. "Implementation of a General Purpose Dataflow Multiprocessor," Ph.D. Diss. MIT Laboratory for Computer Science, Cambridge, Mass. (August 1988).

17. Peyton Jones S.L. *The Implementation of Functional Programming Languages*, Englewood Cliffs, N.J.: Prentice-Hall, 1987.

18. Pingali, K. and K. Ekanadham "Accumulators: Logic Variables Done Right," *Proceedings of the Eighth Conference on Foundations of Software Technology and Theoretical Computer Science, TRDDC*, 1 Magaldas Road, Pune 411 001, India (December 1988).

19. Preparata, F.P. and M.I. Shamos *Computational Geometry: An Introduction*, New York: Springer-Verlag, 1985.

20. Traub, K.R. "A Compiler for the MIT Tagged-Token Dataflow Architecture," Master's Thesis, LCS TR-370, MIT Laboratory for Computer Science, Cambridge, Mass. (August 1986).

21. Traub, K.R. "Sequential Implementation of Lenient Programming Languages," Ph.D. Diss. LCS TR-417, MIT Laboratory for Computer Science, Cambridge, Mass. (May 1988).

22. Traub, K.R. "Compilation as Partitioning: A New Approach to Compiling Non-strict Functional Languages," *Proceedings of the Functional Programming Languages and Computer Architectures*, London (September 1989).

23. Turner, D.A. "The Semantic Elegance of Applicative Languages," *Proceedings of ACM Conference on Functional Programming Languages and Computer Architecture*, Portsmouth, N.H. (October 1981).

24. Wray, S.C. and J. Fairbairn "Non-Strict Languages—Programming and Implementation," *The Computer Journal*, vol. 32, no. 2 (February 1989).

7

Crystal: Theory and Pragmatics of Generating Efficient Parallel Code

Marina Chen   Young-il Choo   Jingke Li

7.1 Introduction

The Crystal project has focused on making the task of programming massively parallel machines practical while not sacrificing the efficiency of the target code. We believe these goals can be achieved by starting from a high-level problem specification, through a sequence of optimizations tuned for particular parallel machines, leading to the generation of efficient target code with explicit communications or synchronization.

The complexity of managing explicit parallelism to produce efficient code remains a major obstacle in the widespread use of the new generation of parallel machines. At the same time, the task of automatically generating parallel programs appears to be extremely difficult and costly except for a very restricted class of problems. Recognizing these issues, we seek a balance between the automatable and the effort required of the programmer.

Our approach to automation is to design a compiler that classifies source programs according to the communication primitives and their cost on the target machine and that maps the data structures to distributed memory, and then generates parallel code with explicit communication commands. Regarding those classes of problems for which the default mapping strategies of the compiler are inadequate, we provide special language constructs for incorporating domain specific knowledge and directing the compiler in its mapping. When formulated mathematically, many algorithms exhibit natural parallelism. However, once they are implemented in a sequential language, the extraction of parallelism requires sophisticated techniques. For example, the work in parallelizing Fortran has been quite successful for vector processor machines and shared memory multiprocessors, but it remains to be seen whether it can be extended to massively parallel machines.

Our approach to parallel programming is to use a purely functional language that resembles mathematical notation, with higher-order operators and data structures, thereby making the extraction of parallelism far simpler, and allowing us to focus on the global communication issues for massively parallel machines. The simpler semantics of the language allows us to formulate a rigorous theory of program optimization that is indispensable both in the automatic analysis of communication patterns and the explicit specification of user-defined mapping strategies.

In the following sections, we give an overview of the programming methodology that underlies the approach, the Crystal language needed to specify and reason about parallel computation, the equational theory of Crystal, and optimization issues for the compiler.

7.1.1 THE PRINCIPLE FEATURES OF CRYSTAL

In order to develop a theory of the language that is useful in practice, the language must have clean semantics and orderly algebraic properties. The model of communication must truly reflect the physical characteristics. It must be abstract enough to be conceptualized by the programmer and simple enough to be incorporated into a compiler.

To this end, we have defined the Crystal functional language with special data types that embody locality and structural information in both the problem and the physical domains. The novel data types are *index domains*, which embody the geometric shape of data structures such as multidimensional arrays, trees, and hypercubes, and *data fields*, which generalize the notion of distributed data structures, unifying the conventional notions of arrays and functions.

Since index domains embody the shape of a data field, the geometry of the set of indices indicates the distribution of the data elements. Therefore, a mapping from one index domain to another, called an *index domain morphism* (or just morphism), can be used to represent the change of shape of the distributed data fields. This is at the heart of the global optimization of Crystal programs. Once a suitable morphism has been chosen, a systematic transformation of the program results in a new program with improved behavior.

The language allows different levels of abstraction: atomic functions for sequential computation on a single processor; data fields for data parallel computation; and higher-order functions for combining data parallel components. Of course, the higher-order functions can be considered atomic at the next level of the hierarchy. But such power of abstraction is obtained at the expense of target code performance—in particular, for the SIMD type of machines. Reformulating a high-order Crystal program using data fields (first order functions defined over index domains) is analogous to turning general recursive definitions into tail recursive ones. You gain efficiency at the expense of abstraction and elegance. The first order version is conceptually more complex because the parallel structure of an algorithm must be directly exposed. (For example, an FFT network in its entirety must be defined as an index domain.) The high-order version uses recursion to do the trick (for example, only the basic butterfly pattern is defined, and the FFT network is generated by way of recursion).

7.1.2   PROGRAMMING METHODOLOGY

The programming methodology underlying our approach to parallel computation centers on the interpretation of functions (data fields) as distributed structures and program transformations that modify such structures until they can be efficiently mapped onto the physical processors, keeping in mind the cost of data communication.

The programs are written in a functional language with special constructs for expressing data parallelism and locality. We claim that notions of efficiency and optimization for massively parallel machines must incorporate the complex cost of interprocessor communication and hierarchical memory access. We represent this by a *reference metric*, which is used by the compiler in its optimization procedures. In addition, the reference metric provides the programmer with a suitably abstract model of the target architecture, allowing the programmer to explore and devise high-level algorithmic strategies, taking advantage of the global characteristic of the underlying machine without dealing with the error-prone micro-management of resource allocation and synchronization.

The performance of parallel computing ultimately depends on the matching between the logical structure of the program and the underlying physical structure of the machine. The mutual interaction of data distribution, execution time, communication overhead, and storage constraints makes the task of finding a good match extremely complex. We deal with this complexity by using a theory of the language in which optimizations can be represented formally as equational program transformations and a model of communication cost for the underlying architecture.

The process of designing parallel programs has both formal and informal aspects. The formal aspect, such as program transformation, is mechanizable. For example, once an index domain morphism is specified, the derivation of the new data field from the original definition is automatable. Note that there are no restrictions on the shape of the domain nor on the domain morphism itself, as long as it has an inverse.

The informal aspect requires insight into the behavior of the algorithm, sometimes even a lemma or two. For example, in the parallel version of the prime sieve algorithm [45], the partitioning of the index domain relies on knowledge of the prime number distribution. Except for very restricted classes of problems, determining the right domain morphism requires insight.

The role of the compiler design is to formalize and automate the process of finding appropriate morphisms. One finds classes of programs that are broad enough to encompass interesting and critical application areas, yet restrictive enough to allow the compiler to give a reasonable solution within a reasonable amount of time and resource.

In the general case where the compiler is limited in its capability (since it cannot prove general theorems automatically), the next best thing is to provide a language and programming environment in which the insight of the programmer can be expressed and implemented. For example, the specification of domain morphisms allows new data fields to be automatically derived. The Crystal metalanguage [15] provides such capabilities.

7.1.3   AN EQUATIONAL THEORY FOR PROGRAM TRANSFORMATION

The theory of Crystal consists of *equations* over program expressions and equational inference rules satisfying functional and lambda-calculus identities. Using lambda-abstraction, we treat definitions as equations with simple left-hand sides.

Unlike the conventional program transformational systems where folding and unfolding are applied only to expressions, leaving the extension of the expression unchanged, the equational theory allows us to derive new programs that are equivalent (in some precise way that will be defined) but extensionally different from the original. This more general framework for program transformation appears necessary in order to express the new optimizations that a parallelizing compiler must do.

7.1.4   THE CRYSTAL APPROACH TO COMPILATION

The Crystal functional language radically simplifies the data dependency analysis necessary for synthesizing parallel control structures. The interpretation of the index domains and data fields admits efficient storage management which, in conventional function language implementations, is difficult to do.

The novel compilation techniques include synthesis of parallel control structures, automatic layout and distribution of data, generation of explicit communication from program reference patterns, and global optimization between parallel program modules. Unless the programmer explicitly provides such information, these techniques are necessary for any compiler targeting distributed memory architectures. For problems that are dynamic in nature, the redistribution of data and tasks is handled by the runtime system, utilizing both the static analysis obtained at compile-time and the dynamic dependency and profile of computation gathered during the execution.

The results of the various compiler optimizations can be formulated as mappings between index domains. Given such a mapping, the compilation corresponds to the transformation of the program using the equational theory into an equivalent program that is better matched to the physical structure.

In dealing with the two related issues of minimizing communication overhead and determining data layout and load distribution, the compiler first determines the relative location of the data structures in a virtual domain and then aggregates contiguous parts of the data structures to be mapped into a single processor so as to convert as many references in the source program as possible into local memory access. For the remaining references requiring interprocessor communication, the compiler tries to match the reference patterns with a library of aggregate communication operators and chooses the ones which minimize network congestion and overhead.

7.1.5   OVERVIEW OF THE CHAPTER

We will introduce the major new constructs of the Crystal functional language for data-parallelism. An example of a Crystal program implementing the Gaussian elimination algorithm is given. We then present the equational theory for program transformation. Next, we introduce the structure of the compiler and describe in greater detail the specific modules of the compiler dealing with dependency and phase decomposition, domain alignment, parallel control structure synthesis, and generation of explicit communication. Finally, we present some performance results and discuss additional language and compiler issues.

7.2   The Crystal Functional Language

In this section we describe the essential features of the Crystal functional language and its model of parallel computation.

Briefly, the language provides various data types and operations over them, a set of constructors for defining new data types, functional abstraction for creating functions, and function application. A program is a set of possibly mutually recursive definitions. The syntax has been kept simple, with most language constructs expressed in prefix notation, except for simple arithmetic functions, which are infix, and the list and set comprehension that uses the standard set comprehension notation with keywords added.

Though the language is purely functional, allowing no side effects, we have compiler directives for specifying resource allocation and other intentional issues that can be used by the compiler in generating efficient parallel code.

In the following sections, we introduce a few programming constructs that are important for parallel programming, including the key notion of *domain morphism*. *Index domains* are abstractions of the "shapes" of composite data structures, which in most current programming languages are not first-class objects. *Data fields* generalize the notion of distributed data structures, unifying the conventional notions of arrays and functions. *Communication forms* defined over an index domain are a means of specifying the data dependencies, and the inverse of a communication form (defined precisely later) provides useful directives for optimizing inter-processor communication. *Hyper-surfaces* are for specifying the boundaries of index domains. Finally, *domain morphisms* describe the reshaping of index domains aimed at optimizing data or control structures for efficiency reasons as well as the necessary mapping from the logical structure of the problem to the physical domain of machine and sequencing in time.

7.2.1   CRYSTAL PROGRAMS

A Crystal program consists of a set of mutually recursive *definitions* and *directives*. In the interactive version, an expression is evaluated in the standard environment augmented by the definitions. In the compiled version, input is indicated by calling the special function StdIn and output is done by defining the special function StdOut.

A *definition* has the form

```
<identifier> : <type-expression> = <expression>
```

and binds `<identifier>` to the value of `<expression>` evaluated in the current environment augmented simultaneously with all the other definitions. The type information is used by the compiler in the allocation of resources.

7.2.2   EXPRESSIONS

Expressions are inductively built up from the constants and the identifiers by function application, both prefix and infix, the primitive data structure forms, the set and list comprehension, and the conditional expression. For any type expression T, $e:T$ indicates that the value of e is of type T.

Functions.   Given any expression $\epsilon[x]$, which may or may not contain the variable x, $\mathsf{fn}(x):T\{\epsilon[x]\}$ denotes a function whose value at v of type T is the value of ϵ evaluated in the current environment with x bound to v.

Local Definitions.   An expression may also be provided with a local environment:

$$\epsilon \ \mathsf{where}\{\ d_1 \ldots d_n\ \}$$

indicates that the expression ϵ is to be evaluated in the current environment augmented with definitions d_i.

Conditional Expression.   The general form for the conditional expression is

$$\left\{ \begin{array}{c} b_1 \rightarrow e_1 \\ \vdots \\ b_n \rightarrow e_n \end{array} \right\}$$

where the b_i's are Boolean expressions, known as guards, and the e_i's are expressions of the same type. The value of the conditional expression is e_k if one b_k is true and otherwise undefined. A special symbol, denoted else, represents the conjunction of the negation of the other guards.

When more than one guard is true, an arbitrary choice leads to nondeterminism, which will not be addressed here.

An ASCII form for the conditional is

```
if b1 then e1
|| b2 then e2
|| b3 then e3
fi
```

However, in this paper we will use the more appealing two-dimensional representation for the conditional.

Reduction Operators.   Let $f : T \times T \to T$ be an associative function over some data type T and let $l = \text{list}\{l_1, \ldots, l_n\}$ be a list with elements from T. The operator reduce is defined by

$$\textbf{reduce}(f, l) = f(l_1, f(l_2, \ldots f(l_{n-1}, l_n) \ldots))$$

The operator scan is defined by

$$\textbf{scan}(f, l) = \text{list}\{m_1, \ldots, m_n\}$$

where $m_1 = l_1$, and $m_{i+1} = f(m_i, l_i)$. Note that reduce can also be defined over sets, but scan cannot since it assumes an ordering of the elements.

Minimalization Operator.   A special operator is needed to simulate while-loops where the bounds are not known. We use the *minimalization operator* or the *μ-operator*, where $\mu(i){:}D \{p[i]\}$ denotes the smallest member of D that satisfies $p[i]$, a Boolean predicate [39].

7.2.3   INDEX DOMAINS

An *index domain D* consists of a set of elements (called indices), a set of functions from D to D (called communication operators), a set of predicates, and the communication cost associated with each communication operator.

In essence, an index domain is a data type with communication cost associated with each function or operator. The reason for making the distinction is that index domains will usually be finite and they are used in defining distributed data structures (as functions over some index domain), rather than their elements being used as values. For example, rectangular arrays can be considered to be functions over an index domain consisting of a set of ordered pairs on a rectangular grid. Also, the elements of an index domain can be interpreted as locations in a logical or real space and time over which the parallel computation is defined. So we classify index domains into certain *kinds* (second order types) according to how they are to be interpreted (for example, as time or space coordinates).

The time coordinates can be detected by the compiler and implemented as a loop whose body may contain assignments to array elements if such a side effect can be done safely. A *time domain* can be semi-infinite and depends on the function that is being defined over it. For each execution, those domain elements that are actually generated during computation are controlled by the use of the minimalization operator. Minimalization over a semi-infinite domain corresponds to unbounded minimalization, which simulates while-loops.

Basic Index Domains.   Examples of basic classes of index domains include the interval, the hypercube, and tree domains:

- □ An *interval domain*, denoted interval(m, n), where m and n are integers and $m \le n$, is an index domain whose elements are the set of integers $\{ m, m+1, m+2, \ldots, n \}$ with the usual integer functions and predicates. The communication operators are prev : $i \mapsto i - 1$ and next : $i \mapsto i + 1$, with communication cost 1. The operators lb and ub return the lower bound (m) and the upper bound (n) of the interval domain respectively. When $m \ge n$, we define the index domain to be the same except that prev and next have reversed meaning.

- □ A *hypercube domain* of dimension n, denoted hcube(n), is an index domain with 2^n elements of the form $(x_0, \ldots, x_{n-1})$, where each x_i is either left or right (or just 0 or 1), and communication operators hcnb(j, k), for j an element of the data type and $0 \le k \le n - 1$, which maps the element j to its neighbor along the kth dimension, each with unit communication cost. Predicates are left?(k) and right?(k), for testing whether an element is on the left or right half of the kth dimension.

- □ A *tree domain*, denoted tree(r, S), where r is some name and S is a set of names, is an index domain whose elements are in S with enough other elements to form a binary tree with root named r and the elements of S at the leaves. The communication operators are left, right, and parent each with unit communication cost, and the predicates are leaf? and root?. The tree structure of tree domains may be further constrained to be a balanced tree, denoted tree-b(r, S), or left or right associative trees, denoted tree-l(r, S) and tree-r(r, S), respectively.

Index Domain Constructors.   Given index domains D and E, we can construct their product $(D \times E)$, disjoint union (coproduct) $(D + E)$, and function space $D \rightarrow E$, in the usual way.

Data-Dependent Index Domains.   Since index domains are first class objects, it is possible to define a new index domain as the value of a recursively defined function. For example, let B be some index domain, and $\phi[A(f(x))]$ be some index domain expression. Then

$$A = \mathsf{fn}(x) : T \left\{ \begin{array}{l} b_0(x) \rightarrow B \\ b_1(x) \rightarrow \phi[A(f(x))] \end{array} \right\}$$

defines an index domain for each x in T, with suitable guards b_0 and b_1. In this way, quite complex, data-dependent index domains can be constructed.

Hyper-Surfaces.   Hyper-surfaces define the boundary of domains where functions take on special values. The idea is to elevate boundaries of domains to be semantic entities and promote a programming style where the same semantic entity has a single syntactic entity corresponding to it. This way, the repetitive occurrence of related Boolean expressions for testing a particular boundary often seen in programs can be eliminated. The notion of hyper-surface makes the algebraic program transformation easier and more elegant, and also helps the compiler recognize domain boundaries and do optimizations such as aligning multiple data structures and reducing storage use. For more details see [14].

7.2.4   THE KINDS OF INDEX DOMAINS

As discussed above, it is useful to indicate how an index domain is to be interpreted by "typing" index domains with "kinds" (second-order types). Analogous to the first-order typing, $D[\mathscr{K}]$ will mean that the index domain D is of kind $\mathscr{K}$. The following are the kinds we have found useful for compiler optimizations:

□ The *universal kind* ($\mathscr{U}$) include all kinds of index domains as well as other data types, such as the integers and the reals.

- The *temporal kind* ($\mathcal{T}$) are index domains used for representing time coordinates (subkind of $\mathcal{U}$).
- The *spatial kind* ($\mathcal{S}$) are index domains used for representing space coordinates (subkind of $\mathcal{U}$).
- The *processor kind* ($\mathcal{P}$) are index domains representing processor coordinates (a subkind of $\mathcal{S}$).
- The *memory kind* ($\mathcal{M}$) are index domains representing memory locations within a processor (a subkind of $\mathcal{S}$). A memory hierarchy can be introduced with subkinds $\mathcal{M}_i$ of $\mathcal{M}$, where i ranges over the levels of the memory hierarchy.

7.2.5 INDEX DOMAIN MORPHISMS

Index domain morphisms formalize the notion of transforming one index domain into another, with the kinds of the domains indicating the change of interpretations.

Definition. Let D and E be two index domains. An *index domain morphism* is a function g from D to E such that for all elements x and y in D, if there exists a composition τ of communication operators $\tau_1 \circ \tau_2 \circ \cdots \tau_k$ over D such that $y = \tau(x)$, then there is a composition τ' of communication operators $\tau'_1 \circ \tau'_2 \circ \cdots \tau'_{k'}$ over E such that $g(y) = \tau'(g(x))$.

The extra constraint is to ensure that if there is a path in the first domain from x to y, then there is a path from $g(x)$ to $g(y)$.

Reshape Morphisms. For any index domain morphism $g : D \to E$, a *left inverse*, if it exists, is an index domain morphism $h : E \to D$ such that $h \circ g = 1_D$, the identity morphism over D. If g is also a left inverse of h (that is, $g \circ h = 1_E$), then h is called the *inverse* of g and is denoted by g^{-1}. A morphism that has an inverse is commonly known as an isomorphism but here will be called a *reshape morphism* to emphasize the idea of "reshaping" one index domain into another.

To require the existence of the left inverse implies that a reshape morphism must be bijective. However, we can easily derive a reshape morphism from an injective domain morphism by restricting the codomain as follows: Given an injective domain morphism $g' : D \to E$, the image of D under g', denoted image(D, g'), is an index domain whose elements are the image of the elements of D and whose communication operators are those of E. Clearly, $g : D \to$ image(D, g'), derived from g', now has a well-defined left inverse.

Here are examples of some useful reshape morphisms:

An *affine morphism* is a reshape morphism that is an affine function from one product of intervals to another. Affine morphisms unify all types of loop transformations (interchange, permutation, skewing) [2, 4, 8, 43, 44], and those for deriving systolic algorithms [26, 34, 38, 13]. For example, if $D_1 = \text{interval}(0, 3)$ and $D_2 = \text{interval}(0, 6)$, then $g = \text{fn}(i, j) : D_1 \times D_2\{(j, i) : D_2 \times D_1\}$ is an affine morphism that effectively performs a loop interchange.

Another example illustrates a slightly more interesting codomain E of the morphism g by taking the image of a function g'.

$$D_0 = \text{interval}(0, 3)$$
$$D = D_0 \times D_0$$
$$E = \text{image}(D, g') \text{ where}\{ \ g' = \text{fn}(i, j) : D\{(i - j, i + j)\} \ \}$$
$$g = \text{fn}(i, j) : D\{(i - j, i + j) : E\}$$
$$g^{-1} = \text{fn}(i, j) : E\{((i + j)/2, (j - i)/2) : D\}$$

Whenever it is legal to apply this affine morphism to a 2-level nested loop structure—consistent with the data dependencies in the loop body [1, 2, 6, 7, 11, 43]—a structure that is similar, but "skewed" from the original, is generated. The most common case is when elements of the inner loop can be executed in parallel but only half of the elements are active in each iteration of the outer loop. In this example, the index domain E has holes, and so guards in the loops must test whether $i + j$ and $i - j$ are even, since only these points correspond to the integral points in D.

Index domains often need to be partitioned with related elements in the same partition. In general, let $\equiv$ be an equivalence relation over some index domain D, let $E(i) = \{ x \in D \mid x \equiv i \}$ be the equivalence class of i, and let I be a set of representatives. A *partition of D* modulo $\equiv$ is a reshape morphism

$$g : D \to \sum(i{:}I)\, E(i)$$

where $\sum$ denotes a generalized sum over all the $E(i)$'s.

When $E(i) = E$ for all i in I, then $\sum(i{:}I)\, E(i)$ is isomorphic to $I \times E$, and a partition $g : D \to I \times E$ is called a *uniform partition* of a domain D.

For example, If $D = \text{interval}(0, 11)$, $D_1 = \text{interval}(0, 3)$, and $D_2 = \text{interval}(0, 2)$, then

$$g = \text{fn}(i) : D[\mathscr{S}]\{(i/3, i \bmod 3) : D_1[\mathscr{P}] \times D_2[\mathscr{M}]\}$$

is a uniform partition that distributes the elements of an index domain of the spatial kind as follows: the 12 elements are partitioned into three blocks of four elements each, each block is assigned to a processor, and each element in a block is assigned to some memory location.

There are numerous other forms of reshape morphisms ranging from "piece-wise affine" morphisms for more complex loop transformations [33], to those that are mutually recursive with the program (to be transformed) for dynamic data distribution.

Refinement Morphisms.   A domain morphism that does not have an inverse is called a *refinement morphism*. Though we shall not deal with them here, refinement morphisms are useful in representing more complex relationships between domains, such as the transformation of one-to-many broadcasts into binary tree broadcasting [15].

7.2.6   DATA FIELDS AND DATA FIELD MORPHISMS

Data fields generalize the notion of distributed data structures and recursively definable functions.

Definition.   A *data field* is a function over some index domain D into some domain of values V.

Usually, V will be the integers or the floating point numbers; however, for higher-order data fields, it can be some domain of data fields. Data fields unify the notion of distributed data structures, such as arrays, and functions. A parallel computation is specified by a set of data field definitions, which may be mutually recursive.

To illustrate the use of data fields, consider the following program segment written in some imperative language (assuming there are no other statements assigning values to A):

```
float array A(0..n,0..n);
if i=0 or j=0 then A:=e1;
for i:= 2 to n do {
    for j := 2, n do {
        A(i,j) := A(i-1,j) + A(i,j-1) } }
```

Let V be the data type of floating point numbers. In the notation of data fields, the above is written as

$$D_0 : \text{domain} = \text{interval}(0, n)$$
$$D : \text{domain} = \text{prod-dom}(D_0, D_0)$$
$$a : \text{dfield}(D, V) = \text{fn}(i, j) : D \begin{Bmatrix} i = 0 \vee j = 0 \rightarrow e_1 \\ \text{else} \rightarrow a(i - 1, j) + a(i, j - 1) \end{Bmatrix}$$

New data fields can be derived using index domain morphisms.

Definition.   A *data field morphism* induced by an index domain morphism $g : D \to E$, is a mapping

$$g^* : (E \to V) \to (D \to V) : a \mapsto a \circ g$$

where $D \to V$ and $E \to V$ are sets of data fields.

Given a data field $a : D \to V$ and a domain morphism $g : D \to E$, what we generally want is to find the new data field $\hat{a}$ such that $g^*(\hat{a}) = a$. In order to solve this equation we need the inverse of g—that is, g needs to be a reshape morphism. Then given g and g^{-1}, we can formally derive $\hat{a} = g^{-1^*}(a) = a \circ g^{-1}$.

7.2.7   COMMUNICATION FORMS

In asynchronous, distributed-memory multiprocessors, communication at the hardware level requires the sender to know the receiver's address, while the receiver only needs to know that a message is arriving. In writing parallel programs in a functional language, where the formal parameters range over the processor addresses, it is easy to determine for each receiver the sender's address, but determining for each sender who the receivers are requires inverting the expressions in the function calls.

Consider the following simple (and incomplete!) data field definition

$$a = \mathsf{fn}(i){:}D\{b(\tau_1(i)) + c(\tau_2(i))\}$$

where D is an index domain interpreted as processor locations. In order to compute the value of the data field a at location i, we need the values of b from location $\tau_1(i)$ and c from location $\tau_2(i)$. If inverses could be found for the function τ_1, then a single send would suffice from location j to $\tau_1^{-1}(j)$, rather than the bidirectional "request" followed by a reply.

For the compiler of any parallel language without explicit "send" and "receive" commands, the communication patterns must be extracted and its inverse derived or provided by the user in the form of directives.

We introduce the notion of a communication form in order to formalize the communication pattern and derivation of the inverse form.

A *communication action* from index domain D to E is a pair (s, t) (also written $s \mapsto t$), where $s \subseteq D$ is the *source set* and $t \subseteq E$ is the *target set*. The intuition is that each member of the source set is sending a message to each member of the target set. A set of communication actions is called a *communication form*. The *inverse* of a communication action, denoted $(s, t)^{-1}$, is (t, s). The inverse of a communication form F, denoted F^{-1}, is defined to be the set of the inverses of the communication actions in F.

A communication action is *one-to-one* if both the source and the target sets are singletons. The others are called *aggregate communication actions*. A communication form is said to be *one-to-one* if it consists of one-to-one communication actions and for each source set there is a unique target set—that is, it defines a one-to-one function from D to E. The others are *aggregate*.

We can regard a surjective function from D to E as an aggregate communication form, where each communication action has a singleton target set and the source sets are disjoint. Similarly, an injective function can be thought of as a communication form, where each communication action has singleton source and target sets.

For example, any injective function $b : D \to E$, defines a communication form $B = \{ (i, b(i)) \mid i \in D \}$, and $B^{-1} = \{ (j, b^{-1}(j)) \mid j \in b[D] \}$, where $b[D] \subseteq E$ denotes the image of D under b.

7.2.8   INPUT AND OUTPUT

Parallel input and output for parallel programming languages is an area in need of further research and experiment. In this chapter we define a very simple scheme by using special reserved data field names.

Parallel input is achieved by calling the special function $\mathsf{StdIn}(D, n)$, where D is an index domain and n is a natural number. The value of the function is a data field with shape D, and which is the nth in the input stream. For example,

$$a = \mathsf{StdIn}(\text{dom-of}(a), 0)$$
$$b = \mathsf{StdIn}(\text{dom-of}(b), 1)$$

inputs the first set of values to the data field a and the second set to b.

Parallel output is achieved by defining a special function *StdOut* over some interval index domain. For example,

$$StdOut : \text{dfield} = \text{fn}(n):\text{interval}(0, 2) \left\{ \begin{array}{l} n = 0 \to a \\ n = 1 \to b \\ n = 2 \to c \end{array} \right\}$$

causes the data fields a, b, and c to be output in this order.

7.2.9   COMPILER DIRECTIVES

Directives are used to specify various intentional aspects of the computation that cannot easily be expressed in a purely functional language.

- *Domain Morphisms:* Declarations of new index domains and domain morphisms indicating that the data fields should be reshaped, and the new program should be run.
- *Communication Forms:* Used by the user to specify the inverse of communication forms that cannot be derived by the compiler.
- *Common Index Domains:* One of the most important optimizations is the alignment of data fields so that they are allocated over the same set of processors. For example, the directive common$\{a, b, c\}$ indicates that the data fields a, b, and c have the same shape and should be aligned; that is, for all i in dom-of(a), $a(i)$, $b(i)$, and $c(i)$ should be allocated to the same processor.
- *Index Precedence:* For multidimensional index domains, it may be necessary to specify the precedence of the indices when implemented as sequential loops. For example, the directive precedence $(a, \{2, 3, 1\})$ specifies that the second coordinate is the outermost loop, the third is next outermost, and then the first coordinate is the innermost loop.
- *Dynamic Scheduling:* In general, the compiler attempts to map the computation to the physical processors statically when possible. The directive dynamic$\{a, \ldots, c\}$ indicates that the mapping to the processors for the data fields a, ..., c should be done dynamically.

7.3   An Example of Crystal Programming

A Crystal program implementing the standard Gaussian elimination algorithm with partial pivoting is shown in Figure 7.1 with the input and output shown in Figure 7.2. In the forward elimination phase, the program iterates over the columns of the input matrix. In iteration k, a pivot element is chosen from the elements in column k at or below the diagonal—for example, element (j, k)—and rows k and j are exchanged. Then the elements in the column below the diagonal are eliminated using the pivot element. In the back substitution phase, the resulting vector is obtained in n steps, where n is the input matrix size.

! Gaussian elimination

! Index Domains

D_0 : domain = interval$(1, n)$

D_1 : domain = interval$(1, n + 1)$

D_2 : domain = interval$(0, n)$

D : domain = prod-dom(D_0, D_1, D_2)

! Forward Elimination:

a : dfield$(D, V) =$

  $\text{fn}(i, j, k):D$

$$\left\{ \begin{array}{l} k = \text{lb}(D_2) \rightarrow A_0(i - 1, j - 1) \\ \text{else} \rightarrow \\ \quad \left\{ \begin{array}{l} i = k \rightarrow a(ipivot(k), j, k - 1) \\ i = ipivot(k) \rightarrow a(k, j, k - 1) - a(i, j, k - 1) * fac(i, k) \\ \text{else} \rightarrow a(i, j, k - 1) - a(ipivot(k), j, k - 1) * fac(i, k) \end{array} \right\} \end{array} \right\}$$

! Pivot Elements and Indices

$ipivot$: dfield$(D_0, V) =$

  $\text{fn}(k):D_0\{\text{reduce}(\max, \text{list}[\, l:D_3 \mid \text{abs}(a(l, k, k - 1)) = apivot(k)\,])\}$

$apivot$: dfield$(D_0, V) =$

  $\text{fn}(k):D_0\{\text{reduce}(\max, \text{list}[\, \text{abs}(a(l, k, k - 1)) \mid l:\text{interval}(k, n)\,])\}$

! Elimination Coefficients

fac : dfield$(\text{prod-dom}(D_0, D_0), V) =$

  $\text{fn}(i, k):\text{prod-dom}(D_0, D_0)$

$$\left\{ \begin{array}{l} i \leq k \rightarrow 1.0 \\ i = ipivot(k) \rightarrow a(k, k, k - 1)/a(ipivot(k), k, k - 1) \\ \text{else} \rightarrow a(i, k, k - 1)/a(ipivot(k), k, k - 1) \end{array} \right\}$$

! Back Substitution Stage:

x : dfield$(\text{prod-dom}(D_0, D_0), V) =$

  $\text{fn}(i, j):\text{prod-dom}(D_0, D_0)$

$$\left\{ \begin{array}{l} i = j \rightarrow (a(i, n + 1, n) - psum(i, j + 1))/a(i, j, n) \\ i < j \rightarrow x(i + 1, j) \end{array} \right\}$$

$psum$: dfield$(\text{prod-dom}(D_0, D_1), V) =$

  $\text{fn}(i, j):\text{prod-dom}(D_0, D_1)$

$$\left\{ \begin{array}{l} i = n + 1 \rightarrow 0.0 \\ i \leq j \rightarrow psum(i, j + 1) + a(i, j, n) * x(i, j) \end{array} \right\}$$

FIGURE 7.1
A Crystal Source Program for Gaussian Elimination with Partial Pivoting.

! Input and Output for Gaussian Elimination.

n : int $= 4$

$$A_0 : \text{dfield} = \left\{ \begin{array}{l} 2.0, 1.0, 3.0, 4.0, 29.0 \\ 1.0, 0.0, 0.0, 1.0, 5.0 \\ 3.0, 1.0, 1.0, 0.0, 8.0 \\ 5.0, 2.0, 0.0, 1.0, 13.0 \end{array} \right\}$$

$StdOut = \text{list}[\, x(1, j) \mid j{:}D_0\,]$

FIGURE 7.2
Initialization and Output for Gaussian Elimination.

For comparison, a Fortran program with the same functionality is shown in Figure 7.3. A major difference in the two implementations is the use of pointers to locate the pivot elements in the Fortran program while these elements are moved to the diagonal positions in the Crystal program.

Due to the functional nature of Crystal, the two programs look quite different in several respects. First, data fields in a Crystal program may have higher dimensionality than the corresponding arrays in a Fortran program due to the use of explicit iteration indices in place of multiple assignment to the same array elements. In Crystal, the space of iterations is considered part of an index domain. For example, the index domain D in the Gaussian elimination program consists of three components, where the third component D_0 is the space over which the time index k ranges. Parallelization is made easier this way. However, those domain components that can be interpreted as being sequential must be identified in order to reuse storage and compact the higher dimensional array. In the end, arrays in a Crystal program will be implemented with pretty much the same amount of storage as its Fortran counterpart.

The style of functional programming also forces the use of more arrays than would a standard, sequential Fortran program because of the lack of side-effecting constructs. For example, the data fields *fac* and *psum* in the Gaussian elimination example would not be needed in a Fortran program. However, when parallelizing such a Fortran program, extra arrays will be created in order to allow more parallelism. Thus a functional program has some of the parallelizing transformations already built-in at the source program level.

```
          program Gauss
C (datain,dataout,input=datain,output=dataout)
          parameter      (MAXN = 200) (NP = 16)
          integer        n, pivot, i, j, k, idx(200)
          real           maxelm, sum, m
          real           xAry(200), aAry(200,200)
C         /* Input matrix data */
          read (*,*) n
          read (*,*) ((aAry(i,j), j = 1, n), i = 1, n)
          read (*,*) (aAry(i,n+1), i = 1, n)
          do 100 i = 1, n
              idx(i) = i
100       continue
C         /* Forward elimination */
          do 2000 i = 1, n-1
C            /* Find a pivot element */
             pivot = i
             maxelm = abs(aAry(idx(i),i))
             do 1200 k = i+1, n
                if (maxelm .LT. abs(aAry(idx(k),i))) then
                    pivot = k
                    maxelm = abs(aAry(idx(k),i))
                end if
1200         continue
C            /* Exchange rows if needed */
             if (pivot .NE. i) then
               k = idx(pivot)
               idx(pivot) = idx(i)
               idx(i) = k
             end if
             do 1600 k = i+1, n
               m = aAry(idx(k),i) / aAry(idx(i),i)
                do 1550 j = i+1, n+1
                 aAry(idx(k),j)=aAry(idx(k),j)-m*aAry(idx(i),j)
1550            continue
1600         continue
2000      continue
C         /* Back Substitution */
          do 4000 i = n, 1, -1
             xAry(i) = aAry(idx(i),n+1) / aAry(idx(i),i)
             do 3400 j = i-1, 1, -1
               aAry(idx(j),n+1) =
    :              aAry(idx(j),n+1) - xAry(i) * aAry(idx(j),i)
3400         continue
4000      continue
          print *, (xAray(i),i=1,n)
          stop
          end
```

FIGURE 7.3
Gaussian elimination with partial pivoting in Fortran.

7.4   Program Transformation

Data fields and domain morphisms are semantic entities that are represented in a programming language. Semantically, a new data field can be defined as the composition of a data field and a domain morphism. In this section we describe an equational theory that allows the representation of the new data field to be obtained by manipulating the representations of the given data field and domain morphism. First, we introduce the equational theory; we then then describe the steps in the program transformation using the representation of reshape morphisms.

7.4.1   EQUATIONAL THEORY

By an *equational theory* of a programming language we mean a set of valid equations or *algebraic identities* in the language ($M = N$) along with *inference rules* for deriving new equations from old.

The following are algebraic identities from the equational theory of Church's lambda calculus [10]:

$$\mathsf{fn}(x){:}T\{M\} \;=\; \mathsf{fn}(y){:}T\{M[x/y]\} \qquad (\alpha)$$
$$\mathsf{fn}(x){:}T\{M\}(N) \;=\; M[x/N] \qquad (\beta)$$
$$\mathsf{fn}(x){:}T\{M(x)\} \;=\; M \quad (x \text{ not free in } M) \quad (\eta)$$

where M and N are expressions and T is a type-expression: The α and β rules are well understood, but it turns out that η-abstraction and reduction are essential in order to simplify expressions containing functions.

The following is a list of a minimal set of algebraic identities for a functional language with function-abstraction, the conditional expression and composition of functions, where F and H are function expressions, and B is a Boolean function expression. Recall that $\{B \to H\}$ denotes a conditional expression. Some of these identities are listed in Backus's work on FP [5], though the key difference is that he does not have any involving explicit function-abstraction.

$$F \circ \{B \to H\} \;=\; \{B \to F \circ H\} \qquad \text{(l-dist-comp-if)}$$
$$\{B \to H\} \circ F \;=\; \{B \circ F \to H \circ F\} \qquad \text{(r-dist-comp-if)}$$
$$\{B \to H\}(x) \;=\; \{B(x) \to H(x)\} \qquad \text{(dist-app-if)}$$
$$\mathsf{fn}(x)\{B(x) \to H(x)\} \;=\; \{\mathsf{fn}(x)\{B(x)\} \to \mathsf{fn}(x)\{H(x)\}\} \quad \text{(dist-abs-if)}$$

The following is a list of the basic inference rules, including the usual ones for *equality* (reflexivity, symmetry, and transitivity), and *substitution*, as well as those obtained from *application*, *abstraction*, and *composition.* Let $M[H/K]$ denote the new term with H replaced by K, the substitution operation of the λ-calculus.

$$M = M \qquad \frac{M = N}{N = M} \qquad \frac{M = L \quad L = N}{M = N}$$

$$\frac{M = N}{M \circ F = N \circ F} \qquad \frac{M = N}{H \circ M = H \circ N} \qquad \frac{M = N}{M[H/K] = N[H/K]}$$

$$\frac{M = N}{\text{fn}(x)\{M\} = \text{fn}(x)\{N\}} \qquad \frac{M = N}{M(L) = N(L)} \qquad \frac{M = N}{L(M) = L(N)}$$

In an equational theory, a definition is a simple equation where the left-hand side is a single variable and the right-hand side is some expression that may contain the same variable (recursive definitions). In the framework of [12], a definition enriches a theory with a new operator and a new equation. For a mutually recursive set of function definitions, we consider the functions that are implicitly defined as satisfying all the defining equations in the enriched theory.

7.4.2 A STRATEGY FOR OBTAINING NEW DEFINITIONS

With the equational theory providing the algebraic identities and the inference rules, we can formally transform the original program into a more efficient one.

For simplicity, we begin with a program consisting of one definition:

$$a = \text{fn}(x) : D\{\tau_1[a]\},$$

where $\tau_1[a]$ is an expression in x possibly containing a. Through an abuse of notation, we also use a to denote the data field defined. Next, let the reshape morphism g and its inverse be given by

$$g = \text{fn}(x) : D\{\tau_2 : E\} \quad \text{and} \quad g^{-1} = \text{fn}(y) : E\{\tau_3 : D\}.$$

Semantically, what we want is a data field $\hat{a}$ satisfying $\hat{a} = a \circ g^{-1}$. However, merely executing the program g^{-1} followed by a does not decrease the communication cost. What we want is a new definition of $\hat{a}$ that does not contain either a, g, or g^{-1}. A strategy for obtaining a new definition for $\hat{a}$ from the definitions of a, g, and g^{-1} is the following:

1. Using the identity $a = \hat{a} \circ g$, replace all occurrences of a with $\hat{a} \circ g$ in the definition of a.
2. Using a combination of unfoldings of g and g^{-1} and various other identities given in the theory, eliminate all occurrences of g and g^{-1} from the result of the first step. A very useful transformation

turns out to be the η-abstraction, where we provide a function with dummy arguments in order to unfold it.

EXAMPLE 7.1: Reshape Transformation

We illustrate the transformation strategy using the data field *ipivot*.

1. Start with the definition of *ipivot*:

$$ipivot = \mathsf{fn}(k):D_0\{\mathsf{reduce}(\mathsf{max},$$
$$\mathsf{list}[\,l:\mathsf{interval}(k,n) \mid \mathsf{abs}(a(l,k,k-1)) = apivot(k)\,]\}$$

2. Replace the left-hand side with the right of these equations

$$ipivot = \widetilde{ipivot} \circ g_{ipivot}$$
$$apivot = \widetilde{apivot} \circ g_{apivot}$$
$$a = \breve{a} \circ g_a$$

in the definition of *ipivot* to get

$$\widetilde{ipivot} \circ g_{ipivot} =$$
$$\mathsf{fn}(k):D_0\{\mathsf{reduce}(\mathsf{max}, \mathsf{list}[\,l:\mathsf{interval}(k,n) \mid$$
$$\mathsf{abs}(\breve{a} \circ g_a(l,k,k-1)) = \widetilde{apivot} \circ g_{apivot}(k)\,])\}$$

3. Right-compose both sides of the above equation with g_{ipivot}^{-1}, and then simplify the left-hand side:

$$\widetilde{ipivot} =$$
$$(\mathsf{fn}(k):D_0\{\mathsf{reduce}(\mathsf{max}, \mathsf{list}[\,l:\mathsf{interval}(k,n) \mid$$
$$\mathsf{abs}(\breve{a} \circ g_a(l,k,k-1)) = \widetilde{apivot} \circ g_{apivot}(k)\,])\}) \circ$$
$$g_{ipivot}^{-1}$$

4. Unfold the compositions and then unfold $g_a(l,k,k-1)$ and $g_{apivot}(k)$:

$$\widetilde{ipivot} =$$
$$(\mathsf{fn}(k):D_0\{\mathsf{reduce}(\mathsf{max}, \mathsf{list}[\,l:\mathsf{interval}(k,n) \mid$$
$$\mathsf{abs}(\breve{a}(l,k,k-1)) = \widetilde{apivot}(\mathsf{lb}(D_0),k,k)\,])\}) \circ$$
$$g_{ipivot}^{-1}$$

5. Eta-abstract the expression on the right-hand side by $(i, j, k):D$:

$\widetilde{ipivot} =$

$\mathsf{fn}(i, j, k):D\{[(\mathsf{fn}(k):D_0$

$\{\mathsf{reduce}(\mathsf{max}, \mathsf{list}[\, l:\mathsf{interval}(k, n)\, |$

$\qquad\qquad \mathsf{abs}(\tilde{a}(l, k, k - 1)) = \widetilde{apivot}(\mathsf{lb}(D_0), k, k)\,])\}) \circ$

$g_{ipivot}^{-1}](i, j, k)\}$

6. Unfold g_{ipivot}^{-1}:

$\widetilde{ipivot} =$

$\mathsf{fn}(i, j, k):D\{(\mathsf{fn}(k):D_0$

$\{\mathsf{reduce}(\mathsf{max}, \mathsf{list}[\, l:\mathsf{interval}(k, n)\, |$

$\qquad\qquad \mathsf{abs}(\tilde{a}(l, k, k - 1)) = \widetilde{apivot}(\mathsf{lb}(D_0), k, k)\,])\})$

$\left\{ \begin{array}{l} j = k \wedge i = \mathsf{lb}(D_0) \to k \\ j \neq k \vee i \neq \mathsf{lb}(D_0) \to \bot \end{array} \right\}\}$

7. Distribute the function over the conditional and beta-reduce:

$\widetilde{ipivot} =$

$$\mathsf{fn}(i, j, k):D\left\{ \begin{array}{l} j = k \wedge i = \mathsf{lb}(D_0) \to \\ \quad \mathsf{reduce}(\mathsf{max}, \mathsf{list}[\, l:\mathsf{interval}(k, n)\, | \\ \qquad\quad \mathsf{abs}(\tilde{a}(l, k, k - 1)) = \widetilde{apivot}(\mathsf{lb}(D_0), k, k) \\ j \neq k \vee i \neq \mathsf{lb}(D_0) \to \bot\,]) \end{array} \right\}$$
$\qquad\qquad\qquad\qquad\qquad\qquad\qquad\qquad\qquad\qquad\qquad\qquad\qquad\qquad\qquad \square$

7.4.3   THE CRYSTAL METALANGUAGE

Since the program transformations used above are all mechanizable, we have defined a *metalanguage* in which these transformations can be defined, and which furthermore allows the user to experiment with other transformations. In this section we indicate only the features of the metalanguage, for more detail see [15, 46].

Constructors and Selectors.   Meta-Crystal borrows ideas from ML [20] and 3-Lisp [42]. It consists of basic constructors and selectors for each of the constructs in Crystal and operations that manipulate programs and a set of operations for manipulating the programs, such as folding and unfolding, substitution, and normalization or beta-reduction. Using *meta-abstraction*, the reshape transformation can be defined in terms of primitive manipulations of the constructs.

Common Expressions.   When identical expressions evaluate to the same value in different definitions, the expression should be evaluated only once. The metalanguage will detect this and transform the expression into a "memoized" version. An expression τ is replaced with $\mathsf{memo}(l, \mathsf{quote}\{\tau\})$, where l is a unique label for the expression. For example,

$$a = \mathsf{memo}(l_1, \mathsf{quote}\{f(y) + z\}) \times 5$$
$$b = \mathsf{memo}(l_1, \mathsf{quote}\{f(y) + z\}) \times 4$$

memoizes the common expression $\ulcorner f(y) + z \urcorner$. Memoization is also applicable to the intermediate language.

Replication.   A metalanguage transformation that eliminates the communication of a value by replicating it at compile time. Given $a : D \rightarrow V$ and domain E, $\mathsf{replicate}(a, E)$ produces a new function $\hat{a} : D \times E \rightarrow V$.

7.5   The Structure of a Crystal Compiler

The compilation techniques developed for Crystal include synthesis of parallel control structures, automatic layout and distribution of data, generation of explicit communication from program reference patterns, and global optimization between parallel program modules. The structure of a Crystal compiler is depicted in Figure 7.4. In the following section, we give a brief description of each part.

7.5.1   DEPENDENCY

Two types of dependency analyses form the basis for various compilation techniques of Crystal: the *call dependency* between data fields (functions) and the *communication dependency* among indices of the index domains. Call dependency is useful in many ways—for instance, in decomposing a program into *phases* and determining the control flow of the target program. Communication dependency provides information for data accessing patterns and storage requirement. Based on this information, the compiler determines how an index domain can be reshaped and mapped to the domain of processors and time sequences by appropriate morphisms.

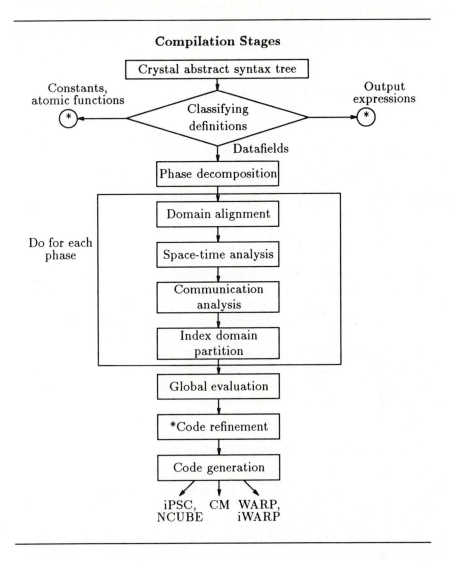

FIGURE 7.4
The Structure of a Crystal Compiler.

7.5.2   INDEX DOMAIN ALIGNMENT

Index domain alignment addresses the issue of reducing data movement between processors that arises due to cross-references among different data fields. The problem of alignment is formulated as finding a set of suitable *reshaping* functions that map the index domains of these data fields into a common index domain.

7.5.3   SYNTHESIS OF PARALLEL CONTROL STRUCTURE

Dependency analyses are influential in determining the *temporal* and *spatial part* of an index domain. The purpose is threefold: (1) to find independent computations that can be done in parallel, (2) to allow *a priori* scheduling of time-dependent computation in an iterative manner, and (3) to determine the values of a data field that can be destructively modified in a safe manner in order to ensure efficient reuse of memory.

7.5.4   DISTRIBUTED DATA MOVEMENT PRIMITIVES

Crystal treats global operations such as array movement with permutations, transposition, reductions, scan, broadcast, scatter and gather, etc. as low-level primitives of a multiprocessor machine. In this view, the Crystal compiler translates high-level code into low-level primitives, be they von-Neumann-style machine instructions or distributed data movement primitives. Like traditional compilers that use estimated cost of instruction sequences for optimization purposes, the costs of these distributed data movement primitives are estimated and used extensively in the compilation stages.

7.5.5   PROBLEM AND DOMAIN PARTITIONING

To ensure appropriate granularity of parallelism, an index domain must be partitioned into a number of subdomains where computation in a given partition is done sequentially. To do partitioning well is perhaps one of the most interesting and difficult compilation problems. We have developed a two-level partitioning strategy [31] where a local strategy is applied to each program phase and global strategy links the different phases.

Local Optimization.   This local strategy is based on the principle of minimizing surface (communication cost) to volume ratio (a fixed amount of computation) as illustrated by Fox et al.[19] with an image processing example where only nearest neighbor communication occurs.

Our techniques are more general and refined since the compiler must consider more general patterns of dependency and choose appropriate communication primitives. The list of primitives includes local memory access, neighboring communications, individual "send/receive" commands, pipelining, and the above-mentioned global distributed data movement routines. The cost functions of these communication primitives are given in a parameterized form with respect to the message size, the number of processors participating in the communication, and the elapsed time of the computation between communications. For each specific target machine, the terms of a cost function are defined according to the algorithmic implementation of the primitive while the coefficients of the terms are determined from experimental data using the least squares fit.

Since data partitioning affects which communication gets *internalized* (for example, a communication becomes a memory access), the estimation of computation cost cannot be performed until a particular partitioning strategy is chosen. A solution to this circular problem is to allow a set of *standard* partition strategies to be considered. For each standard partition strategy, we eliminate those communications that are internalized and estimate the cost of the rest.

Global Optimization.   At the global level, multiple program phases are linked by considering the total cost. Central to this level of optimization is the data movement between phases, which often contribute a large fraction of the total communication overhead. We have developed four types of linking mechanisms: (1) *spatial alignment*, which aligns the spatial parts of the domains of the phases first and then maps the resulting aligned domain to the space of processors and the memory within processors; (2)*domain remapping*, which takes the spatial part of each domain and maps it separately to the processors and memory; (3) *duplication*, in which a phase is duplicated and computed redundantly in space so as to reduce communication; and (4) *interleaving*, in which two phases are executed concurrently.

7.5.6   MAPPING INDEX DOMAINS TO PHYSICAL PROCESSORS

We have considered reshaping, aligning, and partitioning of index domains. The next step is to map elements of index domains to physical processors. Different index domains will require different embedding into the target network of processors. We also consider dynamic mapping where processors request tasks (and data) from a master queue as in the implementation of self-scheduled do-loops [21].

7.5.7   CODE GENERATION AND REFINEMENT

Finally, a code generator is employed for each different target language or machine. The analyses and optimizations are performed at the level of Crystal source and the intermediate language. Thus they are independent of the target language. However, since cost estimation plays a central role in a Crystal compiler, the modeling of optimization problems and the heuristics for solving them often must be hand-tooled for each specific target machine to obtain desired performance.

A compiler generating a parallel target program must also produce efficient sequential code for each processor. Traditional compiler optimization techniques are used to refine the sequential code.

7.5.8   COMPARING A CRYSTAL COMPILER WITH A PARALLELIZING FORTRAN COMPILER

Since our goal is to implement Crystal as efficiently as some of the imperative languages, it is most relevant to discuss some of the differences and similarities between a Crystal compiler and a parallelizing Fortran compiler [3, 9, 16, 18, 27, 32, 36, 37].

Dependencies existing in a Crystal program are evident from the program text because of its functional nature, which thus radically simplifies the analysis. For the same reason, a Crystal compiler need not deal with problems such as aliasing, which arises in a language with side-effects. On the other hand, a parallelizing Fortran compiler needs sophisticated data dependency and interprocedural analysis.

The functional nature of Crystal also has quite an impact on the scheduling of computations. Fortran systems are designed to interchange the nesting hierarchy of loops and to parallelize them, while the Crystal compiler must devise the control flow of the program from scratch. Functionality is an advantage since the greater flexibility permits the compiler to utilize all the parallelism. The down-side of this (the lack of explicit sequencing) is that a significantly greater amount of effort is necessary in optimizing the sequential code to match what a good programmer might write.

Another point relates to the target machines used. So far, parallelizing Fortran compilers have not addressed data distribution, since shared-memory machines are assumed. The Crystal compiler is targeted to machines with distributed memory. A Crystal compiler performs *index domain alignment* to minimize the cost of communication due to crossreferences between arrays, *domain partitioning* to determine the assignment of an aggregate of elements to each processor, and *communication synthesis* to choose the most efficient communication primitives. These new techniques will be described below.

Consider the Gaussian elimination example. One major difference between the Fortran and Crystal approaches is in detecting operations and communication such as scan, reduction, broadcast, etc., which can be done in parallel. Examples would include the reduction operations in the computation of the pivot elements, broadcasting of the pivot row, and the elimination of coefficients. A Crystal compiler will generate code that uses fast parallel routines on the hypercube multiprocessor to carry out these operations while most of the parallelizing Fortran compilers would produce sequential code in this case.

7.6 Dependency and Phase Decomposition

In Crystal, we have a particular approach of dividing a compiler into stages of analyses, syntheses, and optimizations. We have also described the programming methodology of how a programmer can use Crystal's various functional abstractions to divide a problem into small and manageable sub-problems where known algorithmic techniques may apply or new ones may be devised. In addition to these two very important issues is the problem of finding a suitable program unit upon which a compiler can operate most efficiently. At issue here is the coupling of the effect of optimization on different parts of the program.

It turns out that a set of data fields used by a programmer for specifying a data parallel algorithm often has an additional internal structure defined by the call dependency indicating that the elements of a certain subset of the data fields are more closely coupled with each other than with others. The objective of phase decomposition is to allow the optimization of the communication cost defined by the data fields within each such subset to take precedence over that in different subsets. A phase is a program unit used in aligning and partitioning an index domain. Global optimizations are then applied to link multiple phases together.

We begin with a few definitions of various notions of dependency. Consider the Crystal program:

$$f : \text{dfield} = \text{fn}(x):D_1\{\tau_1[f, g]\},$$
$$g : \text{dfield} = \text{fn}(x, y):D_2\{\tau_2[f, g]\}.$$

An *instance* of a definition is an equation formed by the application of both sides of the definition to some argument. An *instance* of a program is a set of instances of each of its definitions. In the case of the above program, an example of an instance is

$$\{ f(2) = \tau_1[f, g](2), \ g(2, 5) = \tau_2[f, g](2, 5) \}$$

where 2 is in D_1 and $(2, 5)$ is in D_2.

In the following, let P be a program defining a set of data fields

$$f_i : D_i \rightarrow V_i, \text{ for } 0 \leq i \leq n - 1.$$

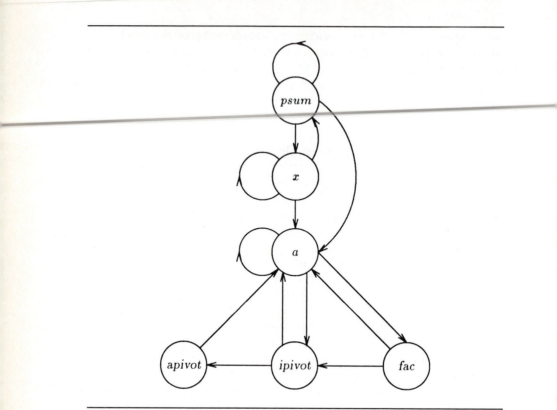

FIGURE 7.5
A Call Dependency Graph.

The value $f_i(x)$ is said to be *data dependent* on the value $f_j(y)$ if there exists an instance of program P with $f_i(x)$ occurring on the left hand side of an equation and $f_j(y)$ occurring on the right hand side. Data field f_i is said to be *call dependent* on data field f_j if x exists in D_i and y in D_j such that $f_i(x)$ is data dependent on $f_j(y)$.

A *call dependency graph* derived from program P, denoted by $G(P)$, consists of nodes labeled by the data fields defined in P, and arcs (directed edges) constructed as follows: If data field f_i is call dependent on data field f_j, then there is an arc going from the node labeled f_j to the node labeled f_i.

Figure 7.5 illustrates the call dependency graph of the program in Figure 7.1. Representing dependencies of programs by directed graphs is widely used [17, 28, 35].

Let the set of data fields f_i, for $0 \leq i \leq n - 1$ be over the same index domain D. We say that the element x of index domain D is *communication dependent* on element y of D if data fields f_i and f_j exist such that $f_i(x)$ is data dependent on $f_j(y)$.

A *communication dependent graph* derived from program P, denoted by $C(P)$, consists of nodes labeled by elements of the domain D, and arcs (directed edges) constructed as follows: If element x in D is communication dependent on element y in D, then there is an arc going from the node labeled y to the node labeled x.

Let the index domain D of the data fields be the product of k interval domains. We now consider D to be a subset of the k-dimensional vector space over the rational numbers. The set of *dependency vectors* derived from program P, denoted by $M(P)$, consists of vectors $x - y$ for all x and y in D such that x is communication-dependent on y.

Now we can define the notion of a phase of a program.

Definition. Let P be a program and S a subgraph of its call dependency graph $G(P)$. The nodes of S are labeled by a subset of data fields defined by P. The subprogram that defines these data fields is denoted by Prog(S). In the case where S is a *maximal strongly connected component*, we call Prog(S) a *phase* of program P.

The program in Figure 7.1 has two phases. The first defines data fields a, *ipivot*, *apivot*, and *fac*, and the second defines data fields *psum* and x.

7.7 Domain Alignment

In Crystal, domain alignment can be either explicitly given by the programmer along with the program or generated by the compiler automatically. In the latter case, the problem of *index domain alignment* is formulated as finding a set of suitable alignment functions that map the index domains of the arrays into a common index domain so as to minimize the cost of data movement due to crossreferences between the arrays.

7.7.1 ISSUES IN ALIGNMENT

The following example illustrates conflicting goals for alignment:

$$a : \mathsf{dfield} \; = \; \mathsf{fn}(i, j) : D\{\phi_1(b(i, j - 2))\}$$
$$b : \mathsf{dfield} \; = \; \mathsf{fn}(i, j) : D\{\phi_2(a(j, i))\}$$

where ϕ_1 and ϕ_2 are functions. Whether $a(i, j)$ is aligned to $b(i, j)$ or not, communication due to these two reference patterns cannot both be reduced at the same time. Thus the alignment problem must be formulated as an optimization problem where references may carry different weights depending on their patterns.

Now let us look at a slightly more involved example where a reduction operator occurs in the definition of data field a:

$$a : \mathsf{dfield} \; = \; \mathsf{fn}(i, j){:}D\{\mathsf{reduce}(+, \mathsf{list}[\, b(k, i) \mid k{:}\mathsf{interval}(0, n-1)\,])\}$$
$$b : \mathsf{dfield} \; = \; \mathsf{fn}(i, j){:}D\{\tau[i, j]\}$$

We consider first the simple scenario of mapping one element per processor. For each $(i, j) \in D$, a set of elements of b is referenced. If we store $a(i, j)$, $b(i, j)$ at processor (i, j), then for each i we must do a reduction across the ith column of elements of b and distribute the result along the ith row. Alternatively, if $b(j, i)$ is stored in processor (i, j), only a reduction operation over a row is needed, provided the processors are connected by networks such as hypercubes, butterflies, etc., because the broadcast can be achieved at the same time as a side effect of reduction [25, 23]. Thus alignment is related to the communication routines specific to the interconnection network of the target machine. In the next section we will discuss the abstract machine model and reference metric upon which we based our formulation of and solution to the alignment problem.

Next, for the same example, suppose each domain is partitioned into sub-domains, each of which is mapped to a processor. By aligning $a(i, j)$ with $b(j, i)$ for all (i, j) in D (that is, transposing b), and partitioning the domain along the first dimension (mapping a row into a processor), there will be no communication involved at all since the reduction operations now take place within a single processor. However, if $a(i, j)$ and $b(i, j)$ are mapped to the same processor, some communication must occur no matter how partitioning is done. We want to point out here that choosing the right partitioning strategy so as to "internalize" as many communications as possible is considered in a separate *domain partitioning* stage in the Crystal compiler and is beyond the scope of this chapter. This example illustrates that alignment always helps in reducing cross-references from a to b, independent of domain partitioning.

The following example illustrates a reference pattern whose first component is a nonlinear expression.

$$a : \mathsf{dfield} \; = \; \mathsf{fn}(i, j){:}D\{b(j^2 - j, i + j)\}$$
$$b : \mathsf{dfield} \; = \; \mathsf{fn}(i, j){:}D\{\tau[i, j]\}$$

Though it might be possible to align a and b in such a way as to avoid communication, the cost of evaluating the extra conditional and the nonlinear expressions generated by the alignment process may exceed the cost of communication. Thus there are some tradeoffs involved in doing alignment. We will discuss the class of alignment functions under our consideration.

Finally, any compilation technique is limited by what is known at compile time, and alignment is no exception. Below is an example where a reference pattern contains an indirect reference $a(i, j-1)$ whose value may not be known until the program is in execution. Hence such communication patterns shall not be taken into account by the alignment algorithm.

$$a : \mathsf{dfield} \; = \; \mathsf{fn}(i, j) {:} D\{b(a(i, j-1), \tau_1)\}$$
$$b : \mathsf{dfield} \; = \; \mathsf{fn}(i, j) {:} D\{\tau_2[i, j]\}$$

7.7.2 ALIGNMENT MORPHISMS

A compiler, in the absence of application specific knowledge, is limited in the type of morphisms it can generate. We consider the following morphisms and their composition for the simplicity of their symbolic forms and their usefulness.

A *permutation morphism* is a domain morphism

$$g : D_0 \times \cdots \times D_{m-1} \to D_{q_0} \times \cdots \times D_{q_{m-1}}$$

defined by $g(i_0, i_1, \ldots, i_{m-1}) = (i_{q_0}, i_{q_1}, \ldots, i_{q_{m-1}})$, where $(q_0, q_1, \ldots, q_{m-1})$ is a permutation of $(0, 1, \ldots, m-1)$.

An *embedding morphism* is a domain morphism

$$g : D_0 \times D_1 \cdots \times D_{m-1} \to D_0 \cdots \times D_{m-1} \times D_m \cdots \times D_{n-1}$$

of the form

$$g(i_0, i_1, \ldots, i_{m-1}) = (i_0, i_1, \ldots, i_{m-1}, f_m(i), \ldots, f_{n-1}(i))$$

where $i = (i_0, i_1, \ldots, i_{m-1})$ and $f_j : D_0 \times D_1 \cdots \times D_{m-1} \to D_j$ for $j = m, \ldots, n-1$.

Let D and E be interval domains. A domain morphism $g : D \to E$ is said to be a *shift morphism* if g is of the form $g = \mathsf{fn}(i){:}D\{i - c\}$ where c is an integer.

Let $D = \mathsf{interval}(l, u)$ and $w = u - l + 1$. A domain morphism $g : D \to D$ is said to be a *cyclic shift morphism* if g is of the form $g = \mathsf{fn}(i){:}D\{((i - l - c) \bmod w) + l\}$ where c is an integer. Similarly, g

!{ Domain morphisms for aligning index domains }!

$$ga : \text{morph} = \text{id}(D)$$

$$g_a^{-1} : \text{morph} = \text{id}(D)$$

$$g_{fac} : \text{morph} = \text{fn}(i,k):\text{prod-dom}(D_0, D_0)\{(i,k,k):D\}$$

$$g_{fac}^{-1} : \text{morph} = \text{fn}(i,j,k):D\left\{ \begin{matrix} j = k \rightarrow (i,k) \\ j \neq k \rightarrow \bot \end{matrix} \right\} : \text{prod-dom}(D_0, D_0)$$

$$g_{ipivot} : \text{morph} = \text{fn}(k):D_0\{(\text{lb}(D_0), k, k):D\}$$

$$g_{ipivot}^{-1} : \text{morph} = \text{fn}(i,j,k):D\left\{ \begin{matrix} j = k \wedge i = \text{lb}(D_0) \rightarrow (k) \\ j \neq k \vee i \neq \text{lb}(D_0) \rightarrow \bot \end{matrix} \right\} : D_0$$

$$g_{apivot} : \text{morph} = g_{ipivot}$$

$$g_{apivot}^{-1} : \text{morph} = g_{ipivot}^{-1}$$

FIGURE 7.6
Alignment Morphisms for Gaussian Elimination.

is said to be a *conditional shift morphism* if g is of the form

$$g = \text{fn}(i):D\left\{ \begin{matrix} (i - c) \leq l \rightarrow \bot \\ \text{else} \rightarrow i - c \end{matrix} \right\}$$

where c is an integer. A *compound shift morphism* is the product of two shift morphisms (cyclic or conditional) where the product of two functions f and g is defined as $f \times g = \text{fn}(i, j)\{(f(i), g(j))\}$.

Let $D = \text{interval}(l, u)$ and $E = \text{interval}(-u, -l)$. A *reflection morphism* is a domain morphism $g : D \rightarrow E$ of the form $g = \text{fn}(i):D\{-i\}$.

A *conditional reflection morphism* is a domain morphism $g : D \rightarrow D$ of the form

$$g = \text{fn}(i):D\left\{ \begin{matrix} -i < l \vee -i > u \rightarrow \bot \\ \text{else} \rightarrow -i \end{matrix} \right\}$$

The formulation of the alignment problem and a fast heuristic algorithm for its solution is presented in [30]. The alignment morphisms for the first program phase of Gaussian elimination appear in Figure 7.6 where the four pairs of alignment morphisms and their inverses are used to map the index domains of the four data fields into the common index domain D. The first pair is an identity morphism, and all others are embedding morphisms.

! Transformed version with index domain aligned

n : int $= 4$

D_0 : domain $=$ interval$(1, n)$

D_1 : domain $=$ interval$(1, n + 1)$

D_2 : domain $=$ interval$(0, n)$

D : domain $=$ prod-dom(D_0, D_1, D_2)

$\widetilde{a}$: dfield$(D, V) =$

$\quad$ fn$(i, j, k):D$

$$\left\{ \begin{array}{l} k = \mathsf{lb}(D_2) \rightarrow A_0(i - 1, j - 1) \\ \mathrm{else} \rightarrow \left\{ \begin{array}{l} i = k \rightarrow \widetilde{a}(\widetilde{ipivot}(\mathsf{lb}(D_0), k, k), j, k - 1) \\ i = \widetilde{ipivot}(\mathsf{lb}(D_0), k, k) \rightarrow \\ \quad\quad \widetilde{a}(k, j, k - 1) - \widetilde{a}(i, j, k - 1) * \widetilde{fac}(i, k, k) \\ \mathrm{else} \rightarrow \widetilde{a}(i, j, k - 1) - \\ \quad\quad \widetilde{a}(\widetilde{ipivot}(\mathsf{lb}(D_0), k, k), j, k - 1) * \widetilde{fac}(i, k, k) \end{array} \right\} \end{array} \right\}$$

$\widetilde{ipivot}$: dfield$(D, V) =$

$\quad$ fn$(i, j, k):D$

$$\left\{ \begin{array}{l} j = k \wedge i = \mathsf{lb}(D_0) \rightarrow \\ \quad\quad \mathsf{reduce}(\max, \mathsf{list}[\, l{:}\mathsf{interval}(k, n) \mid \\ \quad\quad\quad\quad \mathsf{abs}(\widetilde{a}(l, k, k - 1)) = \widetilde{apivot}(\mathsf{lb}(D_0), k, k)\,]) \\ j \neq k \vee i \neq \mathsf{lb}(D_0) \rightarrow \perp \end{array} \right\}$$

$\widetilde{apivot}$: dfield$(D, V) =$

$\quad$ fn$(i, j, k):D$

$$\left\{ \begin{array}{l} j = k \wedge i = \mathsf{lb}(D_0) \rightarrow \\ \quad\quad \mathsf{reduce}(\max, \mathsf{list}[\, \mathsf{abs}(\widetilde{a}(l, k, k - 1)) \mid l{:}\mathsf{interval}(k, n)\,]) \\ j \neq k \vee i \neq \mathsf{lb}(D_0) \rightarrow \perp \end{array} \right\}$$

$\widetilde{fac}$: dfield$(D, V) =$

$\quad$ fn$(i, j, k):D$

$$\left\{ \begin{array}{l} j = k \rightarrow \left\{ \begin{array}{l} i \leq k \rightarrow 1.0 \\ i = \widetilde{ipivot}(\mathsf{lb}(D_0), k, k) \rightarrow \\ \quad\quad \widetilde{a}(k, k, k - 1) / \widetilde{a}(\widetilde{ipivot}(\mathsf{lb}(D_0), k, k), k, k - 1) \\ \mathrm{else} \rightarrow \widetilde{a}(i, k, k - 1) / \widetilde{a}(\widetilde{ipivot}(\mathsf{lb}(D_0), k, k), k, k - 1) \end{array} \right\} \\ j \neq k \rightarrow \perp \end{array} \right\}$$

FIGURE 7.7
The Transformed Crystal Program with Aligned Index Domain.

After the compiler generates all the necessary alignment morphisms, the metalanguage processor takes the source program and in turn generates the transformed program as shown in Figure 7.7 where all data fields are now defined over a common index domain.

7.8   Synthesis of Parallel Control Structure

From the functional definitions of a Crystal program, we want to generate target parallel programs in C or Fortran with explicit communication commands. The technique we use to generate the control structure of the target program is called *spatial and temporal-coordinate analysis.*

We first provide some background for solving this problem. Given a Crystal program phase, after the alignment stage all index domains of the data fields will be aligned. The communication dependency graph of the program is a directed graph, which may or may not contain cycles. Suppose the graph is acyclic. Then we can define the notion of the *wavefront number* of a node: the maximum path length leading into the node from some source node, where a source node is one that does not have any incoming edge. A wavefront is just the set of all nodes with the same wavefront number. It turns out that there is a natural *maximally parallel* scheduling [26] for the program where the computation proceeds from one wavefront after another in order of increasing wavefront numbers. More realistic schedules that take into account resource constraints can then be generated based on this ideal schedule.

Being able to find a schedule at compile-time has many obvious advantages, for example, in reducing memory usage by multiple assignments to a given variable, in achieving better load balance, and in eliminating context switching at run-time. However, most useful programs are likely to have communication dependency graphs that are cyclic.

There are three possible reasons for a communication graph to be cyclic: (1) the combined effect of two references in two different conditional branches, (2) a reference to the same domain element but with a different data field name, and (3) a self reference to the same domain element with the same data field name. Only the third case is a true self-reference and indicates an incorrectly written program. For the first case, the compiler can resolve the cycles by analyzing the predicates when they are of certain restricted form (for example, linear expressions of the indices). In the second case, the cycles can be resolved with the help of the call dependency graph. Other compiler techniques may still sharpen the analysis, but in general, there will be run-time dependent cases where the compiler cannot resolve the cycles. A solution to this problem is to use a data-flow model for executing the program.

In such a paradigm, nodes of the communication dependency graph are thought of as processes, which are suspended if the required data are not available and become active when required data are available. Note that in this situation, *load balancing* is much harder to predict and often adds additional overhead.

The purpose of the spatial and temporal coordinate (STC) analysis is to break the cycles in the communication dependency graph when possible, and then create a control structure for the target program. A component of an index domain is labeled either as temporal or spatial, corresponding to a direction along which either a sequence of computations proceeds or parallelism occurs, respectively. Not surprisingly, there can be many different ways of such labeling. Our approach is to let the compiler generate a small number of different labelings ("optimal" with respect to certain criteria). A global cost evaluation will then determine a particular choice.

7.8.1   DEFINITIONS AND REPRESENTATION OF DEPENDENCY VECTORS

In the following section, we present the STC algorithm that finds the *temporal* part of the index domain. For simplicity, this algorithm does not deal with conditionals. A few definitions first.

In the following, let P be a program defining the data fields f_i : $D \to V_i$ for $0 \le i \le n$, where D is the product of k interval domains. Let $M(P)$ be the set of dependency vectors of P. We now consider D under the Cartesian coordinate system, and we denote the unit basis vectors by $e^0, e^1, \ldots, e^{k-1}$.

A dependency vector $x = (x_0, x_1, \ldots, x_{k-1})$ of P is said to be *positively oriented* with respect to the unit vector e^i if $x_i > 0$, and it is *negatively oriented* if $x_i < 0$ and *orthogonal* if $x_i = 0$.

Let the components of an index domain be labeled by natural numbers $0, 1, \ldots, k-1$ where k is the dimensionality of domain D. Component (dimension) i of index domain D is said to be *positively (negatively) orientable* if for all x in $M(P)$, x is positively (negatively) oriented with respect to e^i.

Component i of index domain D is said to be *partially orientable* if no two dependency vectors x and y in $M(P)$ are such that x is positively oriented while y is negatively oriented with respect to e^i.

Component i of index domain D is said to be *inorientable* if there exist two dependency vectors x and y in $M(P)$ such that x is positively oriented while y is negatively oriented with respect to e^i.

Since the patterns of references occurring in a program affect the scheduling and communication cost of the target program, a compiler must perform extensive analysis and optimization based on the dependency vectors. The general form of a dependency vector of program P defined at x is

$$(x_1 - \tau_1[f_1, \ldots, f_n, x], \ldots, x_k - \tau_k[f_1, \ldots, f_n, x]),$$

where $x = (x_1, x_2, \ldots, x_k)$ is an element of the index domain D. At compile time, the values of such a dependency vector may not be known. Hence there is a need for a compile-time representation of the dependency vectors.

For each component $x_i - \tau_i$ of a dependency vector, its *symbolic form* is as follows:

1. 0, when $\tau_i = x_i$;
2. c or $-c$ for some positive integer constant c, when $\tau_i = x_i - c$ or $\tau_i = x_i + c$;
3. v or $-v$, when τ_i is an integer valued expression whose value either is indeterminable at compile time or may range over a set of values. The sign of the value is explicitly specified if it can be determined at compile-time.

A *symbolic dependency vector* is defined to be a dependency vector with each of its components replaced by its symbolic form. Given a symbolic dependency vector s, its *scope* is the set of elements x in D where there exists a dependency vector at x that has pattern s.

Figure 7.8 consists of a list of the symbolic dependency vectors derived from the program in Figure 7.7 (phase one, with aligned domains) along with the pair of dependent data (the left-hand side followed by the right-hand side). We omit the predicates. Internal to the compiler, the scope of a pattern is represented by a set of restricting predicates over the index domain D.

In the following discussion the term "dependency vector" will mean "symbolic dependency vector."

7.8.2   THE STC ALGORITHM

The algorithm for labeling spatial and temporal coordinates (STC) works by choosing one temporal component at a time. Those components that are not chosen at the termination of the algorithm are spatial. In each iteration of the algorithm, some arcs of the call graph are removed, and the set of dependency vectors are being reduced to a smaller subset. To define exactly when an arc of a call graph can be removed, we present the following definition.

Definition.   Consider a program P whose data fields are over the same index domain D, which is the product of k interval domains. In the call

$(0,0,1)$	$\widetilde{a}(i,j,k)$	$\widetilde{a}(i,j,k-1)$
$(v,0,1)$	$\widetilde{a}(i,j,k)$	$\widetilde{a}(\widetilde{ipivot}(\mathsf{lb}(D_0),k,k),j,k-1)$
$(v,0,1)$	$\widetilde{a}(i,j,k)$	$\widetilde{a}(k,j,k-1)$
$(v,v,0)$	$\widetilde{a}(i,j,k)$	$\widetilde{ipivot}(\mathsf{lb}(D_0),k,k)$
$(0,v,0)$	$\widetilde{a}(i,j,k)$	$\widetilde{fac}(i,k,k)$
$(v,v,1)$	$\widetilde{apivot}(i,j,k)$	$\widetilde{a}(l,k,k-1)$
$(v,v,1)$	$\widetilde{ipivot}(i,j,k)$	$\widetilde{a}(l,k,k-1)$
$(+v,v,0)$	$\widetilde{ipivot}(i,j,k)$	$\widetilde{apivot}(\mathsf{lb}(D_0),k,k)$
$(+v,v,0)$	$\widetilde{fac}(i,j,k)$	$\widetilde{ipivot}(\mathsf{lb}(D_0),k,k)$
$(v,v,1)$	$\widetilde{fac}(i,j,k)$	$\widetilde{a}(k,k,k-1)$
$(0,v,1)$	$\widetilde{fac}(i,j,k)$	$\widetilde{a}(i,k,k-1)$
$(v,v,1)$	$\widetilde{fac}(i,j,k)$	$\widetilde{a}(\widetilde{ipivot}(\mathsf{lb}(D_0),k,k),k,k-1)$

FIGURE 7.8
Symbolic Dependency Vectors Derived from the Transformed Gaussian Elimination of Figure 7.7.

dependency graph $G(P)$, for each arc from the node labeled f_j to f_i, let $V(f_i, f_j)$ be the set of dependency vectors $x - y$, where for all $x, y \in D$, $f_i(x)$ depends on $f_j(y)$.

1. Initialize $R := G(P)$ (the call dependency graph of program P), $S = M(P)$ (the dependency vectors), and $l = 0$. Let Q be the set of orientable dimensions of domain D. For each arc a in the set of arcs of R, initialize $A(a) := V(f_i, f_j)$, where a is from the node labeled by data field f_j to the node labeled by data field f_i.

2. While R is cyclic and Q is non-empty do:

   a. Increment the value of l;

   b. Choose an orientable coordinate (call it j) in Q that is temporal. Let $t(l) := j$ (we say that the lth level temporal index is ranging over the jth component of domain D) and set $Q := Q - j$;

   c. Let Z be the set of dependency vectors that are oriented with respect to the unit basis e^j. Set $S := S - Z$ and $A(a) := A(a) - Z$, for all arcs $a \in R$;

   d. Reduce R (which means remove an arc a from the graph if $A(a)$ is empty).

This algorithm finds all of the temporal components of the index domain; the remaining components are spatial.

EXAMPLE 7.2: We now apply the STC algorithms to the first phase of the Gaussian elimination example. The graph R is initially assigned to the phase 1 part of the call dependency graph in Figure 7.5 and S is assigned to the dependency vectors listed in Figure 7.8. We found component 2 of the index domain D to be the only orientable coordinate. The set Z happens to be the union of the following sets: $V(\tilde{a}, \tilde{a})$, $V(\widetilde{apivot}, \tilde{a})$, $V(\widetilde{ipivot}, \tilde{a})$, and $V(\widetilde{fac}, \tilde{a})$. So, the arcs $\tilde{a} \mapsto \tilde{a}$, $\widetilde{apivot} \mapsto \tilde{a}$, $\widetilde{ipivot} \mapsto \tilde{a}$, and $\widetilde{fac} \mapsto \tilde{a}$ can all be removed from R, which becomes acyclic and the algorithm terminates. Thus the algorithm results in a single temporal dimension (component 2) and two spatial dimensions (component 0 and component 1). □

7.8.3   SKETCHING THE TARGET PROGRAM

The above analysis enables us to sketch in the following the structure of an equivalent imperative program of the Crystal source program. The main translation step is in generating the assignment statements that update the values of array a, which, in the imperative program, is now a two-dimensional instead of three-dimensional array. This collapsing of a higher dimensional array into a lower dimensional one can be done only when some of the domain components are labeled temporal. In this example, component 2 (indexed by formal variable k) of index domain D is labeled temporal. Since component 2 of all dependency vectors has a constant value 1 or 0, with proper ordering of the assignment statements, the two-dimensional array a can be updated without using any temporary storage.

```
! Gaussian elimination

dom D₀ = interval(1, n);
dom D₁ = interval(1, n + 1);
dom D₂ = time(0, n);
dom D = product-dom(D₀, D₁)
array(D, float) a, apivot, ipivot, fac;

for (k:D₂) {
  forall (i:D₀, j:D₁) {
    apivot(i, j) := ···;
    ipivot(i, j) := ···;
    fac(i, j) := ···;
    a(i, j) := ···        } }
```

At the end of synthesizing parallel control structures, we are essentially at the same point as any parallelizing Fortran system after the dependence analysis stage where all potential compile-time detectable parallelism has been discovered. One can think of an intermediate program generated at this stage as a parallel program for multiple processors with a global shared memory. What remains to be done is to distribute data to each processor and generate appropriate communication between them.

7.9   Data Layout and Communication Synthesis

The distribution of data over the individual memory on each processor is done in two stages: (1) mapping the program data structure to a virtual network, and (2) embedding the virtual network into the physical network. Specifically, we consider virtual networks that are multidimensional grids and use the standard Gray code embedding of a grid into a hypercube.

The mapping from data structures to the virtual network consists of (1) *partitioning* the program data structures into appropriate grain sizes in such a way that communication overhead is reduced and workload is balanced, and (2) determining the relative locations of data structures so as to minimize inter-processor communication (we call this process *domain alignment*).

Finally, all references to data structures must be translated to local memory accesses or inter-processor communication. The communication forms of the intermediate program are then matched with a library of aggregate communication routines and those that minimize network congestion and overhead are chosen. The cost of inter-processor communication is modeled by a communication metric on which optimizations are based.

7.9.1   THE MAIN IDEA: USING AGGREGATE COMMUNICATION

Our communication synthesis approach is based on matching program references with aggregate communication routines called *communication primitives* at compile time. The original ideas of aggregate communication routines are from Fox *et al.* [19], and Johnsson [24] and Ho [22]. They have developed a collection of efficient communication routines for hypercube machines and have shown that programs using these routines are far more efficient than those using asynchronous message passing (that is, individual send and receive pairs) in many scientific and engineering applications.

The effect of using aggregate communication routines can be shown through a simple example. The following is a program segment written in a parallel C-like notation with Crystal domain constructs.

```
dom D₀ = interval(0, n);
dom D₁ = interval(1, n);
for (t:D₀) {
    forall ((i:D₁, j:D₁)) {
        a[i][j][t] = a[i][3][t − 1] + a[i][j][t − 1] } }
```

Suppose that the iterations of the above nested forall loops are assigned to different processors. Denote each processor by a pair (x, y), and let processor (x, y) be responsible for a range of iterations specified by the intervals $E_I = $ interval$(I_l(x, y), I_u(x, y))$ and $E_J = $ interval$(J_l(x, y), J_u(x, y))$. The target code using aggregate communication routines would look as follows. Function idx-to-pid$(i_1, \ldots, i_n)$ translates an index tuple $(i_1, \ldots, i_n)$ to the identifier of the processor to which the computation associated with the tuple is assigned. Code for processor (x, y) is

```
for (t:D₀) {
    spread(idx-to-pid(∗, 3, t), a[∗][3][t − 1]);
    for (i:E_I) {
        for (j:E_J) {
            a[i][j][t] = a[i][3][t − 1] + a[i][j][t − 1] } } }
```

A column broadcast routine spread is placed outside of the i and j loops. The broadcast routine spreads the third column of array a—that is, $a[i][3][t − 1]$, $1 \leq i \leq n$—to all other columns. More specifically, broadcasting takes place concurrently and independently within all the rows of the processor network. Each of the processors on which a segment of column 3 resides spreads the segment to other processors in the same row. Each processor will receive a segment of the column $a[i][3][t − 1]$, $I_l(x, y) \leq i < I_u(x, y)$, in a single message.

Global data movements such as the broadcast shown above occur quite frequently in application programs. If such data movement patterns can be identified from the source program, we can then issue calls to runtime communication routines that are both algorithmically optimized and carefully handcrafted for performance on the specific target machine.

7.9.2   AN OVERVIEW OF THE APPROACH

The communication synthesis module consists of three components, as shown in Figure 7.9. The first component is for analyzing reference patterns of the program and matching them with suitable communication routines. The second component deals with scheduling and synchronization of **send** and **receive** pairs, as well as synchronization of global aggregate communication routines. The third component handles the problem of partitioning the index domain of the input program over the target processors. The technical details for distributing data and generating explicit communication commands are contained in [29].

We include in Figures 7.10, 7.11, and 7.12 a portion of the compiler-generated target C code with explicit communication.

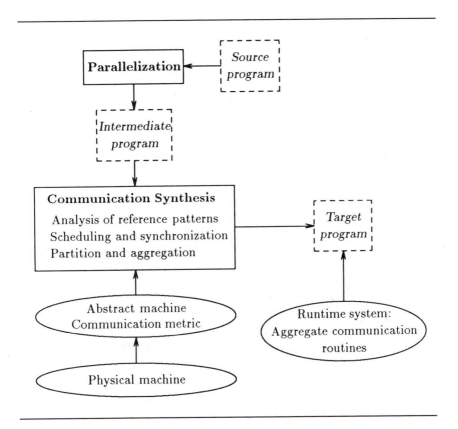

FIGURE 7.9
A High-Level View of the Communication Synthesis Module.

```
/* Declarations ... */

main(){

  crecv(INIT_MSG,param,40);

/* Constant definitions ... */
/* Initializations          */
  init_params();   init_a0();

/* Main computation and communication steps */
  for ((k=0); (k<kmax); k++){
    if (k>0) compute_apivot(k);
    if (k>0) compute_ipivot(k);
    if (k>0) bcast_ipivot(k);
    if (k>0) bcast_a2(k);
    if (k>0) compute_fac(k);
    if (k>0) bcast_fac(k);
    compute_a(k);
    bcast_a3(k);
    bcast_a1(k);
  }
  bcast_a4();
  if (ia!=(ni-1)) recv_x();
  if (ja!=(nj-1)) recv_psum();
  compute_x_etc();
  if (ia!=0) send_x();
  if (ja!=0) send_psum();
  csend(DONE_MSG,tbuf,64,my_host,host_pid);
}

/* initialization: setting up the partitioned data
 * and allocating storage */
init_params(){
  imin = 1; jmin = 1;  lmin = 1;
  imax = n; jmax = n+1;lmax = n; kmax = n;

  i_bz = (((imax-imin)/ni) +1);
  j_bz = (((jmax-jmin)/nj) +1);
  unit_sz = sizeof(float);
  ia = (my_node/nj); ja = (my_node%nj);
  i0 = 0;  jj0 = 0;
  i1 = block_ubound(imax-imin,ia,i_bz,ni,i0);
  jj1 = block_ubound(jmax-jmin,ja,j_bz,nj,jj0);

  a0 = alloc_float_2d_array(imax,jmax);
  a = alloc_float_3d_array(i_bz,j_bz,kmax+1);
  a_g1 = alloc_float_1d_array(jmax+1);
```

FIGURE 7.10
Highlights of the Compiler Generated iPSC/2 C Code (I).

```
/* similarly a_g2, a_g3, a_g4 */

  apivot = alloc_float_1d_array(kmax);
  ipivot = alloc_int_1d_array(kmax);
  fac = alloc_float_2d_array(i_bz,kmax);
  fac_g = alloc_float_1d_array(i_bz);
  x = alloc_float_2d_array(i_bz+1,j_bz+1);
  psum = alloc_float_2d_array(i_bz+1,j_bz+1);
  bcbuf1 = alloc_float_1d_array(max(jmax+1,i_bz*j_bz));
  sbuf = alloc_float_1d_array(max(i_bz+1,j_bz+1)); }

/* example of a data transfer using
 * csend and crecv primitives */
bcast_ipivot(k) int k;
{ int ja1;
  ja1 = gidx_to_ia(jmax-jmin,j_bz,nj,k-jmin);
  if (ia == 0 && ja == ja1){
    ipivot_g = ipivot[k] ;
    csend(200, &ipivot_g, sizeof(int), -1, my_pid) ;}
  else
    crecv(200, &ipivot_g, sizeof(int)) ; }
```

FIGURE 7.11
Highlights of the Compiler Generated iPSC/2 C Code (II).

We now conclude the description of the compiler with the performance of a target program for Gaussian elimination.

7.10 Some Performance Results

Figure 7.13 shows the speedup of the compiler-generated program from the source program in Figure 7.1. The experimental data are obtained as follows: The problem size (that is, matrix size) is first fixed. The same problem is then run on a different number of processors, from one to 64. When running on more than one processor, column partition of the matrix is used.

Let T_1 denote the elapsed time of a program running on a single processor, and let T_k be that on k processors. The speedup is computed as $speedup = T_1/T_k$. Five sets of data are plotted, each corresponding to a different problem size. The speedup of this program is not terrific. The culprits are those collective communication primitives (broadcast and

```
/* example of a data transfer using one of the
 * aggregate communication routines float_cdata_bcast */
bcast_fac(k)
int k;
{  int i,j,j3,ja1;
   ja1 = gidx_to_ia(jmax-jmin,j_bz,nj,k-jmin);
   if (ja==ja1){
      j3 = local_idx(jmax-jmin,j_bz,nj,k-jmin);
      cnt = 0;
      for ((i=i0); (i<i_bz); i++)
         bcbuf1[cnt++] = fac[i][k];  }
   else
      cnt = i_bz - i0 ;
   float_cdata_bcast(ja1,bcbuf1,fac_g,cnt,nj,my_node,my_pid);
}


/* example of the computation for a subblock of the matrix */
compute_a(k) int k;
{ int i,j;
  i2 = global_idx(imax-imin,ia,i_bz,ni,i0+1);
  for ((i=i0); (i<i1); i++,i2++){
     j2 = global_idx(jmax-jmin,ja,j_bz,nj,jj0+1);
     for ((j=jj0); (j<jj1); j++,j2++){
        if (k==0)
a[i][j][k] = a0[(i2-1)][(j2-1)];
        else
if (i2<k)
  a[i][j][k] = a[i][j][k-1];
else
   if (i2==k)
     a[i][j][k] = a_g2[j];
   else
     if (i2== ipivot_g)
       a[i][j][k] = (a_g1[j] - (a[i][j][k-1] * fac_g[i]));
     else
       a[i][j][k] = (a[i][j][k-1] - (a_g2[j] * fac_g[i]));}}}
```

FIGURE 7.12
Highlights of the Compiler Generated iPSC/2 C Code (III).

reduction) used for partial pivoting, where the cost of sending a message
of some unit size increases as the number of participating processors
increases. The communication time, in spite of the decrease in the size
of the messages, stays the same while the amount of computation in

Programs	1	2	4	8	16	32	64 *Nodes*
Handwritten	3.82	2.72	1.63	1.14	1.07	1.11	1.21
Compiler	10.08	5.75	3.64	2.65	2.21	2.05	2.11
Ratio	2.6	2.1	2.2	2.3	2.1	1.9	1.7

TABLE 7.1
Gaussian Elimination on iPSC/2. Matrix Size: 127×127.

Programs	1 *Node*	2 *Nodes*	4 *Nodes*	8 *Nodes*	16 *Node*
Handwritten	0.51	0.41	0.32	0.34	0.39
Compiler	1.47	0.96	0.72	0.63	0.62
Ratio	2.9	2.3	2.2	1.9	1.6

TABLE 7.2
Gaussian Elimination on iPSC/2. Matrix Size: 63×63.

each processor decreases linearly as the number of processors increases. Consequently, the overhead of communication (with respect to some unit computation) increases and results in a speedup that is far from linear. This is an example where one needs to be careful not to be overeager in using more processors.

Tables 7.1 and 7.2 contain the comparison of the performance of a compiler-generated program and a handcrafted program for computing Gaussian elimination with partial pivoting on the Intel iPSC/2 hypercube multiprocessors. The compiler generated program is obtained with all the optimization switches turned on. The handcrafted program is written directly by an experienced programmer familiar with iPSC/2. Figures given in the tables indicate the total elapsed time, in *seconds*, of a program running on different numbers of processors for a fixed problem size.

A factor of two to three inefficiency in the compiler generated program can be attributed to two reasons. One is that the compiler generated program is more flexible and works for different data partitions (for example, row, column, or block partition). The handcrafted version, however, is optimized for a particular partition. The advantage of the former is that it gives the user the extra control in experimenting with different partitions. The compiler can be improved to produce more efficient code in this respect by performing partial evaluating and optimizing the target code once a specific way of partitioning is chosen.

The other factor is in the optimization of the sequential code. The handcrafted program uses pointers extensively while the compiler-generated code tends to do more data copying. We are constantly being reminded that a parallel program generator must also be good at optimizing sequential code.

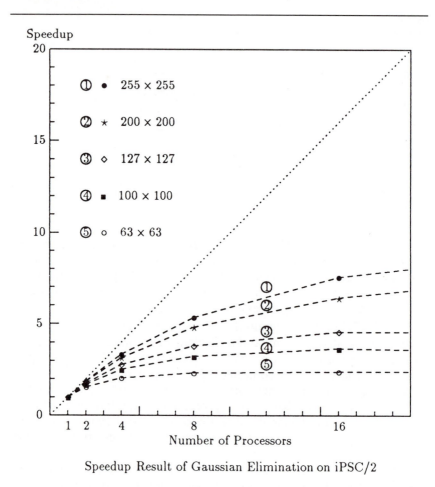

Speedup Result of Gaussian Elimination on iPSC/2

FIGURE 7.13
The Speedup of a Compiler-generated Program Computing Gaussian Elimination with Partial Pivoting.

7.11 Future Work

7.11.1   LANGUAGE AND SEMANTICS

The Crystal language allows functions to be defined over index domains that can be defined and treated as first class objects. Thus we need a formal semantics in which user defined types are interpreted as new semantic domains, or subdomains of the universal domain.

A more curious phenomenon is the interplay between a function and the domain over which it is defined. Consider the following program in which the minimization operator is used to define the domain using the function f over that same domain:

$$D_1 = \text{interval}(0, n)$$
$$D_2 = \text{interval}(0, \mu n : D_1 \, \phi[f, n])$$
$$f = \text{fn } i : D_2\{\tau\}$$

In general this may not be well defined, but in special situations, where the minimization is used to simulate a "while-loop," it seems that the extension of the domain can proceed simultaneously with the definition of the function. It will be interesting to see what kind of higher-order fixed point can be developed to handle this type of recursion that spans objects of different orders.

In trying to model parallel computation, we have been led to define a notion of data type as a collection of elements with operations where some sort of metric is defined on the elements and special functions called *communication functions* that preserve locality are used to model the movement of data.

Another area for further research is in the model for parallel I/O.

The main drawback of the functional approach is in dealing with asynchronous and nondeterministic behavior. We believe it will be possible to develop rules to transform functional descriptions into more efficient programs utilizing side effects in a controlled manner.

7.11.2   COMPILER DESIGN AND RUNTIME SUPPORT

We offer three comments on the Crystal compiler. First, the current implementation of the compiler is only for a subset of the language, without higher order functions taking data fields as arguments. To support the full-blown language, we need at least a dynamic storage manager that can support the dynamic creation of data fields.

Second, the analyses and optimizations we described here are the basics that are absolutely necessary to get a compiler to produce target code with reasonable performance. The analyses can still be sharpened and there is room for improvement in the compiler optimization algorithms. But before doing that, being able to test the compiler extensively with a variety of applications will point out which stage of compilation needs improvement the most and where the greatest payoff may be in using more sophisticated algorithms. We also need more work on comparing the compiler-generated program with the handcrafted program simply to learn more about what should be optimized.

Third, compilers are always limited in dealing with dynamic situations where information is not available at compile-time. We are working on integrating the Crystal compiler with runtime support for load balancing [40, 41] and dynamic partitioning.

7.11.3   NONDETERMINISM

The introduction of asynchronous and nondeterministic behavior to a functional language like Crystal greatly complicates its semantics. By their nature, functional languages cannot handle the kinds of algorithms where a global variable is updated and tested asynchronously by the subprocesses to determine further computation.

Rather than introduce side effects and explicit nondeterministic constructs, our approach is to weaken the definition of functions to include equations that may not be inductive—that is, the standard evaluation strategy for functions may not terminate nor even produce any partial values. As equations over the space of functions, however, they may have many solutions. It's just that they cannot be computed in the standard way.

In this framework the task of the compiler is to analyze the program and introduce the necessary control structures and operations that will yield the right solution. Side effects and global variables may be used to implement the program.

In many situations, nondeterministic behavior may be preferable in that the processes are not required to be synchronized unnecessarily. In this situation, the kinds of operations on global variables need to be monotonic under a suitable notion of ordering that preserves the meaning of the computation. For example, updating a variable with better and better values can be done asynchronously without harm.

Since Crystal data fields are defined over index domains, the semantics of the index domains needs to be generalized to *dynamic domains*, which can be thought of as being defined at successive stages of the computation, and whose elements can be used in the computation of another data field before the whole domain is fully defined.

A program using dynamic sets and monotonic operators can be interpreted to mean the solution to the equation, in the mathematical sense, or as the sequence of nondeterministic operations that produces the result making efficient use of resources.

7.11.4 PROGRAMMING ENVIRONMENT

From a Crystal programmer's point of view, debugging should not make any difference whether the target is a sequential machine or a parallel one. The burden of providing such capabilities therefore falls on a debugger that can monitor a parallel target program. Performance debugging is another difficult problem. We think that the various analyses of dependencies and estimation of costs used by the compiler must be brought to bear on solving these problems.

Another issue to be addressed is programming in the large. Crystal has environments as first class objects. Future research is needed to use this feature for modularizing a program and supporting separate compilation.

7.12 Acknowledgments

We would like to thank Ron Pinter for numerous discussions on compilation techniques, in particular, on global optimizations. Janet Wu and Cheng-Yee Lin have contributed a great deal to the implementation of the compiler as well as writing application programs. We thank Michel Jacquemin and Lee-chung Lu, Wei Shu, and Min-you Wu for many helpful discussions. Our thanks also go to John Smagula for composing the figures.

References

1. J.R. Allen. *Dependence Analysis for Subscript Variables and Its Application to Program Transformation.* Ph.D. thesis, Rice University, April 1983.

2. J.R. Allen and K. Kennedy. "Automatic loop interchange." *Proceedings of the SIGPLAN'84 Symposium on Compiler Construction,* pp. 233-46. ACM, 1984.

3. J.R. Allen and K. Kennedy. "PFC: a program to convert Fortran to parallel form." In Kai Hwang, ed., *Supercomputers: Design and Applications,* IEEE Computer Society Press, 1985, pp. 186-205.

4. J.R. Allen and K. Kennedy. "Automatic translation of Fortran programs to vector form." *ACM Transactions on Programming Languages and Systems* (1987) 9(4):491-542, 10.

5. J. Backus. "Can programming be liberated from the von Neumann style? A functional style and its algebra of programs." *Communication of the ACM*(1978) 21(8):613-41.

6. U. Banerjee. *Data Dependence in Ordinary Programs.* Master's thesis, University of Illinois at Urbana-Champaign, November 1976.

7. U. Banerjee. *Speedup of Ordinary Programs.* Ph.D. thesis, University of Illinois at Urbana-Champaign, October 1979.

8. U. Banerjee. "A theory of loop permutation." Technical report, Intel Corporation, 1989.

9. U. Banerjee, Shyh-ching Chen, and D.J. Kuck. "Time and parallel processor bounds for Fortran-like loops." *IEEE Transactions on Computers* (September 1979) C-28(9):660-70.

10. A. P. Barendregt. *The Lambda Calculus: Its Syntax and Semantics.* New York: Elsevier North-Holland, 1981.

11. M. Burke and R. Cytron. "Interprocedural dependence analysis and parallelization." *Proceedings of the SIGPLAN '86* (1986).

12. R. M. Burstall and J. A. Goguen. "Putting theories together to make specifications." *5th International Joint Conference on AI* (1977), pp. 1045-58.

13. Marina Chen, Young-il Choo, and Jingke Li. "Compiling parallel programs by optimizing performance." *Journal of Supercomputing* (July 1988) 1(2):171-207.

14. Marina Chen and Young-il Choo. "Domain morphisms." Technical report, Yale University, August 1990.

15. Young-il Choo and Marina Chen. "A theory of parallel-program optimization." Technical Report YALEU/DCS/TR-608, Dept. of Computer Science, Yale University, July 1988.

16. R.G. Cytron. "Doacross: Beyond vectorization for multiprocessors." *Proceedings of the 1986 International Conference on Parallel Processing (St. Charles, Ill. Aug.19-22),* New York: IEEE Press, 1986, pp. 836-844.

17. J. Ferrante, K.J. Ottenstein, and J.D. Warren. "The program dependence graph and its use in optimization." *ACM Trans. on Programming Languages and Systems* (1987) 9(3):319-49.

18. J.A. Fisher, F.R. Ellis, J.C. Ruttenberg, and A. Nicolau. "Parallel processing: A smart compiler and a dumb machine." *ACM-Sigplan 84 Compiler Construction Conference.* New York: ACM Press, 1984.

19. G.C. Fox, M.A. Johnson, G.A. Lysenga, S.W. Otto, J.K. Salmon, and D.W. Walker. *Solving Problems on Concurrent Processors.* New York: Prentice Hall, 1988.

20. M. Gordon, R. Milner, and C. Wadsworth. *Edinburgh LCF.* Berlin: Springer-Verlag, 1979.

21. A. Gottlieb, R. Grishman, C.P. Kruskal, K.P. McAuliffe, L. Rudolph, and M. Snir. "The NYU ultracomputer—designing a shared memory parallel computer." *IEEE Transactions on Computers* (1983) C-32(2):175-89.

22. Ching-Tien Ho. *Optimal Communication Primitives and Graph Embeddings on Hypercubes.* Ph.D. thesis, Yale University, 1990.

23. Ching-Tien Ho and S.L. Johnsson. "Stable dimension permutations on Boolean cubes." Technical Report YALEU/DCS/RR-617, Dept. of Computer Science, Yale University, October 1988.

24. S.L. Johnsson. "Communication efficient basic linear algebra computations on hypercube architectures." *Journal of Parallel and Distributed Computation*, 4(2), April 1987.

25. S.L. Johnsson and Ching-Tien Ho. "Spanning graphs for optimum broadcasting and personalized communication in hypercubes." Technical Report YALEU/DCS/RR-610, Department of Computer Science, Yale University, November 1987.

26. R. Karp, R. Miller, and S. Winograd. "The organization of computations for uniform recurrence equations." *Journal of the ACM* (July 1967) 14(3):563-90.

27. D. Kuck. "A survey of parallel machine organization and programming." *Computing Survey* (March 1977) 9(1):29-59.

28. D.J. Kuck, R.H. Kuhn, D.A. Padua, B. Leasure, and M.J. Wolfe. "Dependence graphs and compiler optimizations." *Proceedings of the 8th ACM Symposium on Principles of Programming Languages* (1981) pp. 207-18.

29. Jingke Li and Marina Chen. "Generating explicit communications from shared-memory program references." *Proceedings of Supercomputing'90*, 1990.

30. Jingke Li and Marina Chen. "Index domain alignment: Minimizing cost of cross-reference between distributed arrays." *Proceedings of the 3rd Symposium on the Frontiers of Massively Parallel Computation*. IEEE Computer Society, 1990.

31. Jingke Li and Marina Chen. "Index domain alignment: Minimizing cost of cross-reference between distributed arrays." Technical Report 725, Yale University, October 1989.

32. D.B. Loveman. "Program improvement by source-to-source transformation." *Journal of the ACM* (January 1977) 24(1):121-45.

33. Lee-chung Lu and Marina Chen. "A unified framework for systematic applications of loop transformations." Technical report 818, Yale University, August 1990.

34. D.I. Moldovan. "On the analysis and synthesis of VLSI algorithms." *IEEE Transactions on Computers* (November 1982) C-31(11):1121-26.

35. D.A. Padua and M.J. Wolfe. "Advanced compiler optimizations for supercomputers." *Communications of the ACM*, 29(12), 1986.

36. D.A. Padua, D.J. Kuck, and D.H. Lawrie. "High-speed multiprocessors and compilation techniques." *IEEE Transactions on Computers* (September 1980) C-29(9):763-76,

37. D.A. Padua and M.J. Wolfe. "Advanced compiler optimizations for supercomputers." *Communications of ACM* (December 1986) 29(12):1184-201.

38. P. Quinton. "Automatic synthesis of systolic arrays from uniform recurrent equations." *Proceedings of 11th Annual Symposium on Computer Architecture*, New York, 1984, pp. 208-14.

39. H. Rogers, Jr. *Recursive Functions and Effective Computability.* New York: McGraw-Hill, 1967.

40. J. Saltz, R. Mirchandaney, and D. Baxter. "Runtime parallelization and scheduling of loops." *Proceedings of the 1st Symposium on Parallel Algorithms and Architectures, Santa Fe,* 1989.

41. W. Shu and L. V. Kale. "Dynamic scheduling for medium-grained processes." *Proceedings of Supercomputing '89,* November 1989.

42. B.C. Smith. "Reflection and semantics in Lisp." *Proceedings of the 11th Annual ACM Symposium on Principles of Programming Languages,* pp. 23-35, Salt Lake City, Utah, January 1984. ACM Press.

43. M.J. Wolfe. *Optimizing Supercompilers for Supercomputers.* Ph.D. thesis, Dept. of Computer Science, University of Illinois at Urbana-Champaign, 1982.

44. M.J. Wolfe. *Optimizing Supercompilers for Supercomputers.* Cambridge, Mass.: MIT Press, 1989.

45. Min-you Wu, Wei Shu, and Marina Chen. "Partitioning and scheduling of a multiprocessor prime sieve." Technical report, Yale University, 1989.

46. A. Yang. "Design and implementation of meta-Crystal: A metalanguage for parallel program optimization." Technical report, Yale University, 1989.

8

PTRAN — The IBM Parallel Translation System

Vivek Sarkar

8.1   Introduction

PTRAN (Parallel TRANslation) is a system developed at IBM's Thomas J. Watson Research Center to automatically restructure sequential Fortran programs for execution on parallel architectures. This chapter describes the PTRAN system, and its implementation as of the end of 1989. The primary functions of PTRAN are *analysis* [5] and *process formation* [6, 35]. The goal of PTRAN's *analyzer* is to understand the program's control and data dependence patterns as completely as possible. The goal of PTRAN's *process former* is to generate a parallel program that satisfies all dependences while optimally trading off parallelism with overhead in the target multiprocessor.

The scope of this chapter is to provide a survey and a tutorial of the area of automatic parallelization, using the PTRAN system as a case study. This chapter presents the author's impression of what the fundamental issues in compiling for parallelism are, and how these issues are currently addressed by the PTRAN system. Automatic parallelization is a large and active research area—too large to be covered in its entirety by this chapter. However, it is hoped that any lack of completeness will be compensated by the "whole system" view provided in this chapter.

The reader should be able to appreciate how the various optimization techniques discussed come together in a single working system.

This chapter on PTRAN serves as a contrast to the other chapters on parallel functional programming. The input programming language for the PTRAN system is Fortran—the antithesis of the functional languages proposed in this book! However, the goal of compiler analysis for automatic parallelization is to derive the same level of abstraction from a Fortran program as is found in functional languages. It has been observed that imperative languages like Fortran force a programmer to *over-specify* the control flow and data flow in the computation. Automatic parallelization attempts to remove this over-specification by analyzing the program, and building a *program dependence graph* that captures the essential control and data dependences in the program.

The automatic parallelization problem has received a lot of attention from both industry and academia. There are many good reasons for this attention, including the (in)famous "dusty decks" cause. Section 8.9 at the end of this chapter includes the author's opinion on the role of automatic parallelization in future parallel programming systems. In addition, the area of automatic parallelization is relevant to anyone working in the area of parallel programming (implicit or explicit, functional or imperative) because it reveals the capabilities and limitations of automatic compiler optimization. An awareness of these capabilities and limitations is essential in identifying the *fundamental* differences between two parallel programming languages, as opposed to superficial differences that can be eliminated by compiler analysis and optimization. For example, there is no fundamental difference between the following Haskell definition

```
b = array ((1,1),(n,n))
     [ ((i,j), k*a!(i,j)) | i <- [1..n] j <- [1..n] ]
```

and the following Fortran code

```
do i = 1, n
  do j = 1, n
     b(i,j) = k * a(i,j)
  end do
end do
```

The analysis techniques described in this chapter can be used to assist in such comparisons. For instance, a result at the end of Section 8.2 states that the forward control dependence graph of a structured program must be a tree. This result can be used to determine if a given program is structured, whether the program's control structures are built with special syntax like if-then-else, or built with goto statements.

With this characterization, any compilation or optimization technique developed for programs written in a structured programming language can also be applied to structured programs written in an unstructured language. Another characterization is provided in Section 8.4, which states that a program with no output or anti data dependences is purely value-oriented because it has no storage-related dependences. Again, any compilation or optimization techniques developed for value-oriented (or applicative) programming languages are equally applicable to value-oriented programs written in an imperative language.

In addition to the broad issue of studying automatic parallelization to understand the capabilities and limitations of automatic compiler optimizations for parallel processing, there has been a fruitful exchange of ideas between the automatic parallelization and parallel functional programming communities. Recently, data dependence analysis has been used for optimizing the sequential computation of functional arrays [8]. This issue had also been studied for optimizing Fortran 90 array expressions [7, 104]. There is a remarkable similarity between the graphical program representations used in automatic parallelization and in functional programming. In fact, the program dependence graph used for imperative languages like Fortran was inspired by dataflow graphs used for single-assignment languages like VAL and Id [42].

Perhaps the biggest area of overlap between automatic parallelization and parallel functional programming is in process formation. Process formation includes compile-time optimizations for partitioning and scheduling, as well as runtime system optimizations for efficient multiprocessing. The parallel execution models for both automatic parallelization and parallel functional programming are usually based on *deterministic* and *implicit* parallelism. Determinism simplifies the debugging problem, because a sequential execution is guaranteed to yield the same results as a parallel execution of the program. The advantage of implicit parallelism is that the user is not burdened by low-level details like the placement of code and data onto processors in the target system (the para-functional programming approach described in Chapter 5 is a notable exception, since its very essence is that of combining functional programming and explicit parallelism).

Since both automatic parallelization and parallel functional programming approaches mainly target to commercially available general-purpose multiprocessors, there is further overlap in the area of process formation. Though functional and imperative programs have different semantics that lead to different methods for identifying parallelism, once the parallelism in the program has been identified, the problem of mapping the parallelism onto the target multiprocessor system is essentially the same in both approaches. In fact, the partitioner used in

PTRAN [92] is based on an earlier partitioner developed for SISAL [91, 95].

As we discuss the issues involved in program analysis and process formation, we see that each issue has two sides to it, namely *control* and *data*. The program analysis phase begins with the traditional *control flow* and *data-flow* analyses used in compiling for sequential architectures. This information is then refined by *control dependence* and *data dependence* analyses, in order to discover as much of the potential parallelism in the program as possible. The goal of the process formation phase is to generate a parallel program that satisfies all dependences, while optimally trading off parallelism with overhead in the target multiprocessor. We see that there are two ways in which control and data dependences can be satisfied, namely *control sequencing* and *data synchronization*. The actual trade-off between parallelism and overhead is performed by *partitioning* the program, which also has two components: *control partitioning* and *data partitioning*. As we will see, the current implementation of the PTRAN process former is control-driven, in that control sequencing is the mechanism used to satisfy dependences, and control partitioning is the method used to partition the program.

The sections in this chapter are organized as follows. Sections 8.2, 8.3, and 8.4 describe the PTRAN analyzer. Section 8.2 defines the control dependence relation, describes how it can be computed from a control flow graph, and discusses the special variant of control dependence is used in PTRAN. Section 8.3 briefly describes the interprocedural data-flow analysis performed by PTRAN. Section 8.4 defines the data dependence relation as a refinement of data-flow information and discusses how data dependence analysis is performed. Section 8.5 then discusses the Parallel Fortran language generated by PTRAN, as a prelude to Sections 8.6, 8.7, and 8.8, which describe the PTRAN process former. Section 8.6 discusses various ways in which control and data dependences can be satisfied, using sequencing and synchronization mechanisms in the target language. Section 8.7 describes the PTRAN partitioner. Section 8.8 discusses how PTRAN generates the final Parallel Fortran code from a partitioned program dependence graph. Finally, Section 8.9 presents the conclusions of this chapter.

Special care has been taken to accurately represent the work done in the PTRAN project. Any errors or inaccuracies are the sole responsibility of the author. Like the area of automatic parallelization in general, the PTRAN system is a moving target. By the time this chapter appears in print, PTRAN will undoubtedly have some new features that may have been only hinted at in this chapter as possible areas of future work.

8.2 Control Dependence

Control dependence [42] is an important notion in parallel processing because it identifies statements that are known to have identical control conditions. Consider two statements, X and Y, that have identical control conditions: this implies that if statement X is performed in a given program execution, then statement Y must also be performed in the same program execution (assuming that the program does not terminate abnormally between X and Y). Therefore, statement Y can be executed concurrently with statement X, provided there are no data dependences between X and Y. Control dependence reveals potential parallelism that goes beyond loop iterations and can be among any statements (e.g. IF, DO, CALL), within and across procedures, and arbitrarily nested. For this reason, control dependence is an essential component of the PTRAN system.

Subsection 8.2.1 defines control dependence as a relation on nodes in a control flow graph, and Subsection 8.2.2 shows how control dependence can be efficiently computed from the control flow graph. Finally, Subsection 8.2.3 concludes with a discussion of the *forward* control dependence graph, the variant of the control dependence relation that is used in PTRAN.

Throughout this section, the basic unit of computation is assumed to be a control flow graph node, which may represent an operation, statement or basic block. The current PTRAN implementation uses a statement-level control flow graph.

8.2.1 DEFINITION OF CONTROL DEPENDENCE

Before we discuss the formal definition of control dependence, let us informally consider what it means for statement Y to be control dependent on statement X. Clearly, X would have to represent a conditional branch (for example, due to an IF, DO, or WHILE statement), so that the condition evaluated at X can control whether statement Y will be subsequently executed or not. This idea can be captured by thinking of two paths, P_1 and P_2, in the control flow graph from X to $STOP$, such that P_1 includes Y and P_2 excludes Y. We would also have to require that P_2 have no statement, Z, in common with P_1 between X and Y, otherwise Z would be the one controlling Y's execution instead of X.

To formalize this idea, we begin with the definition of a *control flow graph* as presented in [90] and [35]. It differs from the usual definition [42, 2] by the inclusion of a mapping of node types, and a set of labels for edges. The label set $\{T, F, U\}$ is used to distinguish between conditional execution (labels T and F) and unconditional execution (label U).

DEFINITION 8.1

A *control flow graph* $CFG = (N_c, E_c, T_c)$ consists of

- N_c, a set of nodes.
- $E_c \subseteq N_c \times N_c \times \{T, F, U\}$, a set of *labelled* control flow edges.
- T_c, a node type mapping. $T_c(n)$ identifies the type of node n as one of the following values: *START, STOP, HEADER, PREHEADER, EXITS, POSTEXIT, OTHER*.

  We assume that *CFG* contains two distinguished nodes of type *START* and *STOP* respectively, and that for any node N in *CFG*, there exist directed paths from *START* to N and from N to *STOP*. □

CFG is a directed multigraph in which each node has at most two outgoing edges. A node with exactly two outgoing edges represents a conditional branch; in that case, we assume that the edges are distinguished by "T" *(true)* and "F" *(false)* labels. The restriction to at most two outgoing edges was only made to simplify the discussion in this chapter. All the results presented in this chapter are applicable to control flow graphs with arbitrary out-degree e.g. when representing a computed GOTO statement in Fortran, or a case statement in Pascal. In fact, the PTRAN implementation supports control flow graphs with arbitrary out-degree. Note that Definition 8.1 imposes no restriction on the in-degree of a node.

For convenience in the following discussion, we will use the phrase "path from X with label L" to refer to a directed path in *CFG*, that starts at node X with the *CFG* edge labelled L, and ends at the *STOP* node. We can now formally define a relation called control* dependence, based on the ideas discussed at the start of this subsection (the reason for calling this relation "control* dependence" rather than "control dependence" will become clear shortly).

DEFINITION 8.2

Node Y is control* dependent on node X with label L if and only if

1. there exists a path, P_1, from X with label L that includes Y, and
2. there exists a path, P_2, from X with label $L' \neq L$ that excludes Y, and

3. any node strictly between X and Y in path P_1 does not occur in path P_2. $\square$

However, the definition of control dependence from the literature [42] differs from Definition 8.2 above. Instead, it is based on the notion of *post-dominance* as follows:

DEFINITION 8.3

Node W *post-dominates* another node $V \neq W$ if and only if every directed path from V to *STOP* in *CFG* contains W. $\square$

DEFINITION 8.4

[42] Node Y is *control dependent* on node X with label L in *CFG* if and only if

1. there exists a nonnull path $X \xrightarrow{+} Y$, starting with the edge labelled L, such that Y post-dominates every node, W, strictly between X and Y in the path, and

2. Y does not post-dominate X.

The *control conditions of node Y* is the set,

$$CC(Y) = \{(X, L) \mid Y \text{ is control dependent on } X \text{ with label } L\}$$

Two nodes are said to be *identically control dependent* if and only if they have the same set of control conditions. $\square$

The notion of post-dominance is useful in identifying nodes with identical control conditions because if node W post-dominates node V, we know that node W will be executed whenever node V is executed. Post-dominance is the dual of dominance, which is a well-known relation on control flow graph nodes [2]. In fact, post-dominators in a control flow graph, *CFG*, are the same as dominators in the reverse of *CFG*. Note that post-dominance is an irreflexive relation due to the $V \neq W$ constraint in Definition 8.3—a node never post-dominates itself. The choice of an irreflexive definition over a reflexive definition is solely a matter of convenience. Both reflexive and irreflexive definitions of dominance are popular in the literature, for example in [2] and [73] respectively.

Definition 8.2 states that Y is control* dependent on X if during program execution, X can affect whether Y is executed or not. In contrast, Definition 8.4 states that Y is control dependent on X if during program execution, X can *directly* affect whether Y is executed or not. The "direct" nature of control dependence arises from condition 1 of Definition 8.4, which requires that Y post-dominate every node, W, between X and Y. This means that whenever a branch with label L is taken from node X, we must reach node Y. Hence, Y's execution is directly controlled by X. However, in control* dependence, the only requirement is that there be a path from X to Y with label L, for some execution of the program. It may be possible to avoid Y, even after taking a branch with label L from X, due to a conditional branch that appears between X and Y.

Based on this discussion, the question naturally arises: how are control dependence and control* dependence related? The answer is provided by the following theorem.

THEOREM 8.1

1. Control* dependence is the transitive closure of control dependence.

2. Control dependence is the transitive reduction of control* dependence.

PROOF

By induction on path length in CFG. Details of the proof are left as an exercise for the reader.   □

Since transitive closure and transitive reduction [1] are usually defined on binary relations, and control and control* dependence are tertiary relations (due to labels), the notion of transitivity must be extended for Theorem 8.1. When considered as tertiary relations, control and control* dependence are subsets of the cross-product, $\{nodes\} \times \{nodes\} \times \{labels\}$. If such a relation contains the triple (X, Y, L), it means that node Y is control (or control*) dependent on node X with label L. For transitive closure, consider a tertiary relation, R, with the triples $(X, Y, L1)$ and $(Y, Z, L2)$. In our definition of transitivity, R's transitive closure contains both those triples as well as the triple $(X, Z, L1)$. Note that only the first label is retained in the closure. For transitive reduction, we simply discard all "redundant" triples e.g. $(X, Z, L1)$ is redundant in the set $\{(X, Y, L1), (Y, Z, L2), (X, Z, L1)\}$. These are natural extensions to the standard definitions of transitive closure and transitive reduction.

Theorem 8.1 shows that control dependence and control* dependence are very closely related, and that one can always be derived from the other. However, control dependence should be the representation of choice, since it is more space-efficient than control* dependence.

To conclude, we see that both control* and control dependence are general relations, defined for an arbitrary control flow graph. The control dependence graph will be cyclic if and only if the control flow graph is cyclic. However, the nesting structure of the cycles may be different in the control flow and control dependence graphs, as discussed later in Subsection 8.2.3.

8.2.2   COMPUTING CONTROL DEPENDENCE

As in [42], we first extend the control flow graph with a special predicate node, *ENTRY*, that has an edge labelled "*T*" going to *START* and another edge labelled "*F*" going to *STOP*. This is done for convenience, so that every node (except *STOP* and *ENTRY*) is directly or indirectly control dependent on *ENTRY*, in the extended control flow graph.

The first step in computing control dependence is the construction of the *post-dominator tree* of the extended control flow graph, analogous to the construction of a *dominator tree* [2, 73, 76, 83]. Let the *immediate post-dominator* of Y be the closest post-dominator of Y on any path from Y to *STOP*. It is known that each node (except *STOP*) has a unique immediate post-dominator. Therefore, the parent of a node in the post-dominator tree is simply its immediate post-dominator, and *STOP* is the root node of the post-dominator tree. The post-dominator tree, *PDOM*, can be represented by an array, *PDOM.PARENT(1...N)*, where *PDOM.PARENT(X)* is the immediate post-dominator of node X.

Computing post-dominators in the control flow graph is equivalent to computing dominators in the reverse control flow graph; that is, node Y post-dominates node X in *CFG* if and only if node Y dominates node X in *reverse(CFG)*. A straightforward algorithm for constructing the dominator tree in $O(N \times E)$ time was presented in [83], where N and E are the number of nodes and edges in the control flow graph.[1] A practical and more efficient algorithm for constructing the dominator tree was given in [73], where a simple version runs in $O(E \times log N)$ time, and a more sophisticated version runs in $O(E \times \alpha(E, N))$ time ($\alpha(E, N)$ is a functional inverse of Ackermann's function). Recently, a linear $O(N + E)$ time algorithm for computing dominators has been developed [54], though it may be too complicated to use in practice. The algorithm implemented in PTRAN is the simple version of the algorithm in [73], which takes $O(E \times log N)$ time.

---

[1]For convenience, we assume that $E = \Omega(N)$, since $E \geq N - 1$ for a control flow graph that is connected, as in Definition 8.1.

After the post-dominator tree has been constructed, the next step is to compute the control dependence relation. Earlier algorithms for computing control dependence [32, 42] have shown how to enumerate all nodes control dependent on node X with label L, using the control flow graph and post-dominator tree. These algorithms would then build a *control dependence graph*, which includes an edge for every triple of the form (X, Y, L), where node Y is control dependent on node X with label L. In the worst case, the control dependence graph may have $O(N \times E)$ edges, and the algorithms may take $O(N^2 \times E)$ time to construct it.

In recent work [37], we improved the time bound for computing the full control dependence graph from $O(N^2 \times E)$ to $O(N \times E)$, but more importantly, we improved the space bound from $O(N \times E)$ to $O(E)$ by introducing two linear-sized sparse representations that can be used to answer the following questions:

1. What nodes are control dependent on node X?

2. What nodes have the same control conditions as node X?

If, as in PTRAN, this is the only control dependence information that is needed, then these sparse representations with $O(E)$ size can be used instead of the full control dependence graph with $O(N \times E)$ size.

To answer the question, "What nodes are control dependent on node X?", we simply retain *START* and *END* pointers into *PDOM* as follows:

1. Define $CD.START(X, L) = Z$ if and only if there is an edge from X to Z labelled L in *CFG*. $CD.START(X, L)$ represents the start of the list of nodes control dependent on X with label L.
   No extra storage or time is required to compute *CD.START* since the information is already available in *CFG*. We define the name *CD.START* for convenience.

2. Define $CD.END(X, L) = PDOM.PARENT(X)$. $CD.END(X, L)$ represents the (non-inclusive) end of the list of nodes control dependent on X with label L. This list starts at $CD.START(X, L)$ and is traversed by following *PDOM.PARENT* pointers. The list extends up to, but does not include, $CD.END(X, L)$. For convenience, we will represent this list as a half-closed, half-open interval

   $[\, CD.START(X, L), \ CD.END(X, L) \,)$

   Note that $CD.START(X, L) = CD.END(X, L)$ represents an *empty* list, which means that there are no nodes control dependent on X with label L. Note also that the value of $CD.END(X, L)$ only depends on X, and not on L.

No extra storage or time is required for *CD.END* since the information is already available in *PDOM.PARENT*. We define the name *CD.END* for convenience.

All nodes control dependent on X with label L must be totally ordered by post-dominance, and can be enumerated by starting at $CD.START(X, L)$ and going up the post-dominator tree, *PDOM*, visiting all nodes up to but not including $CD.END(X, L)$. The time taken to visit all nodes control dependent on X with label L (i.e. control dependence *successors*) is therefore linearly proportional to the number of nodes visited. Formally speaking, to step through all the nodes that are control dependent on X with label L, we perform the following steps:

1. $Z \leftarrow CD.START(X, l)$
2. **while** $Z \neq CD.END(X, l)$ **do**
   a. /* Z is control dependent on X with label L — process Z as desired */
   b. $Z \leftarrow PDOM.PARENT(Z)$
   end while

Before proving that the $CD.START(X, L)$ and $CD.END(X, L)$ pointers correctly identify the control dependences, we present a lemma stating that either $CD.END(X, L) = CD.START(X, L)$ or $CD.END(X, L)$ post-dominates $CD.START(X, L)$, thus showing that the interval

$$[CD.START(X, L), \ CD.END(X, L))$$

is well-defined.

LEMMA 8.1

$CD.END(X, L) = CD.START(X, L)$ or $CD.END(X, L)$ post-dominates $CD.START(X, L)$

PROOF

(by contradiction, based on a similar result in [41]):
Assume that $CD.END(X, L) \neq CD.START(X, L)$ and that $CD.END(X, L) = PDOM.PARENT(X)$ does not post-dominate node $CD.START(X, L)$. Then there would be a path in *CFG* from $CD.START(X, L)$ to *STOP* that does not pass through $CD.END(X, L)$. Prefixing this path by the edge from X to $CD.START(X, L)$ gives a path from X to *STOP* that does not pass through $CD.END(X, L)$, which implies that $CD.END(X, L) = PDOM.PARENT(X)$ does not post-dominate X, a contradiction. $\square$

THEOREM 8.2

The *CD.START* and *CD.END* pointers correctly identify all control dependences.

PROOF

We will show that the conditions in Definition 8.4 are satisfied if and only if Y occurs in the interval:

$[\ CD.START(X, L),\ CD.END(X, L)\ )$.

1. *IF:* It is easy to see that conditions 1 and 2 in Definition 8.4 are satisfied if Y occurs in $[\ CD.START(X, L),\ CD.END(X, L)\ )$. The required nonnull path p (in *CFG*) for condition 1 would just be

$$X \xrightarrow{+} CD.START(X, L) \xrightarrow{+} PDOM.PARENT(CD.START(X, L)) \xrightarrow{+} \ldots \xrightarrow{+} Y$$

For condition 2, we see that node Y cannot post-dominate node X, since node $CD.END(X, L) = PDOM.PARENT(X)$ post-dominates node Y.

2. *ONLY IF:* Now we assume that conditions 1 and 2 in Definition 8.4 are known to be true, and prove that Y must occur in the interval

$[\ CD.START(X, L),\ CD.END(X, L)\ )$

From condition 1, we see that the path p must be of the form

$$X \xrightarrow{+} CD.START(X, L) \xrightarrow{+} PDOM.PARENT(CD.START(X, L)) \xrightarrow{+} \ldots \xrightarrow{+} Y$$

since $CD.START(X, L)$ is node X's successor in *CFG* with label L. Since p is a non-null path, either $Y = CD.START(X, L)$ or Y post-dominates $CD.START(X, L)$. Therefore, we must eventually reach Y by starting at $CD.START(X, L)$, and following *PDOM.PARENT* pointers up the post-dominator tree.

The only question that now remains to be answered is whether we will reach Y before we reach $CD.END(X, L)$. This is shown to be true by condition 2, which states that Y does not post-dominate X. If we reached Y at or after $CD.END(X, L) = PDOM.PARENT(X)$, it would imply that Y post-dominates X, thus contradicting condition 2.   □

To answer the question, "What nodes have the same control conditions as node X?", we compute *regions* [42] of the control dependence graph as follows:

1. $REGION(X)$ = region number associated with node X.
2. $RHEAD(R)$ = first node in region R.

3. $RTAIL(R)$ = last node in region R.

Two nodes, X and Y, have the same set of control conditions if and only if $REGION(X) = REGION(Y)$. The list of all nodes with the same control conditions as node X is given by the closed interval $[RHEAD(R), RTAIL(R)]$, where $R = REGION(X)$ and the nodes of the interval are enumerated by following immediate post-dominators as before

$$RHEAD(R) \rightarrow PDOM.PARENT(RHEAD(R)) \rightarrow \ldots \rightarrow RTAIL(R)$$

Previous work [42] identified regions by inserting *region nodes* in the control dependence graph in expected time $O(N)$, worst-case time $O(N^2 \times E)$, and worst-case space $O(N \times E)$. The expected time result assumed $O(1)$ time to check (by hashing) if a newly computed set of control conditions is the same as any previously computed set. However, this operation may take $O(N \times E)$ time in the worst case, since there may be $O(N)$ previously computed sets, and each set may have $O(E)$ control conditions. In [37], we present a new algorithm that computes the region data structures $REGION$, $RHEAD$, $RTAIL$ in $O(N \times E)$ worst-case time and $O(E)$ worst-case space. The reader is referred to [37] for further details.

8.2.3   FORWARD CONTROL DEPENDENCE

In this section, we define the *forward control dependence graph*, the variant of the control dependence graph that is used in PTRAN. This definition reflects the current PTRAN implementation, and differs slightly from earlier definitions of forward control dependence presented in [59], [38] and [35]. The forward control dependence graph is computed in two steps: first, the *forward control flow graph* is computed from the original control flow graph, and next, the forward control dependence graph is computed from the forward control flow graph, using the standard control dependence algorithm described in Subsection 8.2.2. The forward control flow graph is an acyclic version of the original control flow graph. The program's loop structure is made evident in the forward control flow graph by the location of *PREHEADER* and *POSTEXIT* nodes. The forward control flow graph is obtained by rewiring the destination of each back edge in the original control flow graph to its corresponding *POSTEXIT* nodes. The major advantages of the forward control dependence graph are that it is consistent with the loop nesting structure of the original control flow graph, and that it is acyclic, thus simplifying the algorithms for identifying non-loop parallelism and for process formation [19, 38, 35].

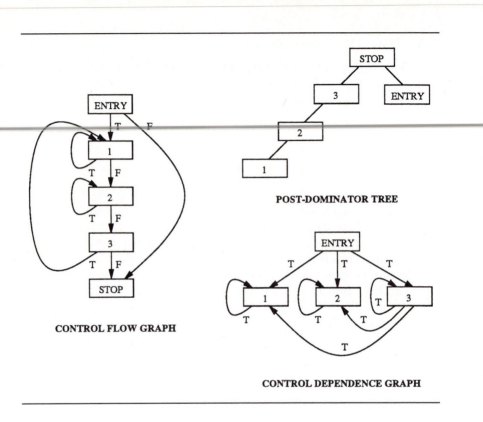

FIGURE 8.1
Original Control Flow Graph, CFG, and Control Dependence Graph, CDG

It is easy to prove that the control dependence graph will be cyclic if and only if the original control flow graph is cyclic. However, the nesting structure of the cycles in the control flow and control dependence graphs may be different in general. Consider the control flow graph shown in Figure 8.1, augmented with the pseudo-edge from *ENTRY* to *STOP* assumed in Subsection 8.2.2. Figure 8.1 also shows the post-dominator tree and the control dependence graph obtained for this control flow graph. Note that the $(1\text{-}2\text{-}3)^+$ loop completely surrounds the $(2)^+$ self-loop in the control flow graph, but this nesting structure is lost in the control dependence graph which has separate $(1)^+$, $(2)^+$ and $(3)^+$ self-loops (the parallel execution semantics of the control dependence graph is given in [94]). This difference in loop nesting structure poses a problem in generating the output parallel program. We have to choose between generating the loop nesting structure present in the original sequential control flow graph or generating the loop nesting structure revealed by the parallel control dependence graph. In PTRAN, we chose to preserve the loop nesting structure of the sequential control flow graph. Since data flow and data dependence analyses are performed with respect to the original loop nesting structure, this choice makes it easier to generate the necessary synchronizations for loop-independent and loop-carried data dependences. It is also much easier to generate sequential code for sequential loops if we preserve the original loop nesting structure in the output.

Given that the loop nesting structure of the output parallel program is to be the same as that of the input sequential program, the main benefit of control dependence is in identifying identically control dependent statements as candidates for *non-loop* parallelism. We need a variant of the control dependence graph that retains the loop nesting structure of the original control flow graph but still identifies potential candidates for non-loop parallelism. The forward control dependence graph was chosen to satisfy these requirements. It is computed from the forward control flow graph, which is acyclic and models a single execution of each loop body in the original control flow graph.

The loop nesting structure of the input sequential program is defined by the *interval structure* [97, 17] of the program's control flow graph. Currently, PTRAN considers only single-entry loops as candidates for parallel execution. This is not a significant restriction in practice. All structured loops (do, while, repeat-until) are single-entry even though they may contain multiple exits; also, most unstructured loops (built out of goto statements) found in real programs are single-entry as well. A multiple-entry loop can be transformed into multiple single-entry loops by *node splitting* [57, 2], which includes a separate copy of the loop with each entry. Node splitting can be done only if the expansion in code size is not prohibitive. For now, PTRAN conservatively marks all multiple-entry loops as sequential. For the purpose of automatic parallelization, a sequential multiple-entry loop can be replaced by a single compound node in the control flow graph, with some incoming (loop entry) control flow edges and some outgoing (loop exit) control flow edges. With this atomic sequential interpretation for multiple-entry loops, all loops in the resulting control flow graph will be single-entry and the control flow graph can be assumed to be *reducible* [3, 57, 100, 2]. The advantage of working with a reducible control flow graph is that it has a unique depth-first spanning tree, and hence a unique *interval structure* that can be easily computed from the control flow graph.

DEFINITION 8.5

[97, 17] A *back edge* in CFG is an edge (x, h, l) such that node h dominates node x (node x is called a *latch node* and node h

is called a *header node*). A back edge defines a *strongly connected region* $STR(h, x)$, which consists of the nodes and edges belonging to all paths from node h to node x, along with the back edge (x, h, l). Consider the set $B(h) \neq \emptyset$ of back edges targetted to header node h. The union of the strongly connected regions defined by the back edges in $B(h)$ is the *interval with header h* denoted by $I(h)$.

Intervals may be nested—interval I_1 being a *subinterval* of interval I_2 if I_1 is a subgraph of I_2. An interval may contain arbitrarily many subintervals. We represent interval nesting by a mapping called *HDR_PARENT*, where $HDR\_PARENT(h_1) = h_2$ indicates that the interval with header node h_1 is an immediate subinterval of the interval with header node h_2. $HDR\_PARENT(h) = 0$ indicates that the interval with header node h is the *outermost* interval.[2] *HDR_PARENT* defines a directed tree on all header nodes. $HDR\_LCA(h_1, h_2) = h_3$ indicates that header node h_3 is the *least common ancestor* of header nodes h_1 and h_2 in this tree.

Finally, we observe that a node may be contained within several enclosing intervals. We use the term, *node n's interval*, to mean the innermost interval containing node n, and define $HDR(n)$ to be the header node of the innermost interval containing node n. □

Definition 8.5 is based on the definition of intervals in [17], which is essentially equivalent to the definitions formulated by Schwartz and Sharir [97] and by Graham and Wegman [49] . However, it differs from the definition of intervals due to Allen and Cocke [4] (also in [57] and [2]), which does not require an interval to be strongly connected. To illustrate the difference between the Schwartz-Sharir and the Allen-Cocke definitions of intervals, consider the control flow graph in Figure 8.1. According to Definition 8.5 (i.e. the Schwartz-Sharir definition), the intervals with header nodes 1 and 2 are $I(1) = \{1, 2, 3\}$ and $I(2) = \{2\}$ respectively. According to the Allen-Cocke definition, the intervals with header nodes 1 and 2 are $I(1) = \{1\}$ and $I(2) = \{2, 3\}$.

After determining the interval structure, the next step is to build an *augmented* control flow graph [35]. Compared to the original control flow graph, the augmented control flow graph makes loop structure evident in the forward control dependence graph via *PREHEADER* and

---

[2]Strictly speaking, there may be several outermost intervals that are not strongly connected together. For convenience, we assume that there is exactly one outermost interval—the one containing the *ENTRY* node. This assumption is satisfied if the outermost interval is only required to be connected rather than strongly connected. One could also add pseudo control flow edges that result in a single strongly connected outermost interval.

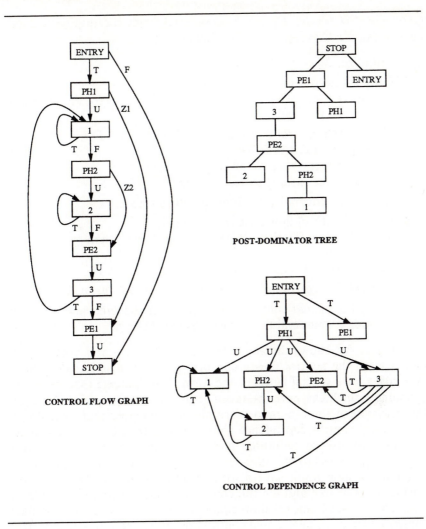

FIGURE 8.2
Augmented Control Flow Graph, $ACFG$, and its Control Dependence Graph, $ACDG$.

POSTEXIT nodes. These extra nodes also provide convenient locations for summarizing data flow information for the loop and moving code out of the loop body. For these reasons, we recommend the use of the augmented control flow graph. Formally, the augmented control flow graph, $ACFG = (N_a, E_a, T_a)$, is computed from the original control flow graph, $CFG = (N_c, E_c, T_c)$, as follows:

1. Initialize, $N_a \leftarrow N_c; E_a \leftarrow E_c; T_a \leftarrow T_c$
2. For each header node h in CFG:
   a. Create a new *PREHEADER* node, ph, add it to N_a, and mark it as h's preheader.
   b. For each control flow edge (u, h, l) in E_c in CFG,
      if $HDR\_LCA(HDR(u),$
      $h) \neq h$ then (we have an interval entry):
        i. Replace (u, h, l) by (u, ph, l) in $ACFG$.
   c. Add an unconditional branch from ph to h.
3. For each control flow edge (u, v, l) in CFG,
   if $HDR\_LCA(HDR(u), HDR(v)) \neq HDR(u)$ then (we have an interval exit):
   a. Create a new postexit node, pe, and add it to N_a.
   b. Replace edge (u, v, l) by edges (u, pe, l) and (pe, v, U).
   c. Add a *pseudo* control flow edge from the preheader node of node u's interval to the new postexit node pe.

Figure 8.2 shows the augmented control flow graph, $ACFG$, obtained from the control flow graph in Figure 8.1. The *pseudo* control flow edges have special labels of the form Z_i to indicate that the corresponding branch can never be taken in the original program. However, the insertion of these pseudo edges provides a convenient structure to the forward control dependence graph, as described below. We assume that we may use an unlimited number of labels of the form Z_i for pseudo edges, so as to maintain the property that all edges from a node in a control flow graph have distinct labels. Figure 8.2 also shows the post-dominator tree and the full control dependence graph for $ACFG$.

The forward control flow graph, $FCFG = (N_f, E_f, T_f)$, is then computed from the augmented control flow graph $ACFG = (N_a, E_a, T_a)$ as follows [36]:

1. Initialize, $N_f \leftarrow N_a; E_f \leftarrow E_a; T_f \leftarrow T_a$
2. For each interval in $ACFG$
   a. Add an *EXITS* node, e, to N_f.
   b. Add *pseudo* control flow edges in E_f from node e to each postexit node pe in the interval.
3. For each back edge (u, h, l) in $ACFG$
   a. Replace edge (u, h, l) in E_f by edge (u, e, l), where e is the *EXITS* node for header h's interval.

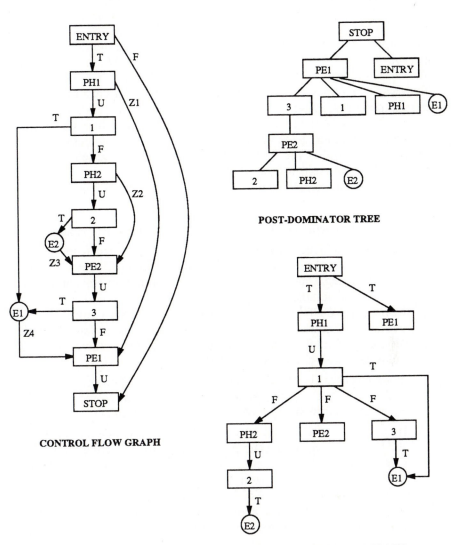

FIGURE 8.3
Forward Control Flow Graph, $FCFG$, and its Control Dependence Graph, $FCDG$.

Figure 8.3 shows the forward control flow graph, $FCFG$, corresponding to the control flow graph from Figure 8.1. The only difference between $ACFG$ and $FCFG$ is that the three back edges in $ACFG$ have been "rewired" to their corresponding $EXITS$ nodes. An $EXITS$ node summarizes all possible paths for the remaining iterations in the interval, and is followed by a branch to all $POSTEXIT$ nodes in the interval. If the interval has a single $POSTEXIT$ node, then the insertion of a new $EXITS$ node is unnecessary since all back edges can be directly rewired to the $POSTEXIT$ node. Having constructed the forward control flow graph, $FCFG$, the forward control dependence graph, $FCDG$, can be directly computed using the algorithm described in Subsection 8.2.2. Figure 8.3 also shows the forward control dependence graph obtained from the forward control flow graph in Figure 8.3.

We now enumerate some characteristics of the forward control dependence graph:

1. $FCDG$ is acyclic. (Follows from the fact that $FCFG$ is acyclic.)

2. If CFG is a structured control flow graph (obtained from begin-end, if-then-else and while constructs only [16]), then $FCDG$ must be a tree. (Each node can have at most one control condition; see [59] for details.)

   Note that $FCDG$ in Figure 8.3 is not a tree because node $E1$ has two control conditions. This is consistent with the fact that the original control flow graph in Figure 8.1 is not structured (because the outer interval has two back edges).

3. Node n is directly or indirectly control dependent on the preheader nodes of all intervals that enclose node n. (Follows from the pseudo edges inserted in step 3.c of $ACFG$'s construction.)

4. If $(x, y, l) \in ACDG$ is an edge in the control dependence graph for $ACFG$ such that all acyclic paths from x to y starting with label l do not include a back edge, then $(x, y, l) \in FCDG$ also. (Since the paths from x to y with label l do not include a back edge, they must be present in $FCFG$ as well. Also, for the path from x to $STOP$ in $ACFG$ that avoids y, there must be a corresponding path in $FCFG$ which may use exit jumps instead of back edges.)

For a structured program, the forward control dependence graph looks quite similar to the program's abstract syntax tree. This is because the control flow information of a structured program is captured accurately by the program's syntax. However, an abstract syntax tree does not correctly identify statements with identical control conditions in unstructured programs. Not only is the control dependence relation more general than an abstract syntax tree, but it also has a simpler execution model and semantics. In an abstract syntax tree, each control structure is assigned a distinct node type with special-case semantics, whereas, in a control flow graph, all control structures are expressed using the same primitives of basic blocks and conditional and unconditional branches. Finally, as described in this section, the forward control dependence graph can be easily computed from the original control flow graph in linear or near-linear time.

In conclusion, the forward control dependence graph is a simple, general and efficient representation of a program's control flow. Experiences with control dependence in the PTRAN system [35] and elsewhere [42, 51, 52, 58, 14] have shown that it is a powerful representation for various analyses, optimizations, and transformations. We strongly recommend using the forward control dependence graph as the compiler's internal representation of a program's control flow.

8.3   Interprocedural Data-flow Analysis

The scope of data dependence analysis in PTRAN is the entire procedure, rather than just a set of nested loops. Since our dependence analysis must span the entire control flow graph, we use *def-use chaining* [2] as the starting point. Def-use chaining is a traditional form of data-flow analysis that links a definition D (i.e. a write access) of variable X to each use U (i.e. a read access), such that there is a path from D to U in CFG that does not redefine X. A *def-use chain* is an ordered pair (D, U), linking a particular definition, D, to a particular use, U. It is simple to extend the notion of def-use chains to *use-def, def-def,* and *use-use* chains.

In PTRAN, we compute def-use, use-def and def-def chains by using a data-flow algorithm based on interval analysis [17, 97]. Moreover, data-flow analysis in PTRAN is performed in an interprocedural framework, which provides more precise data-flow information in the presence of procedure calls [5, 17]. The output of PTRAN's interprocedural data-flow analysis consists of the following:

1. **Summary information for each procedure**
   a. Set of *formal* parameters that are *constant* upon entry
   b. *Aliasing* relationships among *formal* parameters defined in the procedure
   c. Summary USE information — set of *formal* parameters and COMMON block subranges that have *upwards exposed uses* in the procedure [2]

```
PROGRAM MAIN
COMMON // A(100)
   CALL Q(D, 5, F)
   DO I = 51, 100
      A(I) = 1
   ENDDO
END

SUBROUTINE Q(X, M, Z)
COMMON // A(25), B(50), C(25)
   DO J = 1, 10
      CALL R(X, M)
      CALL S(Z)
   ENDDO
END

SUBROUTINE R(X, N)
COMMON // A(50), B(50)
   DO I = 1, 50
      A(I) = X
   ENDDO
END

SUBROUTINE S(X)
   X = 99
END
```

FIGURE 8.4
A Sample Fortran Program — Example of Interprocedural Analysis in PTRAN.

    d. Summary MOD information — set of *formal* parameters and COMMON block subranges that are modified in the procedure

    e. Existence of *history-keeping local variables* i.e. local variables that are upwards exposed

2. **Summary information at each call site**
    a. Summary USE information — set of *actual* parameters and COMMON block subranges that have *upwards exposed uses* in the called procedure [2]

    b. Summary MOD information — set of *actual* parameters and COMMON block subranges that are modified in the procedure

c. Existence of *history-keeping local variables*

3. Data-flow information

a. def-use, use-def and def-def chains within a procedure

An elaborate discussion of the computation of PTRAN's inter-procedural data-flow information is beyond the scope of this chapter. The reader is referred to [18, 5, 17] for further details on the PTRAN approach, and to [101, 102, 20, 22, 11, 10] for other interprocedural summary approaches. Instead, we will discuss an example to highlight the main features of PTRAN's interprocedural data-flow analysis. Figure 8.4 contains a sample Fortran program with four procedures, namely $MAIN$, Q, R and S. The *call graph* of this program simply consists of the three edges $\{MAIN \rightarrow Q, Q \rightarrow R, Q \rightarrow S\}$.

Let us first consider *interprocedural constant propagation*, mentioned in item 1.a above. The constant value 5 is passed to formal parameter M in procedure Q, and then to formal parameter N in procedure R. Therefore, both M and N are constant-valued formal parameters. Next, we observe that the summary USE sets (item 1.c above) for procedures Q, R and S are $\{X\}$, $\{X\}$ and $\emptyset$ respectively; and the summary MOD sets (item 1.d above) for procedures Q, R and S are $\{Z, //(1..50)\}$, $\{//(1..50)\}$ and $\{X\}$ respectively. The notation, "$//(1..50)$", represents a subrange of the blank COMMON block, consisting of the first 50 words. COMMON block subranges provide precise information, in terms of offset and extent, for accesses to COMMON block variables.

We now examine the data-flow information (item 3.a above) computed for procedure $MAIN$. The summary USE and MOD sets for the call to procedure Q are obtained from procedure Q's USE and MOD sets, and are found to be $\{D\}$ and $\{F, //(1..50)\}$ respectively. The MOD set for the assignment to $A(I)$ is simply $\{//(1..100)\}$, based on the offset and extent of array A in the blank COMMON. Since there is an overlap between the MOD sets of the CALL statement and the assignment to $A(I)$, a def-def chain is created between the two statements by data-flow analysis.

However, if we examine the loop bounds of the DO loop in procedure $MAIN$, we realize that the assignment to $A(I)$ will only modify subrange 51..100 of the blank COMMON block, thus making its MOD set disjoint from that of the CALL statement, and eliminating the def-def chain. This kind of observation is specific to the nature of subscript expressions in array accesses, and is beyond the scope of data-flow analysis. However, observations about array accesses are the primary concern of data dependence analysis. Therefore, we can view data dependence analysis as a refinement of data-flow analysis for array accesses. This is the unified approach taken in PTRAN, where data-flow information identifies potential data dependences, and data dependence analysis sharpens the information by eliminating spurious dependences involving array accesses.

8.4   Data Dependence

Data dependence [69, 104], or the lack of it, is the fundamental idea behind parallel processing. Data dependence is a property of the flow of data within a program, just as control dependence is a property of control flow. Consider two identically control dependent statements, S_1 and S_2, that have no data accesses in common: this implies that statements S_1 and S_2 can be performed in any order, without altering the final effect on the data store. In fact, statements S_1 and S_2 can be executed concurrently. When two statements do have some data accesses in common, it becomes necessary to identify the accesses as reads or writes, and to analyze the subscript expressions in further detail, before we can decide if a data dependence exists or not. This decision procedure is called *data dependence analysis*, or simply *dependence analysis*. Dependence analysis dictates not only whether two statements can execute concurrently, but also whether each loop enclosing both statements can be made parallel or not, and whether a proposed code transformation is valid or not.

Data dependence analysis is conservative, in that it may state that a data dependence exists between two statements, when actually none exists. The conservative nature is mainly due to the fact that compile-time analysis must consider all possible execution paths of the program. Another source of conservativeness occurs in subscript expressions that are too complex to be efficiently analyzed by a compiler e.g. non-linear subscript expressions, the use of interprocedural aliases, or pointer references. Conservative analysis is a common feature of compiler optimizations. Even the control dependence analysis described in Section 8.2 is conservative because it assumes that all targets of a conditional branch are potentially reachable. In actual fact, the branch conditions may be such that some branch (or combination of branches) never occurs in any execution of the program.

Though both control and data analyses are conservative in principle, they provide information that is very useful in practice. In fact, control dependence analysis is almost always exact (that is, no spurious dependences are reported), since programmers very rarely write code with unreachable branch targets.[3]

Unfortunately, data dependence analysis is far more conservative than control dependence analysis in practice, though it can be exact or nearly exact in certain restricted cases that have been studied extensively in the literature [13, 104]. In general, data dependences are *may* dependences, because the analysis is conservative. Recent work in register and cache optimizations [21, 81] has identified a need for knowing when a data dependence is a *must* dependence. The bulk of previous work in data dependence analysis has focussed on array accesses embedded in DO loops, with subscript expressions that are linear functions of induction variables. Though this is a restricted case, it has received a lot of attention because of its importance in scientific computing. More recently, there have been efforts to perform dependence analysis on pointer accesses for the automatic parallelization of programs written in languages like Lisp and C [26, 55, 72, 73]. Dependence analysis has also been used for optimizing the sequential computation of functional arrays [8].

8.4.1 DEFINITION OF DATA DEPENDENCE

We begin with the traditional definition of data dependence [70, 104]:

DEFINITION 8.6

Consider two statements, S_1 and S_2, in a control flow graph, CFG. A *data dependence*, $S_1 \delta S_2$, exists between statements S_1 and S_2 with respect to variable X if and only if

1. there exists a path $P : S_1 \xrightarrow{+} S_2$ in CFG, with no intervening write to X, and
2. at least one of the following is true:
   a. **(flow)** X is written by S_1 and later read by S_2, or
   b. **(anti)** X is read by S_1 and later written by S_2, or
   c. **(output)** X is written by S_1 and later written by S_2, or
   d. **(input)** X is read by S_1 and later read by S_2. □

---

[3]A notable exception is when the branch target is a data value (e.g. an assigned GOTO in Fortran or a continuation in Scheme). In this case, control dependence analysis degenerates to data dependence analysis.

Data dependence is an ordered relation $(S_1 \delta S_2)$, and the order is defined by the original control flow graph. This means that data dependence is traditionally defined for a sequential program. However, the definition of data dependence and many of the techniques in data dependence analysis can be extended for analyzing parallel programs as well [29, 78, 79]. Note that the definitions of *flow*, *anti*, *output*, and *input* dependences correspond to the *def-use*, *use-def*, *def-def*, and *use-use* chains discussed in Section 8.3.

A data dependence, $S_1 \delta S_2$, is defined with respect to a given variable, X, and a specific path in CFG, $S_1 \xrightarrow{+} S_2$, that contains no intervening writes to X. Furthermore, a dependence is classified in Definition 8.6 as *flow*, *anti*, *output* or *input*, according to condition 2.a, 2.b, 2.c, or 2.d respectively. Therefore, there may be several data dependences between statements S_1 and S_2, in both directions, depending on the variable involved and the nature of the dependence.

A *flow* dependence is also called a *true* dependence because it involves the flow of the value of X that is written by statement S_1 and read by statement S_2. On the other hand, *anti*, *output*, and *input* dependences are called *storage-related* dependences because they arise from S_1 and S_2 using the same storage location (namely X), even though there is no value being communicated from S_1 to S_2. All storage-related dependences can potentially be eliminated by storage duplication.

Of the four kinds of dependences described above, input dependences can be safely ignored in automatic parallelization because an input dependence consists of two read accesses to the same variable, and these accesses may be performed in any order.[4] Though it is safe to ignore input dependences for *correct* parallelization, it is useful to consider them for *efficient* parallelization e.g. to improve the cache behavior of the parallel program [82] to reduce *hot spots* [81] in memory accesses, or to optimize the data partition on a distributed-memory multiprocessor [9]. The current PTRAN implementation does not compute input dependences, but its data-flow and data dependence analyses can be easily extended to do so, if some future optimization should require input dependence information.

Just as with control dependences, it is possible for there to be a data dependence from a statement to itself (when $S_1 = S_2$), and this can only happen in the presence of a loop. Such a self-dependence indicates a dependence between two separate *execution instances* of the statement. A self-dependence inhibits parallelism between the two execution instances, and hence inhibits parallelism between different

---

[4]One exception, mentioned in [104], is the case of *volatile* variables, whose values may change between successive reads. However, that case can be handled by modelling a read to a volatile variable as both a read access and a write access.

iterations of some enclosing loop(s). Self-dependences are not the only dependences that can inhibit parallelism between loop iterations; in general, a dependence $S_1 \delta S_2$ may be between arbitrary execution instances of statements S_1 and S_2. Clearly, it is essential to characterize a dependence so that we can tell if it inhibits parallelism between loop iterations or not. An exact solution would be to build a dependence graph on the complete iteration space, but such an approach is not feasible at compile-time; run-time approaches have been proposed for special cases [86], though their space and time overhead can become prohibitive. A compile-time characterization should be proportional to the *static* size of the program rather than the *dynamic* size of its execution space. *Data dependence direction vectors* [104] provide a simple and approximate compile-time characterization of dependences among execution time instances and are used in several parallelizing compilers, including PTRAN [18]. *Distance vectors* [71] and *dependence cones* [65] are more precise, and more complex, compile-time characterizations that have also been discussed in the literature. We will only consider direction vectors in our discussion of data dependence analysis, because of their simplicity and their widespread use in practice.

We need to formalize the notion of "execution time instance" before we can present the definition of direction vectors. For a given call to a procedure, multiple execution instances of a statement can occur only as a result of cycles in the control flow graph.[5] As discussed in Subsection 8.2.3, PTRAN uses the interval structure of the control flow graph to identify the loops in the program. Therefore, it is natural to use the interval structure to define the notion of "execution time instances." Interval structure is more general than a set of perfectly nested DO loops (the representation assumed in [104]), because the nesting need not be perfect or linear, and the loops need not be just DO loops.

DEFINITION 8.7

Consider statement S_1 with d enclosing intervals numbered $1...d$ from outermost to innermost. $S_1[i_1, i_2, ..., i_d]$ stands for the execution instance of S_1 corresponding to the i_k^{th} iteration of interval k, $\forall 1 \leq k \leq d$. If interval k is a normalized DO loop (i.e. with initial value and increment both $= 1$), then i_k will equal the value of its index variable. $\square$

---

[5]We consider only multiple execution instances that arise from a given call to the procedure containing the statement. The effect of multiple execution instances due to different calls to the procedure is taken into account by standard interprocedural analysis, which summarizes all effects of a call at the call site. This approach can be extended to recursive calls as well [17], though recursion is not handled by the current PTRAN implementation.

Definition 8.7 defines an execution instance with respect to the iteration *numbers* of all enclosing intervals. In [104], an execution instance is defined with respect to the index variable *values* of all enclosing DO loops, for a set of perfectly nested DO loops. Therefore, it was necessary in [104] to define a function, Θ, to handle the case of negative increments where the index variable decreases as the iteration number increases. We avoid that problem by defining execution instances in terms of iteration numbers instead.

Following Definition 8.7, direction vectors in PTRAN are also defined in terms of interval structure.

DEFINITION 8.8

The *direction vector* of a data dependence, $S_1 \delta S_2$, is the d-tuple $\Psi = (\psi_1, \psi_2, \ldots, \psi_d)$, such that

1. d is the number of intervals that enclose both S_1 and S_2, and
2. each ψ_k is one of { "$<$", "$=$", "$>$", "$\leq$", "$\geq$", "$\neq$", "$*$" }, and
3. for any pair of execution instances of S_1 by S_2, say $S_1[i_1, \ldots, i_d, \ldots]$ by $S_2[j_1, \ldots, j_d, \ldots]$, such that $S_1[i_1, \ldots, i_d, \ldots] \delta S_2[j_1, \ldots, j_d, \ldots]$, we must have $i_k \psi_k j_k \ \forall 1 \leq k \leq d$. □

In Definition 8.8, element ψ_k of the data dependence direction vector, Ψ, corresponds to the kth interval enclosing statements S_1 and S_2. The value of ψ_k represents a subset of $\{<, =, >\}$ that characterizes the direction of the dependence for interval k. $\psi_k = $ "$<$" indicates that the dependence goes in the forward direction for interval k (for example, when $j_k = i_k + 1$). Similarly, $\psi_k = $ "$>$" represents the backward direction. $\psi_k = $ "$=$" means that the dependence does not cross an iteration boundary of interval k. If each ψ_k in Ψ is one of "$<$", "$=$" or "$>$", then Ψ is a *base direction vector*. Other values for ψ_k represent the union of two or more of "$<$", "$>$" and "$=$", thus yielding a *summary direction vector*. $\psi_k = $ "$\leq$" indicates that the dependence may either go in the forward direction or may stay within the same iteration. Similarly, $\psi_k = $ "$\geq$" indicates that the dependence may either go in the backward direction or may stay within the same iteration. $\psi_k = $ "$\neq$" indicates that the dependence does not stay within the same iteration; it may either go in the forward or the backward direction. Finally, $\psi_k = $ "$*$" indicates that the dependence may have any direction — "$<$", "$>$" or "$=$". There is no symbol to represent the empty subset of $\{<, =, >\}$, because it would imply that the data dependence $S_1 \delta S_2$ does not exist.

A data dependence is said to be *loop-independent* if each element of its direction vector is "$=$"; otherwise, the dependence is said to be *loop-carried* [7]. Section 8.6 discusses the issue of identifying the loop(s) that *carry* the data dependence i.e. the loop(s) that must be executed sequentially to satisfy the data dependence.

A direction vector summarizes the conditions under which a data dependence holds. Sometimes, there may be a loss of precision in the summary. For example, if a data dependence holds only in the $(<, =)$ and $(=, <)$ cases, the summary direction vector would be $(\leq, \leq)$, which implies that the dependence also holds in the $(=, =)$ case [18]. It would be inefficient to retain all the base direction vectors for a dependence because there may be as many as $O(3^d)$ of them. The *dependence tree* proposed in [18] is a representation that summarizes base direction vectors as far as possible, without any loss of precision.

As discussed earlier, direction vectors provide a simple and approximate compile-time characterization of dependences among multiple execution instances of statements. In the following subsections, we will see how direction vectors can be used for automatic parallelization and for loop transformations to enhance parallelization.

8.4.2   DATA DEPENDENCE ANALYSIS

The goal of data dependence analysis is to identify all the *data dependences* (Definition 8.6) in a procedure, as well as their *direction vectors* (Definition 8.8). For accesses to scalar variables, data dependence analysis is essentially the same as data-flow analysis. For a given data-flow edge between two references to a scalar variable, there is a corresponding data dependence edge that is classified as *flow, anti, output,* or *input,* depending on whether the data-flow edge is a *def-use, use-def, def-def,* or a *use-use* chain. By default, the direction vector of a scalar data dependence is ("$\leq$", "$*$", ... "$*$"), which simply summarizes all *plausible* directions [18] for the given data-flow edge. The direction vector can be refined to ("$=$", ..., "$=$", "$\leq$", "$*$", ... "$*$") if the source access of the data-flow edge is a definition that is known to be *killed* by subsequent iterations at level i, and the loop at level i is known to have at least one iteration (i specifies the number of leading "$=$"s in the direction vector). Furthermore, the "$\leq$" can be refined to a "$<$" if the data-flow edge has a *backward* direction at level $i + 1$. [6]

---

[6] A data-flow edge links together two accesses to the same variable, say a_1 and a_2, such that there is a simple path from a_1 to a_2 in CFG with no intermediate node that kills the value of the variable. The data-flow edge has a *backward* direction at level L if the path includes a back edge (c.f. Definition 8.5) of the Lth interval in the direction vector; otherwise, the data-flow edge has a *forward* direction at level L.

```
1.              DO I = 1, N
    S1:             A(2*I+1) = ...
    S2:             ...      = A(2*I)
                END DO
2.              DO I = 1, N
    S1:             A(I) = ...
    S2:             ...  = A(I)
                END DO
3.              DO I = 1, N
    S1:             A(I+1) = ...
    S2:             ...    = A(I)
                END DO
4.              DO I = 1, N
    S1:             A(I) = ...
    S2:             ...  = A(I+1)
                END DO
```

Loop Number	def-use $(S_1 \rightarrow S_2)$	use-def $(S_2 \rightarrow S_1)$	def-def $(S_1 \rightarrow S_1)$
1	None	None	None
2	Flow (=)	None	None
3	Flow (<)	None	None
4	None	Anti (<)	None

FIGURE 8.5
Results of Applying Data Dependence Analysis on Data-flow Information.

To illustrate the difference between data-flow and data dependence analyses for array accesses, consider the four Fortran DO loops in Figure 8.5. In all four loops, data-flow analysis will create a def-use chain from statement $S1$ to $S2$, a use-def chain from statement $S2$ to $S1$, and a def-def chain from statement $S1$ to itself. But, as shown in the table, data dependence analysis refines the data-flow information so as to obtain different kinds of dependences for the four loops.

Having discussed what data dependences are, and what data dependence analysis can do, it is now time to describe how the analysis is actually performed. This area has received a lot of attention in the literature, so we will just review the known techniques with appropriate references for the interested reader.

Given a data-flow edge between two references to an array variable X in statements S_1 and S_2, the steps involved in data dependence analysis can be described as follows [30]:

1. Construct a system of *dependence equations*, one for each array dimension, that models a dependence between the two array references.

2. Establish a *context* (constraints based on loop bounds and direction vectors) in which the dependence equations should be tested.

3. Invoke a *decision algorithm* to test the equations for existence of solutions in the provided context.

To *construct the dependence equations* for a given data dependence $S_1 \delta S_2$, we first consider $S_1[i_1, \ldots, i_d, \ldots]$ and $S_2[j_1, \ldots, j_d, \ldots]$ to be arbitrary execution instances of statements S_1 and S_2 respectively. Let the array references in statements S_1 and S_2 be of the form $X(f_1, \ldots, f_m)$ and $X(g_1, \ldots, g_m)$, where m is the number of dimensions in array X, and $f_1, \ldots, f_m, g_1, \ldots, g_m$ are arbitrary subscript expressions. A dependence between the two references is simply modelled by a set of m simultaneous equations: $f_1 = g_1, \ldots, f_m = g_m$. A multi-dimensional array reference, $X(f_1, \ldots, f_m)$, can also be *linearized* [18] into a single address expression, $f_1 * size_1 + \ldots + f_m * size_m$, that defines the offset of the array element in memory, with respect to the base address of the array ($size_l$ is the size of the sub-array addressed by the lth dimension, depending on whether a column or row major storage layout is assumed). Linearization yields a single dependence equation of the form,

$$f_1 * size_1 + \ldots + f_m * size_m = g_1 * size_1 + \ldots + g_m * size_m$$

Linearization is necessary for considering dependences between references to aliased arrays or reshaped arrays [18]. Even if both references are to the same name and have the same shape (the usual case considered in the literature), linearization can be useful for efficiency reasons because the decision algorithms need to be applied only to a single equation instead of m equations. As discussed later, linearization also supports simultaneity of the m equations by coupling them together.

To make the equations amenable for analysis by the decision algorithms, we use the results of constant propagation and induction variable analysis to rewrite each subscript expression as a linear function of the iteration variables, $f_l = a_{l0} + \sum_{k=1}^{d} a_{lk} i_k$ and $g_l = b_{l0} + \sum_{k=1}^{d} b_{lk} j_k$, where the a_{lk} and b_{lk} values are identified as integer constants at compile-time $\forall 1 \leq l \leq m, 0 \leq k \leq d$. If it is not possible to rewrite the subscript expressions in a linear form, then it is usually assumed (conservatively) that the dependence holds in all plausible contexts. Empirical evidence from the Parafrase system [98] shows that about 50 percent of the array references found in real programs have linear subscript expressions. Also, the cause of non-linearity in about 90 percent of the non-linear subscript expressions is due to an "unknown variable" (a variable with unknown value or unknown bounds). This source of non-linearity can sometimes be removed by symbolic elimination, or by considering the unknown variable to be an extra variable in the dependence equations and including in the context any information on the variable's lower and upper bound values.

The only remaining issue in the construction of the dependence equations is that of *simultaneity*. The decision algorithms examine *a single equation* and decide if any solutions exist for the given context. However, we are interested in knowing if the system of *m simultaneous* equations has any solution. A straightforward approach to enforcing simultaneity would be to employ something like a Gaussian elimination algorithm to reduce the system of m equations in $2 \times d$ variables to a single equation in $2d - m + r + 1$ variables ($r < m$ is the number of redundant equations in the system) [66, pages 326-327]. This kind of reduction is also obtained by the generalized GCD test presented in [13]. However, such an approach may be too expensive in practice. Instead, special case optimizations and analysis techniques are used to obtain the effect of Gaussian elimination.

One observation is that the system of equations can be decomposed into disjoint subsystems, so that equations in different subsystems have no variables in common. Each subsystem can be tested independently, thus reducing the number of equations that need to be considered simultaneously by a decision algorithm. A further simplification is to remove all redundant equations from a subsystem. The λ-test [75] has been proposed as an efficient data dependence test for a system of coupled equations, especially if there are only two equations in the system. Linearization [18] also captures the effect of simultaneity and is the approach used in PTRAN for dealing with the coupling of equations. It is sometimes possible for the linearized equation to have a solution when the original system of equations has no solution. Linearization can be made precise by adding bounds constraints to the context (e.g. $lbound_k \leq f_k \leq ubound_k$), which assumes that all subscript expressions stay within their respective array bounds. This assumption was also made implicitly when constructing a separate dependence equation for each array dimension.

Next, we establish the *context* for the dependence equations. The context is a set of constraints on the solution. The decision algorithm has to determine if the dependence equations have a solution that satisfies the constraints specified in the context. The constraints usually imposed on a data dependence test are as follows:

1. The solution must be integer-valued (since the variables represent iteration numbers).

2. $\forall 1 \leq k \leq d$, the values of variables i_k and j_k must lie within the normalized loop bounds of the kth loop:

$$lower_k(i_1, \ldots, i_{k-1}) \leq i_k \leq upper_k(i_1, \ldots, i_{k-1})$$
$$lower_k(j_1, \ldots, j_{k-1}) \leq j_k \leq upper_k(j_1, \ldots, j_{k-1})$$

Note that the loop bound expressions $lower_k$ and $upper_k$ may depend on the iteration numbers of the enclosing loops (e.g. consider a "triangular" loop nest). The fact that the solution must be integer-valued can be used to extend the bounds by ± 1 e.g. $lower_k(i_1, \ldots, i_{k-1}) \leq i_k$ can be replaced by $lower_k(i_1, \ldots, i_{k-1}) - 1 < i_k$.

3. The solution must satisfy the given direction vector constraints. The constraint imposed by direction vector $\Psi = (\psi_1, \psi_2, \ldots, \psi_d)$ is $i_k \, \psi_k \, j_k \, \forall \, 1 \leq k \leq d$ (Definition 8.7). If ψ_k is one of "$<$", "$\leq$", "$>$", "$\geq$", then the constraint has the same form as the loop bound constraints defined above. If ψ_k is "$=$", then the constraint is used to combine the coefficients of i_k and j_k in the dependence equations, thus eliminating i_k or j_k. If ψ_k is "$*$", nothing needs to be done because it does not impose any constraint. The only remaining possibility for ψ_k is "$\neq$". None of the decision algorithms can test for a "$\neq$" constraint directly. Instead, they test for $\neq$ by separately testing for "$<$" and "$>$".

4. The value of each subscript expression must lie within the array bounds for that dimension[7] e.g. $lbound_k \leq f_k \leq ubound_k$. These inequalities impose constraints on the values of variables $i_1, \ldots, i_d$ and $j_1, \ldots, j_d$.

5. If any unknown variables were introduced in the dependence equation to avoid non-linearity, and the variables are known to have

---

[7]Some Fortran compilers allow subscript expressions to fall out of bounds, thus allowing the programmer to address any linearized offset from the base address of the array e.g. the loop "DO I = 1, 100 A(I,1) = 0 END DO" may be used to initialize a 10×10 array. PTRAN has a "respect bounds" option that specifies whether or not the compiler should assume that all subscript expressions lie within their corresponding array bounds.

some bounds constraints (either by range analysis [56] or by Pascal-style subrange type declarations), then the solution must satisfy these bounds constraints as well. These bounds constraints have the same form as the loop bound constraints discussed above.

Except for direction vectors, all the context items listed above can be determined directly from the intermediate program text (which would reflect the results of constant propagation and range analysis, for example). There is no known method for directly obtaining the set of direction vectors for a data dependence. Instead, the decision algorithms are applied separately on different direction vectors to identify the set of direction vectors for which a solution exits. Originally, compilers would simply test for all plausible direction vectors by exhaustive enumeration. PTRAN employs a *hierarchical* approach [18] in enumerating direction vectors—testing needs to be performed on the "<", "=" and ">" cases only if the decision algorithms failed to prove independence for the general "*" case.

After the dependence equations have been constructed and the context has been established, the stage is set to *apply a decision algorithm* to determine if the equations have any solution within the specified context. If no solution exists, then the array references have been proved to be independent. Otherwise, a dependence is assumed for the given context. The decision algorithm should be conservative—when in doubt it should assume that a solution exists. We describe two widely used decision algorithms, the *GCD test* and *Banerjee's inequality*, which are applied to a single dependence equation at a time. Though other decision algorithms have been described in the literature, we feel that they do not provide an improved success rate over these two tests in practice. Empirical measurements [98] suggest that further improvements in the accuracy and efficiency of data dependence analysis will come about by increased knowledge of unknown variables and by extensions for better handling direction vector constraints and simultaneity of equations, rather than from an improved decision algorithm.

GCD Test.   [18, 104, 30] The only contexts relevant to the GCD (greatest common divisor) test are the "=" elements in the direction vector and the fact that the solution must be integer-valued. If ψ_k is "=", then the equality $i_k = j_k$ is used to combine the coefficients of i_k and j_k in the dependence equations, thus eliminating i_k or j_k. After eliminating one variable for every "=" entry in the direction vector, we obtain a reduced dependence equation of the form $\sum_{k=1}^{k=n} c_k v_k = c_0$, where each c_k $(0 \leq k \leq n)$ is an integer constant and each v_k $(1 \leq k \leq n)$ is a variable. We also require that $c_k \neq 0$ for $1 \leq k \leq n$. If $n = 0$ (that is, if no variable in the equation has a non-zero coefficient), then the GCD test degenerates to a simple *constant value* test: a solution exists if and only if $c_0 = 0$.

The GCD test can be stated as follows: *if $GCD(c_1, \ldots, c_n)$ does not divide c_0 evenly, then the equation has no integer solutions.* This result can be derived directly from diophantine equation theory [50]. If $GCD(c_1, \ldots, c_n)$ divides c_0 evenly (this includes the case when $c_0 = 0$), we conservatively assume that a solution exists. There is a *generalized GCD test* presented in [13], which can be applied to a system of simultaneous equations instead of just a single equation.

When testing for a data dependence, PTRAN begins with the GCD test because of its efficiency [18]. However, the GCD test is known to have a low success rate in practice [98]. The low success rate is due to the fact that the GCD of two or more integers is often $= 1$, and the fact that the GCD test ignores all inequalities in the context.[8]

Banerjee's Inequality. [12, 13, 104] Banerjee's inequality complements the GCD test in that it exploits the linear inequalities available in the context but ignores the constraint that the solutions must be integer-valued. As in the GCD test, each "=" direction vector element is used to eliminate one variable, yielding a dependence equation of the form $\sum_{k=1}^{k=n} c_k v_k = c_0$. Let the LHS of the equation define a linear function, $f(v_1, \ldots, v_n) = \sum_{k=1}^{k=n} c_k v_k$. Also, let $\Re \subseteq \mathbf{R}^n$ be the region specified by the inequalities in the context. If we can determine lower and upper bounds on function f in region $\Re$, $b_{low}(f, \Re)$ and $b_{up}(f, \Re)$, then the dependence equation has a real solution in region $\Re$ if and only if

$$b_{low}(f, \Re) \leq c_0 \leq b_{up}(f, \Re) \quad [13]$$

Banerjee's inequality can be used to determine if any *real* solution exists in the specified region. If no real solution exists, it implies that no integer solution exists, which proves independence. However, if a real solution does exist, we conservatively assume that an integer solution exists as well. There's a special case in which the existence of a real solution implies the existence of an integer solution—when $m = 1$ (the array has one dimension) and each coefficient is 1 or -1 ($|c_k| = 1 \, \forall 1 \leq k \leq n$) [12, 13].

The main complexity in using Banerjee's inequality is the computation of the lower and upper bounds, $b_{low}(f, \Re)$ and $b_{up}(f, \Re)$. As a first approximation, we assume that $\Re$ is an n-dimensional rectangle

---

[8]The probability of $GCD(a, b) = 1$, for two integers a and b chosen at random, is $6/\pi^2$ or roughly 60 percent [25].

defined by lower and upper bounds for each variable $LB_k \leq v_k \leq UB_k$. LB_k and UB_k are usually obtained from the loop bounds, though more precise values can be obtained by considering the direction vectors as well [30]. If LB_k (or UB_k) is unknown, then a default worst-case value of $-\infty$ (or $+\infty$) must be assumed. The lower and upper bounds of function f for an n-dimensional rectangle are given by [13] $b_{low}(f, \Re) = \sum_{k=1}^{k=n}(c_k^+ LB_k - c_k^- UB_k)$ and $b_{up}(f, \Re) = \sum_{k=1}^{k=n}(c_k^+ UB_k - c_k^- LB_k)$, where $c_k^+ = \max(c_k, 0)$ and $c_k^- = \max(-c_k, 0)$ are the positive and negative parts of c_k. After attempting the GCD test, PTRAN applies Banerjee's inequality for rectangular regions, with refinements to the lower and upper bounds based on the direction vector being considered [18, 30].

The lower and upper bounds can be further refined by determining bounds for a trapezoidal region instead of an n-dimensional rectangle [13]. A trapezoidal region is defined by inequalities of the form:

$$
\begin{aligned}
p_{10} &\leq v_1 \leq q_{10} \\
p_{20} + p_{21}v_1 &\leq v_2 \leq q_{20} + q_{21}v_1 \\
&\vdots \\
p_{n0} + p_{n1}v_1 + \ldots + p_{n,n-1}v_{n-1} &\leq v_n \leq q_{n0} + q_{n1}v_1 + \ldots + q_{n,n-1}v_{n-1}
\end{aligned}
$$

Such a trapezoidal region naturally models the loop bounds for a nest of loops in which the lower and upper bounds of a loop are linear expressions in the index variables of the enclosing loops. Direction vector inequalities can also be handled, provided they fit into the required triangular structure on the inequalities. Otherwise, approximations of $\pm\infty$ are necessary, just as in the rectangular case.

Figure 8.6 describes the algorithm from [13, pages 56-57] for computing the lower and upper bounds of function f in a trapezoidal region. The notation $(d[k] > 0 \; ? \; d[k] * p[k, 0] : d[k] * q[k, 0])$ is borrowed from the C programming language and represents a conditional expression. The algorithm is inexact in the sense that the lower and upper bounds computed may not belong to the range of the function. However, the bounds computed by the algorithm are more precise than those obtained by a rectangular approximation. Note that the trapezoidal region degenerates to a rectangular region when $p_{hk} = q_{hk} = 0 \, \forall 1 \leq k < h \leq n$, and in that case, the values of b_{low} and b_{up} are the same as the values for the rectangular region.

We conclude this subsection with an example of data dependence analysis. The reader is referred to other references in the literature [104, 13, 18] for further details on the subject. Figure 8.7 contains a Fortran code fragment for the LU decomposition of a dense matrix, based on the algorithm described in [75]. For the sake of simplicity, the code fragment only shows the structure of the elimination phase,

1. /* Initialize */
   $b_{low} := 0$; $b_{up} := 0$;
   for $i := 1$ **to** n **do**
   $d[i] := c[i]$; $e[i] := c[i]$;
   end for

2. /* Iterate */
   for $k := n$ **down to** 1 **do**
   /* Eliminate v_k */
   a. $b_{low} := b_{low} + (d[k] > 0 ? d[k] * p[k, 0] : d[k] * q[k, 0])$;
   b. $b_{up} := b_{up} + (e[k] > 0 ? e[k] * q[k, 0] : d[k] * p[k, 0])$;
   c. **for** $i := 1$ **to** $k - 1$ **do**
       i.$d[i] := d[i] + (d[k] > 0 ? d[k] * p[k, i] : d[k] * q[k, i])$;
       ii.$e[i] := e[i] + (e[k] > 0 ? e[k] * q[k, i] : d[k] * p[k, i])$;
       end for
   end for

3. **return** b_{low}, b_{up}

FIGURE 8.6
Algorithm for Determining Bounds in a Trapezoidal Region.

which is the most time-consuming part of the algorithm. Consider the def-use chain from the a(i,j) reference on the LHS to the a(i,k) reference on the RHS. Data dependence analysis must determine if a dependence actually exists between these references and, if so, the set of direction vectors for which the dependence holds. As discussed above, data dependence analysis proceeds in three steps:

1. *Construct the dependence equations*:
   Let (k_1, j_1, i_1) and (k_2, j_2, i_2) represent the execution instances of the a(i,j) and a(i,k) references respectively. Since a is a two-dimensional array, we have two dependence equations: $i_1 = i_2$ and $j_1 = k_2$.

2. *Establish the context*:
   Let's say that the direction vector being considered is $(=, *, *)$ (which is the only interesting case!). The constraint imposed by this direction vector is the equality $k_1 = k_2$.

```
        parameter (n=100)
        dimension a(n,n)

        do k = 1, n-1
C         ...
C           CODE FOR PIVOTING
C         ...
        do j = k+1, n
          do i = k+1, n
            a(i,j) = a(i,j) - a(i,k)*a(k,j)
          end do
        end do
      end do
    end
```

FIGURE 8.7
Fortran Code for LU Decomposition.

The inequalities defined by the loop bounds are

$$
\begin{aligned}
1 &\leq k_1 \leq 99 \\
1 &\leq k_2 \leq 99 \\
1 + k_1 &\leq j_1 \leq 100 \\
1 + k_2 &\leq j_2 \leq 100 \\
1 + k_1 &\leq i_1 \leq 100 \\
1 + k_2 &\leq i_2 \leq 100
\end{aligned}
$$

Note that these inequalities define a trapezoidal region, as discussed earlier.

We can use the equality $k_1 = k_2$ from the direction vector to eliminate either k_1 or k_2 from the dependence equation and the loop bounds' inequalities. Let's assume that variable k_1 is eliminated. Then, the dependence equations remains unchanged as $i_1 = i_2$ and $j_1 = k_2$, but the inequalities become

$$
\begin{aligned}
1 &\leq k_2 \leq 99 \\
1 + k_2 &\leq j_1 \leq 100 \\
1 + k_2 &\leq j_2 \leq 100 \\
1 + k_2 &\leq i_1 \leq 100 \\
1 + k_2 &\leq i_2 \leq 100
\end{aligned}
$$

Therefore, the decision problem has five variables: k_2, j_1, j_2, i_1, i_2.

3. *Invoke a decision algorithm*:
The GCD test does not prove independence for these decision equations because the constant term is zero. Next, we try to apply Banerjee's inequality on each of the equations. Let us see how this test works on the $j_1 = k_2$ equation (the $i_1 = i_2$ equation is uninteresting because it is easy to see that it has a solution).
To apply Banerjee's inequality, we rewrite $j_1 = k_2$ as $j_1 - k_2 = 0$ and define $f(j_1, k_2) = j_1 - k_2$. Next, we use the algorithm in Figure 8.6 to compute the lower and upper bounds of function f in the trapezoidal region defined by the loop bounds' inequalities. The input values of arrays $c[0 \ldots 5]$, $p[1 \ldots 5, 0 \ldots 4]$, and $q[1 \ldots 5, 0 \ldots 4]$ are $c = [\, 0 \ -1 \ 1 \ 0 \ 0 \ 0 \,]$ and

$$
p = \begin{pmatrix} 1 & & & & \\ 1 & 1 & & & \\ 1 & 1 & 0 & & \\ 1 & 1 & 0 & 0 & \\ 1 & 1 & 0 & 0 & 0 \end{pmatrix} \qquad q = \begin{pmatrix} 99 & & & & \\ 100 & 0 & & & \\ 100 & 0 & 0 & & \\ 100 & 0 & 0 & 0 & \\ 100 & 0 & 0 & 0 & 0 \end{pmatrix}
$$

The algorithm in Figure 8.6 returns $b_{low} = 1$ and $b_{up} = 99$ for this decision problem. Since $c_0 = 0$, these values do not satisfy $b_{low} \leq c_0 \leq b_{up}$, and the decision algorithm has proved independence.

The result of this sample dependence analysis is that no data dependence exists between references a(i,j) and a(i,k) for the $(=, *, *)$ direction vector. In a similar way, guided by the hierarchical approach to dependence testing presented in [18], we can prove that all dependences on array a have "<" as the first element of the direction vector. Therefore, all the dependences can be satisfied by executing the k loop sequentially, and we are free to execute the j and i loops concurrently if it is beneficial to do so (the issue of satisfying dependences is discussed in detail in Section 8.6).

8.4.3   APPROACHES TO REMOVING DATA DEPENDENCES

Subsection 8.4.2 described how data dependence analysis is performed for automatic parallelization. One way to enhance automatic parallelization is to improve the precision of data dependence analysis, in order to make it less conservative. However, it is sometimes possible to *remove* a data dependence from places where a dependence would have been identified, even by an exact test, on the original decision problem. We consider three approaches to removing data dependences:

1. Subscript value analysis
2. Storage transformations
3. Single-assignment languages

Subscript Value Analysis.   In general, the effectiveness of a dependence test can be improved by learning more about the values of variables in the subscript expressions. To this end, PTRAN performs two subscript value analyses that are well-known traditional compiler optimizations:

1. *Constant propagation*: if a variable in a subscript expression is constant-valued, the dependence equation can be simplified by substituting the constant value for the variable. PTRAN performs global constant propagation on the control flow graph, using a variant of the "optimistic" algorithm in [85]. PTRAN's analysis also exploits interprocedural information for constant-valued formal parameters.

2. *Induction variable analysis*: if a variable in a subscript expression is an induction variable [2] in some enclosing loop, the dependence equation can be simplified by substituting an appropriate linear function of the loop iteration number for the variable. PTRAN performs global induction variable analysis on the control flow graph, using an "optimistic" algorithm, similar to the one used for constant propagation [28]. Again, PTRAN's induction variable analysis benefits from the use of interprocedural information for constant-valued formal parameters.

Both constant propagation and induction variable analysis are widely recognized as important subscript value analysis techniques for automatic parallelization. *Range analysis* [56], which determines the lower and upper bounds of variables in subscript expressions, could also help remove potential data dependences. Undoubtedly, other techniques will be developed in the future to further enhance automatic parallelization. One possibility would be to identify *permutation mappings*. For example, if we know that elements $1 \ldots N$ of array L contain a permutation of $1 \ldots N$, then it would be possible to parallelize the following DO loop:

```
DO I = 1, N
   A(L(I)) = A(L(I)) + B(I)
ENDDO
```

Storage Transformations.   As mentioned in Subsection 8.4.1, anti, output, and input dependences are all *storage-related* dependences that can be eliminated by storage duplication. The effect of storage duplication is to introduce the single assignment property into imperative programs, thus giving them a more functional behavior. Some of the techniques developed in this area are as follows:

1. *Scalar expansion* [104, 103, 70] changes a scalar variable into a temporary array variable, so as to remove storage-related dependences on the scalar variable. In practice, the size of the temporary array to only those dimensions necessary for parallelism can be reduced. When used in conjunction with *strip mining* for vectorization [7, 104], the size of the temporary array can be further reduced to the hardware vector length.

2. *Privatization* [19, 38] is a more efficient form of scalar expansion used by PTRAN for concurrent (rather than vector) execution of loops. If a scalar variable is declared *private* in a parallel loop, each iteration is assumed to get its own copy of the variable, thus providing the necessary storage duplication. However, the storage expansion factor for private variables need never exceed the number of processors working on the parallel loop, whereas it equals the number of loop iterations for a temporary array generated by scalar expansion. Besides parallelizing loops, privatization can also be used to enhance general statement parallelism by providing private copies of a variable to different groups of statements. Both loop-level and statement-level privatization have been implemented in PTRAN [19, 38], and are supported by the PARALLEL LOOP and PARALLEL CASES constructs in the Parallel Fortran language [64] generated by PTRAN (discussed later in Section 8.5).

3. *Static single assignment (SSA)* [34] is a program representation with the following characteristics:
   a. Each scalar variable, V, is given multiple names of the form V_1, V_2, ..., so that no two assignment statements in the program use the same name on the left-hand-side.

   b. ϕ-functions are used to distinguish between incoming values of the same variable from different control flow edges.
   SSA form has been proposed as a convenient data structure for implementing traditional compiler optimizations, where the multiple names are used to assist in program analysis, but do not appear in the output code. However, using multiple names of a scalar variable, V, in the output code will remove all storage-related dependences involving V, though doing so may incur some overhead due to copying. This method of storage duplication is also called *scalar renaming* [33].

4. *Data replication* is a technique in which the same value of a variable is maintained in different storage locations, so as to remove input dependences. As mentioned earlier, input dependences can lead to "hot spots" [80] in memory accesses. Hardware solutions to the hot-spot problem include *broadcast* in bus-based multiprocessors, and *combining* in interconnection networks. In the absence of hardware support, data replication can be used to remove input dependences. A well-known trick in the design of EREW (Exclusive Read Exclusive Write) PRAM [39] algorithms [43] is to perform data replication like a fan-out tree. For example, the following pseudo-code copies X into all elements of array $A(1..N)$ in $O(logN)$ time on $O(N)$ processors:

$A(1) := X$
for $d := 1$ **to** $\lceil log_2 N \rceil$ **do**
    forall $i := 2^d$ **to** $min(2^{d+1} - 1, N)$ **do**
        $A(i) := A(\lfloor i/2 \rfloor)$
    end
end

After this replication, the N copies of X can be accessed in parallel by N processors.

Single-Assignment Languages.   Yet another approach to removing storage-related dependences is to write the original program in an applicative language like SISAL [77] or Haskell [62], rather than an imperative language like Fortran. The advantage of using an applicative language is that all programs must satisfy the *single-assignment rule*, which states that each variable has at most one value assigned to it at run-time. Therefore, this rule enforces *dynamic* single assignment, as opposed to the *static* single assignment property in SSA form. With the dynamic single assignment, a variable is really a name for a value, rather than a storage location. Whenever a new value is computed, it must be assigned to a new variable. Therefore, by definition, single-assignment programs have no storage-related dependences.

However, the single assignment rule is a double-edged sword — it can lead to excessive overhead due to copying and storage duplication. This overhead is most acute in the case of an *incremental update*. Consider the assignment statement $B := A[i : x]$ in SISAL. It says that B is defined to be an array value identical to A, except for the ith value where $B[i] = x$. Semantically, A and B have no storage in common, so all elements of A (except $A[i]$) need to be copied into B. In practice, a *copy avoidance* optimization is performed to eliminate unnecessary copying [24, 46, 47, 61, 84]. Fortunately, recent optimization techniques in compiling SISAL have made it possible for SISAL programs to yield comparable execution times with C, Fortran and Pascal programs [95, 24, 46]. Similar performance results have not yet been obtained for more powerful functional languages like Haskell [62], which rely on demand-driven evaluation more heavily than SISAL does. Copy avoidance optimizations are also necessary when compiling array expressions, as in Fortran 90, or when performing storage replication on arrays.

8.4.4 LOOP TRANSFORMATIONS AND DATA DEPENDENCES

Loop transformations are the driving force behind many of today's vectorizing and parallelizing compilers. A loop transformation typically reorders iterations in a set of nested loops to enhance parallelization. Various loop transformations have been defined over the years to handle different loop nest structures. Some of the commonly found loop transformations are [104]:

- Loop distribution
- Loop fusion
- Loop interchange
- Loop reversal
- Loop skewing
- Loop blocking
- Hyperplane method
- Wavefront method
- Loop alignment
- Strip mining
- Loop unrolling
- Loop iteration peeling
- Loop collapsing
- Index set splitting
- Index set shifting

An important observation about loop transformations is that the *loop transformations do not remove data dependences*. They restructure loops so as to make parallel execution more efficient (e.g. by reducing synchronization overhead, by enhancing locality, by reducing setup overhead, etc.). Another way of stating this observation is that loop transformations would have no effect on program parallelism when targetting to (say) an ideal dynamic dataflow machine with infinite resources and no synchronization or communication overhead.

The standard approach in using loop transformations is to apply them on the input program in some predetermined sequence, though the same transformation may need to be applied more than once due to opportunities created by other transformations. For instance, the Parafrase system [68] has a control file that is used to specify the sequence of transformations. However, this approach has two serious drawbacks:

1. It does not address the issue of what final loop structure is desired for a given loop nest, and how to select the best sequence of transformations to get there. Instead, the transformation sequence is specified in an *ad hoc* manner at the start of compilation.

2. It can be very inefficient because all loop transformations are applied to all loop nests.

Both problems will be further exacerbated as more and more loop transformations are included in the system.

The problems with this standard approach serve as evidence that transformations pose a harder problem than analysis in a parallelizing compiler. Analysis is simpler because the object being analyzed does not change, whereas transformations are faced with an ever-changing view of the world. Because of this difference, PTRAN chooses to perform many transformations (e.g. constant propagation, induction variable substitution, privatization, loop parallelization, partitioning) as quasi-transformations that generate lookaside tables rather than modify the program representation. The effect of a quasi-transformation is made manifest during code generation, when the lookaside tables are used to control the output parallel code. The quasi-transformational approach has its limitations, however. For instance, loop distribution transforms a single loop into multiple loops and can be applied recursively on nested loops. Each of the resulting multiple loops will be analyzed and transformed separately, yielding different results in general. It would be very awkward to represent the output of loop distribution as a lookaside table. Instead, it would be more appropriate to transform the program representation (control flow, control dependence and data dependence graphs) to represent the output of loop distribution. Recently, loop distribution has been added to the PTRAN system as a full-fledged loop transformation, rather than a quasi-transformation. After loop distribution, we can still implement transformations like loop parallelization and loop fusion as quasi-transformations with lookaside tables.

For a transformational system to be successful, it should have global properties that can be proved about the ordering of transformations and the final configurations. Thus far, such global properties have proved elusive in the loop transformations performed by parallelizing compilers. An alternative to the transformational approach is a two-step *analysis* and *synthesis* approach:

1. *Analysis* — analyze the loop nest and generate a higher-level canonical representation e.g. *dependence cones* [65] for summarizing dependences between execution instances of the loop body, *reduction clauses* [77] for summarizing reduction operations. The higher-level representations summarize information about execution instances without committing to any execution orderings.

2. *Synthesis* — synthesize the "best" transformed code directly from the high level representation, based on available parallelism and the overhead parameters of the target multiprocessor. *Supernode partitioning* [65] provides a framework for performing this kind of synthesis from a dependence cone representation, though their work does not state specifically how the synthesis should be performed.

The above description of the analysis-synthesis approach is deliberately vague because this is a discussion of an open problem. However, there are some isolated research efforts that should provide answers to different pieces of the puzzle in the future:

□ As mentioned above, *dependence cones* and *supernode partitioning* [65] provide a framework for the analysis-synthesis approach. Supernode partitioning subsumes most of the common transformations that are applied on a set of perfectly nested loops e.g. loop interchange, loop reversal, loop blocking, hyperplane method [70], wavefront method [104]. However, this work has not yet addressed the problem of how the synthesis should be performed to generate efficient code for a given target multiprocessor.

□ The Crystal compiling system described in chapter 7 in this book provides a solution to the synthesis problem. The Crystal programming language is itself a very high-level program representation, which makes the analysis step unnecessary. The problem of synthesis is attacked by using *index domains* and *data fields*.

□ IF1[99] is a high-level, value-oriented, graphical intermediate language for SISAL [77] and other applicative languages. Though the lack of a storage model in IF1 makes it too restrictive for languages like Fortran, loops in IF1 have *return clauses* that could also be used in a high-level representation of Fortran loops. Return clauses include *reductions*, *gather/scatter*, and *masks*, all of which would facilitate the analysis-synthesis approach.

□ *Communication overhead* and *data locality* are widely recognized as critical problems that need to be solved for large scale parallel processing to be successful. Some preliminary work has been done on loop transformations for improved data locality e.g. *loop blocking* of nested doall loops [44]. However, this work still needs to be developed into a complete optimization algorithm that can select the final loop partition based on communication overhead and cache size parameters. As proposed in [65], another important extension would be to consider blocking non-doall loops as well.

□ One reason why it is hard to decide on the final structure for a loop nest, is that the best choice depends on other computations in the procedure and even on other procedures in the program. In PTRAN, we have already established global and interprocedural framework for estimating average statement execution times and their variance [90] (discussed later in Section 8.7). This framework should be helpful in providing relative execution times for a given loop nest and other computations in the program.

□ When generating both loop-level and statement-level parallelism, as in PTRAN, it becomes necessary to carefully *partition* the program into tasks so as to optimally trade off parallelism and overhead [91]. Again, the best choice for partitioning a loop nest depends on how the rest of the program is partitioned. We have already implemented a task partitioner in PTRAN [92] (discussed later in Section 8.7) that provides a uniform approach for both statement and loop level parallelism. Currently, the only *loop transformation* performed by the partitioner is *loop chunking*. In the future, we plan to incorporate more general loop transformations (e.g. loop fusion, loop blocking) into this framework for automatic partitioning.

8.5   Parallel Fortran — PTRAN's Target Language

The parallel language generated by PTRAN is a simple extension to Fortran that can express nested structured parallelism. The extension consists of two control structures for parallelism, PARALLEL LOOP and PARALLEL CASES, which are similar to doall and cobegin-coend respectively. These kinds of control structures have appeared in well-known parallel languages (e.g. Concurrent Pascal [53], Occam [82]), and are supported by the IBM Parallel Fortran compiler [64] and the IBM VS Fortran 2.5 compiler.

The PARALLEL LOOP statement denotes the beginning of a parallel loop, in which each iteration may be executed concurrently. Its syntax is like that of the Fortran DO statement—the PARALLEL LOOP statement specifies a target statement label as well as an index variable with expressions for lower and upper bounds. The PARALLEL LOOP statement has an implicit barrier synchronization at the end: the statement following the PARALLEL LOOP construct is executed only after all iterations of the PARALLEL LOOP have completed execution. A PARALLEL LOOP may contain directives of the form CHUNK(n) and PROCS(p). CHUNK(n) stipulates that the loop iterations should be grouped together in chunks of size n, so that each chunk is executed sequentially. PROCS(p) requests p processors to work on the loop. A PARALLEL LOOP may also contain PRIVATE declarations for scalar variables that are used as local temporary variables within a single iteration. As discussed in Subsection 8.4.3, private variables can be used to avoid data conflicts among loop iterations. PTRAN can optionally tag a private variable with a COPYIN and/or a COPYOUT declaration [19, 38], indicating whether the private variable's value should be read in by all iterations at the start of the loop and/or written out by the last iteration at the end of the loop. The COPYIN/COPYOUT feature can make it possible to parallelize a loop that would otherwise have executed sequentially. The COPYIN/COPYOUT feature is not supported by the IBM Parallel Fortran compiler, but it is supported by a back-end for the RP3 developed at the IBM T. J. Watson Research Center. The PTRAN system can also accept programmer-specified PARALLEL LOOP constructs in the input Fortran program.

The PARALLEL CASES statement denotes the beginning of a group of cases (tasks) that may be executed in parallel. It is terminated by an END CASES statement. Each task begins with a statement of the form CASE i, optionally followed by a clause of the form WAITING FOR CASES($n1, n2,$ $\ldots$). i is a positive integer constant that identifies the task being specified. If the WAITING FOR clause is present, it means that task i can start execution only after tasks $n1, n2, \ldots$ have completed. As a simple way of ensuring that the task precedence constraints are acyclic, the WAITING FOR clause is allowed to refer only to tasks that have been previously declared in the current PARALLEL CASES statement. The PARALLEL CASES statement also has an implicit barrier synchronization at the end: the statement following END CASES is only executed after all tasks in the PARALLEL CASES construct have completed execution. As with PARALLEL LOOP, a PARALLEL CASES construct may contain a list of PRIVATE declarations for scalar variables. Each task is given its own copy of a private variable, so as to avoid data conflicts among the tasks. PTRAN can optionally tag a private variable in a PARALLEL CASES statement with a COPYIN and/or a COPYOUT declaration, indicating whether the private variable's value should be read in by all tasks at the beginning and/or written out by the last task at the end.

The PARALLEL LOOP and PARALLEL CASES constructs specify tasks at compile-time, which are created and scheduled at run-time. Note that the parallelism may be arbitrarily nested and may cross procedure boundaries, e.g. when a procedure containing a parallel construct is itself called from within a parallel construct. As with other parallel language systems that support nested parallelism, the IBM Parallel Fortran runtime system begins by creating a fixed number of operating system processes (called "Fortran processors"), usually one for each real processor. After this, all task scheduling is performed by executing Parallel Fortran library routines on the Fortran processors, without requesting any services from the operating system. Each Fortran processor selects work to do from a shared queue. The IBM Parallel Fortran runtime system has been ported to the MVS and VM operating systems [64].

8.6 Satisfying Control and Data Dependences

Now that we have taken a careful look at control and data dependences (Sections 8.2 and 8.4 respectively), we return to our fundamental identity, Control + Data = Program, and consider how a parallel program with known control and data dependences can be executed on a given multiprocessor. In this section, we first discuss various ways in which control and data dependences can be satisfied and then lead up to the *sequencing* approach used in the current implementation of PTRAN [19, 38].

Any dependence (either control or data) from an execution instance of statement S_1 to an execution instance of statement S_2 is a requirement that S_1's execution instance precede S_2's execution instance in all executions of the program. "Satisfying a dependence" means using some mechanism in the parallel execution model to guarantee that the dependence requirement is satisfied in all executions of the program. The mechanisms available for satisfying dependences can be classified as follows:

1. *Control sequencing* consists of using control structures in the parallel program that are capable of sequencing two statements due to their implicit synchronization e.g. doall, cobegin-coend, fork/join, and even normal begin-end sequential execution. A degenerate form of control sequencing, which is guaranteed to satisfy all dependences, is to simply output the original sequential program.

2. *Data synchronization* consists of using synchronization objects like *semaphores* and *full-empty bits* to sequence two statements.

Pursuing the control/data dichotomy, we see that we have control and data dependences, as well as two ways in which to satisfy dependences, namely control sequencing and data synchronization. A simple approach for satisfying dependences is to:

1. Satisfy all control dependences by control sequencing, and

2. Satisfy all data dependences by data synchronization.

Though this approach correctly satisfies all dependences, it is unnecessarily restrictive and may be inefficient in some cases. We observe that dependences, and the mechanisms for satisfying dependences, are two orthogonal issues. In particular, it is also possible to satisfy data dependences by control sequencing, and to satisfy control dependences by data synchronization, as discussed in the following subsections.

8.6.1 SATISFYING DATA DEPENDENCES BY CONTROL SEQUENCING

Consider the following program fragment:

```
S1:    W :=
S2:    X := F(W)
S3:    Y := G(W)
S4:    Z := H(X,Y)
```

If F, G and H are pure functions (i.e. they have no side effects), then the only data dependences are

$$\{S_1 \, \delta \, S_2, \, S_1 \, \delta \, S_3, \, S_2 \, \delta \, S_4, \, S_3 \, \delta \, S_4\}$$

which form a diamond-shaped dag (directed acyclic graph). It is well known that all series-parallel dependence graphs (including the diamond-shaped graph) can be satisfied by nested cobegin-coend and begin-end control structures without any loss of parallelism. We use the PARALLEL CASES notation defined in Section 8.5 to show how the data dependences in the above program fragment can be satisfied by control sequencing:

```
S1:    W :=
       PARALLEL CASES
       CASE 1
S2:        X := F(W)
       CASE 2
S3:        Y := G(W)
       END CASES
S4:    Z := H(X,Y)
```

In this way, all data dependences are satisfied by a careful placement of task creation and termination operations. The control sequencing approach creates only two tasks, whereas the data synchronization
approach would create four tasks and also use four semaphores for data
synchronization. In this case, control sequencing satisfies data dependences more efficiently than data synchronization and does so without
giving up any parallelism.

One of the biggest advantages of control sequencing is that it
can reduce the number of tasks created when there is little parallelism
revealed by the data dependences. For example, this principle is used
at a very fine granularity in the hybrid-dataflow approach [63], in which
a chain of data-dependent instructions are coalesced into a sequential
thread. In previous work [93], we addressed the problem of satisfying all
dependences in a data dependence dag using fork and join operations
only (which is equivalent to using PARALLEL CASES with no WAITING FOR
clauses), so as to minimize the critical-path length of the fork-join code.

8.6.2 SATISFYING CONTROL DEPENDENCES BY DATA SYNCHRONIZATION

A well-known approach to satisfying control dependences by data synchronization is by performing a *dataflow* execution of the parallel program, where control dependences are enforced by data tokens [15].

In the field of vectorizing compilers, *IF conversion* [7] is a commonly used transformation that can convert some control dependences
into data dependences. The resulting code can then be executed in vector
mode, provided the target vector processor can support conditional
vector operations. As an example, consider the following Fortran loop:

```
DO 100 I = 1, N
   IF (A(I) .GT. 0) GO TO 100
      A(I) = B(I) + 10
100  CONTINUE
```

IF conversion makes the conditional branch explicit as a data dependence by introducing a variable, BR1, to store the branch condition
value [7]:

```
DO 100 I = 1, N
   BR1 = A(I) .GT. 0
      IF (BR1) A(I) = B(I) + 10
100  CONTINUE
```

After IF conversion, the loop can be vectorized as follows (using Fortran 90 notation):

```
BR1(1:N) = A(1:N) .GT. 0
WHERE (BR1(1:N)) A(1:N) = B(1:N) + 10
```

Another example of satisfying control dependences by data synchronization is *compile-time scheduling* [87, 91]. Consider a program fragment of the form

```
S1:    X :=
S2:    Y :=
S3:    IF ( F(X) ) THEN
S4:       Z := G(X)
       ELSE
S5:       Z := G(Y)
       END IF
```

where statements $S1$, $S3$ and $S4$ are assigned to processor 1, and statements $S2$ and $S5$ are assigned to processor 2 (for the reason of reducing communication overhead, say). Since this is a compile-time scheduling approach, no tasks can be dynamically created and the parallel program will consist of two threads (one per processor):

```
    PARALLEL CASES
        CASE 1
S1:       X :=
S3:       C := F(X)
          signal(C)
          IF ( C = true ) THEN
S4:          Z := G(X)
          END IF
        CASE 2
S2:       Y :=
          wait(C)
          IF ( C = false ) THEN
S5:          Z := G(Y)
          END IF
    END CASES
```

In this case, the IF condition will have to be computed on processor 1, and communicated to processor 2 by data synchronization, even though it represents a control dependence.

8.6.3   THE CURRENT PTRAN APPROACH: SATISFY ALL DEPENDENCES BY CONTROL SEQUENCING

In the previous subsections, we demonstrated that dependences, and the mechanisms for satisfying dependences, are two orthogonal issues. For simplicity and efficiency, the initial approach taken in PTRAN is to satisfy both control and data dependences by control sequencing [19, 38]. Although this *sequencing* approach is a good start, we know that PTRAN will need the flexibility of both control sequencing and data synchronization in the future. The general problem of satisfying dependences is an optimization problem whose solution depends on the trade-off between parallelism and overhead when using both control sequencing and data synchronization primitives. As discussed later in Section 8.7, the task partitioner implemented in PTRAN provides a general multiprocessor-independent framework for solving this kind of optimization problem. In the future, we plan to incorporate the job of satisfying dependences into the PTRAN task partitioner as well.

The main advantages of using control sequencing to satisfy all dependences in PTRAN are simplicity and efficiency. Restricting the parallel constructs generated by PTRAN to only PARALLEL LOOP and PARALLEL CASES makes PTRAN's execution model simple and portable, and also easy to extend in the future. By not using explicit data synchronization, we avoid possible inefficiencies due to the overhead of extra semaphore operations (other than those necessary for implementing parallel loops and parallel cases). With a view to using explicit synchronization in PTRAN in the future, [89] addresses the problem of satisfying the precedence constraints of a given dag with the minimum number of counting semaphore operations.

The main disadvantage of generating PARALLEL LOOP and PARALLEL CASES as the only parallel constructs is that some parallelism is sacrificed when it cannot be expressed with only these constructs. For parallelism among loop iterations, PARALLEL LOOP cannot support *doacross*-style parallelism [27]. To do so would also require some data synchronization among loop iterations. Therefore, if a loop has any loop-carried dependences, it will be executed sequentially, even though *doacross*-style concurrent execution may have been possible. For statement-level parallelism, PARALLEL CASES can support synchronization only among identically control dependent statements. Therefore, some potential parallelism may be lost due to a dependence between non-identically control dependent statements. For example, consider the sequential code in Figure 8.8. The only data dependence is a flow dependence on variable W from statement S2 to statement S5. However, it is not possible to directly express this dependence by a WAITING FOR

Sequential code:

```
S1:    IF ( C1 ) THEN
S2:      W :=
       ELSE
S3:      X :=
       ENDIF
S4:    IF ( C2 ) THEN
S5:      Y := f(W)
       ELSE
S6:      Z :=
       ENDIF
```

Parallel code:

```
       PARALLEL CASES
         CASE 1
S1:    IF ( C1 ) THEN
S2:      W :=
       ELSE
S3:      X :=
       ENDIF
         CASE 2, WAITING FOR CASE 1
S4:    IF ( C2 ) THEN
S5:      Y := f(W)
       ELSE
S6:      Z :=
       ENDIF
       END CASES
```

FIGURE 8.8
Satisfying a Loop-independent Dependence Using WAITING FOR.

clause in a PARALLEL CASES construct. Instead, the entire IF statement in
$S1$ must precede the entire IF statement in $S4$, as shown in the parallel
code. In this example, control sequencing is insufficient for expressing
the potential parallelism between statements S3 and S6 (for example).

The *sequencing* phase in PTRAN automatically identifies as much
parallelism as possible from the control and data dependences, subject to the constraint that PARALLEL LOOP and PARALLEL CASES with
WAITING FOR are the only constructs that may be used to express parallelism [19, 38]. Sequencing is integrated with *privatization* (discussed

in Subsection 8.4.3), which may eliminate some data dependences by introducing private variables.

The output of sequencing can be described by the following structures:

1. $PARLOOP(l)$ indicates whether loop l can be executed as a PARALLEL LOOP.

2. $SEQSET$ is a set of quadruples of the form (N, L, C_1, C_2), such that child nodes C_1 and C_2 are control dependent on node N with label L in the forward control dependence graph, $FCDG$. $(N, L, C_1, C_2) \in SEQSET$ means that C_2 must be forced to wait for C_1 if the branch condition at node N evaluates to L.

The $PARLOOP$ structure can be computed by examining all the *base direction vectors* of all data dependences in the program. Recall from Definition 8.8 that a base direction vector is one in which each ψ_k is one of "<", "=" or ">". If a ψ_k value is "≤", "≥", "≠" or "*", then Ψ is a *summary direction vector*. It is easy to enumerate all the base direction vectors summarized by a given summary direction vector.

Consider a base direction vector $\Psi = (\psi_1, \ldots, \psi_d)$ defined for a data dependence $S_1 \, \delta \, S_2$, where both S_1 and S_2 are enclosed by loops $l_1, \ldots, l_d$. If each ψ_k is "=", then Ψ imposes no constraints on the concurrent execution of loops $l_1, \ldots, l_d$ (i.e. Ψ is *loop-independent*). Otherwise, let K be the index of the leftmost non-"=" entry in Ψ (ψ_K must be "<", because Ψ is a plausible direction vector). In this case, the data dependence is *loop-carried* at *level K* [7]. Now, consider any two execution instances of S_1 and S_2, say $S_1[i_1, \ldots, i_d, \ldots]$ and $S_2[j_1, \ldots, j_d, \ldots]$, that are compatible with Ψ (i.e. $i_k \, \psi_k \, j_k \, \forall 1 \leq k \leq d$). It can be proved that only loop l_K needs to be executed sequentially to guarantee that $S_1[i_1, \ldots, i_d, \ldots]$ will precede $S_2[j_1, \ldots, j_d, \ldots]$ and hence satisfy the data dependence constraints imposed by direction vector Ψ [7].

Each base direction vector identifies at most one loop that must be executed sequentially. By examining all base direction vectors in the program, we can identify all loops that must be sequentialized, and set $PARLOOP = false$ for each of them. It is important to look for the first non-"=" entry in the base direction vectors rather than the summary direction vectors. For example, we cannot satisfy all the constraints of a $(*, *)$ summary direction vector by sequentializing the first loop with a non-"=" entry (i.e. loop 1). Instead, we need to expand $(*, *)$ into its plausible base direction vectors $(<, <), (<, =), (<, <), (=, <), (=, =)$ to determine that both loops 1 and 2 must be sequentialized. As an optimization, we observe that the set of loops to be sequentialized can be determined by a left-to-right scan of the summary direction vector, without explicitly generating all base direction vectors.

The direction vectors identify the loops that must be sequentialized due to loop-carried data dependences. Other loops may have to be sequentialized due to loop-carried control dependences. For a target language like Parallel Fortran in which the PARALLEL LOOP construct is the only way to express loop parallelism, loops that are equivalent to DO loops with no premature exits are the only candidates for parallelization. To determine if a given loop is equivalent to a DO loop with no premature exits, we need to check if the loop has a single exit, guarded by a conditional that compares the value of an induction variable with a loop-invariant upper bound. All other loops must be sequentialized (with *PARLOOP* set to *false*) due to loop-carried control dependences.

So far, we have discussed how the *PARLOOP* structure is computed to identify the set of loops that can be parallelized. We now turn our attention to non-loop parallelism and discuss how the *SEQSET* structure is computed [38].

As discussed in Section 8.2, non-loop parallelism is based on the forward control dependence graph. Consider node N with children $\{c_1, \ldots, c_k\}$ due to label L in $FCDG$. If the branch condition at node N evaluates to L, we could attempt to execute $c_1, \ldots, c_k$ in parallel by using the PARALLEL CASES construct. However, as illustrated in Figure 8.8, WAITING FOR clauses are necessary to satisfy loop-independent data dependences. We need to sequence children c_i and c_j (i.e. make c_j wait for c_i) if and only if there exists a data dependence $A \delta B$ with an ("=", ..., "=") base direction vector such that there is a directed path from c_i to A and a path from c_j to B in $FCDG$. If c_i and c_j satisfy this condition, then $SEQSET$ must contain all quadruples of the form (N, L, c_i, c_j) such that both c_i and c_j are control dependent on N with label L in the forward control dependence graph.

An algorithm to compute $SEQSET$ in $O(N_f * E_f)$ time is given in [38], where N_f and E_f are the number of nodes and edges in the forward control dependence graph. A more efficient version of the algorithm has recently been developed and implemented in the PTRAN system [31].

8.7 Partitioning

Partitioning is the bridge between *ideal parallelism* and *useful parallelism*. Ideal parallelism is the parallelism revealed in the program by its control or data dependences. Any two execution instances of statements, say $S1$ and S_2, that are not directly or indirectly related by control or data dependences, can *potentially* be executed in parallel. Useful parallelism is a subset of ideal parallelism that is suitable for execution on the target multiprocessor. The best choice of useful parallelism depends on statement execution times, synchronization, communication and scheduling overheads, and resource limits such as the number of processors available.

The sequencing algorithm described in the previous section actually yields an intermediate point between ideal parallelism and useful parallelism, which could be called *usable parallelism*. Usable parallelism is the subset of ideal parallelism that can *potentially* be executed on the target multiprocessor, based on the mechanisms available for satisfying dependences. When generating Parallel Fortran in PTRAN, we decided that the implicit synchronization in the PARALLEL LOOP and PARALLEL CASES constructs would be the only mechanisms that we would use to satisfy all dependences. Hence, the sequencing algorithms mentioned in Subsection 8.6.3 were necessary to identify the usable parallelism. As we consider more general mechanisms for satisfying dependences, the usable parallelism will come closer to the ideal parallelism revealed by the program dependence graph. No matter how the usable parallelism is defined, partitioning is necessary to determine the useful parallelism in the program based on the overhead parameters of the target multiprocessor.

Continuing with the theme of control/data duality, we see that there are two kinds of partitioning that can be performed on a parallel program:

1. *Control partitioning* — partition the program into parallel tasks so as to optimally trade off parallelism and overhead.
2. *Data partitioning* — partition data across tasks so as to further reduce communication overhead.

There is a close interaction between both forms of partitioning; together, they yield a complete partition of the program's control and data structures. This section will only discuss control partitioning, which is the dominant form of partitioning on shared-memory multiprocessor systems and has been implemented in PTRAN. Data partitioning is mainly a subject for future work in PTRAN, though we have done some preliminary work on software-controlled cache coherence [39], and on data partitioning for a cache-based multiprocessor model, where data partitioning is implicitly achieved by appropriately ordering the sequential execution of loop iterations for improved locality.

Control partitioning is necessary to execute a parallel program at an appropriate granularity, for a given target multiprocessor. The problem is to determine the best trade-off between parallelism and overhead.

It is desirable for the partitioning to be performed automatically, so that a parallel program can be written without burdening the programmer with overhead details of the target multiprocessor, and the same parallel program can be made to execute efficiently on different multiprocessors. To this end, the PTRAN partitioner consists of three steps, which are discussed in the following subsections:

1. *Automatic execution profiling* provides average loop frequencies and branch probabilities. We have implemented an optimized counter-based profiler in PTRAN that incurs only about a 5 percent run-time profiling overhead, compared to the original code.

2. *Computation of average execution times* is then performed, based on the forward control dependence graph, execution profile information, and target multiprocessor parameters for the execution times of primitive operations.

3. *Partitioning* is the final step, which uses execution time estimates and target multiprocessor parameters for overhead values, number of processors, etc.

All three steps use the *forward control dependence graph* defined in Subsection 8.2.3. The reader is referred to [92] for further details.

8.7.1   AUTOMATIC EXECUTION PROFILING

Automatic execution profiling is an empirical means of obtaining average loop frequencies and conditional branch probabilities in a program. In some cases (e.g. a DO loop with constant bounds and no premature exits, or an IF condition that evaluates to a constant), it is possible to determine the frequency values at compile-time by program analysis. However, we believe that determining frequency values by program analysis is feasible for only a few restricted cases and should be complemented by empirical profile information wherever compile-time analysis is unsuccessful. In PTRAN, program analysis is used to determine the number of iterations for DO loops with constant bounds and no premature exits. Profile information is used in all other cases.

An execution profiler performs some extra computation at run-time to keep track of average frequency values. There are two standard approaches to execution profiling:

1. *Sampling-based* profilers examine the program counter periodically to get an estimate of the relative execution time spent in each program region of interest.

2. *Counter-based* profilers maintain integer variables that keep track of the total execution frequency of each program region of interest.

Although counter-based profilers are more accurate than sampling-based profilers, there has been a marked preference in the past for using sampling-based profilers. The preference for sampling-based profilers was due to convenience (they can be implemented in the operating system without recompiling application programs) and due to efficiency considerations (their overhead can be controlled by adjusting the sampling interval). However, we describe three important optimizations, based on the forward control dependence graph, which make the more accurate counter-based profilers competitive with sampling-based profilers in terms of efficiency. The three optimizations are as follows (see [90] for details):

1. The first optimization is to maintain one counter per control condition (i.e. a (node, label) pair) in the forward control dependence graph, rather than the naive approach of one counter per basic block. This optimization avoids using separate counters for different basic blocks that have identical control conditions, since they must have identical execution frequencies. A loop frequency is tracked by the counter for the set of identically control dependent forward edges from the preheader node to nodes in the loop body.

2. The second optimization is based on an observation akin to Kirchhoff's laws of conservation: *the sum of the execution frequencies of all branches entering a node must equal the sum of the execution frequencies of all branches leaving the node.* Consider a node, u, that has at least one successor with label l in $FCDG$ for each branch labelled l out of u in CFG (let there be n such labels). After the first optimization, we would assign one counter for each label l from node u. However, we observe that the sum of the execution frequencies of all n labels must equal the execution frequency of node u. Therefore, we need to maintain counters for only $(n - 1)$ of the n labels. Alternatively, we could maintain counters for all n labels and eliminate a counter for one of node u's parents in FCDG. The optimization can also be applied to loops by observing that the sum of the execution frequencies of all loop exits must equal the execution frequency of the loop preheader.

3. Unlike the previous two optimizations, which are purely syntactic, the third optimization uses limited semantic information by identifying DO loops and DO-like loops in the program. The idea is to add the number of iterations to the counter variable once at the start of the loop, rather than incrementing the counter in every

iteration. This optimization can only be performed for DO loops with no premature exits.

These optimizations have been implemented in PTRAN. When invoked with the GENPROFILE option, PTRAN generates a sequential Fortran program that is equivalent to the input program augmented with profiling statements to initialize and update counter variables. This program is then executed on any input set supplied by the user, and the final values of the counter variables are stored in the program database. It is also possible to average the frequency information obtained from different input sets. Execution profile information is very compact (usually < 50 counters per procedure). Also, unlike dynamic program traces, the size of the execution profile information does not depend on the duration of program execution. Preliminary measurements show that the run-time overhead of optimized profiling is ≤ 5 percent, as opposed to an overhead of 15 to 25 percent obtained from naive execution profiling (i.e. maintaining one counter per basic block).

An implicit assumption in these optimizations is that the program's execution does not incur any exceptions i.e. the program does not terminate abnormally before reaching the $STOP$ node in the control flow graph. If an exception is incurred, the counter values should be ignored because they do not represent a complete execution of the program.

An important issue in the methodology of using execution profile information is the "chicken-and-egg" problem: we want to use execution profile information to optimize a program and speed up its execution, but we need to first execute the program to obtain profile information. If the same program will be executed on several different input sets, then profile information from the first k runs should be used to recompile and optimize the program for the $k + 1^{st}$ run. This is a clear win, assuming that a program run takes significantly longer than a program recompilation. Of course, the effectiveness of the profile information depends on the "repeatability" of the program's behavior over different input sets.

Sometimes, a program is tested on several small input sets and then run on a single large input set. In this case, profile information from the small input sets can be *scaled* to approximate the large input set for which profile information is unavailable. The PTRAN profiling system accepts a *scale factor* value from the user, which specifies the factor by which all loop frequencies should be multiplied to approximate the program's execution on the large input set. All non-loop branch probabilities are assumed to be the same. Scaling is an approximation because all loops are assumed to have the same increase in their number of iterations.

Finally, if no profile information is available, then the default approach is to approximate all unknown frequencies by assuming that all loops have the same average number of iterations (given by a parameter AVG_ITERS), and that all branch labels from a node representing a non-loop conditional branch have the same probability. One of the experiments that we plan to do in the future with the PTRAN system is to measure the relative effectiveness of full profile information, scaled profile information, and default profile information, by observing their impact on the speedup of the partitioned programs.

Irrespective of how the frequency information is obtained, it is used to label all edges in the forward control dependence graph with *relative* frequency values, according to the following definition:

DEFINITION 8.9

Given an edge (u, v, l) in the forward control dependence graph, $FCDG = (N_f, E_f)$, the execution frequency of the edge is defined as:

1. (when u is a preheader node and l is the label connecting u to its header node in $FCFG$)
   $FREQ(u, l)$ = average number of times u's header node is executed in one execution of u's interval. In this case, $FREQ(u, l) \geq 0$ represents the *average loop frequency* for u's interval.

2. (all other cases)
   $FREQ(u, l)$ = average number of times that node u takes the branch labelled l in one execution of node u. In this case, $0 \leq FREQ(u, l) \leq 1$ represents the *branch probability* of label l in node u. □

8.7.2   COMPUTATION OF AVERAGE EXECUTION TIMES

In this section, we describe how average execution times can be computed for all nodes in the forward control dependence graph. Having obtained frequency values as described in the previous section, the other necessary input is the execution times of *primitive* operations on the target architecture. We will not discuss the possible techniques for obtaining the costs of primitive operations since they depend on the nature of the target architecture as well as the level of detail available in the intermediate program representation. For the purpose of this description, it is assumed that the (average) local execution time of each node, u, in $FCDG$ has already been estimated and is stored as $COST(u)$.

We define node u's *total* execution time, $SEQTIME(u)$, to be the sum of $COST(u)$ and the frequency-weighted execution times of node u's children in the forward control dependence graph. The computation of $SEQTIME(u)$ is based on two simple rules (see [90] for details):

1. $$SEQTIME(u) = COST(u) + \sum_{(u,v,l) \in E_f} FREQ(u,l) \times SEQTIME\ (v)$$

   This rule assumes that node v's execution time is independent of the path taken to reach node u.

2. If node u is a procedure or function call, then

   $$COST(u) = SEQTIME(ENTRY)$$

   where $ENTRY$ is the entry node of the callee's forward control dependence graph. This rule assumes that the execution time of a procedure call is independent of the call site.

Rules 1 and 2 implicitly dictate how the execution time values should be computed. Rule 1 requires that the nodes be visited in a bottom-up traversal of $FCDG$. Rule 2 requires that the procedures be visited in a bottom-up traversal of the call graph, so that the root procedure (main program) is visited last. For the purpose of this discussion, we assume that the call graph is acyclic, which is a reasonable assumption for Fortran programs. In previous work [88, 91], we discussed how cyclic call graphs and recursive programs can be handled for the single-assignment language SISAL. Those techniques are equally applicable to the partitioning framework described in this section.

In [90], we also described how this approach to computing average execution times can be generalized to compute *execution time variance*. To define variance precisely, let T be the random variable corresponding to the execution time of node v (say). So far, we discussed the computation of v's average execution time, which is the expected value of T, $E(T) = SEQTIME(v)$. By extending rules 1 and 2 above to compute $E(T^2)$ the expected value of T^2, we obtain the variance by using the well-known equation, $VAR(v) = E(T^2) - E(T)^2$. The standard deviation is simply $STD\_DEV(v) = \sqrt{VAR(v)}$.

The computation of average execution times and variance has been completely implemented in PTRAN. The average execution times are used to guide the partitioner, as described in the next subsection. An interesting application of variance information is in determining the optimal *chunk size* [68] for the execution of parallel loops on multiprocessors. Intuitively, when the execution time of the loop body has zero variance, we would prefer to use a chunk size of $\lceil N/P \rceil$ for N iterations on P processors, since that provides perfect load balancing with the smallest overhead. However, when the variance is large, we should move to smaller chunk sizes to get better load balancing, at the cost of increased overhead due to a larger number of chunks. We intend to use the variance information in the near future to guide the run-time system in selecting a chunk size for a parallel loop. Variance information will also be useful in determining if a region of code should be scheduled at compile-time or at run-time. If the variance is small, it means that the execution times are fairly predictable and we can use the compile-time scheduling algorithms from [87, 91] to map computations directly onto the processors; if the variance is large, then the execution times are less predictable and run-time scheduling is a better choice.

8.7.3   PARTITIONING

In this section, we describe how task partitioning is performed in PTRAN, using the forward control dependence graph. Before describing how the task partition is obtained, we need to describe how a task partition is *evaluated*. An important feature of our work is that we present a single objective cost function that can be used to compare two different task partitions and decide which one is better. This is in contrast to other work [23, 60] where the objectives are stated separately as maximizing parallelism and minimizing overhead, without saying how the two should be traded off with each other.

The target multiprocessor parameters that are currently used by the partitioner are as follows. Assume that all time parameters are expressed in the same unit (e.g. as multiples of the processor cycle time).

1. Execution times of primitive operations—these values are used to compute the local execution time, $COST(u)$, of each node (used in Subsection 8.7.2).

2. $P \geq 1$, the average number of processors available to the user. P need not be an integer. For example, P may be set to 3.5 for a four-way multiprocessor in which the system code uses up half the available time slices on one of the four processors. Unlike compile-time scheduling algorithms, the complexity of PTRAN's partitioning algorithm does not depend on the values of P.

3. $T_{startup}$, the start-up overhead of a task.

4. $T_{forkjoin}$, the total fork-join overhead incurred in the parent task (PARALLEL LOOP or PARALLEL CASES) for creating and terminating its child tasks. $T_{forkjoin} = T_1 + k \times T_2$ is defined as a linear function of k, the number of children (i.e. the number of chunks in

a PARALLEL LOOP or the number of cases in a PARALLEL CASES). The values of T_1 and T_2 depend on the target multiprocessor and runtime system.

5. T_{signal} and T_{wait}, the *signal* and *wait* overheads for a WAITING FOR clause in the PARALLEL CASES construct. For each pair of tasks (T_i, T_j), such that task T_j waits for task T_i, T_{signal} is added to task T_i's execution time and T_{wait} is added to task T_j's execution time.

In the future, we will also include cache parameters (cache size, access time, line size, etc.) in this list for consideration by the partitioner.

A task partition is defined for a single procedure. It is simply a mapping from nodes to task numbers, called *TASKID*, that specifies which nodes belong to the same task i.e. node n is mapped to task $TASKID(n)$. By applying the *TASKID* mapping on the forward control dependence graph, we obtain a reduced graph on the task numbers containing the edges

$$E_T = \{(TASKID(u), TASKID(v), l) \quad | \quad TASKID(u) \neq TASKID(v)$$
$$\text{and } (u, v, l) \text{ is an edge in } FCDG\}$$

The only constraint imposed on *TASKID* is that this reduced graph must be a tree; that is, each task must have a single incoming edge and hence a unique predecessor (or parent) task. This constraint is necessary because the parallel constructs in the target language (PARALLEL LOOP and PARALLEL CASES) can only express tree-structured parallel programs. The reduced graph defined by mapping *TASKID* on *FCDG* is called $TASKTREE = (N_T, E_T)$, where N_T is the set of task numbers and E_T is as defined above. If $(T_i, T_j, l) \in E_T$ then T_i is the parent task of a PARALLEL LOOP or PARALLEL CASES construct, and T_j is the child task.

The cost function to be minimized is *PARTIME*, the estimated parallel execution time of the task tree on the target multiprocessor. Though the value of *PARTIME* depends on P, the complexity of computing *PARTIME* is simply linear in the size of the task tree and does not depend on P. The rules for computing *PARTIME* are more complex than the rules presented in Subsection 8.7.2 for computing *SEQTIME*, because *PARTIME* needs to take the parallelism into account as well. We begin with a few definitions:

□ $LABELS(T_u) = \{l \mid \exists (T_u, T_v, l) \in E_T\}$ is the set of labels emanating from task T_u in E_T.

□ $COST(T_u)$ is the average local execution time of task T_u, obtained as a frequency-weighted sum of the local execution times of all nodes in task T_u.

▫ *PARFREQ*(T_u, l) is the *parallel frequency* of the task tree edge from T_u with label l.
If the edge represents a PARALLEL LOOP then *PARFREQ*(T_u, l) is the chunk size, i.e. the number of iterations executed sequentially in one chunk. Otherwise, *PARFREQ*(T_u, l) = *FREQ*(T_u, l) is simply the sequential frequency, or the average number of times the child task is executed for one execution instance of the parent task, T_u.

▫ *OVHD*(T_u) is the total overhead for task T_u, based on the target multiprocessor overhead parameters.

▫ *TOTAL_TIME*(T_u) is the average *total* execution time (including overhead) of task T_u. It is computed like *SEQTIME*(T_u) in Subsection 8.7.2:

$$TOTAL\_TIME(T_u) = COST(T_u) + OVHD(T_u) +$$
$$\sum_{l \in LABELS(T_u)} FREQ(T_u, l) \times \sum_{(T_u, T_c, l) \in E_T} TOTAL\_TIME(T_c)$$

The following rules show how *PARTIME* can be recursively computed for all tasks by a bottom-up traversal of the task tree:

1. *LABEL_CRITPATH*(T_u, l) = critical path length of the T_u's child tasks with label l. The critical path length is based on the precedence constraints defined by the sequencing arcs in *SEQSET*, and is computed by recursively using *PARTIME*(T_c) as the execution time for child task T_c.

2. *LABEL_PARTIME*(T_u, l) = max(*LABEL_CRITPATH*(T_u, l), $\sum_{(T_u, T_c, l) \in E_T} TOTAL\_TIME(T_c)/P$), is the estimated parallel execution time of T_u's child tasks with label l. It differs from the *LABEL_CRITPATH*(T_u, l) because it also uses the number of processors, P, to enforce a lower bound on the parallel execution time.

3. $PARTIME(T_u) = COST(T_u) + OVHD(T_u) +$
$$\sum_{l \in LABELS(T_u)} \max(PARFREQ(T_u, l) \times LABEL\_PARTIME(T_u, l),$$
$$FREQ(T_u, l) \times \sum_{(T_u, T_c, l) \in E_T} TOTAL\_TIME(T_c)/P)$$

is the estimated parallel execution time of task T_u. *PARTIME*(T_u) is obtained from the frequency-weighted sum of the parallel execution times of each of T_u's labels. As in *LABEL_PARTIME*, the max function is used to enforce a lower bound on the parallel execution time by using the value of the number of processors, P.

As with the computation of average sequential execution times, the computation of *PARTIME* is interprocedural. The *PARTIME* value obtained for a partitioned procedure is stored as summary information to be used at all the call sites. This implies that procedures in the program should be partitioned in a bottom-up traversal of the call graph.

PARTIME nicely expresses the trade-off between parallelism and overhead in a way that takes into account the number of processors available on the target multiprocessor. If the granularity of the task partition is too fine, *PARTIME* will be large due to excessive overhead (defined by the *OVHD* values). If the granularity is too coarse, the values of *LABEL_CRITPATH* and *PAR_FREQ* will be large due to loss of parallelism, causing *PARTIME* to be large once again. *PARTIME* is minimized at an optimal intermediate granularity.

Apart from defining an optimal granularity, the estimated parallel execution time defined by *PARTIME* can be shown to provide tight lower and upper bounds on the actual parallel execution time, $PARTIME_{actual}$, of the task partition on the given multiprocessor:

$$(1 - \epsilon) \times PARTIME \leq PARTIME_{actual} < 2 \times (1 + \epsilon) \times PARTIME$$

where ϵ is the relative error in the compile-times estimates of frequencies, execution times, and overhead values. The details of the proof are given in [92]; a similar proof was provided in [91]. This result assumes that the tasks are scheduled with no unforced idleness and that the overhead components of different tasks can be executed in parallel. The factor-of-2 is a worst-case upper bound, based on a result due to Graham [48]. This worst-case upper bound is achieved when the max terms are nearly equal in rules 2 and 3 above. If one term is significantly larger than the other for each max operation performed (as is usually the case), then the upper bound will be $(1 + \epsilon) \times PARTIME$ without the factor of two [91]. The *PARTIME* cost function is a refinement of the $F(\pi)$ cost function introduced earlier in [88, 91]. A comparison of the two cost functions is included in [92].

The partitioning algorithm attempts to minimize the *PARTIME* value of the current procedure. It starts with the finest granularity task partition and iteratively merges tasks, based on the overhead and critical path length values. Tasks are merged using two primitive merge transformations:

1. *merge_siblings*(T_a, T_b) merges tasks T_a and T_b, which are assumed to have the same parent task and label in *TASKTREE*.

2. *merge_children*(T_u, l) merges task T_u and all its child tasks with label l.

The merging is continued until the entire procedure is in a single task, while keeping track of the *PARTIME* values obtained for the intermediate partitions. The partition with the smallest value of *PARTIME* is then reconstructed and passed on to the code generator as the optimized task partition for the current procedure.

The general structure of the partitioning algorithm is as follows (see [92] for details):

1. Start with the finest granularity task tree that places each node in a separate task. If $FCDG$ is not a tree, then any *fan-in* node (i.e. a node with more than one incoming edge in $FCDG$) is merged with its dominator in $FCDG$ along with all intermediate nodes. The resulting graph must be a tree.

2. Repeat steps 3 and 4 until no further merging is possible i.e. until all nodes have been placed in the same task. Store the best $PARTIME$ value obtained among all partitions generated during the following iterations.

3. Pick the task with the largest *average decrease in overhead* (say task T_a) as the first candidate for merging. The "average decrease in overhead" for a task is the decrease in total overhead obtained by merging task T_a, averaged over all possible merging choices for the task.

4. Evaluate the parent, sibling, and children tasks of T_a as candidates for merging. Of these tasks, pick the one (say, T_b) that yields the smallest value of the *critical path length* of the entire task tree, when merged with T_a. Go to Step 2.

5. Reconstruct the partition with the best $PARTIME$ value.

The main issue in the partitioning algorithm is the choice of tasks to be merged in each iteration. In step 3, task T_a with the largest average decrease in overhead is chosen as the primary candidate for merging. The goal of this heuristic is to obtain the largest reduction in the overhead component of $PARTIME$. In step 4, task T_b is chosen as the one that yields the smallest critical path length, when merged with T_a. This heuristic attempts to find a task, T_b, that can be merged with T_a, while giving up as little parallelism as possible. Further technical details on the partitioning algorithm are given in [92].

The partitioning algorithm deals with loop parallelism and non-loop parallelism in a common framework since both forms of parallism contribute to the critical path length, parallel overhead, and $PARTIME$. The problem of finding a partition with the smallest value of $PARTIME$ is NP-complete [92]. PTRAN's partitioning algorithm is an approximation algorithm that works well in practice. It is intractable to use an optimal exponential-time algorithm for both loop parallelism and non-loop parallelism, considering that 500 to 1000 nodes is not an unusual range for the size of the forward control dependence graph.

However, it is tractable to use an exponential time algorithm for loop-only parallelism, since there are usually less than ten parallel loops in a loop nest. In fact, exponential-time loop nest traversal algorithms have been used in commercial vectorizing and parallelizing compilers [96]. The PTRAN partitioner exploits this property of loop-only parallelism by performing a "loop-only prepass" that identifies the optimal set of loops to be sequentialized if there was no non-loop parallelism in the program (that is, if *SEQSET* was a total order rather than a partial order). Loops that were sequentialized in this loop-only prepass are then marked as sequential (by flipping the *PARLOOP* bit), and the general partitioning algorithm is applied as usual. The justification for this approach is that if a loop is made sequential when only loop parallelism is considered, then it should also be made sequential if non-loop parallelism is considered as well. Further details are given in [92].

8.8   Code Generation

This section examines issues associated with generating executable code from the forward control dependence graph, *FCDG*. There are several advantages in using control dependence to drive code generation [35]:

1. Analysis of statement concurrency, followed by control sequencing, results in a partial order on each set of identically control dependent siblings (defined by *SEQSET*) [38].

2. The forward control dependence graph retains the original interval structure of the program.

3. A level of language independence is achieved because the forward control dependence graph can be built for programs written in any language for which control flow relations are decidable at compile-time.

8.8.1   PARALLEL CODE GENERATION

The code generator assumes as input the following structures that specify parallel loops and tasks:

1. *TASKID*(*) is the task mapping of the optimized partition chosen by the partitioner. The partitioner's output also includes a boolean array, *PARLOOP*(*), that specifies which loops should be executed concurrently.

---

procedure *gen_children*(N, L)
/* Generate code for all nodes control dependent on node N due to
label L. Let this set of forward control dependence successors be $C = \{c_1, \ldots, c_k\}$, ordered according to post-dominance. We can assume that
$TASKID(c_i) \neq TASKID(N) \Rightarrow TASKID(c_j) \neq TASKID(N)$, so
that either all successors are in the same task as node N, or they belong
to some task(s) other than $TASKID(N)$. */

1. $PAR\_FLAG := (TASKID(c_1) \neq TASKID(N))$
2. **if** PAR_FLAG **then** Emit "PARALLEL CASES"
3. $T := \{TASKID(c_i) \mid c_i \in C\}$
   /* $T = \{t_1, \ldots, t_m\}$ is the set of tasks corresponding to nodes
   $c_1, \ldots, c_k$. */
4. **for** $b := 1$ **to** m **do**
   a. **if** PAR_FLAG **then**
       i.Emit "CASE b"
       ii./* Compute $T\_PRED(t_b)$, the set of task predecessors of
          task t_b. */
          $$T\_PRED(t_b) := \{ \quad TASKID(c_i) \mid$$
          $$(N, L, c_i, c_j) \in SEQSET \wedge$$
          $$TASKID(c_j) = t_b\}$$
       iii.**for each** task $t_a \in T\_PRED(t_b)$ **do**
          Emit "WAITING FOR a"
          end for
       iv.Emit PRIVATE declarations for all private variables in
          $PRIVT(t_b)$
       end if
   b. **for each** node c_i s.t. $TASKID(c_i) = t_b$ **do**
       call *gen_node*(c_i)
       end for
   end for
5. **if** PAR_FLAG **then** Emit "END CASES"
   end procedure

FIGURE 8.9
Procedure *gen_children*.

2. *SEQSET* is the set of sequencing edges determined by the sequencing algorithm described in Subsection 8.6.3.

3. $PRIVT(t)$ is the set of variables that must be privatized in task t.

4. $PRIVL(l)$ is the set of variables that must be privatized in parallel loop l.

Recall our observation in Subsection 8.2.3 that, for a structured program, the forward control dependence graph is similar to the syntax tree. It is well known how to perform program translation based on a depth-first traversal of a syntax tree (or parse tree) [2]. The PTRAN code generator works in a similar fashion on the forward control dependence graph, though it also generates correct code when the forward control dependence graph is a dag, rather than just a tree. The depth-first traversal is implemented by two mutually recursive procedures, *gen_children*() and *gen_node*(). Since all nodes in the control flow graph (except $STOP$) are directly or indirectly control dependent on $ENTRY$, the code for the entire input procedure can be generated by calling *gen_children*($ENTRY, T$).

Figure 8.9 contains an outline of procedure *gen_children*(N, L). Let $C = \{c_1, \ldots, c_k\}$ be the set of forward control dependence successors of node N due to label L, ordered according to post-dominance. Procedure *gen_children*(N, L) is responsible for generating correct code for nodes $c_1, \ldots, c_k$ and (recursively) the code for their successors in $FCDG$.

Procedure *gen_node*(N) called in step 4.b of procedure *gen_children* is responsible for generating correct code for node N, and (recursively) everything contained within it. It breaks up into a large number of cases depending on what kind of statement is represented by node N. It is beyond the scope of this chapter to describe code generation for all Fortran statement types. Instead, we outline the steps performed by procedure *gen_node* for four representative node types, IF-THEN-ELSE, DO, PREHEADER, and GOTO, in Figures 8.10, 8.11, 8.12, and 8.13.

If the forward control dependence graph has a *fan-in* node with more than one incoming edge, then procedure *gen_node*() will be called many times for that node from different calls to procedure *gen_children*(), thus leading to *code duplication*. The next subsection shows how code duplication can be avoided during code generation from the forward control dependence graph.

8.8.2   CODE GENERATION WITHOUT DUPLICATION

We now discuss how the code generation algorithm from the previous section can be modified to avoid duplication of code. Consider the Fortran program from Figure 8.14 (also used as an example in [90] and [35]). This example has no useful parallelism, so the partitioner will map

---

procedure *gen_node*(*N*)
/* *N* is an IF-THEN-ELSE node with control dependence successors in
FCDG connected by edges with *T* and *F* labels. */

1. Emit code for IF node *N*, "IF *condition* THEN''
2. call *gen_children*(*N*, *T*)
3. Emit "ELSE''
4. **call** *gen_children*(*N*, *F*)
5. Emit "ENDIF''

end procedure

FIGURE 8.10
Procedure *gen_node*(), when *N* is an IF-THEN-ELSE Statement.

---

procedure *gen_node*(*N*)
/* *N* is a DO node. Its only successor with the *T* label in *FCDG* is its
PREHEADER node. */

1. *L* := unique target statement label for DO node *N*
2. **if** *N* is a parallel loop **then**
   a. Emit directive to specify the *chunk size* of DO node *N*
   b. Emit "PARALLEL LOOP *L* *index variable* = *lower, upper, stride*"
   c. Emit PRIVATE declarations for all private variables in
      PRIVL(*N*)
   else
   a. Emit "DO *L* *index variable* = *lower, upper, stride*"
   end if
3. **call** *gen_children*(*N*, *T*) /* Generate loop body */
4. Emit "*L* CONTINUE" /* Generate target statement */
5. **call** *gen_children*(*N*, *F*)

end procedure

FIGURE 8.11
Procedure *gen_node*(), When *N* is a DO Statement.

---

all nodes to the same task, and the output code will be sequential. Applying the code generation algorithm discussed in the previous section to

procedure *gen_node(N)*
/* N is a PREHEADER node with control dependence successors in $FCDG$ connected by edges with T and $Z_1, \ldots, Z_k$ labels. The T label identifies successor nodes that are contained in the interval of which N is the preheader. The $Z_1, \ldots, Z_k$ labels identify the POSTEXIT nodes $P_1, \ldots, P_k$ respectively. */

1. $H :=$ unique header statement label for the interval corresponding to PREHEADER node N
2. **for** $i := 1$ **to** k **do**
   $L_i :=$ unique statement label for POSTEXIT node P_i
   end for
3. Emit "H CONTINUE"
4. **call** *gen_children(N, T)* /* Generate code for the loop body */
5. Emit "GOTO H" /* Generate branch back to the header */
6. **for** $i := 1$ **to** k **do**
   /* Generate code for PREHEADER P_i, if necessary. */
   a. Emit "L_i CONTINUE"
   b. **call** *gen_children(N, Z_i)*
   end for

end procedure

FIGURE 8.12
Procedure *gen_node()*, When N is a PREHEADER Node.

this example, we obtain the code shown in Figure 8.15 (generated by the PTRAN system). Note that Figure 8.15 contains two calls to procedure FOO, even though the original program in Figure 8.14 contains a single call to FOO. This duplication occurred because the call statement is a fan-in node in the forward control dependence graph.

Figure 8.16 contains the generated code from PTRAN when the NODUP option is specified. The main difference is that the call to FOO now has a label associated with it (= 91003), so that the second call to FOO in Figure 8.15 can be replaced by a goto 91003 statement in Figure 8.16. We are able to avoid code duplication by inserting an appropriate goto statement. The details of how this is done are given later.

For our simple example, there is no noticeable difference in code size between Figures 8.15 and 8.16. However, the call to FOO could have been replaced by an arbitrarily large piece of code, which could amount

---

procedure *gen_node*(N)
/* N is an unconditional GOTO statement. It cannot have any successors
in $FCDG$. */

   1. if the target of GOTO node N is a POSTEXIT node P_i with label L_i
      then
         a. Emit "GOTO L_i" /* loop exit */
         end if

end procedure

FIGURE 8.13
Procedure *gen_node*(), When N is a GOTO Statement.

```
10      if (M .GE. 0) then
            if (N .LT. 0) goto 20
        else
            if (N .GE. 0) goto 20
        endif
        call FOO(M,N)
        goto 10

20      Continue
```

FIGURE 8.14
Sample Fortran Program.

to a 50 percent reduction in code size by avoiding code duplication. In the worst case, we could have a sequence of fan-in nodes so that the code size with duplication would be exponential in the size of the input program, but the code size without duplication would just be linear. Note that the goto 91003 statement is a branch into the else part of a structured if-then-else statement. Such branches are not allowed by the Fortran standard, though many compilers allow them. We decided to use this form for improved readability. If it is not allowed by the compiler, we could always translate the structured if-then-else statements to conditional and unconditional branches to obtain a valid Fortran program. This is only an issue when generating source code.

```
91002 Continue
      if (M .GE. 0) then
          if (N .LT. 0)    then
              goto 91001
          else
              call FOO(M, N)
              goto 91002
          endif
      else
          if (N .GE. 0)    then
              goto 91001
          else
              call FOO(M, N)
              goto 91002
          endif
      endif
91001 Continue
```

FIGURE 8.15
Generated Code with Duplication.

The key to generating code with no duplication is to recognize that all identically control dependent nodes are totally ordered by the post-dominance relation (Definition 8.4). This property was exploited by all previous algorithms for constructing the control dependence relation, including our algorithm based on the sparse data structure discussed in Subsection 8.2.2.

Our approach is to generate code for identically control dependent nodes in the same order as post-dominance. If nodes a and b are identically control dependent and node b post-dominates node a, then we must first generate the code for node a and then the code for node b. The code generation algorithm in the previous section may visit the same node more than once, which is exactly why code duplication occurs. To avoid duplication, we generate the code for node n (say) only in the first visit, and also generate a label for the code at that time. In successive visits, we just generate a branch to the label, instead of generating code for node n again. We have proved that this approach of using post-dominance ordering for code generation without duplication always yields correct sequential code. The proof of the theorem is beyond the scope of this chapter.

```
91002 Continue
      if (M .GE. 0) then
          if (N .LT. 0)    then
              goto 91001
          else
91003         call FOO(M, N)
              goto 91002
          endif
      else
          if (N .GE. 0)    then
              goto 91001
          else
              goto 91003
          endif
      endif
91001 Continue
```

FIGURE 8.16
Generated Code Without Duplication.

The final issue we consider is the question: how do we introduce parallelism in our scheme for code generation without duplication? If we are allowed to use an unstructured parallelism construct like the mgoto in [40, 41], then we can avoid duplication without giving up any parallelism by simply using mgoto's instead of goto's [94]. However, if we are generating structured parallel code (like Parallel Fortran in PTRAN), then we may have to give up some parallelism to avoid duplication. The reason for this is that branches are not allowed into structured parallel constructs like PARALLEL CASES and PARALLEL LOOP. By giving up some parallelism, we can instead generate unstructured sequential code with no duplication. However, we can still have structured parallelism around an unstructured region, or even within it, provided that it does not interfere with the branching necessary to avoid duplication.

8.9   Conclusions

Much has been said about the distinction between the *what* and the *how* of computing. One of the main attractions of functional programming seems to be that the programmer only specifies *what* needs to be computed, and leaves the issue of *how* it should be computed to the compiler and run-time system. In fact, the distinction between *what* and *how* is not as clear-cut as it may seem. The low-level issues of program execution (e.g. register usage, low-order versus high-order byte orderings, instruction selection, etc.) are undoubtedly part of the *how*, and should be addressed automatically by the compiler. It would be a mistake to classify the high-level issues of program execution as part of the *how*, in the same way as the low-level issues. Doing so would imply, for instance, that all the sorting algorithms described in Knuth Volume 3 should be subsumed by a single functional program specifying that *what* needs to be computed is a sorted permutation of an input array. Instead, a programming language should allow the user to specify the high-level issues of *how* the program should be executed, namely the algorithms and the data structures.

What about the *what* and the *how* of parallel computing? Once again, a parallel programming language should allow the user to specify the high-level issues of *how* the parallel program should be executed, namely the *parallel* algorithms and the data structures. This opinion was also expressed in the chapter on para-functional programming. Parallel algorithms are usually more complex than sequential algorithms because they also need to address the issues of control and data distribution. Unlike sequential algorithms, there is little agreement so far as to which parallel program execution issues are "high-level" and which are "low-level". Ideally, a parallel algorithm should be designed for a *virtual* parallel architecture, which can then be automatically mapped onto different *real* parallel architectures. This approach has two benefits: the algorithm designer is not burdened by the low-level details of the real architectures, and the same algorithm can be used on different real architectures. The virtual parallel architecture should place no limit on resources like virtual processors, virtual memory, and virtual communication channels. The role of a parallel programming language is to essentially present such a virtual parallel architecture to the user. Just as different sequential programming languages support different sequential computing paradigms (e.g. numeric, symbolic, object-oriented, functional), we can expect that there will be different parallel programming languages to support different parallel computing paradigms (e.g. shared-memory, message-passing, data-driven, demand-driven). For example, in [94] we define a virtual parallel architecture by providing a parallel execution semantics for program dependence graphs.

What then is the role of automatic parallelization? The answer is simple: to provide a migration path from sequential programming languages to parallel programming languages. Clearly, a sequential programming language like Fortran is inadequate by itself as a parallel programming language. However, it is a good starting point because of its success in presenting a virtual sequential architecture to the user for expressing sequential algorithms. Over the years, a parallel Fortran language will undoubtedly emerge that is equally successful in expressing parallel algorithms. Automatic parallelization helps bridge the gap between the two languages by handling the cases where the parallel algorithm is trivially obtained from the sequential algorithm, leaving the programmer free to concentrate on the hard cases which involve designing new parallel algorithms. For instance, experience with real application programs written in Fortran shows that, after automatic parallelization, only a small number of sequential loops remain that are critical bottlenecks to achieving parallel speedup. Automatic parallelization can identify these remaining critical loops, for the user thus avoiding the effort of rewriting the entire program. This savings becomes more significant for larger programs.

To conclude, automatic parallelization is an important technique for balancing the work of parallel programming between the programmer and the compiler. It is a research area that is mature and well understood, and should be exploited in all compilers for parallel architectures. As described in this chapter, automatic parallelization is a general technique that can be performed on programs with arbitrary control flow and data flow. The compiler algorithms for automatic parallelization have been improved over the years so that they are now practical and efficient for large programs. It remains to be seen how much work a programmer will still need to do to obtain useful parallelism from a program, but at least we know how much work he or she will not need to do, thanks to automatic parallelization.

8.10 Acknowledgments

Writing this chapter on PTRAN was a special privilege for me, having joined the PTRAN group relatively recently in 1987. I am indebted to the other members of the PTRAN group — Fran Allen, Michael Burke, Philippe Charles, Jong-Deok Choi, Ron Cytron, Jeanne Ferrante, Edith Schonberg, Dave Shields — for all that I have learned from them.

The structure of this chapter evolved from a lecture entitled "Compiling for Parallelism" which I presented at various universities during 1989 as part of IBM's Lectures in Computer Science series. A draft version of the chapter was used in a two-week course that I taught during March 1990 at the Indian Institute of Science in Bangalore, India. I am grateful for all the comments and suggestions that I received from these audiences. I especially thank Michael Burke and Vasanth Balasundaram for their valuable feedback on earlier drafts of the chapter.

References

1. A. V. Aho, M. R. Garey, and J. D. Ullman. "The transitive reduction of a directed graph." *SIAM Journal on Computing*, 1(2):131-37, 1972.

2. A.V. Aho, R. Sethi, and J.D. Ullman. *Compilers: Principles, Techniques, and Tools*. Reading, Mass.: Addison-Wesley, 1986.

3. F. E. Allen. "Control flow analysis." *ACM SIGPLAN Notices*, 19(6):13-24, 1970.

4. F. E. Allen and J. Cocke. "A program data flow analysis procedure." *Communications of the ACM*, 19(3):137-47, March 1976.

5. F. Allen, M. Burke, P. Charles, R. Cytron, and J. Ferrante. "An overview of the PTRAN analysis system for multiprocessing." *Proceedings of the ACM 1987 International Conference on Supercomputing*, 1987; also published in *Journal of Parallel and Distributed Computing* (Oct. 1988) vol. 5, no. 5, pp. 617-40.

6. F. Allen, M. Burke, R. Cytron, J. Ferrante, W. Hsieh, and V. Sarkar. "A framework for determining useful parallelism." *Proceedings of the ACM 1988 International Conference on Supercomputing*, pp. 207-15, July 1988.

7. J.R. Allen. *Dependence Analysis for Subscripted Variables and its Application to Program Transformation*. Ph.D. thesis, Rice University, 1983.

8. S. Anderson and P. Hudak. "Subscript analysis and compilation of Haskell array comprehensions." *Proceedings of the ACM SIGPLAN 1990 Conference on Programming Language Design and Implementation*, pp. 137-49, June 1990.

9. V. Balasundaram. Personal communication concerning the effect of input dependences on data partitioning for distributed-memory multiprocessor systems, 1990.

10. ——. "A mechanism for keeping useful internal information in parallel programming tools: The data access descriptor." *Journal of Parallel and Distributed Computing*, 9:154-70, 1990.

11. V. Balasundaram and K. Kennedy. "A technique for summarizing data access and its use in parallelism enhancing transformations." *Proc. of the ACM SIGPLAN 1989 Conference on Programming Languages Design and Implementation*, July 1989.

12. U. Banerjee. "Data dependence in ordinary programs." M.S. thesis, University of Illinois at Urbana-Champaign, 1976.

13. ——. *Dependence Analysis for Supercomputing*. Norwell, Mass.: Kluwer Academic Publishers, 1988.

14. W. Baxter and J.R. Bauer, III. "The program dependence graph in vectorization." *16th ACM Principles of Programming Languages Symposium*, pp. 1-11, January 11-13 1989. Austin, Texas.

15. M. Beck and K. Pingali. "From control flow to dataflow." Technical report, Department of Computer Science, Cornell University, October 1989. TR 89-1050.

16. C. Bohm and G. Jacopini. "Flow diagrams, Turing machines and languages with only two formation rules." *Communications of the ACM*, 9(5):366-71, May 1966.

17. M. Burke. "An interval-based approach to exhaustive and incremental interprocedural data-flow analysis." *ACM Transactions on Programming Languages and Systems*, 12(3):341-95, July 1990.

18. M. Burke and R. Cytron. "Interprocedural dependence analysis and parallelization." *Proceedings of the SIGPLAN '86 Symposium on Compiler Construction*, 21(7):162-175, July 1986.

19. M. Burke, R. Cytron, J. Ferrante, and W. Hsieh. "Automatic generation of nested, fork-join parallelism." *Journal of Supercomputing*, 2(3):71-88, July 1989.

20. D. Callahan. "A global approach to detection of parallelism." Ph.D. thesis, Rice University, April 1987. Rice COMP TR87-50.

21. D. Callahan, S. Carr, and K. Kennedy. "Improving register allocation for subscripted variables." *Proceedings of the SIGPLAN '90 Conference on Programming Language Design and Implementation*, pp. 162-75, June 1990.

22. D. Callahan and K. Kennedy. "Analysis of interprocedural side effects in a parallel programming environment." *Proceedings of the First International Conference on Supercomputing*, 1987.

23. M. L. Campbell. "Static allocation for a dataflow multiprocessor." *Proceedings of the 1985 International Conference on Parallel Processing*, pp. 511-17, 1985.

24. David C. Cann. *Compilation Techniques for High Performance Applicative Computation.* Ph.D. thesis, Colorado State University, May 1989. Tech. Report CS-89-108.

25. E. Cesaro. "A result in number theory." Knuth references Cesaro's article of 1881 in vol. 2 of *The Art of Computer Programming*. Reading, Mass.: Addison-Wesley, 1986, p. 302.

26. D.R. Chase, M. Wegman, and F.K. Zadeck. "Analysis of pointers and structures." *Proceedings of the SIGPLAN '90 Conference on Programming Language Design and Implementation*, 25(6):296-310, June 1990.

27. R. Cytron. "Doacross: Beyond vectorization for multiprocessors." *Proceedings of the 1986 International Conference on Parallel Processing*, pp. 836-44, August 1986.

28. —. Personal communication concerning the implementation of induction variable analysis in PTRAN, 1988.

29. —. "On the application of dependence analysis and restructuring techniques to parallel and functional languages." in *Parallel Systems and Computation*, G. Paul and F.S. Almasi eds, New York: Elsevier, 1988.

30. —. Compiling for Parallelism. Tutorial given at the 1989 SIGPLAN Conference on Programming Language Design and Implementation, 1989.

31. —. Personal communication concerning the improved sequencing algorithm in PTRAN, 1990.

32. R. Cytron and J. Ferrante. "An improved control dependence algorithm." Technical report, IBM, 1987. Tech. Report RC 13291.

33. —. "What's in a name? Or the value of renaming for parallelism detection and storage allocation." *Proceedings of the 1987 International Conference on Parallel Processing*, pp. 19-27, August 1987.

34. R. Cytron, J. Ferrante, B.K. Rosen, M.N. Wegman, and F.K. Zadeck. "An efficient method for computing static single assignment form." *Proceedings of the 16th ACM Symposium on Principles of Programming Languages*, pp. 25-35, January, 1989.

35. R. Cytron, J. Ferrante, and V. Sarkar. "Experiences using control dependence in PTRAN." *Proceedings of the Second Workshop on Languages and Compilers for Parallel Computing*, August 1989. Appears in *Languages and Compilers for Parallel Computing*, edited by D. Gelernter, A. Nicolau, and D. Padua, Cambridge, Mass.: MIT Press, 1990.

36. R. Cytron, J. Ferrante, and V. Sarkar. Personal communication concerning the computation of the forward control dependence graph in PTRAN, 1990.

37. —. "Compact representations for control dependence." *Proceedings of the ACM SIGPLAN '90 Conference on Programming Language Design and Implementation*, pp. 337-51, June 1990.

38. R. Cytron, M. Hind, and W. Hsieh. "Automatic generation of DAG parallelism." *Proceedings of the ACM SIGPLAN 1989 Conference on Programming Language Design and Implementation*, pp. 54-68, July 1989.

39. R. Cytron, S. Karlovsky, and K.P. McAuliffe. "Automatic management of programmable caches (extended abstract)." *Proceedings of the 1988 International Conference on Parallel Processing*, August 1988. Also available as CSRD Rpt. No. 728 from University of Illinois, Center for Supercomputing Research and Development.

40. J. Ferrante and M. E. Mace. "On linearizing parallel code." *Conference Records of the 12th ACM Symposium on Principles of Programming Languages*, pp. 179-89, January 1985.

41. J. Ferrante, M. Mace, and B. Simons. "Generating sequential code from parallel code." *Proceedings of the ACM 1988 International Conference on Supercomputing*, pp. 582-92, July 1988.

42. J. Ferrante, K. Ottenstein, and J. Warren. "The program dependence graph and its use in optimization." *ACM Transactions on Programming Languages and Systems*, pp. 319-49, July 1987.

43. S. Fortune and J. Wyllie. "Parallelism in random access machines." *Proceedings of the 10th ACM Symposium on Theory of Computing*, pp. 114-118, 1978.

44. K. Gallivan, W. Jalby, and D. Gannon. "On the problem of optimizing data transfers for complex memory systems." Proceedings of ACM 1988 International Conference on Supercomputing, pp.238-53, July 1988.

45. D. Gannon, W. Jalby, and K. Gallivan. "Strategies for cache and local memory management by global program transformations." *Proceedings of the First ACM International Conference on Supercomputing*, June 1987.

46. K. Gharachorloo, V. Sarkar, and J. L. Hennessy. "Efficient implementation of single assignment languages." *ACM Conference on Lisp and Functional Programming*, pp. 259-68, July 1988.

47. K. Gopinath. "Copy elimination in single assignment languages." Ph.D. thesis, Stanford University, 1989.

48. R. L. Graham. "Bounds on multiprocessing timing anomalies." *SIAM Journal on Applied Mathematics*, 17(2):416-29, March 1969.

49. S.L. Graham and M. Wegman. "A fast and usually linear algorithm for global flow analysis." *Journal of the ACM*, 23(1):172-202, January 1976.

50. H. Griffin. *Elementary Theory of Numbers*. New York: McGraw-Hill, 1954.

51. R. Gupta and M.L. Soffa. "A reconfigurable LIW architecture and its compiler." *Proceedings of the 1987 International Conference on Parallel Processing*, August 1987.

52. R. Gupta and M.L. Soffa. "Region scheduling." *Proceedings of the Second International Conference on Supercomputing*, 3:141-48, May 1987.

53. P.B. Hansen. "The programming language concurrent Pascal." *IEEE Transactions on Software Engineering*, SE-1(2):199-206, June 1975.

54. D. Harel. "A linear time algorithm for finding dominators in flow graphs and related problems." *Symposium on Theory of Computing*, May 1985.

55. L. Harrison. "The interprocedural analysis and automatic parallelization of scheme programs." Technical report, University of Illinois, Center for Supercomputing Research and Development, February 1989. CSRD Rpt. No.860.

56. W.H. Harrison. "Compiler analysis of the value ranges for variables." *IEEE Transactions on Software Engineering*, SE-13(3), May 1977.

57. M.S. Hecht. *Flow Analysis of Computer Programs*. New York: Elsevier North-Holland, Inc., 1977.

58. S. Horwitz, J. Prins, and T. Reps. "Integrating non-interfering versions of programs." *Conference Records of the 15th ACM Symposium on Principles of Programming Languages*, pp. 133-45, January 1987.

59. W.C. Hsieh. "Extracting parallelism from sequential programs." Master's thesis, Massachusetts Institute of Technology, May 1988.

60. P. Hudak and B. Goldberg. "Serial combinators: Optimal grains of parallelism." *Proceedings of Workshop on Functional Programming Languages and Computer Architecture, Nancy, France*, pp. 382-99, September 1985.

61. P. Hudak and A. Bloss. "The aggregate update problem in functional programming systems." *Proceedings of the 12th Annual ACM Conference on the Principles of Programming Languages*, pp. 300-13, January 1985.

62. P. Hudak and P. Wadler et al. "Report on the functional programming language Haskell." Technical report, Yale University, 1988. Research Report YALEU/DCS/RR-666.

63. R.A. Iannucci. "Toward a dataflow / von Neumann hybrid architecture." *Proceedings of the 15th Annual International Symposium on Computer Architecture*, 1988.

64. IBM. "Parallel Fortran language and library reference." Technical report, International Business Machines, March 1988. Pub. No. SC23-0431-0.

65. F. Irigoin and R. Triolet. "Supernode partitioning." *Conference Record of 15th ACM Symposium on Principles of Programming Languages*, 1988.

66. D.E. Knuth. *The Art of Computer Programming: Semi Numerical Algorithms*. Vol. 2. Reading, Mass.: Addison-Wesley, 1986.

67. C. Kruskal and A. Weiss. "Allocating independent subtasks on parallel processors." *IEEE Transactions on Software Engineering*, SE-11(10), October 1985.

68. D. J. Kuck, R. H. Kuhn, B. Leasure, and M. Wolfe. "The structure of an advanced vectorizer for pipelined processors." *Proceedings of CompSAC 80 (Fourth International Computer Software and Applications Conference)*, pp. 709-15, October 1980.

69. D. J. Kuck, R. H. Kuhn, D. A. Padua, B. Leasure, and M. Wolfe. "Dependence graphs and compiler optimizations." *Conference Record of 8th ACM Symposium on Principles of Programming Languages*, 1981.

70. L. Lamport. "The parallel execution of DO loops." *Communications of the ACM*, pp. 83-93, February 1974.

71. J. R. Larus and P. N. Hilfinger. "Detecting conflicts between structure accesses." *Proceedings of the ACM SIGPLAN '88 Conference on Programming Language Design and Implementation*, pp. 21-34, July 1988.

72. J.R. Larus. "Restructuring symbolic programs for concurrent execution on multiprocessors." Ph.D. thesis, University of California, 1989. Technical Report No. UCB/CSD 89/502.

73. T. Lengauer and R. Tarjan. "A fast algorithm for finding dominators in a flowgraph." *ACM Transactions on Programming Languages and Systems*, July 1979.

74. Zhiyuan Li, Pen-Chung Yew, and Chuan-Qi-Zhu. "An efficient data dependence analysis for parallelizing compilers." Technical report, University of Illinois, Center for Supercomputing Research and Development, May 1989. CSRD Rpt. No. 852. Preliminary version appeared in *Proceedings of 1989 ACM International Conference on Supercomputing*.

75. R. E. Lord, J. S. Kowalik, and S. P. Kumar. "Solving linear algebraic equations on a MIMD computer." *Journal of the ACM*, 30(1):103-17, January 1983.

76. E. S. Lowry and C. W. Medlock. "Object code optimization." *Communications of the ACM*, 12(1):13-22, January 1969.

77. J. McGraw, S. Skedzielewski, S. Allan, R. Oldehoeft, J. Glauert, C. Kirkham, B. Noyce, and R. Thomas. "Sisal: Streams and iteration in a single assignment language: Reference manual version 1.2." Technical report, Lawrence Livermore National Laboratory, 1985. No. M-146, Rev. 1.

78. S. Midkiff and D. Padua. "Issues in the compile-time optimization of parallel programs." Technical report, University of Illinois, Center for Supercomputing Research and Development, May 1990. CSRD Rpt. No. 993.

79. S. Midkiff, D. Padua, and R. Cytron. "Compiling programs with user parallelism." *Proceedings of the Second Workshop on Languages and Compilers for Parallel Computing, August 1989.*

80. G. F. Pfister and V. A. Norton. "'Hot spot' contention and combining in multistage interconnection networks." Technical report, IBM, 1985. Tech. Report RC 11061.

81. A.K. Porterfield. "Software methods for improvement of cache performance on supercomputer applications." Ph.D. thesis, Rice University, May 1989. Rice COMP TR89-93.

82. D.R. Pountain and D. May. *A Tutorial Introduction to OCCAM Programming*, INMOS, 1987.

83. P.W. Purdom Jr. and E.F. Moore. Algorithm 430: Immediate predominators in a directed graph. *Communications of the ACM*, 15(8):777-8, August 1972.

84. J.E. Ranelletti. "Graph transformation algorithms for array memory optimization in applicative languages." Ph.D. thesis, University of California at Davis, Computer Science Department, 1987.

85. J. H. Reif and H. R. Lewis. "Symbolic evaluation and the global value graph." *Conference Record of 4th ACM Symposium on Principles of Programming Languages*, 1977.

86. J.H. Saltz, R. Mirchandaney, and K. Crowley. "The Doconsider loop. *Proceedings of the 3rd International Conference on Supercomputing*, pp. 29-40, 1989.

87. V. Sarkar and J. Hennessy. "Compile-time partitioning and scheduling of parallel programs." *Proceedings of the SIGPLAN '86 Symposium on Compiler Construction*, pp. 17-26, July 1986.

88. V. Sarkar and J. Hennessy. "Partitioning parallel programs for macro-dataflow." *ACM Conference on Lisp and Functional Programming*, pp. 202-11, August 1986.

89. V. Sarkar. "Synchronization using counting semaphores." *Proceedings of the ACM 1988 International Conference on Supercomputing*, pp. 627-37, July 1988.

90. —. "Determining average program execution times and their variance." *Proceedings of the 1989 SIGPLAN Conference on Programming Language Design and Implementation*, 24(7):298-312, July 1989.

91. —. *Partitioning and Scheduling Parallel Programs for Multiprocessors*. London: Pitman, and Cambridge, Mass.: MIT Press, 1989. This is a revised version of the author's Ph.D. dissertation published as Technical Report CSL-TR-87-328, Stanford University, April 1987.

92. —. "Automatic partitioning of a program dependence graph into parallel tasks." Technical report, IBM Research, October 1990. Submitted to special issue of IBM Journal of Research and Development.

93. —. "Instruction reordering for fork-join parallelism." *Proceedings of the ACM SIGPLAN '90 Conference on Programming Language Design and Implementation*, pp. 322-36, June 1990.

94. —. "A parallel imperative semantics for program dependence graphs." Technical report, IBM Research, September 1990.

95. V. Sarkar and D. Cann. "POSC — A partitioning and optimizing Sisal compiler." *Proceedings of the ACM 1990 International Conference on Supercomputing*, pp. 148-63, June 1990.

96. R.G. Scarborough and H.G. Kolsky. "A vectorizing Fortran compiler." *IBM Journal of Research and Development*, 30(2):163-71, March 1986.

97. J. T. Schwartz and M. Sharir. "A design for optimizations of the bitvectoring class." Technical report, Courant Institute of Mathematical Sciences, New York University, September 1979. Courant Computer Science Report No. 17.

98. Zhiyu Shen, Zhiyuan Li, and Pen-Chung Yew. "An empirical study on array subscripts and data dependences." Technical report, University of Illinois, Center for Supercomputing Research and Development, May 1989. CSRD Rpt. No. 840. Also in *Proceedings of the 1989 International Conference on Parallel Processing*.

99. S. Skedzielewski and J. Glauert. "IF1 – An intermediate form for applicative languages." Technical report, Lawrence Livermore National Laboratory, 1985. No. M-170.

100. R. Tarjan. "Testing flow graph reducibility." *Journal of Computer and System Sciences*, 9(3):355-65, December 1974.

101. R. Triolet. "Contribution a la parellisation automatique de programmes fortran comportant des appels de procedure." Ph.D. thesis, L'Universite Pierre et Marie Curie (Paris VI), 1984.

102. R. Triolet. "Interprocedural analysis for program restructuring with Parafrase." Technical report, University of Illinois, Center for Supercomputing Research and Development, August 1986. CSRD Rpt. No. 538.

103. M.J. Wolfe. "Techniques for improving the inherent parallelism in programs." Master's thesis, University of Illinois at Urbana-Champaign, 1978.

104. M.J. Wolfe. *Optimizing Supercompilers for Supercomputers*. London: Pitman, and Cambridge, Mass.: MIT Press, 1989. This is a revised version of the author's Ph.D. dissertation published as Technical Report UIUCDCS-R-82-1105, University of Illinois at Urbana-Champaign, 1982.

9

Conclusion

In this chapter, the authors of this book would like to compare the different approaches to parallel programming presented in the previous chapters. However, it is always hard to draw meaningful conclusions when there are many candidates campaigning for a position, which itself is being defined during this process. The matter gets even worse when there are myriad criteria to be considered, some of which are bound to be conflicting. We can address only the relative merits of some prominent features of the presented languages and compilers.[1]

9.1 Application Area

All the examples discussed seem to be geared toward scientific and engineering applications. Due to the lack of nondeterminism in pure functional languages, these languages are naturally confined to the applications that have very little use for true nondeterminism. Some languages, in particular EPL and Sisal, are intentionally designed to be used

---

[1]The authors of the various chapters are the sole providers of any claim about the properties of the corresponding language.

in large-scale, scientific computing, where the user wants to apply all available computing resources to one task. Fortran, the source language of the PTRAN compiler, is also mainly used in scientific computations today. The remaining four languages—Crystal, Haskell, Id and, to some extent, Lucid—strive for general applicability.

9.2   Functional Versus Conventional Languages

A distinguishing feature of functional languages is their ability to "liberate" the programmer from the burden of having to specify mundane details in a program. Imperative languages won notoriety in *over-specifying* programs. In general, over-specification leads to programs that are hard to write and, more importantly, difficult to understand and debug.[2] We hasten to point out that an unabated drive towards the elimination of all details that are not germane to the functional behavior of the computation is not a desirable goal either. To illustrate this point, we have broadly classified programming details as follows:

1. *Algorithmic details:* The details describing a method of the solution. For instance, a program sorting a list can do it by sorting two halves of the list and combining them, as opposed to scanning the entire list at once.

2. *Data structures:* The details specifying an organization of the program's data. For instance, a program sorting a list can represent the input data as a quad-tree as opposed to representing it as an array.

3. *Control details:* The details defining an order of the program's operations. For instance, to sum up all elements of a vector, the program may add up vector elements from the last to the first, instead of adding them from the first to the last.

4. *Type related details:* The details specifying types of the program's variables. For instance, the program may declare vector elements as double precision real numbers as opposed to using integer numbers.

---

[2]However, an over-specified, step-by-step sequential view of computing is quite natural for most programmers and programming tools today. This view really harks back to the definition of the Turing Machine. Given this background, many programmers find it easier to work with an over-specified computation model. Thus, programmers often remark that it is easier to debug a sequential program than to debug a parallel program.

5. *Storage related details:* The details describing representation of the program's variables. For instance, the program may state that two names must be mapped to the same storage instead of occupying different places, or a particular integer variable may be treated as a list of bits and not as an encoded number.

6. *Resource related details:* The details that specify changes in allocation of program's resources. For instance, the program may direct the compiler to execute two particular loops in parallel, to execute a specific code on a particular processor, or to deallocate part of the program's memory at the given point of the program execution.

Clearly the first two classes of details influence the efficiency of computation tremendously and cannot be suppressed in a program specification. On the contrary, languages must provide versatile tools to specify a variety of equivalent algorithms and data structures. One of the challenges of the functional languages is to pass this level of control on to the user without sacrificing the benefits of functional programming. The control and type related details are largely eliminated in functional languages. Much of the cluttering in imperative programs falls into this category. Functional languages encourage the use of functional abstractions in place of control abstractions. They employ type inferencing for consistency checking in place of type declarations. The fifth category, storage related details, have no place in functional languages that are based on the fundamental premise of value transformations. The last category of details is important for both kinds of languages but has not been fully addressed in any language. As argued in Chapter 5, which discusses para-functional programming, this is the kind of detail we would like to provide in all languages.

Automatic parallelization (as in PTRAN) attempts to remove the details of the third, fourth, and fifth class from an over-specified program and derives equivalent annotations that should really fall into the last category. In order to do this right, these annotations must have a precise definition in a language. But once this is available to the user, perhaps there is no need to over-specify (although storage control will still remain a sticky issue and will be a subject of debate for quite some time). Note that the different classes of details stated above can interact with one another in interesting ways. For example, Crystal attempts to employ types as mechanisms in a program specification for parallelization.

Implicit parallelism (in the context of both imperative and functional languages) is in some sense a degenerate solution to take a program and generate an equivalent program with annotations that parallelize almost everything that could be parallelized. However, it does not provide control over the parallelization (and hence on the resource consumption) and this is the reason why every language must support detailed specifications of the last category in order to be practical. However, implicit parallelism provides a migration path from sequential programming to parallel programming in both functional and imperative languages. It helps bridge the gap between sequential languages and parallel languages by handling those cases where the parallel algorithm is trivially obtained from the sequential algorithm, which leaves the programmer free to concentrate on the hard cases that involve designing new parallel algorithms. Annotations are used to express explicit parallelism in many of the functional languages described in this book. In the PTRAN system, the programmer can use explicitly parallel control structures (PARALLEL LOOP and PARALLEL CASES) in the input Fortran program.

9.3   General Language Properties

With the exception of Fortran, every proposal contends that the starting point to a parallel language must be a declarative language, and that the program specification must not be entangled with orders of evaluation. Many properties of the declarative language "substrate" actually have little to do with parallel computation, but they lend themselves to higher degrees of expressiveness and abstractness and tend to impose fewer constraints on order of evaluation, thus being a good basis for parallel computation. Examples and brief descriptions of high-level declarative language features include the following:

  □ Various notions of *typing:*

    – *Strong typing:* Type mismatches are always detected.

    – *Static typing:* Strong typing that is enforced statically (i.e., at compile time). In contrast, *dynamic typing* refers to run-time enforcement of proper typing.

    – *Type inference:* Static typing that is inferred (i.e., user-supplied type signatures are not required).

    – *Polymorphism:* The ability for functions to operate uniformly on arbitrary types.

    – *Overloading:* The ability for functions to operate nonuniformly on specific types.

  □ *Higher-order functions:* Functions that may be passed as arguments to other functions, stored in data structures, returned as results, etc. Also often referred to as "first-class functions." Higher-order functions are useful in that they permit a higher degree of functional abstraction.

□ *Strict* versus *non-strict* semantics. If bot denotes a divergent (i.e., nonterminating) expression, then a function f is *strict* if and only if f(bot) also diverges. Similarly, a datatype constructor is strict if it diverges when any of its components diverges. Languages based on non-strict semantics are generally recognized as being more expressive, but there may be an associated higher cost in implementation. (Although strict versus non-strict is often referred to as eager versus lazy or call-by-value versus call-by-name (or call-by-need), from an abstract semantical perspective, strict versus non-strict is the proper phraseology.)

These various language features are exhibited to varying degrees in each of the functional languages discussed in this book, as discussed below. Indeed many of the features are exhibited in languages that are not purely functional (for example, higher-order functions are one of the hallmarks of Scheme).

Although all the languages presented here except for Fortran are purely functional, their detailed design differs significantly even if parallelism is ignored for the moment.

As far as purely functional properties are concerned, Haskell is the most similar to the purely functional subset of Id—both are non-strict, polymorphic, and higher-order. Indeed, Haskell could serve as a fine substitute in the chapter on Id, except that I-structures would need to be added (although Haskell's array comprehensions are non-strict and serve much of the functionality of I-structures, I-structures provide a certain degree of imperative expressiveness not found in array comprehensions). Conversely, Id could serve as a substitute in the chapter on Haskell, with the para-functional extensions then being added to Id.

Similarly, Haskell shares much in common with Lucid and Sisal, and the para-functional approach would work perfectly well with any of these languages. However, Crystal is different in that respect, since it introduces constructs for data-parallel computation, which can be added to any language. The para-functional approach would actually interfere with the Crystal approach, because in the latter the allocation of resources is determined by the compiler from the logical dependencies, not from annotations. The annotations in Crystal are for specifying the types of domains (spatial and temporal), and the transformations that should be applied at the meta-level via the domain morphism construct.

With the exception of Haskell and Id, there seems to be less emphasis on abstraction. In Crystal, higher-order functions are allowed, but such power of abstraction is obtained at the expense of target code performance. Lucid is not fully higher-order, but since the simplest objects in Lucid are functions, Lucid operators and defined functions are at least the second order. Sisal has stream and reduction abstractions, but the current version does not support higher-order functions. Finally, EPL is first-order.

Sisal is strict, whereas Crystal, EPL, Haskell, Id, and Lucid are non-strict. Haskell and Id use a polymorphic static type system. Crystal and Lucid are dynamically typed. EPL uses type inference and to some extent polymorphic typing, whereas Sisal is based on static, non-polymorphic typing.

As a final comparison, the source language in the chapter on PTRAN is just Fortran. It is a first-generation high-level programming language that lacks the modern features found in the other languages discussed in this book. Fortran has a strict semantics and static user-specified typing. It does not offer polymorphism, overloading, or higher-order functions. However, Fortran is still widely used today because of its familiarity and availability. These are compelling, but wrong, reasons for using a programming language. We hope that the language features and computing paradigms promoted by the other languages in this book will provide the basis for a modern programming language that will eventually replace Fortran.

9.3.1   DETERMINACY

Determinacy of computation seems to be a key issue for all the languages—if determinacy is lost, referential transparency is not very useful.[3] Furthermore, repeatability of most programs, whether functional or not, is highly desirable—nondeterminacy being usually unacceptable. The declarative nature of languages described in this book is the source not only of parallelism, but also of determinacy. Thus the various languages generally ensure identical results, regardless of the number of processors applied to the task. This guarantee also allows programs to be debugged on a uniprocessor using traditional debugging tools, with the assurance that the results will not change when the program is run on a multiprocessor. It should be noted that there can be nondeterminacy in scheduling and distribution of the computation, but the resulting calculation must be invariant.

---

[3]A nondeterministic programming language could still be referentially transparent, based on a multi-valued semantics for nondeterminism. For example, a function call may return one of several values, and this set of values will be the same for all calls to the same function with the same argument.

On the other hand, there are proposals to introduce annotations (Haskell, EPL, Id) to control the resources. Once this door is open, there must be a formal means to ensure that these tools do not introduce any undesirable nondeterminacy (indeed, a formal proof of such determinacy is provided for at least one language—Haskell). Furthermore, nondeterministic constructs seem to be necessary in many "systems" applications (such as schedulers, servers, and other operating system components). Although not discussed in this book, Id provides them to some extent. Crystal's approach to nondeterminism is to weaken the definitions of functions to forms that may not be inductive and then to let the compiler determine a suitable implementation. In EPL, nondeterminism can be achieved through use of communication ports with a fair merge semantics. It is unclear what impact temporal contexts of Lucid have on determinacy.

9.4   Approaches to Parallelism

9.4.1   EXPLICIT VERSUS IMPLICIT PARALLELISM

A parallel programming language should allow the user to specify the high-level issues of *how* the parallel program should be executed—that is, to specify the *parallel* algorithms and the data structures. Parallel algorithms are usually more complex than sequential algorithms because they have to address the issues of control and data distribution. Unlike sequential algorithms, there is little agreement so far as to which parallel program execution issues are "high-level" and which are "low-level".

One approach to this problem is to allow a parallel algorithm be designed for a *virtual* parallel architecture and then be automatically mapped onto different *real* parallel architectures. This approach has two benefits: (1) the algorithm designer is not burdened by the low-level details of the real architectures, and (2) the same algorithm can be used on different real architectures. The virtual parallel architecture should place no limit on resources like virtual processors, virtual memory, and virtual communication channels. The role of a parallel programming language is to essentially present such a virtual parallel architecture to the user. Just as different sequential programming languages support different sequential computing paradigms (e.g., numeric, symbolic, object-oriented, functional), we can expect that there will be different parallel programming languages to support different parallel computing paradigms (e.g., shared-memory, message-passing, data-driven, demand-driven). It seems that hiding some of the details of the parallel paradigm is acceptable, but to generate efficient parallel code, the user must be aware of the global characteristic of the target architecture. Such characteristics can be captured by the reference metric in Crystal.

In all the proposed languages, parallelism is extracted from the data-dependence graphs. Determining the data-dependence of array elements often enables removal of the overhead of array copying and parallel execution of some iterative expressions. The languages enforce single assignment, which means that the major problem is to decide how to exploit the parallelism on a particular architecture.

Three of the presented languages—Lucid, Sisal and Id—are purely implicit. In Lucid a special mode of execution (eduction) and, in the other two languages, smart compilation techniques tailored for specific parallel machines are assumed to uncover the "inherent" parallelism in a program and schedule it for efficient execution. In PTRAN, the goal of compiler analysis is also automatic parallelization to obtain, without user help, the same level of abstraction from a Fortran program as is found in functional languages.

If successful, automatic parallelization is certainly a noble achievement—minimal user interaction and maximal parallelism. However, as argued in Chapter 5 that advocates para-functional programming, this picture is not as rosy as one might think, for several reasons: (1) optimal compilation strategies are generally undecidable, (2) a particular manifestation of parallelism is often not portable between parallel machines, and (3) the more clever a compiler, the more difficult it is for a person to reason about the parallelism—in particular, a programmer who has a certain parallel algorithm in mind must know how to write the code in such a way that the compiler will implement the appropriate parallelization.

For these reasons, a para-functional programming language (based on Haskell or any other functional language) provides explicit mechanisms for the programmer to express mapping and scheduling constraints. One could think of this as a "poor man's approach to parallelism," but it does at least overcome many of the problems mentioned above, without sacrificing the desirable attributes of functional programming. EPL provides a similar mechanism via virtual process annotations, although much is still left implicit, including scheduling. Similarly, Crystal's index domains, data fields and domain morphisms can be thought of as specifying parallel behavior (although again with much more implicit content), and Crystal's "directives" can be thought of as compiler pragmas. In the PTRAN system, the programmer can use explicitly parallel control structures (PARALLEL LOOP and PARALLEL CASES) in the input Fortran program.

9.4.2 PIPELINE PARALLELISM

In Sisal, the *stream* data type has been included to enable the programmer to express a restricted form of parallelism—pipeline parallelism. The main usage of this mechanism is for the programmer interaction with a running program, but it can also be used to capture communication between producers and consumers of a stream of values. Streams are limited to sequential production and access, which distinguishes them from arrays that are much more general in this respect. With regard to program input and output, the user can type part of the input to a program (such as "run for 111 more time steps and print the results") and then type more of the input ("run to completion" or "stop now"). In Crystal and EPL, pipeline parallelism is established automatically, based on the analysis of data dependencies. In EPL the port communication is executed whenever possible in a pipeline fashion with a single record of data sent in each message. In Crystal the granularity of data going through a pipeline is either determined by the domain morphism supplied by the user or derived automatically by the compiler based on the communication cost of the underlying machine.

9.4.3 COMMUNICATION

The concept of processes and communication is absent in all the languages, with the exception of Crystal and EPL.

In Crystal a model of parallel computation includes the following:

□ A notion of data type as a collection of elements with operators
□ A metric induced by the target machine that is defined on the data elements, and
□ Special relations (called communication forms) that preserve locality and are used to model the movement of data.

Modeling parallel I/O is a topic of ongoing research in Crystal. Another issue researched is programming in the large. Crystal has environment as a first class object. Future research is needed to use this feature for modularizing a program and supporting separate compilation.

In EPL the computation is viewed as a configuration—that is, a set of processes cooperating through ports. The fair merge semantics of ports can be used to describe nondeterministic computations. Processes are compiled independently, and the additional dependences imposed by the interprocess iterations are produced for each process in a

configuration. The code for a process may be different for various configurations because the addition of intraprocess dependencies can change
the generated program.

9.5   Abstraction Mechanism and Special Constructs

Any computation can be expressed in almost any language, but being
able to express that computation in a natural and easy manner is something else. One approach is to identify important paradigms in applications and build suitable constructs for them into the language (EPL and
Sisal seem to fall into this class, as does Crystal). The other approach
is to have basic building blocks and to provide facilities, such as higher
order functions and data abstractions, to build arbitrary abstractions
on them. Haskell and Id take the latter approach very strongly. (However, Id does not provide satisfactory abstractions for reductions and
aggregates.)

Array constructions are very general in Id and Haskell but are
somewhat restrictive in Sisal, where the programmer cannot build an
array by specifying the (value, index) pairs.

9.5.1   ITERATIONS

Using recursion to set up parallel function execution (compare the quadtree example in Sisal from Chapter 4) can generate a lot of potential parallelism that may be difficult to exploit, however. In most architectures,
a straightforward implementation that spawns each function call will
incur large overhead that will dominate the run-time and offset most, if
not all, of the gain that parallel execution brings. Even a tagged-token
data-flow machine usually incurs overhead as it recolors each token that
is passed to or from a new context. Thus even a fine-grained machine
might not wish to treat each and every function as a parallel task. Unfortunately, the overhead for each call is easily parallelized. Simply looking
at speedup curves may lead the users to the false assumption that they
have found a good algorithm and implementation, when in fact, a serial
algorithm can take less time.

It is a well-known fact that tail-recursion is semantically and operationally equivalent to iteration, and transformations exploiting this fact
are commonly used in most Lisp and functional language implementations. Parallelism based on loops (or tail-recursion) seems to be an important source of efficiency in parallel execution for many
scientific programs. Thus whichever form the iteration takes (an explicit

loop or tail-recursion), the concept of an iteration plays a crucial role in expressing parallelism in all of the proposed languages. Some languages (Crystal, EPL, Haskell and Lucid) reject the idea of explicit iterative constructs considering them imperative in nature. Others (Sisal, Id) retain the basic iterative constructs to make the language more familiar to programmers accustomed to languages such as Fortran.

9.5.2 ARRAYS

Arrays are often a focal point of many parallel computations, especially in scientific and engineering applications. Each of the presented languages takes a slightly different position in treating them.

In Crystal arrays are generalized as functions over index domains that are first class objects and general domain constructors are provided for specifying user defined domains from basic index domains. It is easy to specify an arbitrary shaped ragged array by using predicates to select the desired elements out of an ambient index domain. Data types for trees, hypercubes, and FFT networks can be declared as subtypes of index domains by defining proper coordinate systems. A domain can be dynamically constructed by using the minimalization operator whereby its boundary is recursively defined with the very function that is defined over it. Such a dynamic domain definition creates a curious phenomenon where the interplay between the function and domain poses the following interesting question in its semantics: What kind of higher-order fixed point can be developed to handle the type of recursion that spans objects of different orders?

In EPL an elementary data structure is a data field defined over a set of ranges. Ranges can be defined by equations and used in definitions of other (sublinear) ranges. An equation defining a range can use a condition that indicates the last element in the range and can refer to the data field being defined. Such an equation is well defined if the evaluation of the condition at one point of the range can proceed before the data field is evaluated in the next point.

In Haskell arrays are defined *monolithically*—that is, all of the index/value pairs are specified at once, with one single array being returned as a result. This is similar to the functional array definitions in Id, except that I-structures are not used and the array thus cannot be incrementally modified after creation. The benefit of this is the retention of referential transparency (I-structures are *not* referentially transparent); the disadvantage is the lack of an *efficient* way to do incremental updates in those cases where it is the most natural thing to do. This disadvantage is not as bad as it seems, primarily because Haskell arrays are *non-strict*, meaning that *recursive* arrays can be well-defined with no termination difficulties (the LU-decomposition program is an excellent example of this). Operationally speaking, all array elements can be computed in parallel, just as they are in Id.

In Lucid arrays are not explicitly identified as such (there are no array declarations in the language and no subscripting, which would allow "array-ness" to be inferred) but many values can be viewed as ragged, incrementally definable, and incrementally modifiable arrays. Moreover, referential transparency is retained, and the eductive implementation does not require contiguous storage. (The array elements can be stored completely independently, allowing distributed implementations.) The efficiency of any implementation will depend critically on the effectiveness of the storage management strategies used.

Sisal includes conventional data structures, including *ragged arrays*, although this decision has both benefits and costs. The benefit lies in the natural way that objects such as triangular and banded arrays can be specified. The cost is that allowing ragged arrays makes it difficult for the compiler to use address arithmetic to access arrays in both the row-major and the column-major directions. A rectangular matrix array type would allow easy access in any dimension and would have the added benefit that garbage collection could be done on the entire matrix, rather than on each row individually. When Sisal arrays are produced by a "forall" expression, each instance delivers an element at the position of the index value of the array generator – which means that every index position receives one, and only one, value. When an algorithm wishes to store into some other position (e.g., a permutation of the indices), it must go through another "for" expression to rearrange the values. The impact of allowing the user to give both the value to be placed and its index position in an array in a strict functional language would affect dramatically the performance on a conventional architecture (i.e., without a support for I-structures). The run-time system would be required to check that no two instances of the loop attempted to define a value at the same index value as well as to ensure that no indices in the range lacked a value. Of course, in the hardware that would support I-structures there would be no loss of efficiency, but none of the machines on which the Sisal system currently runs supports them. Here the language "feature" was driven by implementation issues rather than language design considerations.

9.6   Models of Execution and Supported Architectures

In this section, we compare the three most relevant models of computation in this book: graph reduction, data-flow, and eduction. In the dataflow and eduction models the evaluated program remains unchanged as the evaluation mechanism moves various computational focal points around the program and changes and moves data associated with the program. In the graph reduction model, a main function, together with arguments, constitutes an initial graph. This graph is repeatedly modified by the evaluation mechanism, in various ways and at various points, using graphs representing subsidiary functions, until the graph is "reduced" to an unchangeable form that represents only data. In graph reduction, the graph can grow arbitrarily large and complicated, containing both data and pieces of program, whereas in data-flow and eduction the program should be thought of as unchanging, with data "flowing" over it.

The dataflow and eduction models differ in the ways that the computational focal points are made to move around programs, with dataflow being data-driven and eduction being demand-driven. That is, in the data-flow model the computational focal points "move" because of the presence of the associated data, whereas in the eduction model the presence of data is not sufficient: The computational path must have previously been "greased" or primed by *demands*. For efficiency reasons, eduction stores values (extensions) that can be retrieved using their tags (contexts). The tagging of values is also found in dynamic dataflow (Id), but values are never stored and retrieved (apart from those in I-structures).

To some extent, demands can be thought of as special sorts of data, which has led some to claim that demand-driven evaluation can be described in purely data-driven terms. Some critics of this data-driven description of demand-driven evaluation claim that *real* demand-driven computation needs storage space for data values (and appropriate storage management strategies) that cannot really be provided by data-driven evaluation mechanisms. These critics also feel that the descriptions of demand-driven evaluation in data-driven terms entail much useless computation, which goes against the basic philosophy of demand-driven evaluation – namely that resources should be conserved by performing only tasks that are useful.

To some extent, the distinction between data-driven and demand-driven evaluation is similar to the distinction between two different evaluation strategies in graph reduction—namely applicative order reduction and normal order reduction. As with data-driven evaluation, applicative order reduction (i.e., evaluation of the arguments of a function before evaluation of the function itself) can result in wasted computation. Basically, both forms of evaluation (applicative order and data-driven) can be too eager. One of the lessons learned in functional programming is that it is better to be lazy (i.e., to delay evaluation until strictly necessary), and that sentiment is certainly echoed in the eduction camp.

It is widely but erroneously felt that eduction is synonymous with normal order graph reduction. This view ignores the use of tags in eduction. The tagging of values, and the retrieval of values using the tags, is essential to eduction but is not found in graph reduction. (Tagging is essential in the implementation of intensionality, since the tags represent the contexts and the arguments of intensions.) Moreover, the tagging of values allows eduction to distribute *data* in a way analogous to, but different from, a graph reduction's distribution of *computation*. (Eduction distributes computation also, and at a finer granularity of parallelism than is found in graph reduction.)

Nevertheless, the lines between the various computing-model camps are becoming blurred. Data-flow is approaching both functional programming (because of higher order functions in Id) and eduction (because of the demand-driven evaluation, or invocation, of code blocks in the Monsoon data-flow architecture), and functional languages are approaching data-flow (because of Id-like array comprehensions in Haskell).

The languages described in this book can often be implemented using different computing models. For example, both Crystal and EPL define functions over index domains; thus a set of indexes assigned to a value can be treated as a tag for an eduction style of execution. Moreover, in Sisal, although streams are not synonymous with lazy evaluation, they can be implemented in a lazy style. Nevertheless, there are times when it might be advantageous to evaluate Sisal streams in an eager style, or to merge their evaluation with consumption of the stream. For example, a pseudo-random number generator could very efficiently produce a vector of results on a vector architecture, at the cost of a buffer of the appropriate length (that length being the size of a vector register, or the length needed to reach acceptable efficiency on a memory-to-memory vector architecture). However, lazy evaluation is desirable during input/output to the terminal, so both mechanisms can be profitably used in Sisal programs.

Lucid, on the other hand, is setting off on its own, with intensional (distributed, non-monolithic, and implicit) data structures.

9.6.1 SPECIAL ARCHITECTURES

Generally, the languages in this volume can be run on a variety of multiprocessor architectures. For example, languages such as Crystal, EPL, Haskell, and Sisal attempt to be suitable for a wide variety of parallel architectures. Some of these languages have been implemented on dataflow architectures, bus-shared multi-microprocessors, and multiprocessor vector processors.

With the exception of Id, the proposals do not assume any specific machine features to help realize parallelism without significant overheads. In the case of Id, the contention is that if memory synchronization and low cost process switching are provided, the overheads of parallel computation are tractable.

The Eduction Evaluator is in many ways similar to the various data-flow machines that have been proposed and constructed. The differences, in construction and performance, come from the demand-driven nature of evaluation. It is hoped that the demand-driven features will obviate the excessive resource utilization that has plagued dataflow machines and also allow more control. Having demands of different priorities, for example, would be a natural way to curb an unruly machine.

9.7   Implementation Efficiency

Although the main focus of this book is not on the implementation issues for the various languages discussed, certain implications are apparent. It is well-known that *expressiveness* and *efficiency* have a mutual repelling effect on each other—that is, the more efficient a program is, the less expressive it becomes and vice versa. (By expressiveness we mean specifying the program at a higher level of abstraction, closer to the problem domain and perhaps more succinct, with fewer details that are not germane to the problem per se.) As has been repeatedly expounded in this book, functional languages revel in function abstractions and the consequent by-products of determinacy, succinctness, ease of expression, and so forth. Although these properties have been known for quite some time, not much attention has been paid to these languages because their efficiency did not match ever-growing efficiency of the imperative languages. The central issue has been the extravagance in memory usage that results from the conceptually clean model that deals with values rather than storage cells. Despite many strategies to organize the memory, the overhead required still remained as a major issue. It was indeed quite hard to beat the efficiency rendered by the full control over the locus of execution in conventional programs that also provided enormous opportunities for optimizing the storage and movement of data.

With the advent of parallel computing, a third component is introduced into this conflict, resulting in a tri-polar relationship of mutual repulsion: *expressiveness, efficiency* and *parallelism*. The introduction of the dire need for parallelism into the arena suddenly brought the functional languages into the limelight, as the extraction of parallelism is a matter that functional languages did not have to worry about. Chapter 8 provides a glimpse of how much effort is involved in extracting parallelism from an imperative program (by undoing the sequential specification). The case for parallelizing Fortran is easily understood because it provides speedup measurements against its sequential executions that have been standardized. For functional programs, preliminary comparison of this kind has been discussed in Chapter 7, which discusses Crystal. However, those comparisons were made for Crystal programs written only with data fields—that is, first order functions defined over index domains. Though there appears to be opportunity for developing analysis and optimization techniques to improve the efficiency of high-order abstractions in certain cases, at the current level of compilation technology abstraction at such levels results in the decreased efficiency. In order to be competitive with imperative languages, the performance of functional programs for realistic application must come close enough, consistently, to what a parallelizing Fortran compiler can do.

The closest to the parallelizing Fortran approach is Sisal, because of its stated objective of being close to the prevalent "native" style of coding. Its deviations from conventional languages are minimal: imposition of a single assignment and the elimination of any storage-related features. Consequently, its implementation does not require any special architectural artifacts and in fact it can be implemented equally efficiently. The question of how expressive it is remains open.

Expressiveness and *parallelism* mutually degrade each other in the sense that if all the parallelism must be exposed in the program, it tends to become cumbersome. Perhaps Sisal takes a middle ground in limiting its exposition of parallelism because of its strict semantics. Id, and to a large extent Haskell, take the approach of bringing the two poles of *expressiveness* and *parallelism* into one fold without degrading either. They provide for the finest level of parallelism to be exposed automatically, by allowing every possible operation to be as asynchronous as possible. This approach, however, requires a run-time mechanism to check and defer arbitrary-sized activities until their preconditions are satisfied. One solution is to have data-flow architecture that supports this approach. The challenge here is to manage the explosion of activities under a limited resource setting. More experience is needed to establish the effectiveness of the data-flow solution. An alternative is to rely on conventional sequential machine apparatus for efficient execution of short sequences. The open questions are how efficiently can an architecture switch short sequential tasks and how effective is a compiler in forming large grain tasks out of such programs. Achievement of both expressiveness and parallelism does seem to necessitate at least some memory tagging and checking in the hardware, however small. Whether all the parallelism exposed by the basic asynchrony is really needed for improving the efficiency is a highly moot question.

Even though the two aspects of *expressiveness* and *parallelism* can be amicably fused into a language design, obtaining efficiency is still a sticky problem. This is reflected by the varied efforts in the implementations. For instance, Sisal relies on reference counting techniques to introduce "update in place" operations to avoid high copying overheads. Several proposed compilers—in particular those for Crystal, EPL and Sisal—use rules to transform functional descriptions into more efficient programs utilizing side effects in a controlled manner.[4] Efforts are underway in the Id compiler to incorporate storage deallocation schema by compiler analysis. There are also provisions for regulating the parallel execution of loops, although this may alter the semantics in some pathological situations. The implementation of eduction proposed in Chapter 2 has to deal with the problem of memory management. This was not discussed in the chapter, but it is handled, in practice, by a "retirement age" scheme.

Finally, there seems to be a consensus that all efforts to generate efficient parallel code by whatever transformations are inadequate. A need to take input from the user at compile-time or run-time is inevitable. This is reflected in the arguments given in Chapter 5 on para-functional programming for annotations and in Chapter 7 on Crystal for the user-supplied partition strategies and for integrating the compiler analysis with run-time support. Id language supports user pragmas to direct the compilation.

It is certain that the fruits of functional languages, however attractive they may appear, cannot be reaped until definitive efficiency comparisons are shown against conventional computing. If these languages need unconventional apparatus to achieve their efficiency, the task is that much harder. Thus in the tri-polar relationship discussed above, some compromise must be made in expressiveness and parallelism in order to demonstrate a decisive advantage in efficiency.

---

[4]Crystal programs are transformed by using equational identities that go beyond the extension preserving transformations.

INDEX